ALBERT BANDURA, Ph.D., State University of Iowa, completed his post-doctoral internship at the Wichita Guidance Center and was an Assistant Clinical Psychologist at the University Hospital there. Dr. Bandura is currently Professor in the Department of Psychology at Stanford University, and a Veterans Administration Consultant.

RICHARD H. WALTERS, Ph.D., Stanford University, has been Lecturer in Philosophy at Auckland University College and Consultant Psychologist to H. M. Prison in Auckland, New Zealand. Dr. Walters subsequently became Lecturer in Psychology and Research Associate of the Institute of Child Study at the University of Toronto.

A PSYCHOLOGY SERIES

Edited by

J. McV. Hunt, Ph.D.

PROFESSOR OF PSYCHOLOGY
UNIVERSITY OF ILLINOIS

Adolescent Aggression

A STUDY OF THE INFLUENCE
OF CHILD-TRAINING PRACTICES
AND FAMILY INTERRELATIONSHIPS

By

ALBERT BANDURA
STANFORD UNIVERSITY

and

RICHARD H. WALTERS
UNIVERSITY OF TORONTO

Foreword by

ROBERT R. SEARS
STANFORD UNIVERSITY

THE RONALD PRESS COMPANY • NEW YORK

N.I.S. - 13/12/77

Foreword

The long centuries of pure, unverified speculation about the influence of a child's rearing on his personality seem to have ended at last. For this problem, as for so many others, the day of theory-based empirical investigation has come. Nothing so well verifies the change as this present book.

The coming of science to the field of behavioral development has not been easy. It has not come all in one piece, and not without a good deal of resistance. We still have "experts" whose convictions go beyond their knowledge, and we still have scientists—even some among the best—who sometimes show an unwarranted optimism about the completeness of their theories or the adequacy of their investigations. Nonetheless, the historically separate pieces that have contributed to child rearing theory are being put together into a workable body of developmental science. This present report of research on the origins of aggression is a rewarding example of the productiveness that comes from the combining of testable theory with precise methodology.

There can be no guarantee that a century hence the theory on which Bandura and Walters have built their study will still be in the historical mainstream of whatever is the most promising theory of that day. At the present time, however, it gives more promise than most, and its effectiveness in directing this piece of research—and ordering the findings—adds substantially to the reasonableness of a hope that it may lead to some rather extraordinary advances during the next decade.

Historically, the theory is a compound of two quite separate lines of endeavor. The first was Freud's clinical study of the effects of infantile experience on later neurosis. He and his psychoanalytic colleagues used the therapeutic couch as their microscope for examining the details of the ways in which parental attitudes and practices determined the quality of a child's development. Variables were defined; causal principles relating them to one another were suggested; observations were repeated many times over. Gradually, a theory was evolved to account for the clinical observations. It had the merit of defining and organizing a vast number of newly noted events, but it did not concern itself sufficiently with the *process* of development.

The other line of endeavor was almost simultaneous but, at the time, entirely irrelevant. This was the development of a theory of learning that would account for the detailed mechanics by which life experiences modified the behavior potentials of mammalian organisms. In general. Not specific. Thorndike and Pavlov were concerned with the process of change as such. Thorndike cared little for the changes in children that occurred outside the classroom, and Pavlov seems to have cared even less about changes that occurred in any species outside those that had salivary glands. Both, however, were devoted to the notion that the rewarding, nonrewarding, and punishing experiences of an organism would account for the changes that occurred in its potentials for action. This is what American psychologists have called "learning."

Thus, from psychoanalysis and behavioral psychology, came the two parts of a theory that would account for those aspects of the development of children that were a function of their relations to their parents. Psychoanalytic observation provided the descriptive dynamics and the substantive variables; behavioral psychology provided the theory of process by which these variables were made operative.

The combining of these two came slowly. G. V. Hamilton made the first and most courageous attempt in the Twenties; the Yale group followed in the Thirties; since World War II, it has been anybody's game. Bandura and Walters have added an important piece to the theory in two respects. One is their derivation of the developmental effects of dependency anxiety, as this relates to aggression and the stultification of conscience, and the other is their analysis of the therapeutic implications of these antecedents for the particular syndrome with which they have dealt.

Theory is not the be-all and end-all of science, however. There is still the problem of achieving correspondence between the theoretically expected and the empirically obtained. This is not a philosophical problem; it is the very realistic one of finding an appropriate methodology for testing the predictions made by the theory. This means the construction of measuring instruments, the designing of appropriate comparisons between groups for the control of crucial variables, and the analysis of obtained differences by statistical techniques which specify the degree of confidence that may be placed on theoretically relevant findings.

In both connections—theoretical and methodological—Bandura and Walters have set a new standard for the field of child development. They have grounded their work on a solid body of other investigators' past experiences, but they have gone rather substantially beyond any previous contributions. Their findings with respect to the child-rearing sources of violent aggression constitute not only an important addition to science but will provide a basis for the hope that one of the most tragic and dangerous forms of character distortion may someday be preventable.

ROBERT R. SEARS

Stanford University

Preface

This book is an account of an empirical study primarily designed to identify the child-training factors and family interrelationships that contribute to the development of antisocial aggressive behavior in adolescent boys. In addition, it represents an attempt to apply the theoretical framework and methodology that have been used by Robert R. Sears and his collaborators in studies of nursery school children to an older group of subjects and to a problem that has been more often approached from a socio-legal or psychoanalytic point of view. While throughout the book our primary concern has been to present evidence relating to our theory of the development of antisocial aggression, we have also used the data obtained from our study to provide information about the socialization process itself and about the behavior and attitudes of adolescent boys.

The choice of variables for study was made on the basis of two kinds of prior investigation. On the one hand were the studies of delinquency in which parent-child relationships have found a prominent place; on the other hand were the more theoretically oriented studies, carried out by child psychologists, of the effects of certain child training procedures on the behavior of young children.

Delinquency is essentially a socio-legal concept. It can refer to a variety of acts, ranging from running away from home or joy-riding in a public vehicle to violent physical assault or the deliberate destruction of property, any of which may bring a young person into contact with the law. It is thus not a useful concept for the psychologist who wishes to demonstrate relationships between attributes of behavior. In order to achieve this aim, the psychologist must select a set of variables, each referring to classes of responses or response tendencies that are sufficiently homogeneous to permit quantification, preferably on some unidimensional scale. While aggression appeared to hold some promise of being a useful variable of this kind, delinquency certainly did not. For this and other reasons, we focused our study on the development of aggressive behavior patterns and have used the term "antisocial aggression" to denote acts of a socially disruptive nature—in other words, acts that result in injury or harm to persons or property—without necessarily implying that they are punishable by law.

Another reason for our utilizing the concept of aggression was that a large body of psychological theory and research concerning the development of aggressive behavior in young children already existed and could be readily related to an investigation into the aggressive aspects of legally delinquent behavior. The application of developmental psychology to the understanding of antisocial behavior enables much delinquent behavior to be portrayed as a failure of the socialization process, one that begins almost as soon as the child is born and that continues to influence his behavior during later years. This kind of viewpoint precludes the presentation of delinquency as a problem that emerges only with adolescence, a form in which it has sometimes been presented, for example, in textbooks on adolescent development.

The planning of the study and the writing of the book was a collaborative enterprise. We are extremely indebted to our co-workers, Robert B. Cairns, Marian Hallett Weide, and Thomas N. Weide, both for the part they played in interviewing and for their assistance in drawing up scales and schedules and in selecting the families for study. We are also indebted to the psychology students who undertook the arduous task of rating the interview material: John P. Booth, Rosalee Tucker Clarke, Roberta Knight De Muth, Clyde K. Emery, Jeri Richards Goldman, Carol A. C. Mitchell, Jan

Roberts Pierce, Robert C. Pierce, Howard M. Rosenfeld, and
Britton K. Ruebush. We are especially grateful to Susan
Crandall Florman, who not only served as a rater but also
continued to assist us throughout the project.

The Alameda County Probation Office and the Board of
Education of the City of Oakland provided facilities for our
study. It is not possible to make individual acknowledgments
for all the assistance that was given by the officers and staff
of these organizations. We are especially indebted to Judge
Ralph E. Hoyt, Dr. Clyde E. Sullivan, Dr. Forest Mitchell,
Miss Marion H. Clark, Dr. Jesse Bracy, and Dr. Samuel
Schonfeld.

In the planning of the study we were assisted by Dr. Lois
Meek Stolz and Dr. Robert R. Sears; both of them gave much
time, thought, and effort to the task of making the project a
success. The comments of Dr. Joseph McV. Hunt, general
editor of the series of which this book is a part, were invalu-
able in guiding us through some of the more difficult stages in
the writing.

We are grateful to friends and colleagues at Stanford and
Toronto for constructive and helpful criticisms. We wish also
to express our gratitude to Virginia Varns Bandura and
Bertha Larkin Bull for the help they gave in the preparation
of the manuscript.

The project was in part supported by a research grant (M-
1349) from the National Institute of Mental Health, United
States Public Health Service, and by a National Science
Foundation research grant (NSF C-3045).

Many excerpts from recorded interviews are included in
this book as illustrative material. Names of persons and
places have been changed to preserve the anonymity of the
respondents.

ALBERT BANDURA
RICHARD H. WALTERS

September 1959

Contents

Adolescent Aggression

Chapter 1

Introduction: The Problem and the Method

In seeking out likely determinants of antisocial aggressive behavior it is possible to choose one of two general approaches. The first type of approach involves studying as many kinds of determinants as possible, constitutional, sociological, psychological, and cultural, at one and the same time. Alternatively, one may attempt to control as many factors as possible in order to concentrate on the study of a single class of variables. Control of sociological factors has been effected in a number of studies through the comparison of a group of delinquents with a group of nondelinquents resembling them in social background. This was the approach used by the Gluecks (1950), who at the same time matched their groups in respect to such variables as age and general intelligence.

In the present study an approach similar to the Gluecks' was employed, except that control was effected not solely by matching procedures, but also by selecting subjects in such a way that the possible influence of certain constitutional and sociological factors was reduced or eliminated from the start. Rather than ask, as some previous investigators have done, why certain boys from adverse homes and neighborhoods become delinquent while others do not, it was decided to ask instead why some boys who appear, on the surface, to be subjected to no obvious sociological or constitutional disadvantages show an antisocial pattern of behavior. Prior research strongly suggested that an answer might be found from a study of parent-child relationships. Undoubtedly, constitutional factors such as inherited defect or physical handicap, or sociological factors such as poor housing, inadequate recreational facilities, and a low standard of living, may contribute to the development of an antisocial orientation. There is increasing evidence, however, that in many cases such factors may not themselves be causative agents; their primary importance may lie in the fact that they provide conditions under which the psychological factors conducive to the development of antisocial behavior may more readily operate.

In their approach to the problem of delinquency, sociologists have frequently emphasized the importance of the social environment as a causative factor. Shaw and McKay (1942), for example, brought forward evidence that delinquency rates were highest in deteriorated areas bordering on the central business and industrial districts of large American cities and decreased gradually throughout zones intermediate between these deteriorated areas and the outer suburbs. The high delinquency areas were characterized by a state of social disorganization that involved not only physical deterioration, poverty, and economic dependency, but also an absence of stable neighborhood standards of conduct. The population of such areas included a high proportion of foreign-born and Negro residents and tended to be highly mobile and transient.

It is very evident that conditions such as Shaw and McKay described are conducive to antisocial behavior. Poverty and poor living conditions are likely to arouse frustration and discontent and to foster a hostile attitude to society. In an area of conflicting cultural standards and rapidly changing population, it is difficult for parents, even if they are themselves law-abiding, to impart their own standards of behavior to their children.

> Under these circumstances it is difficult for parents to maintain control over their children, even though the majority try to do so. The parents have to work single-handed without reinforcement from the neighbors. In a stable community each family is known and each child is known in the neighborhood. Reputations have to be maintained, and behavior is governed by neighbors and acquaintances as well as by members of the family. It is this extended reinforcement of standards that is lacking in a disorganized area (White, 1956, p. 385).

Moreover, such areas provide many aggressive antisocial models for the growing boy; in many of the families, the father himself may provide such a model. In homes in which parents are foreign-born, estrangements and misunderstandings between parents and children may develop through the children's rejection of the traditions and customs that the parents have brought from their countries of origin.

The sociological approach, however, does not explain why only a minority of children who live in deteriorated areas have police records (Kobrin, 1951), or why one child in a family becomes delinquent when a sibling does not. Nor can it account for the occurrence of delinquency among children who live in more privileged and more stable neighborhoods. No doubt, as Healy and Bronner (1936) suggest, a partial explanation is to be found in the psychological development of the individual child.

The influence of sociological and child-training factors may be facilitated or intensified by the presence of mental retardation. A mentally retarded child may not fully understand legal restrictions and is less likely to foresee all the consequences of his actions than a child of average intelligence; perhaps, too, he is more readily influenced by associates who are themselves antisocial. In addition, he may feel inadequate and rejected, especially if other members of his family are better endowed. Sometimes, of course, the mental retardation is an accompaniment of cerebral damage which may at the same time prevent or destroy inhibitions that are ordinarily set up by social training.

Since sociological and intellectual factors may facilitate the development of antisocial aggression, control of these factors was necessary in order to assess the role of child-training variables in this developmental process. This was effected through setting up rather stringent criteria for the selection of subjects for inclusion in the study.

METHOD

The data on which the study was primarily based were obtained from interviews with fifty-two adolescent boys and their parents. Twenty-six of the boys had histories of aggressive antisocial behavior; the remaining twenty-six boys were selected as a suitable comparison group. The study was confined to boys who were of average or above average intelligence, who came from legally intact homes (i.e., homes that were not broken by separation, divorce, or death of a parent), whose parents were steadily employed, and who did not live in deteriorated or high-delinquency neighborhoods. Boys of Negro and Mexican descent were excluded, as were all second generation boys with the exception of one aggressive boy whose parents were born in Canada, and one aggressive and two control boys who each had one British-born parent. Since there had been no language barrier to the acculturation of the parents, it was thought that these latter boys would not have suffered the customary handicaps of second generation children. All the families lived in the same large urban area of central California.

Selection of Families

The aggressive boys were obtained from two general sources. Twenty-one of these boys were secured through the county probation service, the remainder through the guidance department of the major school district of the county. There were many boys available who presented a repetitive, antisocial, aggressive pattern of behavior that had brought them into contact with the law or school authorities. The large majority of these, however, failed to meet the criteria for selection. They either came from homes that were broken in some way, or lived in deteriorated or high-delinquency neighborhoods, or were of low intelligence.

In selecting the boys, more weight was given to case-history material provided by school authorities, probation officers, and guidance workers than to the number and nature of their legal offenses. Even if they had a police record, boys who were described as generally withdrawn, and all boys whose case histories suggested the presence of organic or psychotic involvement, were excluded from the study.

The probation or guidance worker responsible for the boy obtained the consent of the parents for a direct contact to be made by one or another of the interviewers. Approximately 70 per cent of the families with whom contact was made expressed willingness to participate in the study. A few of these, however, were lost through the failure of one or more of the family members to appear at the time of the interview. The original plan was to interview thirty families; difficulties in finding families that met the selection criteria and the inevitable attrition reduced the final number to twenty-six. The boys in these twenty-six families ranged in age from fourteen years, six months, to seventeen years, eleven months, the median age being approximately sixteen and a half years.

Some of the boys obtained through the probation office were in custody at the time of the study; the remainder were currently on probation. Of the latter, a few had previously spent time in a correctional institution. The boys obtained through the guidance service had been in difficulties primarily for truancy and disruptive behavior in school, but had also shown an antisocial pattern outside the school situation; most of them had been, or currently were, on probation, but none had been institutionalized. Thus, the total group consisted mainly of boys who were, at the time of the study, living with their parents, and a few who were temporarily in an institutional setting. The status of the boy at the time of the interview is given in Table 1-1.

TABLE 1-1

STATUS OF AGGRESSIVE BOYS AT TIME OF INTERVIEW

Status	Number of Boys
On probation to County Probation Service,	
No prior commitment to an institution	10
Following release from Observation Camp	3
On probation to California Youth Authority	
Following release from C.Y.A. institution	1
Detained, subsequently committed to California Youth Authority	
No previous commitment of any kind	1
One previous C.Y.A. commitment	1
Detained, subsequently committed to Observation Camp	
No previous commitment of any kind	1
In Observation Camp	4
Under supervision of District Board of Education	
Department of Individual Guidance	5
Total number of boys	26

If the study had included only boys who were currently held in institutions, the answers to the interview questions might have been influenced both by the boys' reactions to institutional treatment and by the parents' reactions to the commitment of the boy. However, if boys who were, or had been, institutionalized had been entirely excluded from the study, some of the most extremely aggressive boys would have been automatically lost. The use of boys of varying legal status probably produced less distorted findings than if the study had included only boys from institutions; at the same time, it insured that a good sample of aggressive boys was being studied.

Selection of the Control Families

The control boys were selected from two large high schools. School counselors were asked to identify boys between the ages of fourteen and seventeen who, in their opinion, were neither markedly aggressive nor markedly withdrawn. They were especially asked to exclude boys with histories of delinquent or disruptive behavior and boys who were social isolates. From the lists of boys provided by the counselors, a group of boys that might provide a match for the aggressive boys in respect to age, intelligence, father's occupational status, and area of residence was selected. It was anticipated that not all families would wish to participate; consequently, a pool of about seventy families was set up.

Letters were then sent out to the parents of boys who had been selected as suitable subjects, inviting them to participate in the study. The letters were sent out under the signature of the principal of the school which the boy attended. About 60 per cent of the families who were approached agreed to participate. From these families a group that seemed to provide the best possible match for the aggressive families was selected for further contact.

Matching Procedures

The criteria that were used in the selection of subjects insured that, for the purposes of comparing the two groups of families, certain possibly relevant factors would be to a large extent controlled. In addition, it proved possible to keep the families individually paired on the basis both of the fathers' occupational status and of the age of the boys.

The age factor was the first consideration in pairing since development is rapid in adolescence over the age range of the boys included in the study. There is little doubt that a better basis for matching would have been the developmental age of the boy. In the absence of facilities for making a prior assessment of developmental age, it was decided, however, that each aggressive boy would be paired with a control who did not differ from him by more than six months of chronological age. Wherever more than one pairing was possible on this basis, the socioeconomic status of the family, as judged by the father's occupation, was used as a secondary basis for pairing. Table 1-2, listing the matched pairs of families, includes the ages of the boys at the

TABLE 1-2

MATCHED PAIRS OF AGGRESSIVE AND CONTROL BOYS

Aggressive Group				Control Group			
Code Number	Age	Occupational Rating of Father	I.Q. Range[a]	Code Number	Age	Occupational Rating of Father	I.Q. Range[a]
1	14-6	3	1	2	14-10	4	1
3	14-7	5	2	4	15-0	5	2
5	14-11	4	3	6	15-5	5	2
7	15-1	5	1	8	15-1	5	2
9	15-1	5	2	10	15-0	5	1
11	15-8	2	3	12	16-2	2	1
13	15-8	6	1	14	15-8	5	2
15	15-11	4	4	16	16-0	4	2
17	16-0	5	1	18	16-4	5	1
19	16-0	5	1	20	15-8	5	2
21	16-2	6	4	22	15-11	6	1
23	16-4	5	1	24	16-2	5	3
25	16-6	4	2	26	16-11	5	1
27	16-7	4	1	28	16-5	2	2
29	16-9	5	2	30	17-1	5	4
31	16-9	4	2	32	16-9	4	2
33	17-0	5	2	34	16-9	4	4
35	17-0	2	2	36	16-8	2	3
37	17-0	2	2	38	16-9	1	5
39	17-3	5	2	40	17-3	5	3
41	17-3	4	2	42	17-0	4	4
43	17-4	4	1	44	17-6	3	3
45	17-5	5	5	46	17-5	4	3
47	17-5	6	4	48	17-7	5	2
49	17-8	4	3	50	17-4	4	4
51	17-11	5	2	52	17-9	5	3

[a] Scaling of I.Q. Range:	Range	Standard Deviation Units	Approximate I.Q. Equivalents
	1	—.75 to —.01	90-99
	2	.00 to .74	100-109
	3	.75 to 1.49	110-119
	4	1.50 to 2.24	120-129
	5	2.25 +	130 +

time of their interview, and the fathers' occupational status. The code numbers of the families are given in this table. Since all references to particular families, including excerpts from the interviews, are identified according to this set of code numbers, the interested reader can readily turn back to this table if he wishes to check on the age of the boy or on other data that are included.

The occupational status of the fathers was assessed by means of the Revised Warner Scale (1949). On this scale a rating of 1 is given to occupations of a professional or managerial nature which carry a high degree of social prestige, and a rating of 7 to completely unskilled laboring jobs. Approximately three-quarters of the families included in the study were given a rating of 4 or 5, which means that the large majority of fathers were employed as skilled laborers or in minor white-collar jobs. Ideally, the occupational rating should be combined with some other measure of social status, for example, the income of the family or the educational level of the parents. However, since this kind of information could not be obtained prior to the interviews, it would not have assisted in the pairing of the families.

Table 1-2 includes an intelligence rating of each boy, based on the mean and standard deviation of the test or tests which had been administered to him. It was not possible within the limits of this study to give each boy an intelligence test; consequently, the information that was available in the boys' court or school records was utilized to obtain intelligence ratings. Estimates of the control boys' intelligence were readily available, since in both schools from which these boys were drawn the Terman-McNemar Group Test of Intelligence was routinely administered each year. The most recent result on this test was accepted as an adequate indicator of a boy's intelligence. On the other hand, estimates of the aggressive boys' intelligence were much less simple. Sometimes several disparate test findings were available for a single boy; in such cases the result obtained from the most recently administered individual intelligence test was accepted. In one instance no intelligence test result was available, and the boy was consequently administered a shortened form of the Wechsler Adult Intelligence Test.

The use of matched pairs of families insured that there would be no significant differences either in mean age between the aggressive and control boys or in occupational status between the two groups of fathers. In addition, as Table 1-3 indicates, no significant difference was found in

TABLE 1-3

COMPARISON OF THE TWO GROUPS OF FAMILIES ON SOME FACTORS
POSSIBLY RELATED TO CHILD-TRAINING PRACTICES

	Aggressive Group		Control Group			
	Mean	S.D.	Mean	S.D.	t	p
Occupational level of father (Revised Warner Scale)	4.38	1.29	4.19	1.52	0.57	N.S.[b]
Number of children in family	3.35	2.02	2.50	0.97	1.90	N.S.
Intelligence rating of boy[a]	2.15	1.14	2.42	1.16	0.86	N.S.
Father's age at birth of boy	29.31	5.27	28.42	5.49	0.55	N.S.
Mother's age at birth of boy	25.50	5.92	25.92	5.11	0.27	N.S.

[a] See Table 1-2.
[b] Not significant.

mean intelligence between the two groups of boys. This table also shows that there was very little difference between the groups of parents in their ages at the time the boys were born.

The two groups of families did not differ greatly in average family size. There was, however, only one control family in which there were as many as five children, whereas in eight of the families of aggressive boys there were five or more children. At the other extreme, there were more only children among the aggressive boys (Table 1-4). In Table 1-5 the ordinal position of the children in their families is given; there were more first-born children among the control boys, but the over-all difference between the groups is very small and obviously not significant.

Information about the number of children in a family was not always available until the parents were interviewed. Consequently, family size could not be fully controlled. It

TABLE 1-4

FAMILY SIZE

	Over Four Children	Two to Four Children	One Child Only
Aggressive group	8	13	5
Control group	1	22	3

Chi-square $= 8.258$
$p < .02$[a]
Mean (total group) $= 2.92$
S.D. $= 1.64$

[a] This p (probability) value indicates that, if there were no true difference between the groups, the reported result would have been obtained by chance less than twice in a hundred times. Probability values subsequently given may be interpreted in an analogous manner.

TABLE 1-5

ORDINAL POSITION OF CHILDREN IN FAMILIES

	Oldest Child	Middle Child	Youngest Child	Only Child
Aggressive group	10	7	4	5
Control group	16	5	2	3

was impossible to assess the extent to which family size currently affected the economic status of the families. In some large families, the older children were already married or were contributing to the total family income. In two very large families, on the other hand, the children were all still young and there were undoubtedly some economic problems in spite of the fathers' steady employment in fairly well-paid occupations. However, even if family size had been controlled, there would have been other factors, such as the efficiency of the family housekeeping, that might have affected economic status and whose influence it would have been impossible to assess.

Since note was taken of the mothers' occupations, as well as of those of the fathers, information was available concerning the number of mothers in each group who worked outside the home. Twelve control mothers, and nine mothers of aggressive boys, were gainfully employed at the time when the study took place; the remainder occupied themselves solely as housewives. In this respect the groups obviously differed very little.

Presentation of the Study

It was decided to present the study to the parents as an attempt to understand the problems of adolescent boys. As far as circumstances allowed, the study was structured similarly for both groups of parents. It was explained that some boys had difficulty in adjusting during adolescence, whereas other boys appeared to have few problems at this time. The control parents were told that a sample of boys who had shown good adjustment to the school situation was being included in the study, and that their sons had been suggested for inclusion by the school authorities. They were not told, however, that a group of aggressive or delinquent boys was also being included, since it was felt that information of this kind might influence their responses to the interview questions. The parents of the aggressive boys, on the other hand, were told that the study was concerned with boys who had had some difficulties during adolescence and that the purpose was to gain information which might eventually be of help to parents and to teachers. The boys were all told that the purpose of the study was to find out more about young people of their age so that their problems could be better understood.

The confidential nature of the interviews was stressed. It was made quite clear to both the parents and the boys that the interview material was being identified only by means of a code number, and that any information that they gave would not be communicated to other family members or to the agencies with whose help the study was being conducted.

The Interviews

The three members of each family were interviewed separately and, in most cases, simultaneously by three different interviewers. In the case of boys who were currently in detention, it was decided to interview the boy at a time convenient to the institution in which he was held and to interview the parents as soon afterward as possible. Since under these circumstances there was no possibility of communication between boy and parent concerning the interview material, this was not felt to be an important departure from the general procedure. In three instances, owing to illness or similar emergencies, it proved impossible for all three members of a family to be interviewed at the same time. There was no evidence, however, that in these cases there had been any communication concerning the content of the interview.

All respondents were interviewed by a member of their own sex. One interviewer conducted all the mother interviews, one all the father interviews, while the third conducted all the interviews with the adolescents. Interviews were recorded on Gray audographs which were left in full view of the respondents.

The interviews were of a semistructured type. In such interviews a standard series of questions is asked in a prescribed order. The questions are, however, open-ended; they permit the respondents to answer in as much detail as they choose and to express themselves in their own way. The main purpose of the semistructured interview is, in fact, to encourage freedom of expression while at the same time insuring that the interviewer obtains information on all the topics to be studied.

The parent interview schedule (Appendix A) was very similar in form to that used by Sears, Maccoby, and Levin (1957) in their study of the child-training practices of mothers. It consisted of forty-three questions, each followed by a series of probes which could be used by the interviewer if the answer to the original question had not supplied all the relevant information.

The adolescent interview schedule was also of a semistructured type. In this case, however, no model existed and a considerable amount of preliminary work was required to produce a set of questions that would both elicit the information that was desired and be fully understood by the majority of the adolescent boys. This schedule, in its final form, consisted of forty questions, most of which were followed by a fairly lengthy set of probes designed to obtain very specific information about the boys' behavior and attitudes (Appendix B).

The Rating Scales

The parent interviews were rated on 61 five-point rating scales (Appendix C), many of which were modeled on those used by Sears, Maccoby, and Levin (1957). With one exception, a three-point scale designed to assess the boys' preference for one parent rather than the other, the 85 adolescent scales also were defined by five points (Appendix D). Raters were allowed to give intermediate ratings, e.g., to rate 3.5 if they felt that, according to the definition of the scale points, a rating of 4 was too high and a rating of 3 was too low. Thus, in effect, the interviews were actually rated on nine-point scales, each scale being defined by five points. Since two raters rated each interview and their ratings were combined for the final analysis of results, the measures that were used in this analysis fell on a seventeen-point scale, ranging from 2 to 10 for each measure.

The scale points were, as far as possible, defined by reference to fairly specific classes of behavior. This insured that they would be given a consistent interpretation by the raters and undoubtedly was an important factor in producing high inter-rater agreement. Scale 38, designed as a measure of the extent to which parents encouraged their sons to come to them to seek help, will serve as an example of the kind of scale that was used.

1. Not at all permissive. Actively discourages boy from coming for help or advice of any kind. Boy should learn to stand on own feet, must solve own problems.
2. Slightly permissive. Will be supportive or directive only in emergencies. Boy generally should stand on own feet, make own decisions.

3. Parent expects boy to work out most things for himself. Little encouragement to come for help, although may be supportive or directive when boy does come for help.
4. Generally permissive. On rare occasions encourages boy to work out things for himself. Usually encourages coming to parent.
5. Entirely permissive. Always encourages boy to come for help and advice. Always supportive or directive.

Since most scales were designed to measure particular aspects of behavior, ratings could ordinarily be made from fairly well-defined sections of the interviews. Other scales, however, referred to more general aspects of the child-training process, or to fairly generalized attitudes or feelings on the part of one or another member of the family. Although specific questions were included in the interview schedules to elicit information for rating on these latter scales, relevant material might appear almost anywhere within the interview, and the total content had therefore to be taken into account in making a rating. This, for example, was the case with all measures of the strength and quality of the affectional relationships between family members.

Included in the parent schedules was a number of questions designed to elicit an account of the boys' behavior; similarly, in the adolescent schedule was included a number of questions designed to elicit an account of the parents' behavior. Thus, in some cases, it was possible to have two estimates of a single variable, for example, the extent to which a parent used physical punishment. The overlapping scales may be regarded as checks on the validity of the data that were obtained. On the other hand, they may perhaps be more profitably considered as potential indicators of discrepancies between the boys' perception of their own behavior and the parents' perception of the behavior of their sons, and vice versa. In addition, in a few cases measures of both parents' behavior were secured from the interviews of both mothers and fathers. For example, the warmth of the mothers toward their sons was estimated both from the statements made by the mothers themselves and from the fathers' statements about the relationship between the boys and their mothers. In such cases, it was felt that a more reliable measure of the behavior or attitude under consideration could probably be obtained by averaging the ratings obtained from the two sets of interviews (mid-parent ratings).

Rating Procedures

Six advanced psychology undergraduates were trained as raters. These were divided into pairs, one man and one woman in each, and each pair was assigned to rate one of the sets of interviews, i.e., mother interviews, father interviews, and adolescent interviews. In this way, through the use of independent interviewers and independent pairs of raters, any possibility of the content or ratings of the interview of one member of the family influencing the content or ratings of the interview of another member was eliminated. Unfortunately, owing to a prolongation of the study beyond the anticipated date of completion, it proved impossible to retain the original pair of raters for all the boys' interviews and two new raters, one male and one female, had to be obtained. In training the two substitute raters, an effort was made to insure that a consistent interpretation of the scales was maintained.

Ratings were made directly from recordings. The rater was supplied with rating sheets bearing the numbers of the scales. He listened to the interview and made ratings as he listened. He was permitted to hear the interview as many times as he wished and to adjust ratings already made in the light of relevant information which came from a later portion of an interview.

The rating of interviews directly from recordings has advantages that are not present when ratings are made from transcripts. The raters are able to take into account not only what the respondents say but also the tone of voice in which they speak and other indicators of emotion which accompany the spoken word. Perhaps equally important, listening to interviews is less boring than reading them, so that the motivation and attention of the raters are more likely to be maintained.

The Thematic Deviation Test

In addition to being interviewed, the boys in the study were administered a projective test designed primarily to assess their reactions to socially deviant behavior. The test consisted of ten pictures and eight incomplete stories, each depicting a situation in which an adolescent boy either is tempted to carry out an act which is of a socially deviant nature or is actually performing such an act. Except for minor changes, the incomplete stories are the same as those developed by Allinsmith and Rhodes (Allinsmith, 1954) for a study of moral standards. The pictures and the incomplete stories are presented in Appendix E. This test was administered by a fourth interviewer. Since it was found that the interview and testing together might take over three hours, these procedures were not ordinarily carried out in a single session.

The projective test was regarded as supplementary to the boys' interviews; consequently, the latter were ordinarily carried out first, and arrangements were then made for the boys to be given the test at a later time. Unfortunately, two boys, one aggressive and one control, were unwilling to take the test; for these two boys the interviewing procedure may have been too anxiety-provoking.

The boys' responses were recorded either on tape or on a Gray audograph. The analysis of this projective material was too difficult to make from recordings; consequently, the stories were transcribed. Owing to mechanical difficulties, the fidelity of four test protocols was too poor for adequate transcripts to be made. Thus, transcripts were available for only twenty-one aggressive and twenty-five control boys.

The test pictures were presented to the boys in a standard order. They were asked simply to make up a story to each picture. However, if a boy merely described the picture, he was encouraged to develop a story with a definite outcome. Only one standard probe was used. If a boy did not spontaneously describe the thoughts and feelings of the characters in the story, he was asked, "And how are they thinking and feeling?" The incomplete stories were presented after the pictures. The interviewer simply read the first part of the story and then asked the boy to continue. Again the boy was asked, if necessary, to state how the characters were thinking and feeling.

The test was scored independently by two scorers, one male and one female, neither of whom had rated any of the interview material. The boys' test responses were scored in terms of a set of categories which it was thought would provide indices of the extent to which the boys' behavior was regulated either by fear or by guilt. Some additional categories that seemed relevant for the study of the development of self-control were also used. The categories are described and discussed in Chapter 6 of this book.

Since some of the pictures and stories were likely to elicit fantasy material of a sexual or aggressive nature, it was decided to utilize such material as a supplement to the information obtained from the interview questions about sex and aggression. The scoring categories that were employed for this purpose are described in Chapters 3 and 4.

STATISTICAL ANALYSIS OF DATA

Reliabilities of Ratings

The reliabilities of the interview ratings were estimated by means of the Pearson product-moment correlation coefficient (r). For the mother interviews, the inter-rater reliabilities ranged from .67 to .98, with a median reliability of .91. For the father interviews, with the exception of one scale which proved completely unreliable owing to the lack of variability of one set of ratings, the range was from .64 to 1.00, with a median reliability of .82. The reliabilities for the adolescent scales were based on the ratings of four raters; Rater A overlapped in her ratings with Rater B and Rater D, whereas Rater D overlapped in his ratings with both Rater

A and with Rater C. The reliabilities are nevertheless comparable with those of the parent ratings; they ranged from .61 to .96 with a median reliability of .83. The inter-rater reliability of each scale is indicated in Appendices C and D. Because it was suspected that the inclusion of an extreme group might have artificially raised reliabilities, a sample of reliabilities based on ratings of the control families only was obtained for all three sets of interviews. For the most part, these reliabilities were comparable to those based on the total group of respondents, median reliabilities being .91 and .79 for the ratings for mothers and fathers, respectively, and .78 for the adolescent ratings.

Reliabilities of scores on the deviation test were also obtained in the form of product-moment correlation coefficients. The reliabilities for the various categories ranged from .61 to .95, the median reliability being .86.

Differences Between Groups

The significance of differences between the mean ratings of the groups of mothers, fathers, and adolescents was in most cases estimated by means of the t-technique for correlated data (McNemar, 1955). For some measures, e.g., deviation test scores, data were not available for all fifty-two cases; in such cases the data were treated as uncorrelated, and a t-test for the difference between independent means was employed. In most instances a specific hypothesis was being tested and, when this was the case, the benefit of a one-tail test was claimed. Some scales were, however, included not as bases for prediction, but as a means of obtaining information which might clarify other findings or suggest further hypotheses about parent or adolescent behavior. A two-tail test was consequently employed when the significance of differences on the latter measures was being tested. Unless otherwise stated in tables of results, a one-tail test was used; where a two-tail test was applied, a note is included to this effect. In cases where the difference between means had been found to be significant between the .05 and .01 levels, an additional test was made utilizing a non-parametric technique (Siegel, 1956). A Wilcoxon signed-rank matched-pairs test was ordinarily used; when data had been regarded as uncorrelated, the Mann-Whitney U-test was substituted. Probability values based on these non-parametric tests are reported in subsequent tables only when they differ from those obtained by the use of the t-test.

Correlational Analyses

Intercorrelations between some of the mother, father, and adolescent measures were obtained by means of the Pearson product-moment formula. In addition, some of the parent measures were correlated with measures obtained from the adolescent interviews. Correlations were calculated separately for data obtained from the control families and for data obtained from the families of the aggressive boys. If corresponding correlations based on these two sets of data were in the same direction and did not differ significantly, they were averaged by means of an r to z transformation. Correlational analyses were carried out only as a means of supplying additional information to clarify that obtained from the tests of the significance of the differences between the mean ratings, or when these latter tests could not by themselves supply the information that was sought.

THEORETICAL ORIENTATION

For many years the only comprehensive theory of personality development was the psychoanalytic theory. Although Freud and his followers provided many provocative ideas concerning personality development, many of their concepts were poorly defined and their propositions were not, for the most part, stated in a form in which they could be readily verified. In recent years considerable progress has been made in relating psychoanalytic hypotheses to the more precise terminology of the behavior theories developed by experimental psychologists. Propositions put forward by psychoanalysts, often in very general terms, have been made testable by defining the concepts in terms of behavioral referents and by specifying more clearly the conditions under which these referents might be expected to occur. Application of the reinforcement theory of Hull (1943) to problems of social learning (Dollard *et al.*, 1939; Miller and Dollard, 1941; Whiting, 1941) paved the way for an integration of the psychoanalytic and Hullian approaches for the systematic study of the socialization process (Dollard and Miller, 1950; Mowrer, 1950; Sears *et al.*, 1953; Whiting and Child, 1953).

Some Basic Concepts

The socialization process consists of the development of habitual response patterns that are acceptable in the society in which the individual lives. The learning of such *habits*, or cue-response associations, requires the presence of some kind of *drive* or motivating process and the occurrence of a reward or *reinforcement*. Any action sequence may be analyzed in terms of *instrumental acts* that lead toward the goal, and the final drive-reducing *goal-response*.

MOTIVATIONAL FACTORS

A *drive* is a strong stimulus that instigates the organism to act. At birth the infant is motivated by a relatively narrow range of instigators that constitute the *primary or innate drives*. Such drives are associated with basic physiological processes, and reduction of the strength of instigation is essential if the organism is to survive. Most physiological processes, e.g., respiration, are self-regulatory, and consequently have no drive value except under unusual circumstances that interfere with their operation and give rise to pain. On the other hand, the infant's need for nutrition is not automatically regulated; nor is the child automatically protected from most external noxious stimuli that give rise to discomfort and pain. Thus, relief from distress is, in the early stages of the child's life, invariably mediated by the

actions of adults in the child's environment; it is the association of other persons, particularly the mother, with the
reduction of the strength of primary drives that provides
the foundation of the socialization process.

Because of their frequent association with relief from
physical discomfort, certain *environmental events* such as
the mother's nurturant behavior acquire *secondary reward*
value. Such events thus become capable of functioning in
the same way as primary rewards in the establishing of habit
patterns. The process by which some events gain secondary
reward value can be readily observed. For example, by four
weeks of age a hungry child may stop crying as soon as he
is picked up by his mother, and by sixteen weeks his crying
will cease when he sees her enter the room (Gesell and Ilg,
1943). He has learned to associate her presence and activities with relief from pain. By the time he has matured
sufficiently for active social training to have effects, his
mother's demonstration of affection can serve to reinforce
actions that she wishes him to reproduce. Socialization is
greatly facilitated by the development of learned rewards.
Rewards associated with the reduction of primary drives
cannot be long withheld if the child is not to suffer serious
physical harm; in comparison, secondary rewards can be
manipulated very freely and effectively in training a child.

Moreover, the anticipation of rewards appears sometimes
to have motivational properties. The child, to continue the
example given above, will actively seek his mother's presence; very early in infancy, he will cry until he is held, even
when he is not apparently in physical discomfort or pain.
Since he has learned to want formerly neutral events, he may
be said to have developed a *learned* or secondary motive.
One of the most important learned motives is *anxiety*, or the
anticipation of pain. Originally neutral events that are associated with painful stimulation acquire the capacity of
arousing to a greater or lesser degree the complex physiological and emotional changes that are originally aroused
by pain. These internal responses can then serve to instigate
behavior which will be reinforced if it results in a state

of relief. Learned motives are thus tendencies to produce or avoid formerly neutral environmental events with which primary rewards and discomforts have been repeatedly associated.

It is possible that anxiety may provide a major part of the motivational properties of all secondary motives. Thus, dependency behavior is most strongly elicited when a child is about to be separated from his mother; such behavior may be elicited primarily by the child's anticipation of the recurrence of painful states experienced during his mother's absence at a stage of life when he was entirely dependent upon her for relief from discomfort. Similarly, aggressive behavior, usually depicted as a response to frustration, may be activated by the anticipation of pain that might result if the goal response were indefinitely prevented from occurring.

The extent to which anxiety provides a motivational component of all secondary motivational systems cannot be fully determined from the research that has been carried out up to the present time. There can be no doubt, however, of its paramount importance in the socialization of the child. Once anxiety has been attached to threats of physical pain and deprivation of secondary rewards, the parents have many additional means for training and controlling the child.

THE TRAINING PROCESS

Parental training involves both the encouragement of socially approved patterns of behavior appropriate to the child's age level, and the discouragement of habits that could earlier be tolerated, or even welcomed, as necessary stages in learning.

In the first place, the child must learn the complex routines that are associated with the satisfaction of primary needs in adult life. Thus, for example, he must learn to use a spoon or fork, and to go to the bathroom to eliminate. Such learning involves the acquisition of new instrumental acts. Since the primary reward remains the same, teaching of these new and arduous techniques is accomplished largely through the use of secondary rewards, for example, approval or affection.

In addition, the child must be taught other skills not associated with the reduction of primary drives and perhaps also new motives for behavior. Here, again, the parents must rely to a large extent on secondary rewards; indeed, the only primary rewards that can usually be employed are especially attractive foods, the giving of which has ordinarily been associated with affection and approval. The effectiveness of secondary rewards is dependent on the quality and intensity of the relationships between the child and his parents. If the child has developed strong emotional ties, social training by means of secondary rewards will be considerably facilitated.

The elimination of socially disapproved habits can be accomplished in two ways. They may be either consistently left unrewarded or actively punished. If the parents ignore a socially disapproved act, thereby letting it go unrewarded, and if at the same time there are alternative rewarded means of obtaining gratification, the unrewarded behavior will gradually die out, or *extinguish*.

Active punishment may also lead to the disappearance of socially disapproved behavior. Its effects are, however, far more complex. If a child is repeatedly punished for some socially disapproved habit, the impulse to perform the act becomes, through its association with punishment, a stimulus for anxiety. This anxiety then motivates competing responses which, if sufficiently strong, prevent the occurrence of, or *inhibit*, the disapproved behavior. Inhibited responses may not, however, thereby lose their strength, and may reappear in situations where the threat of punishment is weaker (Estes, 1944). Punishment may, in fact, prevent the extinction of a habit; if a habit is completely inhibited, it cannot occur and therefore cannot go unrewarded.

Punishment can assist in changing instrumental acts if the goal-response is permitted or approved. The temporary inhibition of the disapproved behavior presents an opportunity for eliciting and rewarding approved means to the goal. Thus a combination of punishment and reward may facilitate training in some areas. If, however, punishment is very severe, it may influence all the child's means of reaching the goal, even those that are approved. In this way a whole system of behavior may become associated with anxiety. A child who has been severely punished for soiling his pants may become anxious about all acts of elimination, no matter if they are conducted in an approved way.

In addition, punishment may prevent the learning of behavior that is not permitted when the punishment is administered but is permitted at some later time in life. Such an effect is most likely to occur when a whole system of behavior, including the goal-response, meets disapproval. Thus, a child who has been punished for all expressions of sexual curiosity may be rendered so anxious about sex that he remains incapable of any satisfying sexual relationships even in later life when such behavior is expected of him.

Generalization and Discrimination

The task of socialization would be extremely difficult if a child had to be taught appropriate behavior for every specific situation. Habits learned in one situation will, however, transfer, or generalize, to other situations to the extent that the new situations resemble the situation in which the habit was learned. This principle of learning has been assumed in previous discussions without being made explicit. It was assumed, for example, in the discussion of rewards and punishment, and especially when the effects of anxiety were described.

In the earliest months of life habits generalize very readily. Thus there is a stage when the hungry child stops crying on being picked up by any adult; it is not long, however, before such responses are made only to the mother or to other persons who have participated in feeding and otherwise caring for him. Much of the child's learning involves an increasing capacity to make discriminations of this kind. He must learn, for example, that certain instrumental acts and goal-responses are permitted, while other, perhaps rather similar, acts are not allowed.

Discrimination learning is achieved through the concurrent operation of both reward and non-reward or of both reward and punishment. It is greatly facilitated by the use of verbal cues. Before the child has learned to attach appropriate labels to objects and events, generalization will occur on the basis of superficial and often misleading appearances. The classifications of objects and events reflected in the basic vocabulary of a language have, for the most part, been made on the basis of some functional similarity; as a result, the child who has learned appropriate responses to verbal cues can profit from the experience of others without having to go through an extensive period of trial and error learning.

Socialization must, however, begin before the child has mastered verbal skills. During this early period of life, parents are sometimes forced to resort to restrictive or punitive measures merely to insure that the child does not come to harm. For example, the parents cannot at this stage explain to a child that it is dangerous for him to run out on the street. If they punish him when he does this, he may become fearful even of going on the sidewalk. It is difficult, then, in the absence of verbal cues, to indicate specifically for what behavior the child is being restrained or punished. It is at this period that the parents are most likely to make the child anxious about goal-responses when they intend only to prevent or change some instrumental acts.

It is believed that conflicts may readily be learned during this preverbal stage (Dollard and Miller, 1950). Superficially, two situations or acts may appear very similar. For reasons he cannot understand the child is punished in one case, rewarded in another. Consequently, in any new situation similar to either of these two, competing responses will be aroused, one which impels the child to approach the goal, one which impels him to avoid it. These unverbalized (unconscious) conflicts can be the source of many problems during later life.

Conditions for the Development of Antisocial Aggression

The aggressive boys were so selected that they might be regarded as representing a somewhat extreme group of adolescents in respect to aggressive behavior of an antisocial kind. It was assumed that this aggression was a manifestation of a learned motive developed over a period of years, first in interaction with the child's parents and other authority figures who may in some respects be regarded as parent-surrogates. It was further assumed that the conditions for the development and establishment of aggressive behavior patterns are to be found in the parents' techniques of handling the child, both in early years and in current situations.

In order for the socialization process to be effective, certain minimal conditions must be present. The primary condition is the development of a dependency motive whereby the child learns to want the interest, attention, and approval of others. These secondary rewards may then be made conditional on the child's conforming to the demands and prohibitions of his parents and society.

If the dependency is present but few socialization demands are made on the child, rather than learning to conform to society he learns to expect and demand immediate and unconditional gratifications (Levy, 1943). Therefore, the establishment of dependency, although a necessary condition for socialization, is not a sufficient one. Socialization pressures in the forms of demands and restrictions are also needed.

Socialization defects are not always manifested in hostile, destructive patterns of behavior. The hobo, the bohemian, the "beatnik," reject the value system of the culture but do not necessarily aggress. It appears that frustration arising from a lack of affectional nurturance and a punitive attitude on the part of one or both of the parents is an essential condition for the occurrence of generalized antisocial aggression (Bender, 1947; Bowlby, 1946; Friedlander, 1949; Goldfarb, 1945; Lewis, 1954).

If both parents are completely rejecting and extremely punitive, a child may remain almost completely unsocialized (Hewitt and Jenkins, 1946). However, this extreme condition is probably rare. More often, the child's relationship with one or the other parent remains relatively intact. In this case, even though the child develops an aggressive antisocial pattern of behavior, partial socialization is usually achieved; thus the child ordinarily shows some capacity for forming emotional relationships and some control over his behavior.

Another condition that may contribute both to the failure of socialization and to the development of hostility and resentment is the occurrence of inconsistency in parental disciplinary practices (Glueck and Glueck, 1950). If the father and mother markedly differ in the demands and expectations that they make on the child or in their methods of discipline, or if one parent or both parents show inconsistency in these areas, no clearly defined standards of behavior are available to the child. Moreover, under these circumstances attempts to curb or direct the child's behavior are likely to evoke resentment and hostility.

If dependency is developed and conformity to the parents' wishes is consistently enforced, internalization of values should occur. However, these values will not be socially acceptable if the parents do not conform to the demands of the culture. Consequently, the quality of the parental models has an important influence on the socialization process (Johnson and Szurek, 1952; Giffin, Johnson, and Litin, 1954).

There are, of course, other conditions that facilitate socialization. These include the amount of contact that the child has with the socializing agents and the use of disciplinary techniques that involve the withholding of secondary rewards, such as approval or affection, while still keeping the child in the dependency relationship.

The specific hypotheses that are put forward in later chapters of this book were derived from a consideration of ways in which the socialization process might be disrupted and of the conditions that seemed to facilitate the development of aggression. Some of these hypotheses relate to more general qualities of the parents' behavior, such as their warmth or rejection; others to their handling of specific aspects of the boys' behavior. They are concerned both with the development of secondary motivational systems and with the role of reward, non-reward, and punishment in modifying the boys' behavior.

In testing hypotheses about child-training antecedents of aggressive behavior, one should ideally commence by identifying families in which the conditions supposedly conducive to the development of aggression are clearly present and other families in which these conditions are clearly absent, and then appraise the incidence of aggressive disorders among the children in both sets of families. However, this procedure has practical difficulties. To be carried out effectively it would require an extensive preliminary survey of families and the conducting of a longitudinal study commencing at or before the birth of the child and continuing into adolescence. Though postdictive studies, such as this one, have their limitations—the main one being that it is impossible to tell in how many cases the hypothesized conditions are present and antisocial aggression does not occur —they can nevertheless serve to point to factors, some necessary, some sufficient, for the development of antisocial aggression.

Chapter 2

Dependency

The theory of antisocial aggression that is offered in this book assumes that such a disorder originates primarily from the disruption of a child's dependency relationship to his parents. In the first place, the frustration of the child's dependency needs through a lack of affectional nurturance on the part of one or both of his parents provides the child with continuing instigation to hostility and aggression. The disruption of the dependency relationship also has important effects on the course of the socialization process. Although a certain amount of socialization of a child takes place through direct training, most of the values and standards that will eventually govern his behavior are acquired through imitation of the important adults in his life. A child who lacks close dependent ties to his parents can have little opportunity or desire to model himself after them and to internalize their standards of behavior. In the absence of such internalized controls, the child's aggression is likely to be expressed in an immediate, direct, and socially unacceptable fashion. Thus an impaired dependency relationship may not only be a source of aggressive feelings, but may also limit a child's capacity to handle such feelings adequately once they are aroused.

A Theory of the Development of Dependency

During his infancy a child is completely helpless and dependent upon others for his survival. While he is incapable of caring for himself, he very quickly learns effective ways of getting the help of others. A cry will bring his mother to attend to his needs. Since his mother's nurturant response brings physical relief, such attention-seeking behavior may be strongly established. As the child grows older he learns to talk and thus has at his disposal a more effective means of communicating his specific needs. He no longer merely cries or becomes restless in order to get help; instead he asks for it directly.

During this period the child not only learns dependency habits but, in addition, the association of his mother's presence with his primary gratifications leads to the development of a dependency motive. His mother feeds him whenever he is hungry, changes him when he is wet, warms him when he is cold, and comforts him when he is in pain. Since she is thus repeatedly associated with satisfying drive-reducing experiences, the positive qualities of these experiences become attached to the mother herself. She thus acquires secondary reward value for the child, and at times her mere presence may be satisfying to him. The child has learned to want his mother in addition to the satisfactions of his physical needs. He now clings to her, follows her about, continuously demands her presence and attention, and seeks her help and recognition. He becomes rivalrous, possessive, and unwilling to share his mother's attention and affection. He also resists and becomes upset at being separated from her, and may, even during infancy, refuse primary gratifications and develop severe feeding disturbances if separation occurs (Escalona, 1945).

While initially the child's dependency is welcomed and fostered, as he grows older his parents strive to bring about certain modifications both in the form and in the objects of his dependency (Heathers, 1955). The physical, clinging forms of expression tend to be discouraged by his parents, and instead the child learns to express dependency in more mature forms such as in seeking his parents' interest, help, and recognition, usually in relationship to his accomplishments. At the same time, he is encouraged to emancipate himself to some degree from his parents and to seek the attention and interest of his peers.

Thus, another aspect of the changes that occur with age is the gradual development of independence. Although his dependency may be fostered during infancy, the child is later expected to become increasingly independent and self-sufficient. The discrepancy between the requirements of childhood and those of adulthood can create conflicts, which may become severe in adolescence. These conflicts have received a great deal of attention in the literature (Hurlock, 1955; Josselyn, 1955; Mohr and Despres, 1958). Their severity will, however, depend on the extent to which independence training has been successfully accomplished during the child's earlier years; indeed, for many children such conflicts may be no more evident in adolescence than they were in childhood.

It is generally believed that during adolescence there is a relatively sudden transfer of dependency from adults to peers, which intensifies the dependency-independence conflict. However, there is evidence to suggest that for most children there is a gradual transfer of dependency from adults to peers that commences very early in life. For example, Heathers (1955) compared the dependency behavior of two-year-old and four-year-old children and found that even over this age range there was a decrease in dependency on teachers and an increase in dependency on peers.

Although a progressive transfer of dependency takes place throughout childhood, in many important areas the majority of adolescents still remain dependent on their parents for advice, help, and emotional support. If an adolescent has basically secure dependency relationships with his parents and other adults, whom he thus can fall back on in times of need, he is better able to take initiative in matters in which he is unpracticed and thus learn to become increasingly self-sufficient and independent. The absence of such secure relationships may, on the other hand, effectively prevent him from establishing strong dependency relationships even with his peers.

Dependency Anxiety as a Reaction to Rejection and Punishment

A characteristic that has been frequently noted among aggressively antisocial boys is their inability to form and maintain stable, dependent, affectional ties to others. They tend to be emotionally guarded or indifferent. Moreover, they are likely to show marked resistance to entering into any close dependency relationship. This absence of affectional, dependent behavior either may spring from an initial failure to develop emotional responsiveness to others or may represent an inhibition of dependency behavior because of the anxiety which its expression arouses.

The amount of *affectional nurturance* that a child receives presumably influences the amount of dependency behavior that he develops. If a mother responds nurturantly to her child's needs, gives him a great deal of attention, and spends much time in affectionate interaction with him, the child's capacity for responding dependently increases. This is borne out by the studies of Levy (1943), who found that the mothers of overdependent children were highly indulgent and oversolicitous. In these cases, however, dependency was not only fostered, but actually accentuated, by the mothers' active discouragement of their children's efforts to gain some independence.

Owing to a young child's weakness and inability to care for himself, he must be offered at least a certain amount of parental care. Therefore, almost all children develop a dependency motive to some degree. However, if from infancy a child is rejected and receives little affectional nurturance, his dependency strivings may be only weakly developed. Several studies have been reported in which it was found that institutionally reared children, who had been severely deprived of maternal nurturance, became socially unresponsive, affectionless, and nondependent (Bowlby, 1951; Goldfarb, 1943; Lowrey, 1940; Spitz, 1945). Similar effects have also been noted in noninstitutionalized children who had experienced early and prolonged separations from their mothers (Freud and Burlingham, 1944). Either these children had never acquired dependency motives or, if they had, their dependency had been partially extinguished under prolonged and severe isolation from personalized contact.

Another factor that may influence the extent to which a child displays dependency behavior is the amount of *frustration or punishment of dependency* that he experiences. Once a dependency motive is established, any rejection or ignoring of a child is likely to increase his dependency needs and to motivate attempts at obtaining dependency gratification (Gewirtz, 1954; Gewirtz and Baer, 1958*a*, 1958*b*; Hartup, 1958). Goldfarb (1945) found that some deprived children showed incessant and indiscriminate clinging and excessive demands for affection and attention, while others appeared apathetic and showed little dependency behavior. These apparently contradictory findings could readily be explained if there were evidence that the deprived children who displayed much dependency behavior had initially received more personalized care than those who were apathetic. Assuming that this initial nurturance had served to develop a dependency motive, the subsequent lack of continuous emotional contact in an institutionalized setting would have the effect of intensifying the dependency needs of these children and thus of increasing their efforts at gaining dependency gratification. Of course, if their efforts continued to go unrewarded, dependency behavior would undoubtedly extinguish. Thus, in order to interpret findings about deprived children, one should know both how much personalized care they had received, particularly during the first few months of their lives, and the degree to which any efforts they had made to obtain dependency gratification had gone unrewarded or had been punished.

While frustration and punishment of dependency behavior may intensify, at least temporarily, a child's efforts at gaining dependency gratification, they also serve to create anxiety about dependency and thus to produce conflicts in this area. The amount of dependency behavior that a child displays at a given time is consequently a function both of the strength of his dependency motive and habits and of the strength of his dependency anxiety. In fact, under conditions of severe punishment, anxiety may be so strong as to inhibit almost all overt dependency.

The effects of frustration and punishment on dependency behavior have been investigated by Sears *et al.* (1953), who found that maternal punishment and lack of nurturance tended to increase the incidence of dependency behavior in preschool boys, but to decrease the incidence of dependency behavior in preschool girls. This led the authors to postulate a curvilinear relationship between the severity of the mothers' frustration and punishment of dependency and the amount of overt dependency behavior shown by their children. It was assumed that the girls, by virtue of their greater identification with the female parent, had adopted their mothers' sanctions and demands as their own to a greater extent than had the boys. Thus, although there was no difference between the boys and girls in the actual amount of punishment and frustration that they had received, the mother's punishment might have had a greater psychological impact on the girls because of the addition of self-punishment. When the girls were thus regarded as more severely punished than the boys, the findings supported the assumption of a curvilinear relationship (Figure 2-1).

Whiting and Child (1953) have provided some additional evidence concerning the influence of frustration and punishment on dependency behavior. They found that adult anxiety concerning dependency was positively related to the severity with which dependency had been socialized. In

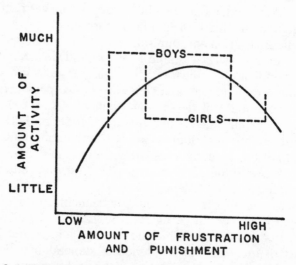

FIGURE 2–1. HYPOTHESIZED RELATIONSHIP BETWEEN AMOUNT OF FRUS-
TRATION OR PUNISHMENT AND AMOUNT OF ACTIVITY (DEPENDENCY)
ENGENDERED BY IT (After R. R. Sears, *et al.*, 1953).

addition, their index of dependency anxiety was negatively
related to the degree of indulgence of dependency needs
before socialization commenced.

While affectional privation on the one hand, and punishment and frustration on the other, may both make a child
nondependent, their effects are somewhat different. In the
severely deprived child who has never experienced any affectionate care, dependency motivation is presumably undeveloped. On the other hand, the child who has experienced
some nurturance, but at the same time has experienced
considerable frustration and punishment, may have developed some capacity and desire for dependency, even though
he is blocked by anxiety from behaving dependently. There
is a good deal of clinical evidence that suggests that the lack
of dependency involvements of many delinquents is due to
conflict, rather than to a failure to develop dependency
needs. The presence of conflict is suggested by the behavior
of delinquents during the course of psychotherapy. Whereas

initially they are likely to be distant and distrustful, when their anxieties are reduced they often display intense dependency behavior (Ackerman, 1944; Bloch, 1952).

Aggression as a Reaction to Dependency Frustration

Frustration created by neglect and rejection frequently elicits anger and aggression. The young child whose needs are urgent, and who at the same time is relatively helpless in caring for himself, will inevitably be frustrated if he does not receive a great deal of attention and care. The most direct evidence that children respond to dependency frustration with aggression comes from the Iowa study of Sears and his collaborators (1953), who found a positive relationship between a lack of maternal nurturance and the incidence of aggressive behavior in boys.

The critical importance of affectional deprivation and rejection in the formation of aggressive disorders has been demonstrated by numerous investigators. Longitudinal studies of institutionally reared children, who had experienced early and severe affectional deprivation, have revealed a high incidence of aggressive disturbances (Goldfarb, 1945; Lowrey, 1940). A lack of adequate affectionate dependency relationships in the history of delinquents has been reported by Healy and Bronner (1936) as a result of a comparison of delinquent children with their nondelinquent siblings, and also by the Gluecks (1950), who compared delinquent with nondelinquent boys. In addition, in an intensive study of a large group of psychopathic children, Bender (1947) found that an early disruption of their dependency on their mothers as a result of separation, neglect, or rejection was the major family background factor in their histories.

Some recent studies, notably those of Bowlby and Friedlander, have not only further confirmed the relationship between dependency privation and aggression, but have also shown that dependency frustration plays a more important role in the development of aggressive disorders than in the development of other forms of behavior pathology. Bowlby (1946), who compared the early family relationships of delinquents with those of otherwise disturbed but nondelinquent children, found that a high proportion of the delinquent children had suffered prolonged separations from their mothers during early childhood, whereas the nondelinquent children had experienced relatively stable and uninterrupted mother-child relationships. Friedlander (1949) reports a similar finding based on a comparison of delinquent and neurotic children.

Although non-nurturance and rejection of a child's dependency needs appear to be important preconditions for the development of antisocial aggression, not all children who are rejected develop aggressive disorders. For instance, withdrawal, overdependency, excessive conformity, and pervasive anxiety may also occur as reactions to rejection (Goldfarb, 1945; Wolberg, 1944). Perhaps the differential effects of rejection are a function, in part, of the severity of the rejection and of the age at which it occurs. Where rejection is less severe and some affection is demonstrated, the child may learn to expect some affectionate responses from his parents. If these affectional rewards are made conditional on his conformity to parental demands, the child may strive to win and maintain his parents' affection by avoiding reactions to frustration that are likely to meet with parental disapproval. Under such conditions a pattern of anxious conformity is more likely to develop than a pattern of aggressiveness. For example, Sears *et al.* (1957) found that mothers who expressed openly what affection they felt for their children but yet had an underlying rejection of them that was expressed through the use of withholding love as a means of discipline, and who were intolerant of aggression, had children who responded with marked dependency.

Goldfarb (1943) compared the behavior problems of adolescents who had been reared during the first three years of their lives in institutions with those of adolescents raised in foster homes in which they presumably had experienced more continuous affectionate care. The institutional children manifested predominantly aggressive disorders, while hyperaggressiveness was rarely found among the foster-home children. On the other hand, those foster-home children who developed problems presented a pattern of shyness and timidity.

In comparing the family backgrounds of overinhibited and aggressive children, both Hewitt and Jenkins (1946) and Lewis (1954) found that early and severe rejection, particularly maternal rejection, was predominant in histories of aggressive children. On the other hand, the parents of over-inhibited children tended to be lacking in warmth, but not completely rejecting, and to make their affection contingent upon the children's conformity to rather severe socialization demands.

A child who is severely frustrated and rejected has little or nothing to gain through controlling the anger and aggression that the frustration provokes. His aggression at least brings temporary relief and may, at the same time, force others to attend to him. While there are other factors, some of which will be discussed later, that also contribute to the development of aggressive behavior patterns in children, there is nevertheless strong evidence that early and severe frustration of a child's dependency needs through rejection is an important precondition of antisocial aggression.

HYPOTHESES

While the general hypotheses concerning the role of dependency in antisocial disorders were based upon clinical observation and prior studies of delinquency, the specific predictions stemmed largely from the theory and research of Sears and his collaborators.

One set of hypotheses was concerned with aspects of the parents' behavior that might contribute to the development of the dependency motive. It was predicted that the parents of the aggressive boys would, in general, show less warmth and affection toward their sons and would be more rejecting than would the control parents. Since the aggressive boys came from families that were relatively intact, it seemed unlikely that they would have experienced the nearly complete deprivation of affectional nurturance that had been suffered by some of the hyperaggressive children described in the literature. Because they had received a certain amount of continuous parental care, it was assumed that the aggressive boys would have to some degree developed a dependency motive.

Once a dependency motive is acquired, the extent to which dependency behavior is manifested overtly is probably determined by the nature of the parents' handling of such behavior. Consequently, hypotheses relating to the parents' handling of the boys' dependency behavior were advanced. It was predicted that the parents of the aggressive boys would be less permissive of dependency behavior, and that they would be more punitive when such behavior occurred. These predictions were based on the conception of the aggressive boy as being fearful of dependency involvements as a result of being continuously frustrated and punished for his dependency strivings. It was assumed that the control parents were average parents in their tolerance of dependency; that, although they would discourage overdependency, they would provide the emotional support which an adolescent needs and thereby maintain their sons' dependency behavior. On the other hand, it was assumed that the greater frustration and punishment of dependency by the parents of the aggressive boys had served to reduce the incidence of such behavior in their sons. These predictions are in accordance with Sears' paradigm of a curvilinear relationship between the amount of frustration and punishment of dependency and the incidence of overt dependency, inasmuch as relatively strong dependency strivings were expected in a group of moderately frustrated boys (Figure 2-1, p. 38).

It was predicted that the aggressive boys, as a result of repeated rebuffs, would feel more rejected by their parents than would the control boys. Since, through such experiences, they would develop expectations of being disappointed and punished in dependency relationships, it was predicted that the aggressive boys would show less overt dependency on their parents than would their controls, and that they would display more anxiety about depending upon them. While their anxiety about dependency would thus have been first learned in relationship to their parents, this anxiety should generalize and make the aggressive boys fearful of, and resistant to, entering into any close dependency relationships. Thus it was predicted that the aggressive boys would show less dependency on their teachers and their peers, and display more anxiety about becoming dependent on them, than would the control boys.

While it was assumed that the parents of the aggressive boys had created anxiety by their handling of their sons' dependency, it was not assumed that they had necessarily eradicated the boys' motivation to behave in a dependent manner. They had succeeded, it was presumed, merely in reducing the overt expression of dependency through the conflict that their rejection and punishment of dependency had created. One form of behavior that clearly typifies a dependency-conflict is negative attention-getting. If a child is fearful of dependency on others, he is apt to avoid direct positive requests for attention and to resort instead to disruptive activity as a way of drawing attention to himself. It was therefore predicted that the aggressive boys would show more negative attention-getting behavior in school than would their controls. Some support for this hypothesis was provided by Sears *et al.* (1953), who found that negative attention-getting behavior in preschool children represented an aggressive way of securing dependency gratification. Although such behavior may gain a child some attention from others, at the same time it tends to alienate the person from whom the attention is gained and thereby further prevents the child from establishing and maintaining a satisfying dependency relationship.

The hypotheses that were advanced referred to the boys' emotional dependency. Although for the sake of completeness a scale was included to measure the extent of the boys' economic dependency on their parents, there seemed no reason to suppose that such dependency would necessarily be related to the other forms of dependency behavior that were measured, and consequently no hypothesis was offered concerning economic dependency.

MEASURES

The boys' *emotional dependency* was assessed in terms of the frequency of behavior that seemed to be aimed at securing a nurturant response from others. The categories of behavior that were chosen for study were *seeking help, seeking praise or approval,* and *seeking the company of others.* This selection was made on the basis of the categories of dependency that were used in the Iowa study of Sears *et al.* (1953). Not all of the categories used in the Iowa study were applicable to adolescents, and most of them needed redefinition in terms of activities that are socially acceptable for adolescent boys. The category of physical contact, for example, was dropped and the category of seeking proximity was replaced by a measure of the boys' tendency to seek the company of others.

Some evidence has been provided by Beller (1955) that, at least for young children, the specific dependency activities of physical contact, seeking proximity, seeking attention, seeking help, and seeking recognition are components of a single motivational system. Consistently positive, if not always large, relationships between the categories of dependent behavior used in the present study suggest that they, too, have at least to some extent a common basis (Table 2-1).

In the present study, one of the main concerns was to assess the extent to which the boys displayed anxiety about dependency. The measurement of *dependency anxiety* poses a somewhat complex problem. The mere absence of dependency behavior in itself does not necessarily indicate anxiety in this area. For instance, a boy may seek little help from his parents either because he is able to cope adequately with his difficulties without their help or because he feels that his parents are not competent to help him. On the other hand, if a boy strongly resists help and assistance even though he is faced with obvious problems that he is unable

TABLE 2-1

INTERCORRELATIONS BETWEEN MEASURES OF DEPENDENCY AND MEASURES
OF DEPENDENCY ANXIETY: DATA FROM BOYS' INTERVIEWS

Dependency on Fathers

	2	3	4	5	6
1. Help-seeking from father	.16	.45	−.30	−.23	−.29
2. Praise-seeking from father		.41	−.30	−.37	−.26
3. Seeking father's company			−.32	−.46	−.29
4. Resistance to father's company				.47	.35
5. Resistance to father's suggestions					.55
6. Resistance to confiding in father					

Dependency on Mothers

	2	3	4	5	6
1. Help-seeking from mother	.31	.59	−.31	−.28	.02
2. Praise-seeking from mother		.56	−.50	−.36	−.10
3. Seeking mother's company			−.50	−.46	−.17
4. Resistance to mother's company				.47	.30
5. Resistance to mother's suggestions					.47
6. Resistance to confiding in mother					

Dependency on Teachers

	2	3	4
1. Help-seeking		.40	−.25	.22
2. Praise-seeking			−.15	−.06
3. Resistance to help				.41
4. Negative attention-getting				

Dependency on Peers

	2	3	4	5
1. Help-seeking from peers	.12	.20	−.39	−.43
2. Approval-seeking		.51	−.03	−.39
3. Seeking company			.00	−.39
4. Resistance to seeking help				.41
5. Resistance to confiding				

Correlations equal to, or greater than, .37 are significant at the .01 level.
Correlations equal to, or greater than, .28 are significant at the .05 level.

to handle on his own, he is probably anxious about being placed in a dependent role. Consequently, one would expect that a scale, for example, measuring the amount of help-seeking behavior would show a negative, but not very high, correlation with a scale measuring resistance to help; and this, in fact, was the kind of relationship that was found (Table 2-1). In addition to the boys' *resistance to accepting help*, their *resistance to spending time in the company of others*, and their *reluctance to trust or confide in them* were regarded as signs of dependency anxiety.

The measure of *negative attention-getting* behavior was used only with regard to the teacher-boy relationship. It showed a significant positive relationship ($r = .41$, $p < .01$) to resistance to accepting help from teachers, which provides some justification of its use as a dependency-anxiety measure. Indeed, the relationships between the measures of dependency anxiety were, in general, even more consistent than those found between measures of dependency (Table 2-1).

The measure of the boys' *feelings of rejection by their parents* took account of the extent to which they felt that their parents lacked interest in them, failed to promote their welfare, or did not seem to enjoy their company. A somewhat similar scale was used to measure the boys' *feelings of rejection by their peers*. This latter scale, however, was not used as a basis for any prediction.

Because of the crucial role generally assigned to the parents' nurturant behavior in the development of dependency, scales were introduced to measure the *extent of the parents' caretaking* activities during the boys' infancy and the amount of time the parents spent in *affectionate interaction* with their sons during the boys' early childhood. In addition, the extent of the parents' affectional demonstrativeness toward their sons was measured by the *warmth* scale which took account of the parent-child relationships from the boys' infancy to their adolescence. A separate measure of the parents' rejection of the boys was included, since it was thought that, although warmth and rejection would be negatively related, they could be somewhat independent factors in the parents' behavior. For instance, a parent might be generally accepting of his son but nevertheless quite undemonstrative. Similarly, a parent might be demonstratively affectionate toward his son but at the same time intolerant and critical of certain of the boy's characteristics. Correlations between warmth and rejection, although significant, were only moderate in size ($r = -.56$ and $-.53$ for mothers and fathers, respectively). The inclusion of both measures was thus justified.

Two aspects of the parents' handling of the boys' dependency behavior were selected for study. One of these, *permissiveness*, referred to the readiness or willingness of the parent to allow dependency behavior to occur, or to continue once it had commenced. In the initial attempt to measure this variable in the pretesting period, considerable difficulty was encountered in devising questions that would elicit information reflecting differences in permissiveness that undoubtedly exist between parents. It was therefore decided to focus primarily on the extent to which dependency was encouraged. Since a parent who is relatively nonpermissive of dependency is unlikely to encourage it, at least a partial measure of permissiveness could in this way be secured.

A measure was also made of the *punitiveness* with which the parents handled the boys' dependency. Difficulties were again encountered in devising interview questions that would elicit relevant data. For the most part, there is no socially approved justification for the discouragement or punishment of dependency behavior such as seeking help, approval, or company. Indeed, for a parent to admit that he ridicules or scolds his child for requesting help or desiring his company is tantamount to admitting callousness according to socially accepted standards. In this respect dependency behavior differs considerably from aggressive or sexual behavior, especially in adolescence. While, at this period, parents are often very concerned to curb a boy's aggressive and sexual impulses and to keep them within socially approved bounds, they are likely to welcome signs of dependency as guarantees of their continuing influence and control. While a parent who is permissive of dependency is unlikely to punish it, a parent who is nonpermissive may discourage or prevent its occurrence in nonpunitive ways, such as making himself less available to his son or by explaining why it would be best for the boy to be on his own. Consequently, a moderate inverse correlation between permissiveness and punitiveness might be expected. Correlations were run between the scale measuring parental encouragement of dependency and the scale measuring parental punitiveness for dependency. The correlations between these two scales were $-.49$ $(p<.01)$ for the mothers and $-.30$ $(p<.05)$ for the fathers. The lower correlation in the case of the fathers was probably due to the limited variability of the ratings of their punitiveness. The relationship between encouragement and punitiveness was therefore similar to the relationship that would have been expected between a permissiveness and punitiveness scale, had a more direct way of estimating permissiveness, other than through degree of encouragement, been devised.

FINDINGS FROM PARENT INTERVIEWS

Affectionate Interaction

It was apparent from the parent interviews that both the aggressive and the control boys had received a good deal of maternal care during their infancy and early childhood. In general, they seemed to have been well cared for, with their mothers assuming most of the responsibility for their upbringing. Both groups of mothers had apparently spent a good deal of their leisure time playing with their sons, reading to them, taking them on walks outdoors, and engaging in other forms of affectionate interaction with them. In this respect there was little difference between the two groups of mothers, either according to their own accounts or according to the accounts given by their husbands (Table 2-2).

The amount of caretaking done by the fathers during the boys' infancy was relatively small and in this respect the

TABLE 2-2

CHILD-TRAINING FACTORS RELATING TO DEPENDENCY: DIFFERENCES
BETWEEN PARENTS OF AGGRESSIVE AND CONTROL BOYS

Scales	Aggressive Group		Control Group		t	p
	Mean	S.D.	Mean	S.D.		
Data from Father Interviews						
Mother's warmth to boy	7.83	1.23	8.44	1.16	1.66	<.10
Father's warmth to boy	6.94	1.56	8.40	1.04	3.65	<.001
Father's rejection of boy	4.63	1.21	3.04	0.76	4.75	<.001
Father's caretaking in boy's infancy	4.46	1.47	4.56	1.59	0.25	N.S.
Father's affectional interaction in boy's early childhood	6.00	1.95	7.04	2.01	1.54	<.10
Mother's affectional interaction in boy's early childhood	8.69	1.56	8.98	1.34	0.66	N.S.
Data from Mother Interviews						
Mother's warmth to boy	7.44	1.43	8.02	1.42	1.62	<.10
Father's warmth to boy	6.38	2.10	7.60	1.64	1.98	<.05
Mother's rejection of boy	4.50	1.29	3.00	1.18	4.27	<.001
Father's caretaking in boy's infancy	4.37	1.16	4.37	1.38	0.00	N.S.
Father's affectional interaction in boy's early childhood	5.77	1.88	6.85	1.93	1.99	<.05
Mother's affectional interaction in boy's early childhood	8.44	1.40	8.96	1.24	1.44	<.10
Combined Estimates						
Mother's warmth to boy	7.63	0.96	8.23	1.16	1.95	<.05
Father's warmth to boy	6.62	1.62	8.01	1.10	3.06	<.01
Father's affectional interaction in boy's early childhood	5.88	1.55	6.96	1.54	2.21	<.02
Mother's affectional interaction in boy's early childhood	8.57	1.23	8.95	1.06	1.08	N.S.

two groups of fathers did not differ. [They did differ, however, in the amount of time that they had spent in affectionate interaction with their sons during the boys' early childhood.] The joint estimates based on the data of both the
mother and father interviews showed that the control fathers
had spent significantly more time in this interaction ($p < .02$).

This difference was more apparent from the mothers' accounts of their husbands' interactions with their sons than from the accounts given by the fathers. A number of the mothers of the aggressive boys described their husbands as lacking interest in their sons.

I. And how about your husband, how much time did he have to play with him and that sort of thing?
M. (Case 49) Not very much, I'm afraid. He just didn't take time. He, well, I don't know what he will tell you, but he (laughs) didn't.
I. What about week ends?
M. Not very much. Well, unless it was with the whole family, but not just him alone. We used to go picnicking and things like that on week ends, but he isn't the type that will go out and play ball or anything like that.

. . .

M. (Case 25) Well, you know how husbands are. They don't take, I don't think they take the interest in; they have their own interests doing different things you know.
I. How much did he do along these lines?
M. Well, he used to play with him in the evening when he was little, sometimes when he was home. But as I say, he wasn't home too often. He had what you call a swing shift.

More often the situation was one in which the father was away from home for a large part of the boy's waking hours and consequently had had very little contact with his son.

I. And what about your husband, how much time did he have to play with him and that sort of thing?
M. (Case 35) Very little. My husband worked nights, so he would come in at midnight and sleep almost 'till noon the next day. So when he was in bed, I'd have to keep the children quiet and on many instances, after Harold was old enough to go to school, my husband would go back off to work before Harold would come back from school. So, as a child, there was very little association there with the father.

In contrast, not only had the control fathers spent more time with their sons, but their relationships with them had been friendly and pleasant.

M. (Case 40) He always has been very much interested in the children and they adored him. It was a very, very pleasant and happy relationship.

I. How much time did he have to play with him?

M. Well, he had in the evening before they went to bed and the week ends only, you see. But then there always was a very fine relationship. I think that's why he gets along with him so well now.

.   .   .

M. (Case 38) He spent lots of time in the evening with him reading to him, playing games with him, teaching him things. It was the first one, and it was fun. And he also had a father that was wonderful to him, and I think he was trying to do the same for his boy.

The disruption of affectional relationships between the aggressive boys and their fathers that was apparent even in the boys' early years had become more strongly evident by the time that these boys had reached adolescence. As Table 2-2 shows, the difference between the groups of fathers in their current warmth or affectional demonstrativeness was significant, whether ratings were based on the fathers' own accounts or on the accounts given by the mothers. The recurrent theme of distance and coldness between father and son is illustrated in the excerpts below.

I. Can you tell me something about the relationship between Stanley and his father? How much affection would you say they show towards each other?

M. (Case 49) They don't. His father loves him, but he doesn't understand him a bit. To him he's just a teen-ager, and to him all teen-agers are equivalent of the headlines you see. That's his idea, and Stan knows that, I think. I don't know, they just don't get along. They don't fight so much, but the feeling is there you know.

.   .   .

F. (Case 21) No, Arnold is not affectionate. He doesn't care for affection as far as his parents are concerned. Now outside, I don't know.

I. How well do you think you and Arnold know and understand one another?

F. Well, that I cannot say. I don't think he understands us at all, or that we understand him.

I. Do you think you usually know how he feels?

F. Definitely not.

In general, the control fathers had closer and warmer relationships with their sons. Yet they were not too openly demonstrative of their feelings. Their affection was more often expressed through their close companionship with their sons and the sharing of many enjoyable experiences. However, some of the control fathers had very demonstrative affectional relationships with their sons; relationships of this kind were not encountered in any of the families of the aggressive boys. Some examples that illustrate the range of the control fathers' warmth toward their sons are given below.

I. How much affection would you say they show toward each other?
M. (Case 16) Just affection in the tone of voice. They don't put their arms around each other or that sort of thing at all. But there is this good relationship between the two of them.

. . .

I. Do you show your affection toward each other quite a bit or are you fairly reserved?
F. (Case 48) Yes, we don't kiss. We don't do that, but I believe he knows that I think very highly of him. I believe there's more affection there than the average son and average father.

. . .

I. Do you show your affection toward each other quite a bit or are you fairly reserved?
F. (Case 36) Yes, we do something that probably most fathers and sons don't do. I usually kiss him on the cheek when I leave, and a greater number of times when he leaves, he'll come over and kiss me on the cheek. He won't do it when there's anyone around because of the shyness of it. He'll come over and shake my hand or say, "Hello, Dad." But if it's just my wife and myself and Ray in the house, he kisses us both on the cheek.

. . .

I. How much affection would you say they show toward each other?
M. (Case 38) They are very affectionate. He kisses his father each night when he comes home. I mean, he's met at the door by the two youngsters and practically knocked down. . . . So I think for a sixteen-year-old boy that's fairly affectionate to continue it this long.
I. How well do you think they understand each other?
M. Pretty good. His father has been pretty close to him.

Neither the mother ratings nor the father ratings, taken alone, yielded any significant differences between the groups of mothers in their warmth toward their sons. In fact, it was only when the ratings from the mother interviews and from the father interviews were combined that a significant difference between the mothers was obtained on the warmth scale ($p < .05$).

Both groups of mothers almost invariably commented on the gradual changes in the boys' manner of expressing affection from the physical forms of infancy and early childhood, such as hugging and kissing, to the verbal forms that predominated by the time the boys had reached adolescence. One mother described these changes in some detail.

I. Do you show your affection toward each other quite a bit, or are you fairly reserved?

M. (Case 33) Well, he was never; he was up until he was eight years old. He didn't want you to kiss, to hug him or anything like that, so I just would gradually, I would talk instead of hugging him or kissing him like I used to. Like he'd come and crawl on my lap, put his arm around me and kiss me on the cheek. He'd want to be loved a little bit, you know, and then he'd go to play. After he got to where he didn't want you to make over him, why, I tried to more or less, when I felt it was right to show him my affection in other ways.

In most cases, as in the one cited above the changes appeared to have been instigated primarily by the boy himself. During the boys' preadolescent years some mothers noted the boys' increasing uneasiness and resistance to their mothers' physical demonstrations of affection. The boys seemed to avoid close physical contact with their mothers and objected to being kissed or hugged; when they did seek some affectionate response, they were more likely to seek it indirectly through provocative teasing and other attention-getting behavior. These changes in affectionate interaction between mother and son were probably determined to a large extent by the boys' increasing sexual maturation. As a boy approaches puberty his mother's physical affection becomes more capable of eliciting sexual feelings which are, under these circumstances, strictly tabooed. As one of the mothers commented, "He feels he's too big to be kissed and petted."

The aggressive boys, in particular, appeared to be markedly resistant to their mothers' attempts to demonstrate affection.

I. Do you show your affection toward each other quite a bit, or are you fairly reserved?

M. (Case 21) We used to be fairly affectionate when he was smaller, but as he got older, why, he resents affection. I'm inclined to be quite affectionate, and I was hoping that would sort of carry on. Oh, I don't mean extreme, or anything like that. I just don't feel like I can go and put my arms around him any more, 'cause he just, he just resents it. So my husband says, "Just leave him alone. Don't force him." And, of course, I haven't in the last year or so. Just haven't, period.

The greater resistance of the aggressive boys may have been due in part to a factor which has not yet been considered, dependency anxiety. As a later section of the chapter shows, the aggressive boys had developed strong anxieties about dependency which led them actively to resist any close dependency involvements. Their mothers' demonstrations of affection may therefore have been doubly threatening to them. Demonstrative physical affection may not only have been a potential instigator of these boys' sexual impulses but may also have elicited their dependency anxiety. Consequently, it is not surprising that the aggressive boys manifested a strong defensive avoidance reaction.

Dependency on Parents

The data from the parent interviews indicated that the aggressive boys showed considerably less emotional dependency on their fathers than did their controls (Table 2-3). On the other hand, a significant difference between the two groups of boys in their dependency on their mothers was obtained only after the ratings of the two separate measures of dependency, seeking the mother's help and seeking the mother's company, had been combined.

The interviews with the fathers showed that the aggressive boys spent considerably less time in their fathers' company than did the control boys. The aggressive boys generally preferred to spend most of their time alone or in the company of other boys, whereas the control boys often shared some common interests such as sports and hobbies with their fathers and thus more readily spent their leisure

TABLE 2-3

BOYS' DEPENDENCY ON PARENTS: DIFFERENCES BETWEEN
AGGRESSIVE AND CONTROL BOYS

Scales	Aggressive Group		Control Group			
	Mean	S.D.	Mean	S.D.	t	p
Data from Father Interviews						
Extent boy seeks help from father	4.56	1.67	6.92	2.01	4.78	<.001
Time spent in father's company	5.81	1.59	6.71	1.23	2.30	<.02 (.05)ᵃ
Total dependency on father	5.20	1.35	6.80	1.11	4.62	<.001
Data from Mother Interviews						
Extent boy seeks help from mother	6.21	1.95	6.90	1.37	1.40	<.10
Time spent in mother's company	6.88	1.69	7.37	1.13	1.27	N.S.
Total dependency on mother	6.55	1.52	7.13	1.02	1.78	<.05

ᵃ The probability in parentheses is based on the Wilcoxon Test.

time in their fathers' company. The qualitative differences in the father-son relationships, which the ratings alone cannot fully reveal, are well illustrated by the two excerpts cited below. The first excerpt was taken from an interview with a control father, the second from an interview with a father of an aggressive boy.

I. When you and he are alone, what sort of things do you do?

F. (Case 18) He likes to go fishing when I go fishing or something like that. He likes that very much, and occasionally even on my job. When school vacations are on, he goes on my job with me sometimes and stays for the day. He seems to enjoy that. Of course, that can't happen very often because the boss would get put out about it.

I. How do you suppose Roy feels about doing things with you, or being out in your company?

F. He seems to enjoy it. That's, that's the general deal, and we have a lot of fun when we do go out.

.   .   .

I. When you and he are alone, what sort of things do you do?

F. (Case 15) Well, not too much of anything as far as entertaining each other. I like to fish. I've never been able to get him too interested in that. He'll go sometimes for a little while, and then he gets bored with it.

I. How do you suppose Duncan feels about doing things with you, or being out in your company.

F. Well, I guess he's more or less pretty bored most of the time. That's the way it seems to work out.

A similar picture emerged from the fathers' accounts of the boys' help-seeking behavior. The data indicated that the aggressive boys sought their fathers' help less often than did the control boys. As a matter of fact, a few of the aggressive boys practically never turned to their fathers for any form of help.

I. When Duncan is in difficulties, does he ever come to you to talk things over?

F. (Case 15) No, not too much. He's more or less on his own.

I. What kind of things does he come to you about?

F. Well, not a lot of anything, as far as coming to me for help.

I. Suppose he's worried about something, or has gotten into a scrape, does he come to you then?

F. No. Not particularly. He may talk about it, but he just as soon not, if he doesn't have to.

More usually, however, the aggressive boys sought their fathers' help on a few minor matters, and particularly on problems dealing with the repair and operation of their cars, but very seldom sought their fathers' guidance or support in personal problems. Indeed, the car seemed to be the one and only point of contact with their fathers for many of the aggressive boys.

I. When Russell is in difficulties, does he ever come to you to talk things over?

F. (Case 39) To my knowledge, no. He never, unless he had something he was fixing or something like that that he needs help on. Actually, the trouble is he never confides in us.

I. Suppose he's worried about something, or has gotten into a scrape, does he come to you then?

F. No.

I. Are there any other ways in which he asks you to help him out?

F. Small things he has difficulties with, he'll come and ask you about that, but if something is troubling him, actually that he's worried about or anything, then I think he never did confide in either of us. Unless it was something small, you know what I mean.

Had separate ratings been made of help-seeking with personal and with more impersonal problems, the differences between the two groups of boys would undoubtedly have been much more marked.

In contrast to the fathers of the aggressive boys, most control fathers described their sons as frequently calling on them for help and assistance on personal problems.

F. (Case 18) If Roy gets himself in a spot, why, he'll come to me. He usually picks a time when there is nobody there, just I and my wife. And he'll come and tell us what the difficulty is and he'll explain it to us. If it's something he did wrong, he'll admit he did wrong and he'll explain every phase of it so we can understand what happened. . . .

I. Besides worries or difficulties, are there any other ways in which he asks you to help him out?

F. Well, sometimes he gets a little beyond my depth. Like school, for instance. He'll bring problems home that he doesn't understand and try to get me to explain them, and if I can, I will. I won't give him a false explanation. If I don't know, I try to find out what the right answers are. We go into it together. I say, "If you find anything wrong, well, bring it in and we'll put it together and maybe we'll get a solution." It usually works out pretty good that way.

While the ratings of the boys' dependency on their mothers were somewhat lower for the aggressive than for the control boys, there were no marked differences comparable to those found for their dependency on their fathers. Indeed, the parent interviews left the impression that the aggressive boys turned primarily to their mothers in times of need; most of the control boys, on the other hand, turned equally readily to either of their parents.

Dependency Anxiety

Not only did the aggressive boys show less emotional dependency on their parents, but they also showed more anxiety about relating to them in a dependent manner. (Table 2-4). This anxiety, which was inferred from the aggressive boys' resistance to accepting the help and company of their

TABLE 2-4

BOYS' ANXIETY ABOUT DEPENDENCY ON PARENTS: DIFFERENCES
BETWEEN AGGRESSIVE AND CONTROL BOYS

Scales	Aggressive Group		Control Group		t	p	
	Mean	S.D.	Mean	S.D.			
Data from Father Interviews							
Boy's resistance to father's help	6.15	1.69	4.15	1.40	5.16	<.001	
Boy's resistance to father's company	4.65	2.23	3.45	1.73	2.25	<.02	(.03)[a]
Total dependency anxiety	5.79	1.78	3.97	1.33	4.15	<.001	
Data from Mother Interviews							
Boy's resistance to mother's help	6.56	1.43	4.33	1.70	5.20	<.001	
Boy's resistance to mother's company	5.00	2.04	4.08	1.61	1.98	<.05	
Total dependency anxiety	5.79	1.29	4.20	1.49	4.24	<.001	

[a] The probability in parentheses is based on the Wilcoxon Test.

parents, was displayed toward both their mothers and their fathers. Both groups of parents acknowledged the boys' preference for being with peers for such matters as visits, vacations, and leisure-time activities. At the same time, however, the control parents seldom reported any active avoidance of their company. A fairly typical picture was presented by the father in Case 52.

I. How do you suppose Mark feels about doing things with you, or being in your company?

F. (Case 52) I think he likes it. I think he does. That is, he likes it until two or three of his cronies come around and they're all hot for going out there and seeing some hi-fi set that some kid built, and away they go.

In many control families, in fact, both the parents and the boy seemed to derive considerable enjoyment from one another's company on the occasions that they were together.

M. (Case 8) We enjoy the same things and, when we're alone home together, we watch TV and get a lot of pleasure out of that. We like the same types of records and we discuss it and we like the same type of humor. We get an awful lot of enjoyment out of each other's company.

I. How do you suppose Sidney feels about doing things with you, or being in your company?

M. I think he enjoys our company, or he wouldn't be there so much. Of course, part of the time he'll leave and go up to his room, 'cause he's got a lot of studying to do. But he's with us purely because he wants to be.

.   .   .

I. How do you suppose Howard feels about doing things with you, or being out in your company?

F. (Case 46) I think he likes it very much. He likes to be around me as much as he could, and that goes for myself, too.

Indeed, some of the control parents, particularly the fathers, expressed their regret that, as the years passed by, they were inevitably losing more and more of the rewards that their sons' company had brought them.

F. (Case 46) The only thing I'd do differently would be to spend more time with him. Because that's the greatest pleasure in life, children and to be with them. They grow up, and they're gone.

In contrast to this, most of the aggressive boys were at best described as disinterested or indifferent to their parents' company.

I. How do you suppose Arnold feels about doing things with you, or being out in your company?

F. (Case 21) He just seems to be, well, indifferent or not interested. I don't know what, how you really put it into words. You know what I mean. He doesn't seem to be happy or unhappy. He's just going along because I'd like him to go along, and not because he's enjoying it or not enjoying it. He doesn't show it.

At times they showed active resistance to being in the company of their parents, such resistance being most evident when the parents brought pressure on the boys to spend time with them. An example of one boy's strong avoidance of his parents and their equally strong pressure for his company was given by the mother in Case 33.

M. (Case 33) Well, he's got so for a while, he, I told him one time that the only time he came home was to eat and sleep, but he gradually got over that and stayed home a lot and he went with us. Since he came home, there was only one time we insisted that he go with us. He wanted to stay here in town alone while we went up to the country. He wanted to stay the week end by himself. We wouldn't let him because we didn't feel that was right. And we talked with his probation officer and we made Donald go with us. And we talked with him (probation officer) afterwards and he said we did the right thing.

It was evident, however, that the aggressive boys' parents did not usually force their company on their sons and consequently did not in this way elicit strong anxiety reactions. Their attempts to instigate dependency more often took the form of offering advice or recommendations, and the aggressive boys' anxiety was thus predominantly reflected in their resistance to accepting help and counsel from their parents. There were several forms in which this resistance was manifested. One of these forms, and the most common one, involved a blatant rejection of any assistance that might threaten to place the boys in a dependent position. They insisted on coping with problem situations on their own and ignored any help that was offered them; at times they seemed to do the very opposite of what their parents suggested.

I. When you offer Duncan advice or make a suggestion to him, what does he do?
F. (Case 15) In general, he goes ahead and ignores it.
I. Do you feel that he does the very opposite to what you suggest just because you suggested it?
F. Yes, at times he does. He likes to disagree.

                                        •   •   •

M. (Case 45) He'll listen, but generally he wants to make his own decisions. I believe I've often said that, if we suggest one thing, Brian will go in the other direction. Whether he's doing that just to show us he's going to make his own decisions, or whether he really disagrees with us, I'm not very sure.

Another form of resistance was a guarded seclusiveness through which the boys defended themselves against any closeness with others. In describing an aggressive boy, his

parents often referred to him as "distant," "keeping to himself," "shut in," and other terms that suggested that the
boy was difficult to approach. Any attempts to offer him
help or support were met only with strong resistance.

I. When Arnold is in difficulties, does he ever come to you to talk
things over?
M. (Case 21) Well, you mean such as a heart-to-heart talk about something? No, he stays off by himself pretty much. He seems to work
things out by himself. In other words, he doesn't come to us very
often about any kind of problem.
I. Suppose he's worried about something, or has gotten into a scrape,
does he come to you then?
M. He's pulled himself in a shell pretty much. I think he has been
worried about a few things but I can't seem to—like I say, he
doesn't open up.

. . .

I. When Philip is in difficulties, does he ever come to you to talk
things over?
F. (Case 37) No.
I. Suppose he's worried about something, or has gotten into a scrape,
does he come to you then?
F. No.
I. Are there any other ways in which he might ask you to help him
out?
F. Kind of hard to answer. Difficulties, something wrong with his
car he wouldn't hesitate to ask me to help him correct it. Personal
problems, no. He would never, he's too retiring. He wouldn't talk
about them. In fact he would get somewhat upset if you tried to
find out what was bothering him.

In contrast, whenever the control boys encountered a
situation that necessitated some help, they typically accepted
parental assistance or advice with little conflict or anxiety.
In fact, a few of them seemed rather too ready to rely on
their parents. For example, one boy kept a notebook of his
parents' advice and suggestions so that he would have a
constant guide for his behavior. Another example was provided by the father in Case 46.

F. (Case 46) He comes to me for any advice. When anything comes
up, he comes and asks me. I have to be careful about being too
positive about anything, because he believes anything I tell him.

It was noted in the previous section that the two groups of boys did not greatly differ in the extent to which they sought dependency gratification from their mothers. They did, however, differ in the amount of anxiety they displayed about being made dependent on their mothers. In fact, the difference in anxiety between the two groups of boys was as apparent in their interactions with their mothers as it was in their interactions with their fathers.

Parental Handling of Dependency

Both groups of parents tended to emphasize the extent to which they encouraged the boys' dependency and to deny its discouragement through punishment. The fathers, in particular, were prone to deny flatly the use of punishment. In spite of this, some evidence was found to support the hypothesis that the aggressive boys had experienced more punishment for dependency behavior. This was most apparent in the case of the boys' help-seeking behavior, which the mothers of the aggressive boys discouraged and punished to a significantly greater extent than did the control mothers (Table 2-5).

In their interviews, the control mothers typically stressed their constant availability to their sons. They depicted their sons as having developed the expectation that they could always turn to their parents whenever they encountered difficulties that they were incapable of handling on their own or when they were in need of some emotional support.

I. How much have you encouraged him to come to you for help in things like these?

M. (Case 40) I've always told him to always come to us, you know, if there was anything he needed like that. We would always be there to help and guide him as best we could.

I. Have you ever discouraged him from coming because you felt he should stand on his own feet a little more?

M. No. I never have done that.

.   .   .

M. (Case 38) We've always been willing and we've always had time, regardless of what either I or my husband were doing. We'd sit down and take time to answer his questions from the time he was a little fellow.

TABLE 2-5

PARENTS' HANDLING OF BOYS' DEPENDENCY: DIFFERENCES BETWEEN
PARENTS OF AGGRESSIVE AND CONTROL BOYS

Scales	Aggressive Group		Control Group		t	p
	Mean	S.D.	Mean	S.D.		
Data from Father Interviews						
Encouragement to spend time in father's company	6.73	1.51	6.58	0.91	0.43	N.S.
Encouragement of help-seeking	7.92	1.55	8.15	1.41	0.62	N.S.
Punitiveness for help-seeking	2.15	0.77	2.00	0.00	0.97	N.S.
Punitiveness for seeking father's company	2.00	0.00	2.04	0.13	1.48	N.S.
Data from Mother Interviews						
Encouragement to spend time in mother's company	7.08	1.46	7.15	0.90	1.20	N.S.
Encouragement of help-seeking	8.44	1.19	8.69	1.11	0.72	N.S.
Punitiveness for help-seeking	3.52	1.46	2.63	0.96	2.39	<.02 (.05)*
Punitiveness for seeking mother's company	2.50	0.08	2.29	0.80	1.28	N.S.

* The probability in parentheses is based on the Wilcoxon Test.

I. Have you ever discouraged him from coming because you felt he should stand on his own feet a little more?
M. No. No, I don't think so.

Since their dependency had customarily been rewarded by their parents, the control boys were well oriented toward seeking their parents' help. Consequently, there was no longer much need for the control parents to instigate or encourage their sons' dependency. In fact, a number of the control mothers said that they did not encourage their sons to seek their help because they had no need to do so.

I. When Tony is in difficulties, does he ever come to you to talk things over?

M. (Case 30) Oh, yes. He comes batting in the front door. The front door slams. "Hey, Mom. Hey, kids, where's Mom?" "I'm here, honey, what do you want?" "Oh, Mom, I got a parking ticket, doggone it."

I. What do you say?

M. I don't say much. I just listen. Sometimes it's dates. "Hey, Mom, help me out. How am I going to get out of going with so and so? If she calls up, tell her I'm not here." I say, "No. I won't tell her you're not here. You do your own dirty work." "Oh, Mom, please, please. . . ." (laughs)

I. How much have you encouraged him to come to you for help in things like these?

M. Always, always. We expect him to. I don't say I've encouraged him. I mean the kids all know that we expect them to come to us. There's no question about it. If I'm in trouble, I come home to the family. If my husband had a bad day, he comes home and tells the family. If one of my children has trouble, where else would he come but to the family?

Although some mothers of aggressive boys expected their sons to come to them for help with their personal problems, they nevertheless emphasized the importance of the boys' learning to handle these very same problems on their own and of their learning to fend for themselves. Such conflicting parental expectations were not uncommon. A situation in which a boy is both encouraged and punished for the same behavior is certainly liable to make him conflicted. An interaction sequence in which the boy was encouraged to seek the mother's help, yet when he did so was rebuffed, was described by the mother in Case 11.

I. How much have you encouraged him to come to you for help in things like these?

M. (Case 11) Oh, we've told him all along, if he wants help, to come to his dad or me. . . .

I. When Edward has a decision to make, to what extent does he talk it over with you?

M. He'll tell me about it. Sometimes ask me what he should do.

I. What might you say in a case like this?

M. I tell him to make up his own mind. I like them to think for themselves.

As this mother further described her son's behavior it was evident that he had almost completely inhibited his dependency strivings, a solution that seemed to have been adopted by many of the aggressive boys.

I. When Edward is in difficulties, does he ever come to you to talk things over?
M. No. He keeps his own counsel about things.
I. Suppose he's worried about something, or has gotten into a scrape, does he come to you then?
M. No. He keeps it to himself.
I. How about asking you to help him on his schoolwork?
M. Well, he does it so seldom. . . .

In comparison to the control boys, the aggressive boys made few dependency demands upon their parents. It would seem, therefore, that the parents of the aggressive boys would have had less need to discourage dependency behavior and that, if anything, independence training would have been of greater concern to the control families. This, however, did not seem to be the case. In responding to the question on the parents' encouragement of dependency, the parents of the aggressive boys more often stressed the need for the boy to be independent. This further suggested that the aggressive boys had experienced the more severe socialization of their dependency.

I. How much have you encouraged him to come to you for help in things like these?
M. (Case 35) Well, I've never turned him down on anything. I feel in my own mind that he would come. I don't think a person ought to keep encouraging and encouraging a child all the time. I think they should do a few things on their own.

If parents have repeatedly frustrated and punished their children's dependency behavior, the children may give up seeking their parents' help and support. In this case, the parents have little occasion to discourage or punish dependency behavior during their children's later development. There was some evidence that such a process had been operating in the families of the aggressive boys. This would, of course, tend to diminish the differences in punitiveness between the parents of the aggressive boys and the control parents. The fathers of the aggressive boys, in particular, seemed to have had few opportunities for punishing or discouraging their sons' dependency behavior.

I. Have you ever discouraged him from coming because you felt he should stand on his own feet a little more?

M. (Case 49) We have told him that, but we haven't had occasion for it because he doesn't rely too much on us. I don't think he does, anyway.

. . .

M. (Case 21) No, I never discourage him because he never comes, you know, very much and I certainly don't want to discourage what little bit he would come.

. . .

F. (Case 5) We've never had to really press that issue. He's stood on his own feet pretty much.

However, in the case of aggressive boys who were currently striving for dependency gratifications, it was sometimes quite evident that their mothers frustrated and punished their dependency behavior.

I. Have you ever discouraged him from coming because you felt he should stand on his own feet a little more?

M. (Case 45) Oh, yes. I've told him that lots of times. Oh, yes, . . . and his father has told him that many times too. He does depend on us too much, just for the simple everyday things around the house. Just takes them for granted. . . . There have been times when I've become annoyed when he comes to me with his troubles right away. I think, "Well, he's let us down again," and I get up on my high horse. I'll admit that. But I think for the most part I've heard him through before putting in my little speech.

. . .

I. Have you ever discouraged him from coming because you felt he should stand on his own feet a little more?

M. (Case 15) Yes. I've told him that it was strictly his problem. He'd have to work it out to his best advantage, such problems as in school, how to get along and so forth. Yes. I've pointed out to him that he's sixteen now, and he should make his own decisions about certain things and start to think about his future. . . .

I. Do you ever feel he wants to be too much in your company?

M. He doesn't want to be too much in my company, but he demands too much of my attention when he's around in proportion to the amount of attention that I can give him and the little girl. I try to encourage him to spend more time with his father (laughs), but they don't seem to have too much in common as far as discussing things. . . . He gets on my nerves 'cause he constantly demands attention regardless of what I'm doing. He helps himself to anything he sees and wants. He doesn't seem to have much consideration for the rest of the family.

The second of the above excerpts illustrates how dependency needs may be strengthened through repeated frustration. As he was turned away, the boy demanded more strongly the attention and interest that his mother denied him. Finally, he aggressively appropriated objects around the house, which probably led his mother to reject him all the more strongly.

In some instances, although the mothers did not punish their sons' dependency directly, they nevertheless were unwittingly instrumental in associating their sons' dependency behavior with punishment. For instance, instead of supplying their sons with the emotional support that they sought, they would report the boys' problems to their husbands, who in turn would punish the boys for getting into difficulties. This naturally made the boys fearful of confiding in their mothers and reluctant to seek their help.

I. When Stanley is in difficulties, does he ever come to you to talk things over?
M. (Case 49) No. He doesn't like to talk to anybody at such times.
I. Suppose he's worried about something, does he come to you then?
M. No.
I. How about asking you for help on his schoolwork?
M. Very seldom asks for that either, unless he wants me to help him with a book report. But that's not too often.
I. How much have you encouraged him to come to you for help in things like these?
M. Well, by the pattern he has set I don't think I've encouraged him enough, because he doesn't. I would like for him to, but maybe I didn't make my likes known to him. Maybe he just didn't. I don't know why he didn't feel that he could, because I don't think I've ever turned him away. I know sometimes he doesn't confide in me

because he's afraid I'll tell his father. Says he doesn't want to tell me something because he supposed, "You'll tell everything you know to Pa." I get the feeling sometimes that's the reason he doesn't.

. . .

M. (Case 15) Well, I've told him that, "When there's anything you want to know, just come and ask me. I'll tell you to the best of my ability." He said, "Oh, then you'll tell Dad, and then I get scared." He said, "I don't feel like telling you things."

Although some differences were found between the groups of parents in their punitiveness for dependency, it is possible that a more subtle approach than the one used might have elicited a wider range of responses concerning the handling of dependency, and so brought results even more consistent with the hypotheses than those that were obtained. It was noted earlier that the punishment of a child's strivings for a positive social interaction has no social sanction and is unlikely to be openly practised or acknowledged. The operation of reward and punishment may therefore be a more subtle process where dependency is concerned. The general attitude and emotional responsiveness of parents may, in fact, be more important factors in producing dependency anxiety than their handling of dependency behavior. Indeed, parental rejection seems to involve a pervasive form of punishment of the child's attempts to gain emotional support from his parents. If this is so, there can be little doubt that the aggressive boys had experienced many rebuffs in their attempts to gratify their dependency needs. Both the mothers and fathers of the aggressive boys were more rejecting of their sons than were the control parents, the differences being significant beyond the .001 level.

Some empirical evidence that parents who reject their children are also likely to punish them for dependency was, in fact, obtained from the mother interviews. Mothers who rejected their sons tended to punish the boys both for seeking their help ($r = .40$; $p < .01$) and for seeking their company ($r = .29$; $p < .05$). Perhaps because of the small variability in the ratings of the fathers' punitiveness for dependency, the corresponding correlations for the fathers failed to reach significance.

The extent to which the rejecting, non-nurturant behavior of the parents of the aggressive boys was a cause or an effect of the boys' aggression is difficult to determine without a longitudinal study. The parents' attitudes and behavior were certainly influenced to some extent by the boys' current and past behavior. On the other hand, the parents' retrospective accounts of their handling of their sons in early childhood and their descriptions of early parent-child relationships gave considerable support to the hypothesis that parental rejection and lack of nurturance are determinants of aggression. When some of the factors that were associated with the parents' rejecting behavior were examined, the picture became even more convincing.

In most cases the defective parent-child relationship was not an isolated problem, but reflected the parents' inability to establish close relationships with other people. For example, the marital relationships between the parents of the aggressive boys were frequently disrupted. These parents showed less warmth toward, and less acceptance of, each other than did the control parents. This aspect of the family relationships will be discussed in more detail in Chapter 6.

In some instances, the parents of the aggressive boys rejected the boy because he possessed characteristics that they were unable to accept in themselves. One mother revealed considerable awareness of this process.

M. (Case 45) I think that there are certain traits probably in Brian that might remind me of myself, and those are the ones I don't like. There might be some tie-in there.

An example of how a father's early rejection of his son may be an expression of his own emotional problems was given by the mother in Case 21.

I. And what about your husband? How much time did he have for things like this? (Affectionate interaction with boy in early childhood.)

M. (Case 21) He had about the same amount of time as I did to play with him, but actually he didn't have the patience with him. My husband is quite nervous, nervous temperament, and that might account for it.

Occasionally a father's conflicts over his own sex role and masculinity interfered with his ability to accept and to relate closely to his son. The correlations between paternal rejection and other characteristics of the fathers revealed that fathers who rejected their sons tended also to display relatively high sex anxiety ($r = .33$) and to make relatively few demands on their sons for masculinity ($r = -.44$). A father's difficulty in relating to his male child and his strong avoidance of the boy as he showed increasing masculinity was illustrated in Case 15.

I. How much affection would you say they show toward each other?
M. Not a great deal. Duncan likes to be around his father, but they seem to have a difference of opinion in any and all subjects and there's a certain awkwardness between them that doesn't exist between him and my little girl. My husband is a rather distant and reserved person. He's not distant to me or the little girl, but he doesn't, he seems bewildered by the fact that Duncan has suddenly grown up. He doesn't know quite how to approach him. He was very affectionate toward him when he was small. I'd say from twelve years on he began to be a little more awkward in his approach to him.

The foregoing considerations cannot provide a conclusive answer to the question of causality. They do, however, suggest that the attitudes and behavior of the parents of the aggressive boys were not merely reactions to their sons' conduct, but were at least in part antecedent conditions of the boys' aggressive behavior.

RESULTS FROM BOYS' INTERVIEWS

Dependency on Parents

The ratings of the boys' interviews provided strong confirmatory evidence of the aggressive boys' reluctance to enter into dependency relationships. The aggressive boys sought the help and company of their parents to a much lesser degree than did the control boys (Table 2-6). Their

TABLE 2-6

Differences in Dependency Behavior between Aggressive and Control Boys: Data from Boys' Interviews

Scales	Aggressive Group		Control Group		t	p	
	Mean	S.D.	Mean	S.D.			
Extent boy seeks help from:							
Mother	5.33	2.03	6.79	1.71	2.78	<.01	
Father	4.37	1.76	6.96	1.51	5.20	<.001	
Teacher	3.98	1.18	5.25	1.50	3.44	<.01	
Peers	4.73	1.61	6.50	1.16	4.69	<.001	
Extent boy seeks praise from:							
Mother	5.92	1.98	6.35	1.38	0.80	N.S.	
Father	5.58	1.91	6.35	1.66	1.44	<.10	
Teacher	4.98	1.57	7.06	1.10	5.05	<.001	
Seeking parent's company:							
Mother's company	4.52	1.36	5.31	1.35	1.95	<.05	
Father's company	4.96	1.54	6.13	1.81	2.42	<.02	
Extent boy seeks approval of peers	7.02	2.28	8.15	1.15	1.88	<.05	(.06)[a]
Importance of group activity	7.27	2.25	7.04	1.95	0.43	N.S.	

[a] The probability in parentheses is based on the Wilcoxon Test.

lack of dependency was most evident in their relationships with their fathers, a finding that is consistent with the results obtained from the parent interviews. However, the boys' reports suggested that the difference between the groups of boys in their dependency on their mothers was more marked than the interviews with the mothers alone indicated.

In most cases the aggressive boys appeared to turn to their parents only when there was no possibility of dealing with their difficulties without some form of help.

I. How about if you are worried about something or have gotten into a scrape? Do you go to them?

B. (Case 47) No. I usually keep it to myself. . . . Well, if I, if there was really something that I couldn't keep to myself, I think I would go to her (mother) more than to my father.

From the accounts given by some aggressive boys, it appeared that they had completely ceased to depend on their parents.

I. How often would you say you went to your father to talk things over?

B. (Case 33) Never.

I. How about getting him to help you with your schoolwork?

B. No.

I. How about if you were worried about something or had gotten into a scrape? Do you go to him then?

B. No. I never go to my parents.

I. When your parents make a suggestion, do you usually accept it or do you prefer to work it out for yourself?

B. I'd rather work things out for myself. . . .

I. Some fellows go around with their parents quite a lot, for example on trips or to movies. Others don't like this very much. How do you feel about this?

B. I don't go.

In contrast, many of the control boys felt that they could benefit from the parents' experience and readily turned to them for support and guidance.

I. How often would you say you went to your father to talk things over?

B. (Case 28) About, maybe about, do you think I should do this, or about maybe a job, or if he thinks I should take it, or if he thinks I should go someplace or do this, or on money problems or anything, I ask my father.

I. Do you do the same with your mother?

B. Not as much with my mother as with my father. I'm not closer to him than to my mother, but I think what I do, he's done usually and he has more insight into it. . . .

I. Now I'd like to ask you how often you go somewhere with your father.

B. I go with him, not regularly, but not just on special occasions. As much as possible, as much as I want to and, you know, not on vacations, but say there was a picnic yesterday, the office picnic, I usually go. I didn't go yesterday because I was working, but I have gone all the time. Fishing once in a while and football games; he tries to take me. He says he wants me to see everything in life and things he hasn't had the opportunity to. We try to, we do a lot of things together.

The two groups of boys did not differ greatly in the extent to which they sought to win their parents' praise and approval. This may be partly due to the fact that the questioning of the boys on this point was not very detailed, so that ratings had to be made on the basis of unelaborated answers. Moreover, the seeking of approval may have been a less direct and, therefore, a less threatening way of eliciting nurturant behavior from the parents than asking for their help or seeking their company. A boy must make a somewhat direct bid for his parents' company or assistance; he may win their approval through some behavior which involves no direct interaction with them, but which he knows is likely to please them. By thus seeking approval, he may receive some dependency gratification without having to risk a direct rebuff.

Dependency on Teachers

Since attitudes and behavior learned in relation to the parents are commonly transferred to some degree to other authority figures, it was expected that the aggressive boys would show disturbed dependency relations with their teachers. The findings suggest, if anything, an accentuation of their dependency problems in the school situation (Table 2-6). Differences on all scales relating to dependency on teachers were significant beyond the .01 level.

The control boys typically sought and appreciated their teachers' help and advice on a wide range of problems.

I. How do you feel about going to a teacher or a counselor to talk over problems?
B. (Case 36) I think it's the only way to clear things up. I mean, I very frequently do that, especially with teachers that I really get along with. I discuss many things outside the school even like dating, their life, why they teach and stuff like that.

However, these boys sought their teachers' help mainly as an aid in reaching their own solutions to problems, a fact which was stressed by many of them and can be illustrated by the further remarks of the boy who has just been quoted.

I. If a teacher or counselor offers you advice or makes a suggestion, do you generally follow it, or do you prefer to work things out for yourself?

B. Usually, if the basic idea seems good. I like to work things out for myself a lot of times, but I will take advice. Usually it helps you work them out for yourself.

The aggressive boys were, in general, much less inclined to seek their teachers' help. Some of them expressed both their discomfort about the thought of seeking help from teachers and their perplexity over their inability to seek their teachers' help.

I. How do you feel about going to a teacher or counselor to talk over problems?

B. (Case 23) I don't like to.

I. How about asking them for help with schoolwork?

B. No.

I. Does it ever make you feel uncomfortable if you have to get help from a teacher or counselor?

B. I just don't like it. I just, I don't know, I just don't like asking them for help. I don't want to. I don't know why. I just don't like it.

On the approval-seeking scale the difference between the groups of boys was significant beyond the .001 level; this finding forms a contrast to the absence of any appreciable differences for seeking approval from the parents. These divergent findings may be partly due to the fact that this area was explored much more extensively and directly in relation to the teachers, and thus considerably more rateable material was elicited.

Dependency on Peers

On both the help-seeking and approval-seeking scales that related to peers, the control boys secured significantly higher ratings than did the aggressive boys. The sense of security that the peer group may provide was reflected in a number of the control boys' comments.

I. Some fellows like very much to have friends with whom they can talk things over and whom they can trust. Others think it best to rely on none but themselves. How do you feel about this?

B. (Case 40) I like to rely on other people, too. Like you get real close friends, you can always fall back on them.

An acknowledgment of a need to rely on others may be experienced as a confession of inadequacy. Even the control boys laid emphasis on the importance of reaching their own decisions once they had received the support necessary for handling their problems. The provisional acceptance of their dependency seemed, in fact, to help them to achieve the sense of independence they desired.

I. Suppose you were in a jam and needed help. How many friends of your own age have you to whom you could go in a case like that?
B. (Case 26) I can go to anybody in the club, or I can go to a lot of kids in school. I have lots of friends with which to talk over our problems.
I. How often would you say you went to your friends for suggestions on how to do things?
B. I don't do it all the time, but usually when I have an important decision to make, I usually ask a lot of people which would be the right way to do it. I always do that, ask a lot of people and get different ideas and make my own decision.

The aggressive boys were much more likely to minimize the extent to which they sought help and approval or even to respond to the interviewer's questions with a blatant assertion of their independence.

I. How do you feel about asking favors of friends, like lending you money or fixing you up with a date?
B. (Case 25) I want to get my own. If you can't work for it, why have it?

On the group activity measure, designed to assess the extent to which the company of peers was sought, no difference was found between the two groups of boys. This measure, as a matter of fact, proved to be inadequate. From the way in which the boys answered questions about group activity, it became clear that a boy might discount its importance for one of two reasons. De-emphasis sometimes arose from the boy's inability to relate to his peer group, but at other times it seemed to reflect a healthy development of independent interests and judgment.

TABLE 2-7

DIFFERENCES IN DEPENDENCY ANXIETY BETWEEN AGGRESSIVE AND
CONTROL BOYS: DATA FROM BOYS' INTERVIEWS

Scales	Aggressive Group		Control Group		t	p
	Mean	S.D.	Mean	S.D.		
Resistance to receiving help from:						
Teachers	5.65	1.91	3.63	1.33	4.27	<.001
Peers	5.13	2.28	4.00	1.45	1.73	<.05 (.06)ᵃ
Resistance to suggestions from:						
Mother	6.58	1.97	4.60	1.67	3.79	<.001
Father	6.35	2.19	4.11	1.65	3.27	<.01
Resistance to parent's company:						
Mother's company	4.50	2.41	3.81	2.01	1.20	N.S.
Father's company	4.35	2.77	3.17	1.62	1.72	<.05 (.07)ᵃ
Resistance to accounting for activities to:						
Mother	5.23	2.00	3.65	1.53	3.04	<.01
Father	4.96	2.00	3.96	1.61	2.32	<.02
Resistance to confiding in peers	6.27	1.94	4.25	1.54	3.56	<.001
Negative attention-getting behavior toward teachers	6.27	2.33	4.67	1.63	2.81	<.01

ᵃ The probabilities in parentheses are based on the Wilcoxon Test.

Dependency Anxiety

The hypothesis that the aggressive boys would show
strong anxiety about dependency was confirmed (Table 2-7).
This anxiety was equally apparent in their relationships with
their parents, their teachers, and their peers. The aggressive
boys' responses to the interview questions indicated that
the relatively small amount of dependency behavior that
they showed arose less from a mature, conflict-free self-
reliance than from a fearful avoidance of dependency involvements.

The differences between the groups of boys were most
apparent in their relationships to their peers. When dealing
with their relationships to adults, the aggressive boys tended,

for the most part, merely to describe their avoidant reactions. In dealing with their peer relationships, however, the boys tended also to express the feelings of threat and distrust that dependency situations created in them.

Here are the contrasting replies of an aggressive and of a control boy to the same question.

I. Does it ever make you feel uncomfortable if you have to get help from another fellow or can't make up your mind for yourself?

B. (Case 7) Sometimes it does. I don't know, it's just something inside me that don't make me feel very good.

. . .

B. (Case 36) No. That's what friends are, for something. It's a good thing you have them.

The following excerpts from one interview illustrate how anxiety and distrust may underlie the avoidance of dependency involvements.

I. When a friend suggests something to you, do you generally do what he suggests, or do you prefer to work things out for yourself?

B. (Case 33) I prefer to work things out for myself.

I. Does it ever make you feel uncomfortable if you have to get help from another fellow or can't make up your mind for yourself?

B. Yes, it does. It makes me feel like I need somebody around me.

I. How do you prefer to spend your time, alone or in the company of friends?

B. Alone.

I. What sort of things do you prefer to be alone to do?

B. Listen to music, read, walk. . . .

I. Suppose you disagree with a decision, do you usually go along with them (friends), or do you go off by yourself and do what you want to do?

B. Once in a while I go with them, but most of the time I go off by myself.

I. Do you care very much what other guys think of you?

B. No. . . .

I. If your friends don't like some ways you act, do you try to change, or do you think that's your business and not theirs?

B. I try to avoid them. If they don't like the way I act, then I try to avoid them.

I. Would you say you like to have friends to talk things over with and trust in, or do you think it's better to rely on nobody but yourself?

B. I want to rely on myself. I don't want to rely on others.

I. How much do you think you can trust other guys?

B. Not too far.

In their relationships with adults the aggressive boys were inclined to ignore, or even openly reject, opportunities for help and support.

I. How often would you say you went to her (mother) to talk things over?

B. (Case 49) Hmm. Not very often. I'm getting in a jam where I don't talk about it with anyone.

I. Does she ever help you with your schoolwork?

B. No. I've never asked her. She would if I asked her, but I never have asked her.

. . .

I. When a teacher or counselor offers you advice or makes a suggestion, do you generally follow it or do you prefer to work things out for yourself?

B. (Case 15) I can't make up my mind at first, but it seems like when someone gives me some advice I make up my mind to do something else.

Several of the boys, in fact, reported that their parents had given up any further attempts at advice and guidance and had in recent years let them steer their own course.

Occasionally, the boys' uneasiness about having to seek help was as apparent in their relationships to adults as in their peer relationships.

I. How do you feel about going to a teacher or counselor to talk over problems?

B. (Case 25) I don't like to. You know, you feel kind of funny.

. . .

I. Does it ever make you feel uncomfortable if you have to get help from a teacher or counselor?

B. (Case 31) Yes, it does. I think I should be able to do everything myself without anyone else's help.

Negative attention-getting behavior was regarded as symptomatic of conflict in the area of dependency. Such behavior was considerably more frequent among the aggressive boys and took such forms as walking about the classroom, throwing airplanes, frequent questioning of teachers, making loud remarks to other students and otherwise interfering with them. While these are all more or less aggressive forms of behavior, their predominant function appears to be the eliciting of the interest and attention of others. Indeed, little or no personal hostility might be involved.

I. Do you sometimes do things openly in school for which you know you'll get told off or punished?
B. (Case 25) Yes. I used to smoke in the back of the room in Mr. Molt's class. He used to say, "Fellows, I smell smoke." We used to put up an argument and go back and light up again. "Fellows, I smell smoke." He never turned us in, though. He was an easygoing guy. We used to cut up in his class, throw airplanes. One girl had real long pigtails. We used to tie her to the next chair. She'd get up and pull the chair with her. "Oh, my head." (laughs)

The way in which such behavior might be self-defeating, by alienating the boy from the affection of which he already felt deprived, was illustrated by an incident described by the mother in Case 13.

M. Glen, in the last year in school he just seems like he can't get his mind to settle down and go to work. He was always, he's a kid who makes other kids laugh. You know, he'll make faces, making all the kids laugh. Naturally, the teacher doesn't like that because, if she can't calm him down, she can't get the whole room. So Glen will come home and say, "Oh, mother, I just can't, she don't like me, the teacher"; and I try to explain, "How could she like anybody that would act like that?"

In answer to the questions designed to tap dependency anxiety, the control boys, for the most part, gave further evidence of how helpful they found others to be. The conflicts they felt were more likely to be of the approach-approach type, arising from the conflicting attractions of their homes and of peer group activities.

B. (Case 28) When I'm out with my friends, they (parents) object strongly to me coming home too late—and I object to them objecting. Because here again, if you think about it, should a boy stay out, do what his friends do, or go home, not do what his friends do and be an outcast or something like that? It's not that way with me, but I don't want to leave and spoil everything with my friends, and they get home at a certain time, and as far as I know, their parents don't object. My parents, I mean, I'm the only child and there's more feeling toward me, I think, than with other kids that have brothers or sisters.

The consistent differences that were found between the two groups of boys provided evidence that anxiety about dependency that has been developed in relationship to one or both parents may generalize and affect all other relationships. Even more direct evidence was provided by the correlational data shown in Table 2-8. These correlations were obtained by averaging each boy's ratings on the indices

TABLE 2-8

INTERCORRELATIONS BETWEEN MEASURES OF DEPENDENCY ANXIETY:
DATA FROM BOYS' INTERVIEWS

Scale	2	3	4
1. Dependency anxiety in relationship to father	.65	.39	.39
2. Dependency anxiety in relationship to mother		.30	.20
3. Dependency anxiety in relationship to teacher			.31
4. Dependency anxiety in relationship to peers			

Correlations equal to, or greater than, .37 are significant at the .01 level.
Correlations equal to, or greater than, .28 are significant at the .05 level.

of anxiety about dependency on parents, teachers, and peers, respectively, and then intercorrelating the combined ratings.

Feelings of Rejection

It was evidently difficult for the boys to express directly any feelings of rejection that they might have experienced. Even so, it was evident that the aggressive boys felt considerably more rejected, both by their mothers and by their fathers, than did the control boys (Table 2-9). The aggressive

TABLE 2-9

EXTENT TO WHICH BOYS FELT REJECTED BY PARENTS: DIFFERENCES
BETWEEN AGGRESSIVE AND CONTROL BOYS,
DATA FROM BOYS' INTERVIEWS

Scales	Aggressive Group		Control Group			
	Mean	S.D.	Mean	S.D.	t	p
Rejection by mother	3.61	1.80	2.64	1.32	2.29	<.02
Rejection by father	4.48	2.24	2.59	1.29	2.86	<.01

boys were most likely to reveal their feelings of rejection when they were asked if they thought that their parents treated all their children alike.

B. (Case 17) Well, I think she treats my brother a bit (pause), gives him more money. Well, you can just feel that she's treating him a little better by doing things for him, you know.

I. How do you feel about this?

B. Well, I tell her once in a while, "You should treat us all alike"; and she says, "He's older and you're supposed to mind him, do what he wants you to do." Different things like that.

In answer to the more direct questions concerning the extent to which their parents understood, wanted, and took an interest in them, the boys were more likely to block and even to deny feelings of rejection they had revealed in other contexts. However, a few boys who had revealed very strong dependency anxiety also expressed strongly and directly their feelings of rejection. The boy in Case 33, who has already been quoted on pages 72 and 77, expressed his distrust of his parents at the same time as he described their estrangement from him.

I. How much do you feel she (mother) understands you?

B. She doesn't. I don't think she understands me, period. I never rely on her. You know what I mean. . . .

I. How much do you feel he (father) understands you and tries to help you?

B. Not at all. I don't understand him.

I. Do you think he likes having you around?

B. By the way he acts, I don't think he does.

I. How much interest do you think he takes in you?

B. Not too much.

The control boys gave very few indications of any feelings of rejection. Some of them realistically admitted that their behavior might be occasionally irritating to their parents or not fully understood by them. These boys were not usually upset by this situation, and were inclined to express tolerance and understanding of their parents' difficulties. The control boy who is quoted below came from a family in which there was a good deal of warmth between himself and his parents.

I. How much do you feel she (mother) understands you?

B. (Case 28) I'd say 85 per cent. No kidding, I don't think she understands me completely.

I. Do you feel she does her best to help you?

B. Yes. Again, yes.

I. How much interest do you think she takes in you?

B. One hundred per cent.

I. Are there things you really enjoy about your father?

B. Well, he doesn't get angry at me. I mean he's easy-going, does things with me and jokes a lot and doesn't get angry at me if I make a mistake. . . .

I. How much do you feel he understands you?

B. I think my mother understands me a little bit more. Not, gee, not a big difference, just a little teeny bit, maybe between 85 per cent and 84 per cent or 83 per cent, something like that. Gee, I can't express it. There's some things she understands more than my father, some things my father understands more about me. It's really just about the same, I'd say.

I. Does he help you?

B. Yeah, sure. Maybe more than my mother.

I. Does he like having you around?

B. Oh, sure. Yes.

I. How much interest do you think he takes in you?

B. As much as possible.

In spite of the fact that it was not easy for the boys to express feelings of rejection, further indications of the relationship between parental rejection and the development of dependency were obtained from the adolescent interviews. Boys who felt rejected by their fathers were inclined to show little dependency on them ($r = -.63$; $p < .001$). Similarly, boys who felt rejected by the mothers were inclined to show little dependency on their mothers ($r = -.28$; $p < .01$). In addition, boys who felt rejected by their fathers tended to feel anxious both about being dependent on their fathers ($r = .42$, $p < .01$) and about being dependent on their mothers ($r = .28$; $p < .05$). Moreover, the ratings of the boys' dependency on the father made from the boys' interviews correlated $-.30$ ($p < .05$) with the completely independent estimates of the fathers' rejection that were made from the father interviews.

Most aggressive boys did not feel that they were rejected by their peers, and in this respect they did not differ significantly from the control boys. Since they remained distant and aloof from the majority of their peers, they perhaps forestalled some of the rejection that their hostility might have elicited had they sought out the company of their peers more actively. As Table 2-10 indicates, they showed

TABLE 2-10

PEER RELATIONSHIPS: DIFFERENCES BETWEEN AGGRESSIVE AND
CONTROL BOYS, DATA FROM BOYS' INTERVIEWS

Scales	Aggressive Group		Control Group		t	p
	Mean	S.D.	Mean	S.D.		
Extent boy feels rejected by peers[a]	4.65	2.07	3.92	1.56	1.21	N.S.
Warmth toward peers	5.13	1.93	6.44	1.41	2.92	<.01

[a] This scale was not used as a basis for prediction.

less warmth for their peers than did the control boys; from the accounts they gave in their interviews it was clear that they typically associated only with a small group of boys who shared their antisocial orientation.

Economic Independence

Measures of the boys' economic independence were obtained from each of the parent interviews and from the interviews with the boys themselves. There was a good deal of variability in the amount of money the boys earned, but no difference between the aggressive and the control boys was apparent (Table 2-11).

Within the social group from which these boys were drawn it was taken for granted that the parents would provide the boys' basic necessities. Consequently, the motivation to earn additional money was determined less by the boys' attitudes and feelings toward their parents than by

TABLE 2-11

Boys' Economic Independence: Differences between
Aggressive and Control Boys

Scales	Aggressive Group		Control Group			
	Mean	S.D.	Mean	S.D.	t	p
Estimate from father interviews	6.25	2.09	5.46	1.81	1.45	N.S.
Estimate from mother interviews	6.15	2.10	5.62	1.61	0.93	N.S.
Estimate from boys' interviews	5.91	1.91	5.58	1.75	0.02	N.S.

These scales were not used as bases for prediction.

their desire for personal possessions for which the parents
were not likely to provide money. The most frequent situation was one in which a boy earned money for a specific
purpose, such as buying and maintaining a car. Some boys
in both groups purchased items of clothing and supplied
most of their own day-to-day spending money. Their parents, however, were prepared to cover even these expenses
if the boys' earnings should stop.

DISCUSSION

The findings that have been presented in this chapter
show that conditions for the establishment of a conflict in
the area of dependency had been operative in the histories
of the aggressive boys. These boys had received sufficient
affectional rewards from their mothers in their infancy and
childhood for them to acquire a dependency motive. However, their attempts at securing dependency gratifications
from their parents had been also to some extent frustrated
and even actively punished.

Both the parents' and the boys' interviews indicated that
the aggressive boys' attempts to relate to their fathers in an
emotionally dependent manner were met with relatively few
positive responses. The fathers of the aggressive boys showed
less warmth to, and were more rejecting of, their sons than

were the control fathers. During the aggressive boys' early childhood, their fathers had spent relatively little time in affectionate interaction with them, and it was apparent that the disruption of the relationship between these boys and their fathers had begun long before the boys' aggression had brought them into conflict with school and legal authorities.

Much of a child's dependency has as its major goal the eliciting of affection from his parents. If, instead of responding with affection and nurturance, a parent is rejecting and unresponsive, the child's dependency behavior is, in effect, punished. Throughout his childhood, because of pressures on him to make a masculine identification, the male child is encouraged to transfer more and more of his dependency from his mother to his father. As his interests become increasingly masculine, many of the activities in which a boy engages can be more easily shared by a male parent. For example, adolescents' interests center mainly on active sports, cars and mechanical devices, and other acknowledgedly masculine activities such as hunting and fishing. In fact, for an adolescent to participate in activities with his mother may be interpreted as a sign of immaturity. It is not therefore surprising that some boys in the study expressed unwillingness to be seen by their friends in their mothers' company. For instance, one boy who enjoyed his mother's company and liked going to movies with her would nevertheless get her to park the car several blocks away and then walk ahead of her to the theater. In contrast, for an adolescent to participate in his father's activities may be a token that he is attaining adult male status. Thus, while a father's rejection and frustration of his son's attempts to gain his nurturance might be felt to some degree even during the boy's very early childhood, it is probable that the boy's feelings of rejection would become increasingly acute throughout his childhood and early adolescent years.

The mothers of the aggressive boys, while not as lacking in warmth as their husbands, were nevertheless somewhat rejecting and punitive of their sons' dependency behavior. Their relatively greater warmth seemed to encourage their sons to turn to them for the nurturance that the fathers failed to provide, while at the same time their rejection and their punitiveness of the boys' dependency behavior could serve only to reinforce the boys' dependency anxiety. Under home conditions in which their fathers were rejecting and their mothers were inconsistent in their handling of dependency behavior, the aggressive boys had learned to be fearful and avoidant of close dependent attachments.

The aggressive boys were not only blocked by conflict from behaving dependently toward their parents but, in comparison to their controls, showed relatively little dependency on either their teachers or their peers. If his parents are the main sources of a boy's dependency anxiety, one would expect, on the basis of the principle of generalization, that this anxiety would generalize to others with the strength of the anxiety being a function of the degree of similarity of a given person to the parents. Thus, the amount of anxiety generalization from the boy's parents to his teachers is likely to be greater than that from his parents to his peers. If a child is blocked by conflict from gratifying his dependency needs in his relationships with his parents, he will probably turn to other sources that are less threatening to him for such gratification. The fact that, in general, the aggressive boys did not displace their dependency either to their teachers or to their peers makes it reasonable to infer that these boys' anxieties were so strong that they could not freely express dependency even to persons who might not have been punitive and rejecting. Since the aggressive boys did not feel any more rejected by their peers than did their controls, their reluctance to depend on them almost certainly reflected a generalization of anxiety from other situations in which they had been rejected and punished.

It is true that, particularly in his early childhood, a boy cannot completely transfer his dependency to other children since, by virtue of their own immaturity, they can give him only limited help or emotional support. However, as a boy approaches adolescence, his peer group assumes an increasing importance as a source of dependency gratification and as a guide for his behavior. Indeed, as Benedict (1938) has pointed out, with the rapidly changing conditions of life his parents' pattern of behavior may no longer be a very helpful guide for a boy in meeting certain contemporary problems, which in some respects are very different from those of a generation ago. Furthermore, even an adolescent who feels secure in his dependency on adults finds it easier to turn to his peer group for help in some of his day-to-day problems. To some extent, then, adolescents must learn from each other. If, in addition to being unable to accept the help and guidance of adults, a boy is also blocked from accepting the help of his peers, he will have to go through a painful process of trial and error or, as one of the parents put it, "learn the hard way."

Chapter 3

Aggression

The hypotheses which will be presented here are largely derived from the frustration-aggression theory systematically expounded first by Dollard *et al.* (1939). This theory states that aggression is a learned response to frustrating situations, though not the only response to frustration, and that aggressive behavior is reinforced insofar as it proves successful in overcoming frustrations that prevent the satisfaction of biological drives or learned motives. In Chapter 2 evidence was produced that the aggressive boys had experienced more frustration of their dependency needs than had the control boys. These frustrations, however, can account only for the boys' potentiality for displaying aggression; they cannot, alone, account for the amount and kind of aggression that the boys actually displayed. Thus this chapter is, in part, concerned with the extent to which the parents permitted and encouraged their sons to display aggression and with the way in which they handled aggressive behavior when it occurred. In part, it is aimed at exploring further the differences between the two groups of boys.

The aggressive boys were selected for study on the basis of their repeated disruptive, antisocial behavior. To a certain extent, then, any differences in aggression that might be found between the two groups of boys could merely confirm the adequacy of the selection procedure. It was known in advance that most of the aggressive boys had given trouble in school; it was known also that some of them had been troublesome in their homes. However, the extent to which they showed aggressive behavior in their interactions with parents, teachers, and peers, respectively, and the forms that their aggression took, required further exploration. Consequently, many of the interview questions, especially in the adolescent interviews, were aimed at eliciting material that might show how generalized these boys' aggression had become, in what ways these boys responded to frustration or thwarting, to what extent they initiated aggression, and how they felt after they had aggressed.

A Theory of the Development of Aggression

Frustration may be defined as the occurrence of conditions that prevent or delay the attainment of a goal-response. Most of the early frustrations that an infant encounters are due to delay in the satisfaction of his bodily needs and result from his helplessness and inability to care for himself.

When a child is hungry or otherwise in discomfort, it can do nothing except emit motor or vocal responses which appear initially to be completely nonpurposive in character. The crying, restlessness, and flailing of limbs seen in infants seem in fact to be the precursors of later verbal and physical responses that would unhesitatingly be classed as aggressive. The conditions for the development of aggression are thus present for every infant; frustrations are inevitable, and, although infants differ in the frequency and strength of their responses to frustration, all at some time respond by some form of motor or vocal discharge.

As yet, however, the child's responses lack the distinctive characteristics of aggressive acts. It is only when the child has learned to attack persons or objects in his environment in such a way as to injure or damage them that he can be described as aggressing. This transition from a protest response to an aggressive one is possible only when the child has acquired a certain degree of motor control. Since earlier motor discharges have frequently elicited the mother's attention and so have been followed by the removal of discomfort, it is not surprising that the slightly older child will, when frustrated, lash out, flail its limbs, beat on objects, or respond in similarly aggressive ways. At first, however, one may doubt whether there is always or necessarily present any *intent* to hurt or destroy. The aggressive behavior appears to be wholly instrumental, a means of obtaining something that is desired or of getting rid of something that is unpleasant. Only when the child has learned that signs of pain, distress, or injury in another person are frequently followed by the removal of frustrations for himself, so that he now seeks to produce such signs, can one speak of an intent to hurt. Aggressive behavior is under these circumstances still, however, primarily instrumental in character.

Sometimes, as early as the second year of life, a child may display aggression for no other apparent reason than to produce signs of pain or distress in others. Sears, Maccoby, and Levin (1957) suggest two reasons for this sort of behavior. In the first place, the sign of pain in others may have occurred sufficiently often in conjunction with the removal of frustrations to have acquired a secondary reward value. Secondly, an aggressive act may serve to reduce tension resulting from conflict. Since displays of aggression ordinarily meet with parental disapproval or punishment, anxiety is aroused when an impulse to aggress is present. The resulting conflict and tension are reduced when aggression finally occurs. Aggression may thus become a learned response to conditions of tension, and may occur even when the tension-producing situation is not in the first place a conflict in the area of aggression.

At the same time as aggression is being learned, efforts are being made to bring it under control. Socialization of aggression is relatively severe in North American society (Whiting and Child, 1953), and most parents make some attempt to limit their children's aggressive displays through restraint or punishment. When frustrated, the young child quickly resorts to physical violence. As the process of socialization takes effect, he learns to substitute the more readily tolerated verbal means of aggression for physical ones (Goodenough, 1931). Even direct verbal expressions of anger nevertheless meet disapproval, and the child eventually learns more or less subtle forms of expressing aggression that do not involve a direct attack on the instigator. Most adults rarely engage in direct acts of physical violence, and even their verbal attacks tend to be softened or camouflaged to some extent. Very often, indeed, they may display no open aggression, but instead their hostile feelings are expressed in thoughts and fantasies (Lindzey, 1950; Nowlis, 1953; Sears, Hovland, and Miller, 1940; Wright, 1954). This process whereby a more tolerated form of aggression is substituted for a less tolerated one represents a kind of response displacement.

Another form of displacement simultaneously takes place under the pressure of anxiety about possible punishment or disapproval. The primary socializing agents are, of course, the parents, and they are undoubtedly in a position to be the most effective ones. Not only can they impose physical restraint or punishment on the child, but they have a very potent weapon in their ability to threaten the child with withdrawal of their affection and approval. Consequently, aggressive impulses first aroused against the parents, who must frustrate in order to train and control the child, tend to be displaced to other persons and even to nonhuman objects. For example, a child who has been thwarted by his parents may physically attack another child or pet, or damage a toy or household furniture. A similar process of displacement has been demonstrated in studies in which children who were frustrated by adults showed aggression toward peers (Lewin, Lippitt, and White, 1939). This second form of displacement, whereby aggressive acts are diverted from the original instigators to other objects, may be referred to as object displacement.

The process of socializing aggression thus involves training the child to react to frustration in ways that are relatively acceptable. Training is, of course, never completely successful; occasionally, almost every adult responds in an impulsively aggressive manner. The majority, however, learn to avoid for the most part the kinds of aggressive acts that might bring serious consequences for themselves or for the objects of their aggression.

HYPOTHESES

On the basis of the principle of generalization it was predicted that the aggressive group of boys would display more direct aggression than would their controls, whether this aggression was expressed toward parents, toward teachers, or toward peers, and that they would express more hostility toward them during the interviews. It was also predicted that the aggressive group would show less anxiety concerning aggression.

There seemed two definite possibilities concerning the absolute amount of indirect aggression that the two groups of boys might show. It might be that the aggressive boys would display more aggression of all kinds, whether this aggression were direct or indirect in character. On the other hand, it seemed possible that, because of their readiness to express aggression in more direct ways, the aggressive boys would have less need to resort to indirect forms and consequently would express no more indirect aggression than would the control boys.

While childhood frustrations of dependency needs were regarded as the main source of the aggressive motive, the extent to which overt aggression occurs presumably depends also on the parents' handling of such behavior. In their Iowa study, Sears and his collaborators (1953) examined the relationship between severity of punishment for aggression shown toward the mother and the incidence of aggressive behavior in preschool children. They concluded that there was a curvilinear relationship between these variables—most aggressive behavior being shown when the mother had punished the child with moderate severity, least when punishment was very light or very severe. If this finding were generalized to the present situation, the parents of the control group might be expected to be either more light, or more severe, in their punishment of aggression than the parents of the aggressive boys, assuming that the hypotheses concerning the differences in aggression between the groups of boys were confirmed. On the other hand, there is evidence from other studies that would lead to an opposite conclusion, if applied to the present case. The Gluecks (1950), for example, found both overstrictness of discipline and laxness of discipline to be more frequent among parents of delinquents than among parents of nondelinquents. Assuming that such disciplinary practices reflect, among other things, the way in which aggression toward the parent is handled, a curvilinear relationship between parental punishment for aggression and aggression shown by the boy in social situations might again be inferred. This relationship, however, would be the inverse of that found in the Iowa study, with the more aggressive behavior being found when punishment was very light or very severe.

Actually, these findings are not necessarily so contradictory as they might seem from the presentation above. "Laxness of discipline" seems to be more nearly equivalent to what Sears would call extreme permissiveness than to his nonpunitiveness, since the latter does not necessarily imply lack of all restraints. "Severity of discipline," on the other hand, would seem necessarily to imply severity of punishment, though it is not clear to what extent it involves an attempt to prevent undesirable behavior from occurring. In addition, of course, the group of boys studied by the Gluecks was much older than the Iowa preschool children, and parental handling of aggressive behavior undoubtedly is modified by the degree of occurrence of such behavior over a period of years. Any kind of curvilinear relationship between parental punitiveness for aggression and the degree of aggression shown in social situations by the boys, would, however, reduce the likelihood of finding significant mean differences between the parents of the aggressive boys and the control parents in the severity of their punishment for aggressive behavior. While Sears, Maccoby, and Levin (1957) have now produced evidence that suggests that the more severely a mother punishes aggression toward herself, the more aggressive her child tends to be in the home, it was decided to proceed cautiously and make no prediction about parental punitiveness for aggression.

When a child develops a consistently aggressive pattern of behavior, one may suspect that in some way his aggression has been encouraged and reinforced. In order for reinforcement to be provided, aggression must be allowed to occur. Probably, the surest way to prevent a child from learning the efficacy of aggressive patterns of behavior is to make every effort to control aggression from the start by not allowing it to occur. Consequently, it was predicted that the parents of the aggressive boys would be more permissive of aggression than would the parents of the control boys. Supportive evidence for this prediction came from the Harvard study of Sears, Maccoby, and Levin (1957), which revealed a small, but significant, correlation between a mother's permissiveness for aggression toward herself and the amount of aggression her child displayed in the home.

When children are aggressive outside the home, the parents are frequently not at hand and consequently cannot intervene. Their attitudes toward such aggressive behavior may, however, be a strong influence in determining to what extent it occurs. For example, parents who are themselves aggressive may both instigate and reinforce their children's aggression through encouraging and condoning a combative, aggressive attitude toward others. However, even parents who display little overt aggression may directly or indirectly encourage aggression in their children. In fact, Johnson and Szurek (1952) have provided evidence that some parents keep their own antisocial impulses under control, yet at the same time subtly instigate and condone their children's antisocial acts and thereby obtain vicarious gratification of their own repressed antisocial impulses. On the basis of these considerations, it was predicted that the parents of the aggressive boys would encourage aggressive behavior more actively than would the control parents.

MEASURES

In order to study the process of displacement, it was decided not to make any over-all rating of aggression but to create scales for the separate rating of direct physical, direct verbal, and indirect aggression. Moreover, separate ratings were made of aggression toward parents, aggression toward teachers, and aggression toward peers. Thus there were nine main scales for the assessment of aggressive behavior. Ratings of aggression toward parents were made both from the parent and from the adolescent interviews; aggression toward teachers and peers was assessed from the adolescent interviews only.

The scale measuring *physical aggression* took account only of direct physical attacks, such as fighting, striking with the fists or with weapons, or throwing objects calculated to produce bodily injury. Under direct *verbal aggression* was included any form of attack which involved a face-to-face interaction and an undisguised expression of attack or defiance. For example, in this category were included not only name-calling or saying derogatory things to another person but also refusals to obey adults or hurtful criticism, provided these were openly expressed to the person whom it was intended to injure. Under *indirect aggression* were included less direct displays of verbal aggression, such as defamation, refusing favors in order to frustrate the petitioner (a not infrequent technique, it was discovered, of expressing dislike), and inciting others to aggression. Less direct forms of aggression that were expressed in actions rather than in words—for example, deliberately spurning or walking away from another person in order to show distaste for his company and all instances, such as door-slamming and throwing objects to the ground, in which aggression was displaced to nonhuman objects—were also categorized as indirect aggression.

Further estimates of the boys' aggression were obtained through scales which measured the boys' *hostility*. These estimates were based on the extent to which, during their interviews, the boys made disparaging remarks about their parents, teachers, and peers, respectively.

In addition to a measure of the extent to which aggressive behavior was manifested, an attempt was made to gauge the degree to which anxiety concerning aggression was present. It was assumed that with high anxiety there would be a relatively greater amount of indirect, than of direct, aggression so that, if aggression were expressed at all, its form would be more likely to be indirect than direct. Thus a scale measuring *directness of aggression*, which took no account of the absolute amount of aggression, was introduced. If a boy manifests little aggression, this may be because he is exposed to few frustrations or because aggressive responses are inhibited. If whatever aggression he expresses occurs in a direct form, there is a strong possibility that the former explanation holds. In this case he would obtain a high rating on the directness of aggression scale. If, on the other hand, a boy expresses much or little aggression, but all of it in indirect forms, it may reasonably be supposed that some inhibition is occurring. In this case he would obtain a low rating on the directness of aggression scale. Ratings were made of the directness of aggression toward parents, toward teachers, and toward peers.

Three aspects of the parents' handling of the boys' aggressive behavior were measured. Ratings were made of the parents' *permissiveness for aggression* toward themselves, toward siblings, toward peers, and toward adults other than the parents. Parallel ratings were also made of the parents' *punitiveness for aggression*. In addition, a single rating was made of the parents' *encouragement of the boys' aggression* outside the home.

A parent may be quite nonpermissive of aggression, yet not punish for aggressive behavior. He may try to prevent its occurrence by distracting the child or explaining why such behavior cannot be allowed; yet, at the same time, he may refrain from punishing aggressive behavior after it has occurred. On the other hand, a parent who punishes for aggression is displaying a particular kind of nontolerance of aggressive behavior. Some relationship (in an inverse direction) between permissiveness and punitiveness might therefore be expected. Such a relationship was found by Sears, Maccoby, and Levin (1957); in their study the correlation between the mothers' permissiveness for aggression toward themselves and their punitiveness for such aggression was —.46. The correlations between the measures of permissiveness for aggression and punitiveness for aggression used in the present study were all negative but they were not consistently high. For the mothers, the correlations between permissiveness and punitiveness for aggression toward themselves, toward teachers, and toward peers were —.61, —.22, and —.03, respectively. The corresponding correlations for the fathers were —.26, —.41, and —.30.

Correlations between parental encouragement of aggression and permissiveness and punitiveness for aggression are given in Table 3-1. Parents who were permissive of aggres-

TABLE 3-1

CORRELATIONS BETWEEN PARENTS' ENCOURAGEMENT OF AGGRESSION
AND THEIR PERMISSIVENESS AND PUNITIVENESS FOR AGGRESSION

Scales	r
Data from Mother Interviews	
Permissiveness for aggression toward peers	.59
Punitiveness for aggression toward peers	.06
Permissiveness for aggression toward adults	.31
Punitiveness for aggression toward adults	.23
Data from Father Interviews	
Permissiveness for aggression toward peers	.55
Punitiveness for aggression toward peers	—.01
Permissiveness for aggression toward adults	.33
Punitiveness for aggression toward adults	—.23

Correlations equal to, or greater than, .37 are significant at the .01 level. Correlations to, or greater than, .28 are significant at the .05 level.

sion tended also to encourage aggression. However, parents who encouraged aggression were not consistently nonpunitive when aggression had occurred.

RESULTS FROM PARENT INTERVIEWS
Boys' Aggression Against the Parents

Most parents declared that their sons had never displayed any physical aggression against them. Their reaction to the question: "Has he ever struck you?" tended to be one of surprise or dismay, as though an event of this kind were inconceivable. A few mothers of the aggressive boys, however, reported an occasional isolated act of striking or pushing, and this resulted in a small, but nevertheless significant, difference between the groups of mothers in the extent to which they reported physical aggression toward themselves (Table 3-2).

On the other hand, none of the fathers of the aggressive boys reported a physical attack, whereas one control father reported very frequent sparring with his son. Since the raters had been instructed to rate material at its face value, this latter father secured a very high rating for the amount of physical aggression he reported. It was clear, however, from listening to the interview that this father was jocularly referring to playful sparring without intent to hurt, injure, or annoy. In effect, then, no father reported the occurrence of any hostile physical attack upon himself.

Judging from the parents' reports, most boys, both aggressive and control, had answered their parents back or shouted at them, but very few had sworn or used abusive language. Thus the data from the parent interviews did not reveal any difference between the two groups of boys in the amount of verbal aggression that they showed toward their parents (Table 3-2).

Most of the boys' aggression was, according to their parents, quite indirect in nature. The boys most frequently displayed their anger by sulking, slamming doors, walking out of the house, or retiring to another room where on rare occasions they might stamp around, throw objects, or otherwise behave in a noisy manner. From the parent data it appeared that the aggressive boys showed more indirect

TABLE 3-2

Boys' Aggression toward Parents: Differences between
Aggressive and Control Boys

	Aggressive Group		Control Group			
Scales	Mean	S.D.	Mean	S.D.	t	p
Data from Father Interviews						
Physical aggression toward father	2.00	0.00	2.23	0.36	3.15	<.01[a]
Verbal aggression toward father	4.62	2.35	4.13	1.90	0.72	N.S.
Indirect aggression toward father	5.33	1.86	4.23	1.93	1.96	<.05
Data from Mother Interviews						
Physical aggression toward mother	2.35	0.91	2.02	0.10	1.79	<.05 (.07)[b]
Verbal aggression toward mother	5.60	2.08	5.25	1.86	0.62	N.S.
Indirect aggression toward mother	6.31	2.43	5.79	2.28	0.73	N.S.

[a] This difference was produced by the response of one control father who interpreted the interview question as referring to playful sparring between father and son, as well as striking in anger. With the extremely small variabilities this one case was sufficient to produce a significant difference. On the other hand, several of the mothers of the aggressive boys reported some physical aggression by the boy.

[b] The probability in parentheses is based on the Wilcoxon Test.

aggression toward their fathers than did the control boys, but that the two groups of boys did not differ in the amount of indirect aggression that they showed toward their mothers (Table 3-2).

Parental Handling of Aggression

The prediction that the parents of the aggressive boys would be more permissive of aggression was only partially confirmed (Table 3-3). The mothers of the aggressive boys were significantly more permissive of aggression toward

TABLE 3-3

Parents' Permissiveness for Aggression: Differences between Parents of Aggressive and Control Boys

Scales	Aggressive Group		Control Group			
	Mean	S.D.	Mean	S.D.	t	p
Data from Father Interviews						
Permissiveness for aggression toward:						
Father	4.13	1.92	4.40	2.29	0.41	N.S.
Other adults	3.88	0.70	3.94	0.84	0.27	N.S.
Siblings[a]	3.36	2.21	3.33	1.81	0.05	N.S.
Peers	4.52	2.43	4.33	1.95	0.28	N.S.
Data from Mother Interviews						
Permissiveness for aggression toward:						
Mother	6.37	1.72	5.35	1.73	2.06	<.05
Other adults	3.62	1.11	3.90	0.76	1.22	N.S.
Siblings[a]	4.95	1.06	4.91	1.10	0.12	N.S.
Peers	4.92	1.57	5.02	1.36	0.25	N.S.

[a] Based on $N = 21$ and $N = 23$ for aggressive and control groups, respectively.

themselves than were the mothers of the control boys. The groups of fathers, however, did not differ significantly in this respect.

Most parents tended to be intolerant of aggression toward themselves. This was particularly true of the fathers, most of whom would tolerate only the more indirect forms of aggression. The excerpts below are taken from interviews with fathers of aggressive boys.

I. When Arnold gets angry at you, what does he do?
F. (Case 21) Well, he just doesn't talk. He goes in his room and starts playing his records or his piano.
I. Does he ever shout or swear at you?
F. No, he does not.
I. Does he ever answer back?
F. He answers back, yes.
I. How often?

F. Oh about fifty per cent of the time. Maybe once a week.
I. Has he ever stamped out of the house?
F. He has never stamped out, but he has walked out.
I. Slammed doors?
F. He's slammed doors.
I. How much of this sort of thing have you allowed?
F. Well, I haven't condoned any of it. I've jumped him every time he's done it.

. . .

I. How much of this sort of thing have you allowed?
F. (Case 23) I don't allow him to get moody with me because he knows he wouldn't get away with it. They're too smart. They know what they can do and what they can't do.

. . .

I. How much of this sort of thing have you allowed?
F. (Case 29) Well, that's just one of those things that I just won't allow is for him to particularly get out of line with his mother or I, either one. Or if he were to try to use any abusive language or, you know, want to strike one or something like that, I just won't allow it. And he knows it, because I always told him, you know, how to treat us like he should have done and so forth. It's always been that way.

The control fathers were, in general, equally unwilling to tolerate aggression from their sons but were usually more understanding and kindly in their way of responding to it.

I. When Samuel gets angry at you, what does he do?
F. (Case 40) I don't know what his innermost reaction is at all times, but he'll have something to say. It's not always right direct toward me, either. It will come in a roundabout way. But, as I say, he'll probably get moody at times and I've counteracted that. . . .
I. How much of this sort of thing have you allowed?
F. I don't let it progress very far. No, I keep everything pretty well under control.
I. What do you do?
F. Well, as I say, I let it work itself out. If it got out of hand, I would certainly put him in his place. And I think, a given word, he listens. As I say, I never strike him. Never do that.

The mothers in both groups characteristically took a more permissive attitude about aggression toward themselves than did their husbands. A good many of the mothers were prepared to let their sons "blow off steam." However, the control mothers seemed to place definite limits on the amount and kind of aggression they would allow and typically would tolerate little or no aggression of an interpersonal kind.

I. When Mark gets angry at you, what does he do?
M. (Case 50) He usually just goes up into his room. That's it.
I. Does he ever shout or swear at you?
M. Never, never swears at me. He may raise his voice a little bit.
I. Does he ever answer back?
M. Oh, a little. It may issue in a slight argument with him giving his side of it and me giving him my side of it, but he doesn't shout back at me.
I. Has he ever struck you?
M. Oh, no.
I. Has he ever thrown things around the house?
M. No. He may throw a shirt across the room or something like that, but nothing with any weight and that's very light. If he's looking for something and can't find it and he's in a hurry, well, light things may go with him a little bit, but never anything that would do any damage.
I. Has he ever stamped out of the house?
M. Oh, that might have happened once or twice, but not more than that.
I. How much of this sort of thing have you allowed?
M. Not very much. I don't like a display of temper, and he knows it.
I. What do you do?
M. Well, there's been very little actual punishment of any kind. I may just be quiet for a little while. I think that hurts more than anything else. If he knows he's actually hurt me in any way, then he feels very sorry about it. That's all that's needed with him. Just doesn't want to hurt any of us in any way.

In contrast, some of the mothers of the aggressive boys would permit aggression to occur and sometimes do nothing to prevent its recurrence.

I. What have you done about it?
M. (Case 49) You can't do much because by the time Stanley comes back, why, everything's cooled off and the incident is usually forgotten.

. . .

I. How much of this sort of thing have you allowed?
M. (Case 39) He doesn't seem to show his anger in a violent way. Rather than try to coax him and reason him out of it, I just leave him alone and let him work it out in his own mind. So I just let it go.

Some of the mothers in both groups felt none too competent to handle their sons' outbursts of aggression. While the mothers of the aggressive boys were in this case inclined to express an attitude of helpless resignation, the control mothers usually took some steps to prevent the recurrence of aggression.

I. How much of this sort of thing have you allowed?

M. (Case 2) Not very often. And I get after him and I get my husband to talk to him, and he usually does. And my husband always talks with him and somehow, the way he talks to him, I guess he knows how to get around him, and he listens. It seems like the mother always has the boy in front of them all the time, and they sort of resent the fact that I'm always telling them. But they don't feel that way about their Dad and somehow they look up to their Dad, and he knows how to get round them.

No differences were found between the groups of mothers or the groups of fathers in their punitiveness for aggression toward themselves. Nor were there any differences of note between the groups of parents in their handling of aggressions toward peers or toward siblings (Table 3-4). In general, parents were rated somewhat low in permissiveness for aggression toward peers and toward siblings, but very few were found to be highly punitive. Somewhat more drastic measures were likely to be taken when a boy had been aggressive toward one of his siblings than if he had aggressed against a peer who was not a member of the family, but even so punishment was very rarely severe.

The majority of parents were less permissive of aggression toward adults outside the immediate family than they were of any other form of aggression (Table 3-4). Both the parent groups were rated very low on this permissiveness scale, and there was very little difference between the mean ratings of the parent groups. The greater strictness in this connection is precisely what might be expected, for it is a boy's aggression toward adults outside the family that is most likely both to bring serious trouble on himself and to bring the parents into disrepute. A parent whose son is insolent or defiant toward teachers or toward neighbors runs a strong risk of being looked upon as an unsuccessful parent.

TABLE 3-4

PARENTS' PUNITIVENESS FOR AGGRESSION: DIFFERENCES BETWEEN
PARENTS OF AGGRESSIVE AND CONTROL BOYS

Scales	Aggressive Group		Control Group			
	Mean	S.D.	Mean	S.D.	t	p
Data from Father Interviews						
Punitiveness for aggression toward:						
Father	4.71	1.66	4.54	1.54	0.40	N.S.
Other adults	4.87	1.54	4.02	1.00	2.41	<.02 (.03)[b]
Siblings[a]	5.00	3.70	4.90	2.85	0.10	N.S.
Peers	3.06	1.53	3.19	1.59	0.00	N.S.
Data from Mother Interviews						
Punitiveness for aggression toward:						
Mother	5.08	1.79	5.48	1.44	0.94	N.S.
Other adults	5.69	1.43	4.27	0.71	4.52	<.001
Siblings[a]	6.21	0.84	6.15	0.76	0.25	N.S.
Peers	4.88	1.40	5.37	1.27	1.21	N.S.

[a] Based on $N = 21$ and $N = 23$ for aggressive and control groups, respectively.

[b] The probability in parentheses is based on the Wilcoxon Test.

These scales were not used as bases for prediction.

It is not surprising, therefore, that the two groups of parents differed quite markedly in their punitiveness for aggression toward other adults. The mothers of the aggressive boys were, on the average, considerably more punitive than the mothers of the control boys, and while the difference between the groups of fathers was not quite as marked, it was nevertheless significant. As far as the mothers were concerned, the findings, taken as a whole, were thus somewhat similar to those of Sears, Maccoby, and Levin (1957); the aggressive boys had mothers who were both more permissive of aggression toward themselves and more punitive of aggression toward other adults than were the mothers of the relatively nonaggressive control boys.

Ratings on the punitiveness measures are, however, somewhat difficult to interpret. A rating of 2 was given whenever a parent reported that no aggression had occurred, but nevertheless indicated that punishment would be administered in the event of its occurrence. In the case of the control group, aggressive behavior against adults had rarely come to the parents' notice. Consequently, most control parents were given a rating of 2 on the grounds that aggression by the boy had not occurred but that there were indications that the parents would punish if such aggression were brought to their attention.

On the other hand, the parents of the aggressive boys had in many cases been faced with the situation of having to deal with aggression against adults sufficiently serious to be brought to their attention. On the whole, such behavior had not been ignored by them, and consequently the scale demanded a rating higher than 2. Had the scale been set up to take account of the severity with which possible aggressive behavior would have been handled, if and when it occurred, the differences between the groups of parents might have been somewhat reduced or even reversed.

The fact that the parents of the control boys were more likely to train them through reasoning (Chapter 5) could also have contributed to differences between the parent groups on the punitiveness for aggression scale. A rating of 1 on a punitiveness scale was given only if the parent indicated that he would not punish, or had not punished, for aggression. But not punishing when aggression occurred might indicate either that the parent used a nonpunitive technique of control or that he simply did not try to control aggression. It seemed possible that, whereas the parents of the aggressive boys punished their sons' aggression, the control parents might have been using a nonpunitive, but restraining, technique. Individual ratings were consequently examined for any indication that this might be the case. No mothers in either group, however, and only three of the fathers of the aggressive boys and six control fathers had been given ratings of 1 by both raters. It seemed, therefore, that the differences that were found on this particular scale could not be accounted for simply by the fact that the control parents used, or would use, reasoning as a preferred technique of control when aggression was shown against adults. Thus it seemed that the control parents had punished their sons for aggression toward adults less than had the parents of the aggressive boys simply because they had less need to do so.

It was noted during the discussion of hypotheses that, if the parents of the aggressive boys were more (or less) *moderate* in their use of punishment than the parents of the control group, this difference could not be demonstrated by a comparison of *mean* scores on the punitiveness scales. Consequently, the incidence of high, moderate, and low punishment for aggression toward parents, siblings, and peers, respectively, was noted for each group. It was clear from inspection that the differences between the groups of parents, in respect to the distribution of varying degrees of severity of punishment, were negligible. It must therefore be concluded that there were no differences between the groups in the severity of their punishment for aggression, with the single exception of those found on the scale measuring severity of punishment for aggression against adults, and that these latter differences probably occurred only because the control boys had rarely, if ever, displayed any serious overt aggression toward adults.

While the fathers of the aggressive boys would permit their sons to show little aggression toward themselves, they actively encouraged them to show aggression outside the home (Table 3-5). Sometimes the encouragement took the form of a demand that the boy should be able to use his fists.

I. Have you ever encouraged Glen to use his fists to defend himself?
F. (Case 13) In thoughts or physically, or how do you mean? Well, Glen has always been a kid where kids have pushed him over at school. We've had to encourage him, "Now, son, you just stand right up there." That comes right back to the point that he's never played with children until five years ago. In fact, he was the type

TABLE 3-5

PARENTS' ENCOURAGEMENT OF AGGRESSION: DIFFERENCES BETWEEN
PARENTS OF AGGRESSIVE AND CONTROL BOYS

Scales	Aggressive Group		Control Group			
	Mean	S.D.	Mean	S.D.	t	p
Fathers' encouragement of aggression	6.64	1.85	5.06	1.81	2.80	<.01
Mothers' encouragement of aggression	5.37	1.95	4.12	1.25	2.51	<.01

of kid that, when he was small, he'd rather sit down and play paper dolls than get in the yard and play with the boys, kicking a football around. That's just the difference. But lot of times he'd come home and kids would throw a left or right at him and he didn't know what to do about it. I used to want to teach him to protect himself but my wife didn't go for it. She said, "You're putting things in his head," that I was training him to fight. So we dropped it.

This father's method of training was depicted somewhat differently by his wife, and it is easy to see why she felt that she had to intervene.

M. (Case 13) When he was about six or seven years old, all the kids were fussing and fighting and he would never fight. His sister would always have to take up his battle for him. Always fighting. So one day my husband took off his belt and said, "Listen, you're coming home and crying all the time, saying, 'Somebody hit me.'" So my husband was watching through the bedroom window one day and he saw two little boys. They were really fighting him. So he went up, took off his belt, and he said, "Glen, I'm going to tell you something. You're going to whip these boys or else I'm going to whip you." So he made him stand up and fight both of them.

It appeared from the interviews with both his parents that Glen had at first shown a nonaggressive reaction to the frustrations encountered in his home. Had he remained nonaggressive, however, there seems little doubt that his father would have been even more punitive and rejecting than he currently appeared to be. Although, under pressure from his wife, Glen's father had apparently desisted from

openly encouraging him to fight, he continued to demand in
less blatant ways that Glen should accept and enjoy aggression.

F. (Case 13) One day we went to see Bobo Olson fight. We tried to
get him to go. "No, I don't want to go." Well, he hated it. I said,
"No, you're going." Of course, if he didn't want to go, that's fine.
But he'd rather be home calling his friends over the telephone.
That's what just burns me up; it makes me so mad. I never turned
down anything like that when I was a kid. You get a chance maybe
one out of five years to see Olson fight, the champion of the
world, and he turns it down flat.

Glen's father was by no means an exceptional case. Many
fathers of the aggressive boys made it quite clear that they
did not want their sons to be "pushed around."

I. Some people think it is very important for a boy to be able to
stand up for himself, others think boys are only too ready to do
this. How do you feel about this?
F. (Case 49) I think it's very good for a boy to do that.
I. Have you ever encouraged Stanley to stand up for himself?
F. No, I never have. In fact, I've had to stop him a few times, espe-
cially in fights.
I. Have you ever encouraged him to use his fists to defend himself?
F. If it comes to that, yes, I have.
I. What precisely have you done to encourage him?
F. Well, I want him to protect himself. I don't want him to be a
baby and have somebody push him around.

Sometimes, although a father actually denied any encouragement of aggression, it seemed likely from his enjoyment of aggression that encouragement had in fact occurred.

I. Some people think it is very important for a boy to be able to
stand up for himself, others think boys are only too ready to do
this. How do you feel about this?
F. (Case 25) Yes, I think he should stand up for himself.
I. Have you ever had to encourage Carl to stand up for himself?
F. No, no, he's always done that for himself.
I. Have you ever encouraged Carl to use his fists to defend himself?
F. No, never have, no.
I. Has Carl ever come to you and complained that another fellow was
giving him a rough time?
F. Never has, no; and if he can't take it, that's too bad (laughs).
I. Suppose he did, what would you say to him?

F. Well, I'd tell him, if he couldn't fight his own battles that would be too bad (laughs heartily).
I. If Carl got into a fight with one of the neighbor's boys, how would you handle it?
F. Let 'em fight it out (laughs).
I. How far would you let it go?
F. Let 'em go as far as they could.

Most control fathers wanted their sons to assert themselves in socially acceptable ways and, if necessary, to defend themselves against aggression. However, they usually discouraged physical aggression and under no circumstances would they allow their sons to provoke other children.

I. Have you encouraged Eric to stand up for himself?
F. (Case 44) Several years back we used to, just a little bit, to get him to shove himself forward and get his fair share, but there's no particular problem in that direction now.
I. How did you do this?
F. He seemed to more or less naturally grow into it as he grew larger and had more strength and energy and gained confidence in himself through doing things.
I. Have you ever encouraged Eric to use his fists to defend himself?
F. No. No. We have tried to teach him that he should be strong and able to defend himself, but that it's smarter to run away from physical combat than to actually enter into it. . . .
I. If Eric got into a fight with one of the neighbor's boys, how would you handle it?
F. If I thought he was the aggressor, I would take steps towards disciplining him; but if he were attacked, I don't know. Those things are difficult to give an answer to.
I. How far would you let it go?
F. I wouldn't let it keep up at all.

Some of the fathers of the aggressive boys encouraged their sons to show aggression against adults, as well as against other children, although in more subtle ways. They would demand that their sons should stand up for their own rights against adults, would side with the boys against their teachers, and would criticize the school in a way that might justify their sons' aggression against school authorities. The example given below is especially interesting on account of the father's awareness that his own hostility might have led him to instigate his son's aggression.

I. Have you ever had to encourage Edward to stand up for himself?

F. (Case 11) Well, yes, and in about fifty per cent of the time I was wrong. I'll admit that. Two or three times I thought that he was taking something that he shouldn't and I advised him. But it was only my hatred in my heart. I was wrong fifty per cent of the time, and it was just his easy-going way in following what I told him to do.

I. Have you ever encouraged him to use his fists to defend himself?

F. Oh, such little things that come up. Somebody tries to step ahead of him when they shouldn't and I thought it was his part. . . .

I. Has Edward ever complained that a teacher or another adult was being unfair to him?

F. He's made the remark that they have. He hasn't really come down and made an issue of it that they've taken advantage of him, and I do believe that occasionally he was right. In fact, I thought so in a couple of cases. I went and checked with other children, and they said the same thing about the same teacher. All teachers aren't perfect. . . . And we caused an issue about it. We went to school, and the principal of course said, "Teachers are hard to get, you know," and gave that kind of excuse. And we dropped the subject then. But we did want the heads of the department to know that we were complaining about it. We didn't go any further.

I. Have you ever encouraged Edward to stand up for himself against an adult?

F. I've never had that situation happen. But I've always encouraged Edward to stand up for himself when he's right, regardless of the size of the other side.

The control fathers almost invariably discouraged any hostile aggression toward adults. A number of them told their sons never to be impolite or resistant, but simply to let their parents know, if they felt that they were being unjustly treated by adults. If problems arose in the school, most control fathers would explain to their sons the difficulties that the teachers had to face and would simply advise their sons to work harder.

I. Has Alfred ever complained that a teacher or another adult was being unfair to him?

F. (Case 38) Yes, he felt that some of his teachers were unfair. On investigation we have found usually it wasn't true. On occasion some of the teachers weren't as good as they might have been.

I. What did you say to him?

F. I told him that that was one of the things he had to get along with. That there were lots of people in life that he will meet that were unfair, but that he would have to make the adjustment that they would not.

I. Have you ever encouraged Alfred to stand up for himself against an adult?

F. No, I don't think so. Certainly we've encouraged him to discuss with the teachers he couldn't get along with. Discuss his problem with them, how he could be better, how he could get along with it.

I. What would you do if you discovered Alfred was giving a teacher a hard time?

F. We'd explain to him that the teacher was trying to help him get an education and that he was in school to get an education and he wasn't in school to rib the teachers.

The mothers of the aggressive boys not only were more permissive of aggression toward themselves than were the control mothers, but they also more actively encouraged aggression outside the home (Table 3-5). In fact, some of the mothers of the aggressive boys made as strong demands for aggression as did any of the aggressive boys' fathers.

I. Have you ever encouraged Russell to use his fists to defend himself?

M. (Case 39) Yes, when he was in kindergarten. He came home every night for about three weeks; some little boy had picked on him and pounded on him and he'd come home all dusty, dirty and crying. So I told him one night, the next time he came home crying he was going to get a spanking. So the next night he came home, he got as far as the gate, and this kid was still following him. He saw the house and decided he was pretty safe, so he turned on the other little boy and pounded him, and he felt pretty good about it after he stuck up for himself. And I can't remember a time after that when he didn't stick up for himself. He found out he could and then he wasn't afraid. It didn't seem to matter how much bigger than he the other boy was, he'd still, if anything real or fanciful happened, why he'd stick up for himself.

Some of the mothers, while not blatantly encouraging aggression, showed a pervasive tendency to support and condone their sons' aggressiveness.

I. Have you ever encouraged George to stand up for himself?

M. (Case 9) Aggressively? I think they have to stand up for themselves, but I don't think they should start anything unless somebody else starts it (laughs).

I. Have you ever encouraged George to use his fists to defend himself?

M. No, no. I'd rather they didn't. I've always told him, if they do fight, fight fair and square and not with any sticks or anything, just with their fists. . . .

I. Suppose George complained that another boy was giving him a hard time, what would you say to him?

M. I think I'd just tell him to stick up for himself or else, you know, just keep out of his way.

I. If George got into a fight with one of the neighbor's boys, how would you handle it?

M. Well I usually get down to the bottom and see whose fault it was.

I. How far would you let it go?

M. The fight? I'd stop it if they got too vicious. As long as they're fighting with their hands and have nothing in them—if it's fair—I'd just let it go. You know, not till they hurt each other, but I wouldn't let them hit with sticks and things. . . .

I. How do you handle things if they (George and his brother) quarrel?

M. Well, they usually settle their disturbances. They don't quarrel a great deal; they'll horse around. They'll box one another. But usually when they do that, George lets him pummel him. So he doesn't hurt Billy on purpose.

I. Has George ever complained that a teacher or another adult was being unfair to him?

M. Yes, the principal (laughs). I think that's an awful lot of George's trouble. That's why he's aggressive at the principal, which I told him the other day.

I. What did you do about this?

M. Well, I tried to cooperate with the principal for three years until he just picked and picked and picked at that boy. I finally got mad. Boy, what I didn't tell him (laughs). Today I really blame George's aggressiveness and bullying on the teacher. I think that's the cause of it.

I. What have you said to George about it?

M. After the day I had the fight, when I went up to the principal and just told him what I thought, he left George alone from that day on.

I. Have you ever encouraged George to stand up for himself against an adult?

M. Well, I always told him that he should be polite; but I know one day he did get mad at the principal, and I wouldn't blame him. I mean, I had taken so much from him myself that I wouldn't, actually wouldn't have cared if George hit him.

Most control mothers, in contrast, avoided encouraging any aggression of a socially unacceptable nature. They demanded only that their sons should be firm in maintaining their standards and principles and not be too easily influenced by others.

I. Have you ever encouraged Eric to stand up for himself?

M. (Case 16) We have permitted our children to do a great deal of talking as far as they themselves are concerned. If they don't like some rule or regulation, well, they certainly have a right to say what they don't like about it and why they don't like it, even to the extent of being noisy about it. I much prefer, both of us much prefer, that attitude to the attitude of this is it, now take it and be quiet about it.

I. Have you ever encouraged Eric to use his fists to defend himself?

M. No.

I. Has he ever come to you and complained that another fellow was giving him a rough time?

M. Yes.

I. What have you advised him to do about it?

M. Well, I usually tell him that the best way to meet a problem like that is to either avoid the boy or to try to see to it that the boy doesn't dislike him, so that the problem doesn't come up. I never thought that it was my duty to teach him to fight.

I. If Eric got into a fight with one of the neighbor's boys, how would you handle it?

M. The only example of that was at one time when a neighbor boy deliberately tripped him on his bicycle. My husband and I discussed it and then we phoned the other boy and his dad, and the two of them talked about it and that was the end of it. It never went any further.

I. What would you do if you found Eric teasing another fellow or calling him bad names?

M. If he did it when he was small, which would be the only time when he would have—because no normal child of sixteen would do such a thing, I'm sure—but I certainly would have disciplined him for it. But as I say, it's never been any problem.

I. Has Eric ever complained that a teacher or another adult was being unfair to him?

M. Oh yes, particularly teachers.

I. What did you do?

M. If I felt that there could be anything to it, I usually go and talk to the teacher and feel her out, never telling her anything that Eric said, and just see what the lay of the land is, and then I have some basis for talking to him about it. I usually explain to him that the teacher is there for the purpose of teaching him, not for the purpose of either liking or disliking him, and that it's probably

his own guilty conscience for not doing his work that he feels that
the teacher doesn't like him.
I. Have you ever encouraged Eric to stand up for himself against
an adult?
M. There's never been any occasion for such a thing. There's no one
for him to stand up to, except perhaps his father or me. You see,
there's no one else that it would be necessary at all.
I. What would you do if you discovered Eric was giving a teacher a
hard time?
M. I would discipline him.

Most control mothers viewed hostile aggression as a sign
of weakness and urged their sons to try to see the point
of view of other persons rather than to oppose them.

I. Have you ever encouraged Dan to use his fists to defend himself?
M. (Case 26) We've always taught Dan that it takes a bigger man to
keep from getting into a fight than it does to pick a fight, that anybody can fight.

.   .   .

I. What would you do if you found Keith teasing another fellow or
calling him bad names?
M. (Case 50) I would put a stop to it. I would see that he was fair
and treated boys the way he wanted to be treated. . . .
I. Has Keith ever complained that a teacher or another adult was
being unfair to him?
M. Yes, he has. He has complained about teachers. And then there
was a woman in the neighborhood. She wasn't quite mentally
right, and he complained about her. In her case, I explained to
him that she was sick and it's best for him to try to make things
easier for her if he possibly could, and not to be too quick to
criticize her. And he didn't know how she felt. I explained that to
him. As far as the teacher was concerned, I just tried to explain
that she might have her problems, too. He would have to try and
look over her side of it.
I. Have you ever encouraged Keith to stand up against an adult?
M. No, I haven't.
I. What would you do if you discovered Keith was giving a teacher a
hard time?
M. I'd be disappointed in him, and I would be very disturbed about
it. I think if a person tries to put himself in another person's shoes
and tries to think about how the other person feels, and that's
what I try to explain to Keith. "Try to think how the other person
feels. How would you feel if you were having to take the same
treatment that you're giving?" This gets him to think about it.

It seemed that, in the aggressive boys' families, one or other of the parents almost invariably encouraged aggression. Indeed, when the ratings of mothers and fathers were combined to provide an estimate of the total amount of encouragement to aggress that the boys had received from their parents, a highly significant difference between the two groups of parents emerged ($t = 3.66$; $p < .001$).

Some of the most aggressive boys came from families in which both parents encouraged aggression. Case 23 provided an excellent example of a very aggressive boy both of whose parents demanded, instigated, and condoned aggression.

I. Have you ever encouraged Earl to use his fists to defend himself?
F. (Case 23) Yes, if necessary. I told him many times that if someone wanted to fight with him and started the old idea of the chip on the shoulder, "Don't hit the chip, hit his jaw, and get it over with."
I. Has he ever come to you and complained that another fellow was giving him a rough time?
F. Yes.
I. What did you advise him to do about it?
F. I told him to hit him.
I. If Earl got into a fight with one of the neighbor's boys, how would you handle it?
F. That would depend who was at fault. If my boy was at fault, he'd be wrong and I'd do my best to show him that. But if he was in the right I wouldn't want to chastise him.
I. How far would you let it go?
F. I'd let it go until one won. See who was the best man.

· · ·

I. Have you ever encouraged Earl to stand up for himself?
M. (Case 23) Yes. I've taught young Earl, and his Dad has. I feel he should stand up for his rights, so you can get along in this world.
I. How have you encouraged him?
M. I've told him to look after himself and don't let anybody shove him around or anything like that, but not to look for trouble. I don't want him to be a sissy.
I. Have you ever encouraged Earl to use his fists to defend himself?
M. Oh yes. Oh yes. He knows how to fight.
I. What have you done to encourage him?
M. When he was a little boy, he had a little pair of boxing gloves. His dad has been an athlete all his life, so his dad taught him.

I. Has he ever come to you and complained that another fellow was giving him a rough time?

M. Oh yes, when he was younger. I told him, "Go on out and fight it out yourself."

I. If Earl got into a fight with one of the neighbor's boys, how would you handle it?

M. Oh, he should fight it out himself. When he was a little fellow he used to fight with kids. Dad said, "Go on." He used to fight his own battles. . . .

I. What would you do if you found Earl teasing another fellow or calling him bad names?

M. That would be up to Earl. If the other boy wants to lick him, that would be up to Earl. He deserves it.

There was no case in which a control parent instigated or condoned a boy's aggression toward the other parent. On the other hand, a few parents of aggressive boys subtly instigated, and quite clearly condoned, their sons' aggression toward their marital partners.

I. Does he ever answer back?

F. (Case 11) With his mother once or twice a week. With myself, I would say not too often, every two weeks maybe. . . .

I. Has he ever thrown things?

F. No. I say "no," because I haven't seen him throw anything around, although he was to have broken a mop the other day when she asked him to mop the floor. But I didn't see it. I wasn't there. It was between he and his mother. No, he hasn't thrown anything at me or any of that sort of thing. . . .

I. How much of this sort of thing have you allowed?

F. Arguments come up between he and his mother, and I've walked away from it rather than get into it as a third person. I agree with her once in a while and sometimes I disagree. So when you say what have I allowed or what I haven't allowed, it isn't that I have the authority to allow or not allow. Let's put it that way.

RESULTS FROM BOYS' INTERVIEWS

In accordance with predictions, the aggressive boys displayed significantly more physical, verbal, and indirect aggression and more hostility toward their teachers than did the control boys (Table 3-6). In addition, they showed significantly less guilt after an aggressive act had been committed (Chapter 6).

TABLE 3-6

Boys' Aggression toward Teachers: Differences between
Aggressive and Control Boys

Scales	Aggressive Group		Control Group		t	p
	Mean	S.D.	Mean	S.D.		
Physical aggression	2.60	0.91	2.08	0.23	2.67	<.01
Verbal aggression	5.90	2.09	3.90	1.38	3.86	<.001
Indirect aggression[a]	6.58	2.02	4.88	2.06	3.14	<.01
Directness of aggression	5.60	1.77	3.83	1.22	3.87	<.001
Hostility	5.94	1.92	4.12	1.35	3.85	<.001

[a] This scale was not used as a basis for prediction.

Several of the aggressive boys had struck their teachers either with their fists or by throwing objects at them. The majority had sworn at teachers or answered them back.

I. What if he gives you too much homework? Tells you to do some-thing you think is unreasonable?
B. (Case 23) I hit one once and got suspended for it. I got suspended many times.
I. Suppose a teacher punishes you unjustly, what do you do about it?
B. Hits me? I tell him back.
I. If you dislike a teacher, do you ever try to get back at him?
B. What do you mean, like slicing his tires and that sort of stuff? No. No.
I. How often do you try to get back?
B. Pretty often.
I. You mentioned you hit a teacher. What happened?
B. I said, "Hit one, two, three." The teacher said, "Cut it out." He took me in the corner and bounced me around a little bit, and I threw a stomp on him and hit him. That was about eighth grade.
I. Have you ever thrown something at a teacher?
B. No.
J. Sworn at them?
B. Yeah, about twenty times.
I. Answered them back?
B. Yeah.

The following excerpt from an interview with one of the aggressive boys illustrates not only the boy's frank aggression toward his teachers, but also the manner in which his mother supported her son's aggression by coming to his defense when action was taken against him.

I. How often have you felt that a teacher has given you an unfair grade?

B. (Case 25) About three or four times. My English teacher in school used to give me unfair grades. I'd do all my work real good until the last three or four days before the report card, and then she'd flunk me. She wouldn't flunk me, but she gave me a "D," and my Ma wouldn't like that. She'd go up and see her. My Ma would get kind of salty at her, wanted to know why.

I. Would you say anything to a teacher if you felt your grade was unfair?

B. Yeah, I would.

I. What kind of thing?

B. I'd get kind of mad, I guess.

I. Suppose a teacher punishes you unjustly, what do you do about that?

B. Just take it and then go talk to her after, I guess. She'd send me to the office a lot of times for doing stuff I didn't do. She said I did it. We used to throw oranges in the class. She used to blame me all the time, because she knew I used to have an orange in my lunch every day.

I. What if a teacher gives you too much homework?

B. I just didn't do it.

I. Did you complain to the teacher, or would you just not do it?

B. I just didn't do it. Then when she wrote the answers on the board, I just copied down the answers.

I. What if you are told to do something you think is unreasonable?

B. I ask them why.

I. Now, if you dislike a teacher, do you ever try to get back at him?

B. Yeah, we used to put thumb tacks on her chair. She had a Volkswagen. We used to lift it on the sidewalk all the time.

I. When was the last time you got mad at a teacher?

B. I was going to high school. Somebody took some girl's purse or something, and when she came in she complained to the teacher that someone had her purse, and they planted it under my chair. The principal expelled me for it. Wasn't my mother mad! She went storming up to that school. "Let my son back in school," she said. So they let me back in the next day.

I. How often would you say you got mad at a teacher?

B. Not very often. I just didn't want to work, you know. There was a lot of mess-ups. Of course, you know, I wasn't a mess-up, but there was a lot of guys in the room that used to create all sorts of trouble. In biology class I used to throw chalk, and I'd be just wising up to throw a piece of chalk and the teacher'd turn round. "O.K., go down to the office."

I. Have you ever struck or thrown anything at a teacher?
B. A ruler.
I. How many times?
B. Once.
I. When you're mad, have you ever slammed doors or desks and things like that in school?
B. One time I got mad and threw a chair, that was about all.
I. Have you ever sworn at a teacher?
B. No.
I. Answered them back?
B. Yes.
I. How often?
B. When they said I did something, and I didn't do it, you know. When they pick on me or something like that, you know. . . .
I. How many times have you complained to a principal or counselor about a teacher?
B. None. I've only told my Ma. Have her go up and fight it out for me.

This boy's resentment of authority figures is quite clear from the excerpt. It appears not only in his aggressive activities but also in his manner of attributing hostility and unfairness to his teachers. He puts himself on one side of the arena and his teachers on the other, apparently in full confidence that in a crisis his mother will join in and do battle for him.

Often the boys' hostility toward school authorities was manifested in persistent noncooperative and stubborn defiance.

I. If you dislike a teacher, do you ever try to get back at him?
B. (Case 31) I don't really try to get back, but every time they tell me to do something I say, "No."
I. When did you last get mad at a teacher?
B. Last day of school, I got in trouble for turning on a saw in class. I got mad and the next day I didn't go back to school, and the next time I got back they said I cut. . . .
I. How often do you get mad at a teacher?
B. Well, almost once every day. Almost, not quite, maybe one day I wouldn't. . . .
I. Have you ever answered them back?
B. Yes. Sometimes in school I just go outside and sit down. I don't do anything. I just go outside and sit down.

I. What have you found the best way of dealing with a teacher you don't like?

B. Everytime he says he wants me to do something that would help the class, I'll say, "No, I won't do it."

All the control boys appeared to have a generally positive attitude toward school authorities. They typically avoided open clashes with their teachers and tried to resolve any disharmony either by talking things over with them or by working harder in order to win the teachers' approval.

I. How often have you felt that a teacher has given you an unfair grade?

B. (Case 20) Not too often. Once in a while you feel you didn't get a fair shake, but most of the time they give you a fair shake.

I. When you feel you haven't had a fair shake, what do you do about it?

B. I go and talk to the teacher and see if it's a mistake on his part or if it's just that I've been loafing off. . . .

I. Suppose a teacher punishes you unjustly, what do you do about it?

B. I don't do too much. Take what you get, but don't feel too good about it.

I. Would you say anything about it?

B. There's not too much you can do.

I. What if he gives you too much homework?

B. I try to do as much as I can. I go to school and try to do it before school. In that way you don't have to work so much at night. You can do it in the morning. . . .

I. When did you last get mad at a teacher?

B. Oh, let's see. I went out for the basketball team and he kept ignoring me. I mean, I tried to show him by working hard, but he didn't notice me. He knew I was there, but he didn't care too much. I tried to do everything he said. He just didn't seem to do anything. So I decided, well, not to go out, because I don't think he cared. He had the team picked out anyway.

I. If you dislike a teacher, do you ever try to get back at him?

B. There's not too many teachers that I dislike. They're all pretty good. . . .

I. What have you found the best way of dealing with a teacher you don't like?

B. I just try to do everything a teacher asks me to do, like homework or something.

In contrast to the aggressive boys, most of the control boys expressed aggression toward their teachers only in very indirect ways.

I. Suppose a teacher punishes you unjustly, what do you do about it?
B. (Case 2) Well, there's not much I can do, but, I mean, I imagine I could get back at the teacher by spreading around the word that the teacher's no good, and that's probably what I would do.

The hypotheses concerning aggression toward peers also stood up well to statistical tests (Table 3-7). The aggressive boys reported more physical aggression toward peers and expressed this aggression more directly than did the control

TABLE 3-7

Boys' Aggression toward Peers: Differences between
Aggressive and Control Boys

Scales	Aggressive Group		Control Group		t	p	
	Mean	S.D.	Mean	S.D.			
Physical aggression	6.35	2.34	4.08	1.25	4.08	<.001	
Verbal aggression	5.54	1.91	4.81	1.20	1.43	<.10	
Indirect aggression[a]	4.35	2.06	5.94	1.94	2.35	<.05	(.01)[b]
Directness of aggression	7.63	2.11	5.40	2.11	4.16	<.001	
Hostility	5.27	1.72	4.27	0.89	2.50	<.01	

[a] This scale was not used as a basis for prediction.
[b] The probability in parentheses is based on the Wilcoxon Test.

boys. They also expressed considerably more hostile feelings toward peers. The two groups of boys, however, did not differ greatly in the amount of direct verbal aggression they displayed toward their peers. On the other hand, the control boys showed considerably more indirect aggression than did the aggressive boys.

Some of the aggressive boys took obvious pride in their skill at physical attack even when this took a form that most adolescents would deplore.

I. Are there things about yourself that you're proud of, and wouldn't want to change?
B. (Case 29) Motorcycle riding.
I. Is there anything else?
B. Say, something like you're proud of? You probably won't understand, but "stomping." I'm proud of it because, I don't know, all the guys I hang around with do that. Do you know what "stomping" is?
I. No, I don't.

B. Fighting with two feet without using your hands, see. I'm not trying to be conceited or anything, but I know I can use my feet better than all the guys I hang around with, so I wouldn't want to
change that. Like my Dad, he said, "If you know how to fight with
your feet, then it's in your hands, you've got it made," or something
like that. "You never need be afraid of anybody."

Here again in a boy's interview there is evidence of encouragement of aggression by a parent, and this time not
of subtle, but of very direct, encouragement. Yet this father,
as the quotation on page 101 indicates, would tolerate no aggression against himself. In this particular boy's case, there
may indeed have been quite a strong identification with an
aggressive father, so that, while there was little problem with
aggression in the home, the boy accepted and valued aggression as a sign of power and freely expressed it outside
the home.

I. How do you deal with the kind of guy who likes pushing his weight
about?
B. (Case 29) I like them kind of guys in a way, because then in that
way some guys get along better with them because, oh, sometimes
some guy comes along and pushes his weight about and stuff and
makes him fall, you know, pushes him back down. At least he
tried, but some of the guys they don't even try. They just go around
hiding behind everybody's back and stuff.

In contrast, the control boys rarely favored physical means
of settling disputes, and were much more likely to show
irritation or annoyance in indirect ways.

I. Do you ever feel like doing something mean to another fellow?
B. (Case 36) Oh, sometimes, yes.
I. What kind of things make you feel that way?
B. Oh, when somebody should be serious and they are always fooling
around. . . .
I. Suppose you feel this way, what do you usually do?
B. I usually make a joke about it. "Come on, let's get up, let's get
going. We can't sleep here." Something like that, you know. I
mean, I do try and tell him in a way that doesn't seem . . . (trails
off).

While many of the control boys reported getting into fights
when they were of grade school age, their aggression had
been so well socialized by the time they had reached adoles-

cence that they deliberately avoided conflicts with their peers even when others provoked them. The majority, however, were prepared to assert themselves, at least verbally, if they felt that a peer was taking advantage of them.

I. How do you deal with the kind of fellow who likes pushing his weight around?

B. (Case 48) I just let him go ahead and hurt himself. I figure he's not hurting me any, but when he does infringe upon my property, I'll say something about it.

I. What about the sort of fellow who blows his top at you or says things about you you don't like?

B. I usually let it ripe on him because I know he's that type of guy. By blowing his top he's only hurting himself, displaying himself to other people. I just keep quiet. It doesn't bother me, it doesn't bother him.

I. When did you last hit a guy?

B. Oh, I don't know. I think back in sixth grade.

I. Have you ever gotten into a fight since you've been at high school?

B. No. I've evaded them pretty well. I've gotten into them but I've evaded them.

I. How about junior high?

B. No, I haven't. When I was a little kid I was always doing something like that. Sixth grade is the last time.

I. How about blowing your top at a guy?

B. I never blow my top too much. I always try to keep an even temper.

The negative attitude of most of the control boys toward aggressive peers and their unwillingness to associate with them undoubtedly contributed to their relatively high score on the scale measuring indirect aggression toward peers.

The data from the boys' interviews did not yield any differences between the aggressive and the control boys in the amount of overt aggression that they showed toward their parents, nor did they differ in the amount of hostility they felt toward their mothers. Though the aggressive boys felt more hostility toward their fathers than did the control boys (Table 3-8), it was clear that the majority dared not express their aggression too directly.

I. What do you usually do when you get mad at your father?

B. (Case 1) I don't do nothing. I just get mad, that's all. . . .

TABLE 3-8
Boys' Aggression toward Parents: Differences between
Aggressive and Control Boys

Scales	Aggressive Group		Control Group		t	p
	Mean	S.D.	Mean	S.D.		
Physical aggression toward father	2.08	0.38	2.17	0.77	0.51	N.S.
Physical aggression toward mother	2.08	0.38	2.13	0.58	0.35	N.S.
Verbal aggression toward father	5.40	1.95	5.08	1.83	0.62	N.S.
Verbal aggression toward mother	5.31	1.88	5.58	1.89	0.48	N.S.
Indirect aggression toward father	6.38	2.11	5.65	2.02	1.23	N.S.
Indirect aggression toward mother	6.12	2.48	6.04	1.80	0.13	N.S.
Directness of aggression toward father	5.48	1.71	4.88	1.31	1.28	N.S.
Directness of aggression toward mother	5.37	1.86	5.12	1.32	0.58	N.S.
Hostility toward father	5.31	2.22	3.92	1.57	2.21	$<.02$ (.01)[a]
Hostility toward mother	4.83	2.13	4.46	1.59	0.71	N.S.

[a] The probability in parentheses is based on the Wilcoxon Test.

I. Have you ever sworn at him?
B. He'd kill me.

.   .   .

I. Have you ever struck your father?
B. (Case 9) No, I almost did once, but if I did I'd have gotten all beat up.

.   .   .

I. What do you usually do when you get mad at your father?
B. (Case 19) I get mad at them, but I don't show it too much. When I get mad, I try not to show it. . . .
I. Have you ever slammed doors and things like that?
B. When my father's not around, I might. If he's around, I wouldn't. If I go off into another room, he knows I'm mad. I sit there and keep calm and do whatever I was doing. . . .
I. How often do you get mad at your dad?
B. I get angry quite a few times, but I try to get through without showing it.

.   .   .

I. What do you usually do when you get mad at your father?
B. (Case 25) Go up to my room and mope.

I. Have you ever struck your father?
B. No.
I. Thrown things around the house?
B. No.
I. Do you shout at him?
B. Yeah.
I. How often?
B. About three times. I got beaten three times for it.

The aggressive boys seemed to be somewhat less fearful of showing aggression toward their mothers, but they found the more indirect ways of expressing anger to be usually safer and sometimes equally effective.

I. If you get angry with your mother, do you ever stomp out of the house or slam the door of your room or anything like that?
B. (Case 15) No, if I do that—I don't know—I find that it gets her madder. I mean, I can annoy her more if I just act nonchalant-like; calmly walk up to my room, that's what I usually do.

The calculated provocation which appears in the last excerpt was almost entirely absent from the reports of the control boys. At times, of course, the control boys did get angry with their parents, though, like the aggressive boys, they usually expressed their anger only in very indirect ways.

I. What do you do when you get mad at your father?
B. (Case 52) I go up to my room and shadow box.

· · ·

B. (Case 50) I frown and stare off into space.

· · ·

B. (Case 34) I don't do anything rash. I usually walk around the house and don't say anything to anyone.

· · ·

B. (Case 40) Oh gee, we usually argue, never much, nothing violent. I'll stick up for my rights, which I think is right, and so forth.

There were, then, indications within the adolescent interviews that overt aggression had been effectively inhibited both within the homes of the aggressive boys and within the homes of their controls.

Some evidence that aggression generalizes from one situation to another was provided by the consistently positive correlations that were found between aggression toward parents, toward teachers, and toward peers (Table 3-9). These correlations are based on estimates of total aggression

TABLE 3-9

INTERCORRELATIONS BETWEEN MEASURES OF TOTAL AGGRESSION: DATA FROM BOYS' INTERVIEWS

Scale	2	3	4
1. Aggression toward mother	.64	.30	.12
2. Aggression toward father		.34	.16
3. Aggression toward teachers			.44
4. Aggression toward peers			

Correlations equal to, or greater than, .37 are significant at the .01 level. Correlations equal to, or greater than, .28 are significant at the .05 level.

obtained by combining ratings of physical, direct verbal, and indirect aggression.

In general, ratings of the various forms of aggression were positively correlated. Since little physical aggression had been shown toward parents and teachers, the ratings of physical and direct verbal aggression were, in these cases, combined into a single measure of *direct aggression*. This combined estimate of direct aggression correlated with the boys' indirect aggression .57 ($p < .001$), .59 ($p < .001$), and .36 ($p < .02$) for aggression toward teachers, mothers, and fathers, respectively. In addition, physical aggression toward peers correlated positively with direct verbal aggression ($r = .31$; $p < .05$). On the other hand, the correlation between direct verbal aggression and indirect aggression toward peers was approximately zero ($r = .04$), while physical aggression and indirect aggression toward peers were negatively correlated ($r = -.35$; $p < .05$). Undoubtedly, the inclusion of walking away and spurning peers as indices of indirect aggression was partly responsible for the atypical correlations found among the measures of aggression toward peers. It seemed possible that the inclusion of these indices was also responsible for the relatively low correlations between total aggression toward peers and total aggression toward parents. However, while the correlation between direct aggression toward mothers and direct aggression toward peers was .35 ($p < .02$), that between direct aggression toward fathers and direct aggression toward peers was approximately zero. Probably another factor influenced these latter correlations—the boys' fear to show direct aggression toward their parents, particularly toward their fathers.

Further evidence that parents who encouraged aggression outside the home tended to have aggressive children was provided by correlations between the mid-parent ratings of parental encouragement of aggression and ratings of the boys' aggression based on the adolescent interviews. Boys whose parents encouraged them to be aggressive outside the home tended to show more physical aggression toward their peers ($r = .45$; $p < .001$) and more verbal aggression toward their teachers ($r = .35$; $p < .02$). Aggressive boys whose parents strongly encouraged them to be aggressive tended also to display physical aggression toward their teachers ($r = .44$; $p < .05$); a similar correlation could not have been expected for the control boys, since practically none of them had ever shown any physical aggression toward a teacher. Moreover, boys whose parents encouraged aggression were inclined to be verbally aggressive both toward their mothers ($r = .33$; $p < .05$) and toward their fathers ($r = .26$; $p < .07$). They tended, on the other hand, to show relatively little indirect aggression toward their peers ($r = -.36$; $p < .02$), presumably because they felt free to express aggression in direct ways.

If the directness of aggression measures are interpreted as indices of anxiety about aggression, it may also be said that boys whose parents encouraged aggression tended to be somewhat lacking in anxiety about aggression. The mid-parent ratings of encouragement correlated .30 ($p < .05$) with the directness of the boys' aggression toward their teachers, .27 ($p < .06$) with the directness of their aggression toward their peers, and .30 ($p < .05$) with the directness of their aggression toward their mothers. A small, but nevertheless positive, correlation ($r = .20$) was also found between the parents' encouragement of aggression and the directness of the boys' aggression toward their fathers.

Consistent relationships were found between the boys' feelings of rejection and their hostility. Boys who felt rejected by their mothers tended to be both hostile toward their mothers ($r = .48$; $p < .001$) and lacking in warmth for them ($r = -.45$; $p < .001$). Similarly, boys who felt rejected by their fathers were likely to be hostile toward ($r = .68$; $p < .001$), and lacking in warmth for ($r = -.73$; $p < .001$), their fathers. While boys who felt rejected by their peers tended to be hostile toward their peers ($r = .51$; $p < .001$), they were not necessarily lacking in warmth for them ($r = -.14$). It is possible that the ratings of the boys' feelings of rejection and the corresponding ratings for hostility were somewhat contaminated, since the same cues might have formed the basis for both sets of ratings. Such contamination is, however, less likely to have occurred in the case of the correlations between the feelings-of-rejection and the warmth measures, since the ratings of warmth were based on the extent to which the boys demonstrated affection and not merely on their expressed attitudes.

Correlations between ratings of characteristics of the parents, based on the parent interviews, and ratings of the boys' hostility and aggression, based on the adolescent interviews, gave some additional support to the hypothesis that parents who are cold and rejecting tend to have aggressive sons. Ratings of the fathers' hostility toward their sons correlated $.35$ ($p < .05$) with ratings of the boys' hostility toward their teachers, and ratings of the fathers' warmth toward their sons correlated $-.32$ ($p < .05$) with ratings of the boys' total aggression toward their teachers. In addition, the mid-parent ratings of parental warmth correlated $-.33$ ($p < .05$) with the directness of the boys' aggression toward their peers. Moreover, in the control families, boys whose parents were somewhat rejecting tended to show hostility toward them ($r = .46$; $p < .02$). In Chapter 5 further evidence will be provided that parental characteristics that were associated with rejection were also associated with the boys' hostility and aggression.

RESULTS FROM THEMATIC TEST

Although there were no consistent differences between the two groups of boys in the extent to which they displayed overt aggression toward their parents, it seemed possible that the aggressive boys might express more hostility toward their parents in fantasy productions. Some of the thematic test items were clearly capable of eliciting material that might reflect the boys' attitudes toward their parents. However, the items were for the most part too structured to allow the boys to introduce acts of aggression that were not already depicted within the items themselves. Consequently, it was decided to score the protocols simply for the number of times the boys in the stories were depicted as having *hostile thoughts and feelings* about their parents.

The aggressive boys gave significantly more responses indicating hostility toward the father than did the control boys. There was no difference, however, between the two groups of boys in the number of responses indicating hostility toward the mother (Table 3-10). No significance should be attached to the fact that both groups of boys obtained a

TABLE 3-10

FREQUENCY OF HOSTILITY RESPONSES TO THEMATIC TEST:
DIFFERENCES BETWEEN AGGRESSIVE AND CONTROL BOYS

Scales	Rater Reliability	Aggressive Group		Control Group		t	p
		Mean	S.D.	Mean	S.D.		
Hostile feelings toward father	.81	2.00	0.93	1.36	1.16	2.00	<.05
Hostile feelings toward mother	.80	0.81	1.20	0.48	0.81	1.10	N.S.

Probabilities remained the same when Mann-Whitney *U*-tests were employed.

higher rating for hostile feelings toward the father than they did for hostile feelings toward the mother; this difference is largely due to the inclusion of a picture (No. 7) that depicted a boy in the act of raising his fist to his father.

When the aggressive boys gave a response that could be scored for hostility toward the father, they tended to express the hostility in a vehement and generalized manner.

B. (Case 43) The boy's father told him that he couldn't have some money to go out tonight. When the father turns his back, the boy raises his fist, clenches his fist at him. The boy is angry. He's thinking that he's very angry because his folks wouldn't give him any money, and he's worrying that he can't get any money to go out with his girl tonight. The father turns around and sees him waving his fist. Well, the father doesn't know what to do, because the kid clenched his fist at him. But the father thinks to himself that he, if he's doing the right thing. And the boy, it's hard to say. I guess he's, he's mad at his father. He hates his father.

• • •

B. (Case 23) Kid's going to beat hell out of his old man, looks like. The kid and the old man have just had an argument. The kiddy is getting pretty crazy. He must have talked some nasty trash to the old man. Looks like he's calling his old man out, and the old man keeps walking ahead. I guess the kiddy wanted to go to a dance and used the old man's car or something. The old man won't let him. The old man makes him stay home or beats the hell out of him, I guess. Well, the kid's thinking he wants to beat the shit out of the old man.

In contrast, the control boys tended to depict the story-character's anger as a temporary response to frustration and they sometimes mentioned that the father might, in fact, have been frustrating the boy for his own good.

B. (Case 38) Looks like they're having some kind of discussion that turned into an argument, maybe about getting the car. His dad has finally laid down the law and said, "No, you can't and there isn't anything more to it." The guy, he doesn't seem to think it's quite fair; he's getting a raw deal. So he's mad. I think he'll probably cool off afterwards and realize he got a right deal, but it doesn't seem fair then. And his dad, he really wants to do whatever it was but—for some reason, for his own good or something—he shouldn't do it. He just, he doesn't want to particularly give the kid a rough time, but yet he still wants to do what's best for him all round. The boy was kind of hot-headed then, because he was all set on doing something. He probably had his plans all made, and then all of a sudden his parents won't let him go through with it. So he's just gonna have to let it ride over or talk it out peacefully.

Had the stories been rated for the intensity of hostile responses, the difference between the groups would undoubtedly have been much greater.

DISCUSSION

The inconsistency with which the parents of the aggressive boys handled their sons' aggressive behavior may have been an important factor in fostering the boys' antisocial aggressive orientation. On the one hand, both the mothers and the fathers of the aggressive boys encouraged their sons' aggression outside the home, while the mothers, through their relative permissiveness of aggression toward themselves, allowed opportunities for aggression to occur, and so to be reinforced, in the home. On the other hand, the fathers of the aggressive boys were very nonpermissive of aggression toward themselves, and both they and their wives had from time to time punished their sons for aggression, particularly for aggression toward adults. Since their parents encouraged aggression in some circumstances, the punishment that the aggressive boys received probably served merely to make them more hostile and resentful.

It was nevertheless clear, both from their own accounts and from the accounts given by their sons, that the parents of the aggressive boys had succeeded almost as well as the control parents in inhibiting their sons' direct aggressive behavior within the home. On the other hand, the boys' interviews revealed that the aggressive boys felt more hostility toward their fathers than did the control boys. Since they were apparently strongly motivated to aggress against their parents, particularly their fathers, and were also fearful of expressing direct aggression toward them, one might expect that the aggressive boys would displace some of their aggression to persons outside the home. In respect to role similarity the teacher is more like the parent than is the peer, and con-

sequently object displacement might be expected to occur
primarily to teachers and only secondarily to peers. At the
same time, response displacement had been occuring within
the home, the boys' aggression toward the parents being for
the most part shown only in relatively indirect ways. Consequently, aggressive responses might be expected to take
on more direct forms under conditions of lessened anxiety
such as might be found outside the home. Thus, in order to
interpret the findings about the boys' aggression, it is necessary to take into account the operation both of object and of
response displacement.

Miller (1948) has provided a theoretical model for the displacement of responses under conditions of strong and weak
anxiety. According to Miller's paradigm (Figure 3-1), an in-

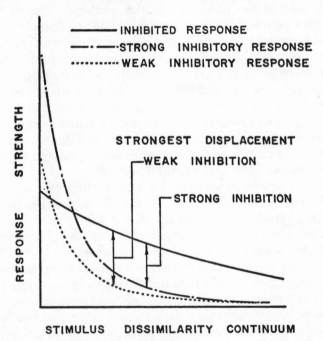

FIGURE 3–1. THEORETICAL MODEL FOR THE DISPLACEMENT OF OVERT
RESPONSES UNDER CONDITIONS OF WEAK AND STRONG INHIBITION (After
N. E. Miller, 1948).

hibitory (anxiety) response generalizes less than the response that it inhibits so that, in situations that are slightly dissimilar from those in which a conflict was originally learned, the inhibited response will be somewhat less strongly inhibited than it was in the original conflict situation. If one imagines a continuum of situations which are increasingly dissimilar from the original situation, there will be some point on this continuum at which the inhibited response will be just as strong as the anxiety response that inhibits it. From this point on, the original response is consequently not prevented from occurring. The point on the continuum at which the originally inhibited response first occurs will, of course, shift to the right as the strength of the inhibitory response increases and shift to the left as the strength of the inhibitory response decreases.

By subtracting the height of the curve representing the strength of the inhibitory response from the height of the curve representing the strength of the inhibited response, it is possible to represent the strength of the overt response that might be expected at any point on the dissimilarity continuum. If the strength of the inhibitory response increases, the point of maximum strength of the overt response is shifted to the right; on the other hand, if the strength of the inhibitory response decreases, the overt response will reach maximum strength at a point closer to the vertical axis to the left of the diagram. Obviously, the effect of increasing or decreasing the strength of the originally inhibited response would be analogous to the effect of decreasing or increasing, respectively, the strength of the inhibitory response (Figure 3-2).

It is possible to interpret response strength in terms of the probability of the occurrence of a particular kind of response —in the present case, in terms of the probability of the occurrence of aggression. The curve for the inhibitory response will now represent the strength of anxiety about aggression, whereas the curve for the originally inhibited response will represent the strength of the instigation to aggression or the potentiality for displaying aggressive behavior.

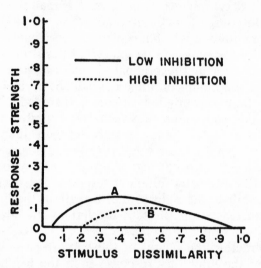

FIGURE 3–2. STRENGTH OF DISPLACED RESPONSES UNDER CONDITIONS OF STRONG AND WEAK INHIBITION (After J. W. M. Whiting and I. L. Child, 1953).

Two sets of curves of this kind could be set up, one referring to object displacement, one to response displacement. In the first case, the points of the dissimilarity continuum would represent objects increasingly dissimilar to the original instigators of aggression; in the second case, these points would represent responses increasingly dissimilar to the most direct kinds of aggressive response. An attempt will be made to combine the effects of object displacement and response displacement into a single theoretical model for the explanation of the findings concerning the boys' aggression, taking into account the Sears-Whiting conflict-drive theory. This theory has been employed to explain variations in the relative strength of displaced aggressive responses, both for children (Sears *et al.*, 1953) and in the myths of primitive societies (Whiting and Child, 1953), that Miller's paradigm, in its original form, would not have predicted. The conflict-drive theory, stated in its barest terms, claims that a state of conflict is in itself drive-producing and that the drive it produces summates with the aggressive drive to increase the strength of the motivation to respond aggressively. Brown and Farber (1951) have dealt with the problem of emotion as an intervening variable in somewhat similar terms. In the presence of frustration they assume that there occurs an irrelevant or frustration-produced drive which summates with, and so adds strength to, the drive that has been frustrated. Thus the probability of the occurrence of an overt response is increased under conditions of high frustration.

Although the present case is not completely parallel to that considered by Whiting and Child, an extension of their theoretical model (Figure 3-3) will serve to illustrate the kind of processes that are assumed to be at work. In place of the

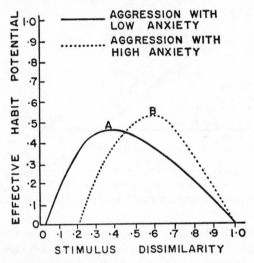

FIGURE 3–3. THEORETICAL MODEL OF EFFECTIVE HABIT POTENTIAL OF AGGRESSION, WITH HIGH AND LOW ANXIETY ABOUT AGGRESSION (After J. W. M. Whiting and I. L. Child, 1953).

single curves used by Whiting and Child for their high and low anxiety groups, two curves are required for each group of boys, one representing the direct expression of aggression, one the indirect expression (Figure 3-4). Actually, two curves are not adequate to express all possibilities; theoretically, a new pair of curves would be required for each point on the continuum of directness-indirectness of response. The present findings can, however, be dealt with in terms of the curves as drawn.

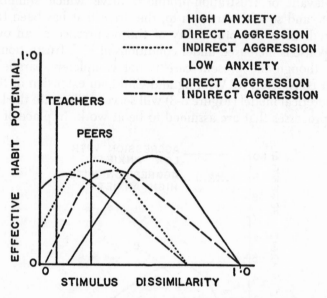

FIGURE 3–4. THEORETICAL MODEL OF EFFECTIVE HABIT POTENTIAL OF AGGRESSION UNDER CONDITIONS OF HIGH AND LOW ANXIETY ABOUT AGGRESSION, WITH ALLOWANCE FOR RESPONSE DISPLACEMENT.

The original instigators to aggression, it was assumed, are the parents. These, as such, are represented by a zero point on the dissimilarity continuum; following Whiting and Child, objects that are completely dissimilar to the original instigators are located at the extreme right of the baseline, represented by 1.0. Teachers, as adults in a parent-surrogate role, have been located close to the parents on the continuum; peers have been placed further to the right, but still, as human beings approaching adulthood, closer to the zero point than to the extreme right of the baseline. Much of the extreme right of the diagram might be expected to refer to nonhuman and inanimate objects.

Most of the findings fit this model. There were no consistent differences between the groups of boys in the extent to which they expressed aggression against the parents. The aggressive boys, however, showed much more aggression toward their teachers than did the control boys, whether this aggression took a direct or an indirect form. For aggression toward peers, the findings are more complex. The aggressive boys employed much more physical aggression, i.e., aggression of the most primitively direct kind, than did the control boys. The difference between the two groups of boys was much smaller for direct verbal aggression, with the aggressive boys showing somewhat more aggression of this kind. In contrast, the control boys showed more indirect aggression toward peers. It seemed that the control boys' anxiety about aggression was sufficiently reduced when they were interacting with their peers to permit them to express considerable aggression, though only in indirect forms. The aggressive boys, however, in their interactions with peers, apparently reduced their aggression by direct means and thus had less instigation to express their aggression by indirect ones.

The conflict-drive theory, if adopted to explain these findings, would need elaboration. It would have to be assumed that conflict increased instigation to aggress in both groups of boys, but that it added to the existing instigation to a greater or lesser extent according to the relative strength of the instigation to aggress and the strength of anxiety at any point on the dissimilarity continuum. In this way, the effects of the conflict-produced instigation might be most apparent in the aggressive boys in their strongly aggressive reactions to their teachers, but be more apparent in the control group in the pattern of their aggressive behavior toward their peers.

Logically, it should follow from the above discussion that, if the differences between the groups were examined for even more indirect forms of aggression than were covered by the indirect aggression scales, a clear difference should begin to emerge between the groups; the aggressive boys would be expected to express more of this kind of aggression toward their parents. Such a trend can be seen in the fantasy data. The aggressive boys expressed more hostile thoughts and feelings to the fantasy father in their thematic test stories than did the controls.

In this exposition it has so far been assumed that the only difference between the groups of boys was a difference in the amount of anxiety they felt about aggression. It has previously been argued, however, that they also differed in the extent to which they were motivated to aggress. Consequently, the theoretical model that has been drawn up must be interpreted as reflecting differences between the groups of boys that are a joint function of differing levels of anxiety and of differing instigations to aggress.

So far, the possibility that anxiety may be qualitatively, as well as quantitatively, different in the two groups of boys has not been considered. In Chapter 2, however, it was claimed that a disruption of the dependency relationship between a boy and his parents might prevent the internalization of parental standards of behavior, and evidence was produced that dependency relationships were disrupted in the families of the aggressive boys. Consequently, it might be expected that the aggressive boys would be restrained more by fear of punishment from behavior that was not acceptable to their parents, while the control boys might be restrained to a much larger extent by anticipation of feelings of guilt.

The findings about the boys' aggression toward their parents fit in well with this expectation. The aggressive boys were reported as showing more *direct* aggression toward their mothers than the control boys, but more *indirect* aggression toward their fathers. As will be shown in Chapter 5, the aggressive boys, in general, perceived their fathers as the more punitive of their parents. Fear of punishment may consequently have prevented the aggressive boys from showing aggression directly toward their fathers, even though they were apparently more hostile to their fathers than they were to their mothers.

Let us now consider a possible complicating factor for any paradigm for displacement. Assuming that one group of boys is controlled by fear of punishment from an external agent, and that a second group of boys is controlled by anticipatory feelings of guilt, would different predictions be made for the two groups under certain conditions? It seems that they would. When the subjective probability of being discovered was small, one might expect that the fear-controlled group would transgress, whereas the guilt-controlled group would resist temptation. If this argument is correct, in order to predict whether antisocial behavior will occur, knowledge is required not only of the *strength* of inhibitory mechanisms, but also of their *kind*. In other words, knowledge of the strength of more than one variable is needed.

At the present time, in the absence of controlled experimentation, there is no possibility of an extension of the theoretical model for displacement that would take into account qualitative differences in inhibitory mechanisms. However, some speculations, which may not be substantiated by further research, may be offered.

Successful socialization seems to require a process of response displacement rather than a displacement of the original response to another object. In the latter case, the displaced response may be just as primitive, and just as socially disruptive, as the original response; the only difference may be that someone other than the original instigator suffers. This is especially evident when the displaced response is an aggressive one. Outside their homes the aggressive boys showed much less response displacement than did the controls, and it is the directness, perhaps as much as the quantity, of their aggression that makes them stand out as antisocial personalities. Control that is predominantly based on fear, it is suggested, may lead to little modification of response; it may affect predominantly the choice of object against which the aggression is expressed. An acceptance of this point of view would involve qualitatively distinct forms of anxiety, one form of anxiety being associated with a modification of response, the other form with the choice of object against which the socially unacceptable behavior is expressed. This theory is offered as an alternative to the one to which the findings about the boys' aggression have provisionally been fitted. It will be further supported by findings that are reported in Chapter 6.

Chapter 4

Sex

There is evidence that aggressive antisocial persons sometimes display markedly deviant sex behavior (Cleckley, 1955; Henry, 1941). Such behavior may be one facet of a generalized rebellion against social standards (White, 1956); in other words, the deviant sexuality may be largely motivated by hostility to social prohibitions. On the other hand, certain socialization defects may facilitate the occurrence both of antisocial aggression and of socially disapproved sexual behavior. Thus, since the aggressive boys in this study were expected to present a defective conscience development (Chapter 6), they were expected to express their sexual, as well as their aggressive, impulses with greater freedom and less consequent guilt than the control boys.

Psychoanalysts have frequently interpreted antisocial acts in terms of underlying sexual conflicts (Alexander and Healy, 1935; Bromberg, 1948; Fenichel, 1945; Friedlander, 1947; Lindner, 1944) and have brought forward impressive clinical evidence that sex and aggression are sometimes associated in antisocial behavior. Moreover, the forms in which sexuality is expressed seem often to reflect the strength of aggressive and dependent impulses and of conflicts in the areas of aggression and dependency. It seemed possible, therefore, that the pattern of interrelationships among sex and these other motivational systems might differ for the two groups of boys.

A relationship between masturbation and feelings of rejection has sometimes been noted in individual case histories; masturbation has been described as a reaction to frustrated dependency needs and as an attempt to compensate auto-erotically for the feeling of being rejected and unloved by others (Phillips and Smith, 1953). Moreover, Jenkins and Hewitt (1944) have depicted unsocialized delinquents, whose parents were severely rejecting, as engaging in excessive masturbation. Consequently, it was decided to investigate not only the extent to which the boys had engaged in premarital sex relationships and homosexual behavior but also how frequently they masturbated.

The decision to include measures relating to sex behavior and training arose less from their possible relevance to the general theory of aggressive behavior that is offered in this book than from a wish to investigate some of the claims that have been made about sex behavior among aggressive personalities. Consequently, the only hypothesis that was put forward concerning the sex measures was that the aggressive boys would show less guilt and anxiety about their sex behavior than would the control boys.

The inclusion of measures relating to the boys' sex behavior and attitudes and to the sex training given by their parents provided an opportunity to extend psychological investigations into this important area of adolescent development. There have been few studies of the sexual behavior of adolescents in which adolescent boys have served as subjects. Most prior studies have relied upon the reminiscences of adults gathered either through questionnaire or through interview methods. In contrast, the data obtained in this study consist of the recorded responses of adolescents within the context of questions devoted to other topics. No indication was given in advance of the interviews that the matter of sex behavior would be brought up, and consequently the boys were not volunteers insofar as their answers to the sex questions were concerned. However, no pressure was exerted on the adolescents to give details of their sexual experience. Although some of the questions were quite direct, care was

taken not to disturb the boys unduly, and there is no doubt
that some of them were evasive, and probably untruthful, in
their answers. On the other hand, many were surprisingly
ready to answer questions about their sexual behavior and
attitudes and supplied a good deal more information than
the questions were designed to elicit.

The parent interviews provided information concerning
parental handling of sexual behavior during the boys' infancy and childhood and, in particular, an indication of
parental attitudes toward sexual behavior during the boys'
adolescence. This information, obtained in a systematic fashion from both fathers and mothers, is of considerable interest in its own right.

Because much of the information that was obtained
through the sex questions cannot be found in most books on
adolescent development, it is presented in some detail even
in cases where a difference was not found between the aggressive and control boys or between their parents.

Sexual Development and Training

Behavior that has sexual implications, at least in the eyes
of adults, can be observed from the earliest years in almost
every child. Male infants have erections; children of both
sexes finger their genitals, engage in acts of exhibitionism
and voyeurism, and at times in sexual play with other children. Some of these acts have sexual significance only in a
particular cultural setting. To appear in the nude before
strangers or children of the opposite sex can have no particular significance in a society in which children ordinarily
wear no clothes. Other acts, however, such as infantile masturbation and sexual experimentation with other children,
are more obviously related to adult sexuality wherever they
occur.

Childhood sexual behavior, however, is quite different in
character from that which develops with the onset of
adolescence.

> The sexual life of the younger boy is more or less a part
> of his other play; it is usually sporadic, and (under the

restrictions imposed by our social structure) it may be without overt manifestation in a fair number of cases. The sexual life of the older male is, on the other hand, an end in itself, and (in spite of our social organization) in nearly all boys its overt manifestations become frequent and regular, soon after the onset of adolescence (Kinsey, Pomeroy, and Martin, 1948, p. 182).

Moreover, the social consequences of sexual play during adolescence are potentially much more serious than they are during earlier years. While the attainment of full reproductive maturity is a gradual process and occurs later than the outward signs of puberty (Ford and Beach, 1951), there is always the possibility that sexual intercourse may lead to pregnancy. Sexual behavior is, of course, not unique in its increased social danger during adolescence. A physical attack by an adolescent boy can result in permanent injury or even death, consequences which are far more serious than those customarily resulting from the sexual act. The average adolescent, nevertheless, is probably more poorly prepared to cope with sexual impulses than with impulses of any other kind, not only because of the relatively sudden biological changes that occur, but also because the process of socialization in our culture provides the adolescent with few or no opportunities of learning through progressive experimentation to express sexual impulses in forms that will be permitted him when he reaches adult status. This is in contrast to the social training of aggression and dependency, of which certain attenuated forms are not only tolerated but under some circumstances actually approved.

> Here (in the realm of sexuality) it is neither a question of teaching new habits to replace earlier ones nor of controlling and regulating competition, but rather of inhibiting, during part or all of childhood, all goal-directed behavior and gratification (Mowrer and Kluckhohn, 1944, p. 112).

The adolescent is consequently beset with sexual urges which he has no socially approved means of reducing. As

Sears, Maccoby, and Levin (1957) have pointed out, the
growing child is given little opportunity of learning even to
identify these urges, which are to become rapidly strengthened during adolescence. Children are frequently not provided with proper labels for parts of the body involved in
sexual functioning, for sexual behavior, or for sexual feelings.
It is no wonder, then, that the adolescent is sometimes confused, embarrassed, and threatened by the tensions that
accompany unsatisfied sexual impulses. Even if he wants to
talk about his problems in this area, he must feel not merely
hesitant, but even incompetent, to speak of them. This in-
competence was clearly reflected in many of the interviews
with the boys in this study. The boys who were most open
and frank about their sexual experiences tended also to be
the most crude; those who refrained from using the slang
of the peer group usually had difficulty finding the vocabulary with which to conceptualize their experiences.

MEASURES

Scales were set up to assess three aspects of the boys' sexual behavior: *heterosexual* experiences, *masturbation,* and
homosexual experiences. In many ways it would have been
advantageous to report findings in terms of frequency of
occurrence of each of these kinds of sexual behavior. However, since almost all other measures were being made by
means of five-point scales, it was felt that the raters' task
would be simpler if the same method was retained for the
measures of sexual behavior. Some supplementary data in
terms of incidence of occurrence have been derived from
the ratings and are given within the chapter. A measure was
also taken of the extent to which boys had received *sex information* from their parents, relative to the amount of sex
information they had received from other sources. Finally,
a rating was obtained of the *sex anxiety* of the boys. The
latter rating was based on two kinds of data. If a boy said
that he had held himself back when he was tempted to engage in sexual behavior, or that he was worried about his

sexual acts, this was taken as an indication of the presence of anxiety. In addition, signs of disturbance within the interview itself, for example, blocking in any way in response to sex questions, were also given weight in determining the ratings.

From the parent interviews measures of parental *permissiveness* and *punitiveness for sexual behavior* were obtained. Four permissiveness scales were employed. Two measured the parents' permissiveness for masturbation and sex play with other children, respectively, during the boys' childhood years; the other two measured the parents' current permissiveness for masturbation and heterosexual experience—in other words, their readiness to accept and allow sexual activity during the adolescent period.

It seemed unlikely that many occurrences of sexual behavior, except perhaps during very early childhood, would have come to the parents' notice; consequently no attempt was made to set up punitiveness scales parallel to the four permissiveness scales. Instead a single punitiveness scale was employed that took into account parental punishment for sexual behavior of any sort. Raters reported considerable difficulty in rating on this over-all punitiveness scale and were convinced that important information was being lost. Nevertheless, rater reliabilities were high (.94 for the mother interviews, .93 for the father interviews), and the use of more specific scales would have certainly required too many ratings based on inferences about how the parents would have acted, had they discovered their sons engaging in specific kinds of sexual behavior.

A rating of the *parents' sex anxiety* was also obtained from the parent interviews. This rating was based partly on the parents' accounts of their own reactions to their sons' sexual behavior, and partly on signs of emotional disturbance when sexual matters were discussed. In addition, the parents were asked to what extent they felt that their sons were worried about sexual matters, and, on the basis of their responses to this question, a rating was made on a scale assessing the *parents' estimate of the boys' sexual anxiety.*

RESULTS FROM PARENT INTERVIEWS

Early Sex Training

The handling of early forms of sex behavior by the parents of the aggressive boys did not differ significantly from that of the control parents (Table 4-1). Both groups of parents

TABLE 4-1

PARENTS' HANDLING OF BOYS' SEX BEHAVIOR: DIFFERENCES BETWEEN PARENTS OF AGGRESSIVE AND CONTROL BOYS

Scales	Aggressive Group		Control Group			
	Mean	S.D.	Mean	S.D.	t	p
Data from Father Interviews						
Permissiveness: sex behavior in early years	3.60	1.45	4.35	1.91	1.56	N.S.
Permissiveness: masturbation	4.88	2.05	5.38	2.74	0.70	N.S.
Permissiveness: heterosexual behavior	8.02	1.30	7.13	1.58	2.14	<.05 (.02)[a]
Punitiveness	3.85	1.53	3.62	1.68	0.47	N.S.
Data from Mother Interviews						
Permissiveness: sex behavior in early years	3.42	1.44	4.25	2.14	1.60	N.S.
Permissiveness: masturbation	3.46	1.59	4.08	1.73	1.15	N.S.
Permissiveness: heterosexual behavior	5.44	1.94	5.10	1.75	0.65	N.S.
Punitiveness	6.19	1.94	5.38	1.88	1.37	N.S.

[a] The probability in parentheses is based on the Wilcoxon Test.
These scales were not used as bases for prediction.

were typically nonpermissive, but nonpunitive, for early sex behavior. Variations in parental attitudes were, nevertheless, encountered within both groups, and the primary aim of the discussion that immediately follows is to illustrate some typical attitudes rather than to point up differences between parents of aggressive boys and parents of controls.

The ratings of early sex training were based on questions concerning modesty training, childhood masturbation, and sex play with other children. The responses of mothers to

questions on these topics have been well documented by
Sears, Maccoby, and Levin (1957). The fathers in this study
had little to say concerning early training. Consequently
these topics will be dealt with only briefly here.

MODESTY TRAINING

As children, most of the boys had been compelled at least
to wear shorts when they were not being bathed or toiletted.
Some mothers frankly indicated that they thought it was im-
proper for a child to appear without clothes; a few seemed
on the surface to have no objection to the child's being seen
in the nude, but nevertheless brought forward some reason
why he had not been allowed to run around in this
condition.

I. When Raymond was a small child, how did you feel about letting
    him run about indoors without his clothes on?
M. (Case 36) No clothes? Well, he always wore a diaper because I
    thought it would be too messy otherwise. I mean that would be
    why he always wore a diaper until he got to the point where
    he was beginning to be broken, and then he wore underpants and
    he wore a little shirt. I mean, I didn't do more than that unless he
    went out or somebody came over. He always wore a diaper.

MASTURBATION

Almost all fathers denied having seen their sons masturbate, though some remarked that their wives may have witnessed this kind of thing. In fact, a good proportion of the
mothers had observed some masturbation when their children were very small. The more usual method of dealing
with this problem was to distract the children's attention
by providing them with some other plaything or by simply
removing their hands from their genitals. A few mothers had
slapped their children's hands whenever such behavior occurred, thus presumably producing a conditioned avoidance
response, at least in the mothers' presence. The more severe
parents admitted spanking older children or sending them
to bed, but the majority preferred not to make an issue of
the matter and merely directed their children's attention to
some other activity while avoiding mention of the act they
were correcting.

I. What did you do when you noticed him playing with himself?
M. (Case 33) Nothing other than give him something, a toy or something, to distract him, keep his hands busy.

SEX PLAY WITH OTHER CHILDREN

The majority of parents denied any occurrence of sex play with other children. Those who had observed such play had all intervened at some point. Mothers were markedly nonpermissive about childhood sex play, and it was clear that many had exercised close and continued surveillance over the children's play-groups.

I. How about sex play with other children. Did this ever come up?
M. (Case 3) There was one time when he was about four years old.
I. What did you do about it?
M. He got a spanking and then I watched him closely. In fact, I always did watch the boys if they were with girls.

The following excerpt illustrates the customary denial of the occurrence of sex play, the generally nonpermissive attitude of parents, and, in addition, their determination not to make an issue of sex matters.

I. How about sex play with other children, did this ever come up?
M. (Case 34) No.
I. Would you have allowed this or do you think you would have done something about it?
M. Well, I certainly would have discouraged it. I don't think as far as small children are concerned that it's good to make an issue of anything like that to any great extent, because that only impresses it on their minds. But I think they should be watched a little more carefully.

In view of the amount of parental supervision many of the children had received, it is strange that so little sex play had been observed. One suspects that parents prefer not to see these things or at least to interpret them in other terms.

Parents who had witnessed sex play were very ready to blame other people's children for its occurrence. They apparently felt that any display of sexual curiosity or interest on the part of their children was evidence of their own failure to train their children properly.

I. How about sex play with other children, did this ever come up?

M. (Case 35) Well, in a kind of roundabout way, and I have always felt in my own mind that there was this other little boy involved, and we discussed it. It was the other little boy was the instigator of it, so I watched them very closely since then. I think he was nine or ten or something like that then, and I never found any inkling or traces of anything like that. I did feel in my own mind that Harold was clean morally. I believe he is.

. . .

M. (Case 29) Yes. Back in Riverport we had a little girl. She was mentally ill, she wasn't right at all, and she'd take my two boys out in the fields and take down their pants and play with them.

I. What did you do about it?

M. Well, I got a petition up to have her put away, but her parents wouldn't sign it, wouldn't consent to it. So finally I moved away myself.

This last excerpt illustrates a not infrequent parental belief that sexual curiosity is a sign of mental abnormality.

Information Control

Parents varied a great deal in their readiness to impart sexual information to their children. Very few of them were, however, prepared to be completely frank about all matters. As one mother (Case 9) put it: "I mean I've told him all about childbirth, how the baby was born. But, of course, intercourse is kind of ticklish." Some parents, influenced no doubt by modern books on sex education, would tell the child that intercourse is "something nice and very beautiful," yet at the same time would respond with shock when the child attempted to satisfy his curiosity about details, and would discourage any further talk about the matter.

I. How about sex play with other children, did this ever come up?

M. (Case 28) Yes, when he was about six or seven. He came in the house one day, and we were reading and he was giggling and looking at us. We lived in Hillside at the time. And I said: "Hugh, why are you laughing like that?" He said one of the boys across the street told him something. It sounded silly to him. He couldn't understand it and continued like this. So I asked him, "Which boy," and he told me about some family who moved across the street that were not of a—I don't know where they came from, from Oklahoma. Not that there's anything against people from Oklahoma, but I mean just that type of family, very dirty. And I asked, "What did he say to you?" So he said that his father lays on top of his mother. And he said, "I cannot see Daddy lying on top of you." I just couldn't understand it. "And that's how babies come." So then he started asking questions. Of course my husband was just shocked. I mean, he just turned white. So we started to tell him that that wasn't a silly thing: that, that when he was old enough to understand that will be explained to him, but just to forget about it; and if any of the boys or the girls he ever played with discussed anything like that, just to walk away and not listen, because it would be told to him in a nasty way; and life and birth and so forth was a very beautiful thing, and not to be laughed at or dirty remarks about it. And that was the end of that.

Several of the mothers stated that they felt that a father should take the main responsibility for imparting sex information to a boy, but acknowledged that their husbands were no more prepared to do this than they were themselves.

I. From whom do you think it is best for a boy to get information and advice about sex matters?

M. (Case 9) I think their father should, you know, take them over and tell them. Of course, I have told him most of it because his father gets embarrassed, but so do I. But I've told him (laughs). His father thinks the less they know the better, but I don't agree with him.

One motive for not imparting sex information is, of course, the anxiety of the parent that the boy might utilize the information to assist him in his sexual experimentation.

I. How do you feel about young fellows who go all the way with girls?

F. (Case 5) Well, I'd like to hold it off as long as possible. Let's put it this way. I don't happen to be one who believes in pouring them full of what they should do to protect themselves and so forth. I happen to believe, I don't believe in all this school education. I think it's overdone, to a great extent.

I. What is the best way, do you think, for a young fellow to learn about sex?

F. Well, I think a certain amount should be done that way, but too much education leads to a little less fear of it; a little less fear of it makes it a little easier. When it gets a little easy, why you don't worry about it.

Some fathers, however, had been quite free in giving information, though such information was almost inevitably ac-

companied by warnings of possible dangers should the boy
become involved in sexual acts.

I. How has he become aware of this (the father's views on sexual
   matters)?
F. (Case 30) Because I tell him. Any problems he has, I told him.
   Anything—sexually or anything like that—he wishes to know, I can
   tell him, because I've been fourteen years in the Navy and I
   learned a lot (laughs).
I. What is the best way, do you think, for a young fellow to learn
   about sex?
F. Well, I think the best way is for his parents to tell him right from
   the time they begin to understand. Tony has been prompted right
   from the time I thought was the time to tell him.
I. What sort of information have you given?
F. Well, I sat down in his room and told him. I said, "You, of course,
   have seen the difference between male and female." I said, "The
   only bad thing about male and female is that there's no mating
   season. It's just one of those things. It's one of those things you
   have to be very, very careful about. When you grow up and you're
   a single man, you have to be very, very careful of what you could
   cause. You could ruin your whole life and your family too. It's
   something that can bring disgrace upon you and your own family,
   and yet it's one of the most beautiful things in the world. If it
   wasn't for that, you wouldn't be here, my boy." And I think that's
   the best way to tell them.

A good deal of misinformation was imparted to the boys
by some fathers and mothers. Some of this misinformation
came from attempts to evade truthful answers to the boys'
questions about sex; the remainder mainly took the form of
threats of what might happen if the boy engaged in sexual
activity.

I. What sort of information have you given him?
M. (Case 28) Oh, I don't think I've given him information with the
   exception of when he was a little boy. "Where do babies come
   from?" And I just said, "A seed was planted in the woman," And
   he asked me why the woman was so fat, and I told him that the
   child was there and it was born. "How did it come?" And I just
   explained that God made a way for the baby to come from me.
   And I said, "When you're old enough, you'll be able to understand."

While the mother quoted above was evasive in her replies
to her son's curiosity, her husband was both moralistic and

free in his use of threats based on false information. The mother told how she found her son's bed spotted. She spoke to her husband, who assured her that this was a natural occurrence. She nevertheless asked her husband to talk to the boy. "So he did, and when my husband started to talk to him, Hugh said, 'Oh, Dad, I know all those things.' But my husband said, 'Do you know all those things in a decent way and not in a sordid way?'" A quotation from this father's protocol will help complete the picture of the kind of sex education that was given in this family.

I. Suppose you found him doing this (masturbating) now, how would you feel about it?

F. (Case 28) If we saw him indulging in that right now? Well, let me tell you this, Tom (this father constantly addressed the interviewer by his first name), I laid stress upon this, that he should never touch his body. I told him that it could result, Lord forbid, in insanity, and I says, "Nature will take care of those things." I say, "Never, as long as I know it, Hugh, do you indulge in a thing like that." Then he gave me some answer in biology. I've been out of school so long, Tom, that I couldn't contradict just what he was mentioning, but he knows the consequences of indulging in that.

Perhaps parental inadequacies in imparting sex information have been overemphasized by the above selection of quotations. Not all parents were as evasive, inconsistent, moralistic, or threatening as some of those who have been quoted. Many did their best, often in spite of their own inadequate sex education, to impart straightforward, factual information about sex to their sons. They sometimes sought out books that might provide the information that they did not feel competent to impart.

I. What is the best way, do you think, for a young fellow to learn about sex?

M. (Case 4) Well, I think, by reading a good book on the subject. At the present I am looking for one. I think at the library they do have wonderful books on the subject. I couldn't begin to explain it as well as they have, and as clearly as they do.

• • •

I. From whom, do you think it best for a boy to get information and advice about sex matters?

M. (Case 4) The parents.

I. To what extent has Norman come of his own accord and asked
   you things?
M. He hasn't, any.
I. What sort of information have you given?
M. To be very honest, I haven't given any really. Oh I know Norman
   knows quite a bit about it, the facts of life. But I haven't really
   gone into it. I really should. I realize I'm being lax there. But I've
   been looking in the library for a particular book which I have seen
   two girls read. Yet I haven't been able to find it for him.

Another substitute for directly imparting sexual information
was the provision of pets.

M. (Case 49) He used to like to raise rabbits. There again was where
   he learned a lot about sex too, from these rabbits. He could learn
   more from them than I could have told him, in a different way of
   course.

Unfortunately, most of these well-intentioned parents put
off the provision of sex education so long that the boys had
already picked up sex information from other, often less
trustworthy and reputable, sources. In fact, from some parents' remarks it seemed that they gave information to their
sons only after they began to suspect that the boys were
already learning "too much" from other sources.

Attitudes toward Adolescent Sex Behavior

No clear-cut difference was found between the groups of
parents in their permissiveness for childhood sexual behavior. The same was true also for permissiveness for masturbation during adolescence (Table 4-1). In both cases,
however, the control parents were rated as slightly more
permissive. In contrast, the aggressive boys encountered in
their families a somewhat more permissive attitude toward
adolescent heterosexual behavior than did the control boys.
In fact, fathers of aggressive boys proved to be significantly
more permissive of heterosexual behavior than were the
control fathers.

Differences between fathers and mothers were, however,
far more marked than differences between aggressive and
control parents. Whereas mothers tended to be somewhat

nonpermissive of sexual behavior during adolescence, many fathers showed a great deal of understanding of the urges and temptations that their sons might feel.

ATTITUDES TOWARD MASTURBATION

Very few parents both expressed the view that masturbation was a completely natural occurrence and also accepted the implications of this view in relation to their own sons.

I. What did you do when you noticed him playing with himself?

F. (Case 48) I just explained to him that it wasn't a harmful thing as long as it wasn't overdone and quite a common thing as long as it's not overdone.

I. Suppose you found him doing this now, how would you feel about it?

F. We've explained to him that it isn't unnatural for a young man to have nightly ejaculations. That is, not nightly, but if he did so, why, not to worry about it. Not to fret about it.

. . .

I. Suppose you found him doing this now, how would you feel about it?

M. (Case 36) Oh, I'd do nothing about it. I'd feel it was perfectly normal.

Even while verbalizing the belief that masturbation was a normal occurrence, several parents clearly felt uneasy about the possibility that their sons should be displaying this supposedly normal behavior.

I. Suppose you found him doing this now, how would you feel about it?

F. (Case 25) No, wouldn't, because, wouldn't do nothing, because that'd be just natural. But he never has, that's one thing, I think.

. . .

F. (Case 2) Well, we're supposed to believe it's a normal thing, I guess. I don't know, but I would discourage him all I could.

The belief that masturbation may lead to insanity, formerly a prevalent fear, was very rarely expressed directly. However, the belief apparently lingers on in an attenuated form, for a number of parents felt that masturbation could be mentally, as well as physically, harmful. The father quoted below actually regarded as old-fashioned the view that masturbation causes insanity, yet believed that masturbation weakened and confused the thought processes.

I. Suppose you found him doing this now, how would you feel about it?
F. (Case 18) I explained. I even got a book, a very good book written by a very good doctor on the subject. I sat down and read it and I explained it to him, what it meant, each word. I got to where he understood it. I didn't go about it, some of the older people say it drives you crazy, and all that stuff. I explained just exactly what it does to you. It's weakening to lots of things other than your health. It also weakens your health, and your thinking ability becomes kind of muddled up where you're doing things like that. So I explained it to him in that way.

Particularly prevalent, especially among mothers, was the belief that adolescent masturbation is an indication of some form of physical abnormality.

I. Suppose you found him doing this now, how would you feel about it?
M. (Case 27) Well, I know it would be very serious and I believe, I mean, I would take him to a doctor. Find out what was causing it.

. . .

M. (Case 13) Well, naturally I'd take him to a doctor. I mean there's something ailing him. People just don't go around doing that unless there's something wrong with them.

ATTITUDES TOWARD HETEROSEXUAL BEHAVIOR

The contrast between mothers and fathers was much more marked when heterosexual behavior was discussed. Mothers were for the most part quite disturbed by the thought that their sons might possibly engage in any premarital sex play, whereas most fathers regarded petting as a normal and inevitable event, and some expressed the view that they would not be too surprised to learn that their sons had had intercourse.

Some mothers were clearly shocked and horrified by the idea that their sons might engage in premarital sex relations.

I. How do you feel about young fellows who go all the way with girls?
M. (Case 22) Oh, I think that's terrible. I don't think it should be allowed. Of course, we don't always know; but I think in my case,

if ever it happened with Bruce, I should know. It's one of those things. He has an open face. He would tell us everything. He would look so guilty that we'd know right off the bat. I know there isn't anything like that.

                                    •   •   •

M. (Case 4) Oh, I'd be shocked. I know it's the wrong thing to say but, oh, I'd be horrified. I feel Norman knows better than that, that he should be a gentleman at all times.

Most mothers who had faced the possibility that their sons might engage in heterosexual play had attempted to arouse sufficient anxiety about the possible consequences of intercourse to deter them from going this far.

I. Suppose you found that George had now begun to play around with girls, how would you feel about it?
M. (Case 9) Well, we've already talked to him about that. I told him that sex was for marriage. That when you were married, that sex was for marriage and to produce children, and that you never should do anything to a little girl because she could always get into trouble. And that a lot of little girls had committed suicide over that by getting into trouble with a boy. And I told him—he was fourteen—I told him, "You're kind of young, George, but I'll tell you, if you ever got a little girl into trouble, you'd marry her. I don't care whether she was white, black, or what else she was. There will never be a baby coming into the world without a name."

Even the more tolerant mothers obviously feared that a pregnancy might result from a possible misdemeanor on the part of their sons.

I. Suppose you found that Raymond had now begun to play around with girls, how would you feel about it?
M. (Case 36) Well, I don't really know. More than anything else I would feel that, if a girl got pregnant, it would be horrible if he had to get married at this time, and that would be the thing that would upset me terribly. I understand that it's perfectly normal for a boy of his age to have sexual relationships. I guess I wouldn't be pleased, because I feel he's a little too young to know exactly what to do and how to do it. I think he's a little young. I guess I'm wrong, but that's how I feel.
I. Does Raymond know how you feel?
M. In a way, yes, I think so, because we discussed somebody at his school that had to get married, and I said to him, "Heavenly Day, I hope you don't go and have to get married, and I become a grandmother with you at sixteen."

Some mothers accepted petting as an inevitable and natural occurrence, but still resorted to close surveillance as a precaution against the possibility that intercourse might occur.

I. How about petting, how do you feel about that?

M. (Case 29) Well, I don't think it's wrong. I think, if he doesn't do it in the home, he's going to go out and do it behind my back. He has his girl friend come in the house about once a week or so, and they spend an evening together. Of course, I'm always there. I mean, I'm near, so that's something.

I. How do you feel about a boy who goes all the way with a girl?

M. Well, I think they should wait until they are married. Of course, I know many of them don't; but of course it depends on the girl herself, for if she lets the boy, he's going to make advances.

Obviously there are times when the boy cannot be thus watched. One device by which mothers attempted to extend control beyond the home was the institution of double-dating in the belief that such an arrangement would lessen the probability of sex relations.

I. Are there any things which Alfred might do in this way that would make you particularly upset?

M. (Case 38) Yes, if I felt he was going too far or if he were parked with a girl this age, I'd be upset. That's the reason he usually goes double or triple dating, and we figure that's much safer; and I think when there's a group like that there's less likelihood of the other. We don't mention the other, but when he first started dating we'd say, "Why don't you call up so-and-so, and take them also? It's more fun." Because we felt that at thirteen or fourteen, when he first started dating, it was hard to keep a conversation going and he'd get started that way and no, they don't go single-dating. It's not fun. If he doesn't call somebody, some of his boy-friends call, "Let's double-date."

This excerpt once more illustrates parental reluctance to speak openly and directly about sexual matters; it illustrates, too, the rationalizations that the parents sometimes provided for their attempts to protect their sons' virginity.

One mother stood out for her highly permissive attitude toward heterosexual behavior. In this case, however, one might suspect that the mother was receiving vicarious gratification from the boy's sexual escapades.

I. Suppose you found that Donald had now begun to play around with girls, how would you feel about it?

M. (Case 33) Well, in fact, I know he has been; and once or twice he hasn't come right out and said, but he did make the remark that, if he was, that's one thing he wouldn't go about bragging about, and especially who the party was or anything like that. And he said that he knows all about it.

I. How about petting, how do you feel about it?

M. Well, I think they all, all young people, especially right now more than they used to in years back. They have more opportunity now; and I don't know, I've never thought much about it. They're all going to more or less, some time or another.

I. How do you feel about young fellows who go all the way with girls?

M. Well, I don't think that's right, but if the two are agreeable, why, there's not much at that age that a person can say or do. . . .

I. Do you think that Donald is worried at all about matters that have to do with sex?

M. Sometimes I used to wonder a little, but my father-in-law talked with him and he seemed to feel that Donald knew more than he did (laughs heartily).

I. What is the best way, do you think, for a young fellow to learn about sex?

M. Well, we have always tried to answer all of his questions, simple and direct as we possibly could. I always felt the best place to get his information was to get it at home, get it right.

I. To what extent has Donald come of his own accord and asked you things?

M. He used to ask questions a lot, but then as he got older, naturally, where all the other youngsters are congregating at corners, whispering and talking and telling things, he gradually worked away from that.

I. What sort of information have you given?

M. Well, as I said, I always tried to answer all his questions as direct and honest as I could in words that he could understand and as far as he asked. I felt, as he got to where he was more curious and wanted to find out more, he would ask the questions, and I more or less waited for him to ask.

Some of the fathers of the aggressive boys were surprisingly permissive of heterosexual behavior.

I. How do you feel about young fellows who go all the way with girls?

F. (Case 13) This one girl he went out with didn't have a good reputation, and there were four boys and two girls; and he told me everything that happened, and it wasn't nice. I, I wasn't a bit pleased about it at all, and I sat down and I had a nice long talk with him.

I said, "Son, I know you're a young man, and I think you're too young; but if you must do something like that, for crying out loud, go by yourself. Don't go in a bunch." I tried to put it to him in a very nice way. I said I didn't think there was anything abnormal about it. Of course, I know they take it in school now and they talk about it. There's no keeping it a secret, and I know those kids know more than I did when I got married, I guess. But it's just the way they go about it. It's not nice, and I told him. I tried to make him understand.

Apparently this father would not have been at all disturbed had the boy not participated in a six-person orgy. One wonders, in fact, whether he, like the mother in Case 33, did not himself get some satisfaction from his son's behavior. Had the boy not felt that a detailed account of what happened would have· been somewhat acceptable, it is unlikely that he would have so freely related the events to his father.

Other fathers in this group seemed to feel that, if the boy could conquer the girl, then there was little to be said or done.

I. How would you feel if you found that Donald had now begun to play around with girls?
F. (Case 33) Well, if he didn't, I think he'd be, at his age he'd be kinda, something wrong here (laughs). I think, a kid gets sixteen years old, why, they kind of feel out their oats.
I. How do you feel about young fellows who go all the way with girls?
F. Well, that I don't know. It's up to the girl, I guess. That's the way I look at it. If she's willing to go all the way, why, that's the way it's going to be.

.   .   .

I. Suppose you now found that Earl had begun to play around with girls, how would you feel about that?
F. (Case 23) He's getting pretty big; I suppose he is. I don't know; I just take it for granted that the other kids, at his age. I don't know.
I. How about petting, how do you feel about that?
F. All kids do that. I don't think I can stop that.
I. How do you feel about young fellows who go all the way with girls?
F. Well I don't approve of it naturally, but there's always two sides to that, too. If a girl is not willing, he can't get very far. I don't know what he could do about it. It's kind of natural, you know.

While some of the control fathers were equally tolerant, there was usually no sign that they would regard intercourse as a personal conquest on the part of their son. They were more inclined to view such an event as a mutual yielding to natural urges on the part of both boy and girl.

I. How do you feel about young fellows who go all the way with girls?
F. (Case 52) Well, I think it's the individual and the girl. I don't know just how to explain it. I think it's perfectly natural. You've got an urge there. Young boys and young girls get hungry just like I do. Some of them are strong and resist, and others are not strong and they give in. You can't condemn anybody for relationships. I don't care whether it's fourteen or forty. They have feelings. Who can control their feelings? I can't. They were given to us. Churches and everything say that they were given to us for specific use, but that would apply in some cases, but in some cases it don't.

Even while appreciating the strength of the temptation to engage in intercourse most of the control fathers indicated that they definitely did not wish it to occur.

I. How do you feel about young fellows who go all the way with girls?
F. (Case 30) Well, I don't think it's—well, there are two sides to that question. The girl has something to do about that too. You can't blame it all on the boy. After all, any boy is only human and it's a fifty-fifty proposition. Partly the girl's fault and partly the boy's. I think I don't agree with it all, and, oh well, I was taught right from wrong and I always knew when to stop and I never in my life got into any trouble. If they do, I'm sorry. I'm going to give them marching orders. They know.

      •   •   •

I. How about petting, how do you feel about that?
F. (Case 48) Well, we never forbid him, because we understand that young men at seventeen or eighteen, perhaps the drive is at its strongest ebb, and we do realize that sometimes they go beyond what they naturally, what's best for them. We've tried to show them the danger of pregnancy which might result in early marriage when they're not prepared for it financially, and we've taught them that restraint is certainly the best policy. We've shown them that there are many unwed mothers that, whose lives were partially ruined or where children are born out of wedlock. It causes great problems on the taxpayers as well as the parents of the girl. Oftentimes marriages are unhappy where they're forced into marriage. Tell him it's better to restrain than heavy petting.

Not all fathers, of course, were as permissive or understanding as those who have so far been quoted. Perhaps the most usual attitude was to expect and permit some petting, but to draw the line at premarital intercourse.

I. How would you feel if you found that Arthur had now begun to play around with girls?
F. (Case 10) Well, being fifteen, I figure it would be normal, but—er—there are limitations there.
I. How about petting, how do you feel about that?
F. There are no restrictions on that at all.
I. How do you feel about young fellows who go all the way with girls?
F. Well, I feel that it isn't any good. That's about all I can say about that. I don't have much use for those.

Parental Sex Anxiety

Parental sex anxiety was clearly reflected in many of the excerpts already quoted. Especially, perhaps, it was shown by the conscious inability of many parents to provide the growing boy with an adequate background of sex information. It was shown, too, by the importance that many parents attached to not making an issue of sexual matters when training had to be imposed. Not making an issue of these matters usually means not talking about them. Consequently, during their earlier years, many boys must have been confused and bewildered by the prohibitions that were imposed. Occasionally a parent's anxiety seemed to be manifested in a misunderstanding of terms, the meaning of which should have been obvious in the context of the sex questions. Such distortion can be best illustrated from one of the pretest interviews.

I. What did you do when you noticed him playing with himself?
F. Oh, I never let him play with himself. I used to get right down on the floor and play with him.

Of course, parents are to a large extent victims of the society of which they are members. If parents attempt to be "progressive" and teach a child to label his sexually significant activities and feelings, they are always faced with the possibility of their neighbors' disapproval, and even of ostracism, when their child communicates, as he almost inevitably will, his newly-acquired vocabulary to his peers.

Many parents undoubtedly were doing their best to be "enlightened" in sexual matters, yet their own training prevented them from being completely acceptant of the views they verbally expressed. This point has been illustrated by quotations from the protocols of parents whose expressed views seemed to reflect the teachings of pediatricians such as Spock (1946), yet who could not fully accept the possibility that their own child might engage in activities which they had learned to label "normal."

To judge from ratings made on parallel scales, mothers were generally more anxious than their husbands (Table 4-2).

TABLE 4-2

Sex Anxiety Measures: Differences between Parents of Aggressive and Control Boys

Scales	Aggressive Group		Control Group		t	p
	Mean	S.D.	Mean	S.D.		
Father's sex anxiety	4.98	1.55	4.52	1.44	1.01	N.S.
Father's estimate of boy's sex anxiety	2.39	1.09	2.15	0.77	0.87	N.S.
Mother's sex anxiety	7.42	1.84	6.81	2.00	1.08	N.S.
Mother's estimate of boy's sex anxiety	3.31	1.73	2.98	1.52	0.74	N.S.

These scales were not used as bases for prediction.

Since an interviewer of the same sex as the parent was employed, this difference between mothers and fathers cannot be attributed to the conditions of the interview. It is possible, however, that men talk to men more freely about sexual matters than women talk to women, and the difference may be accounted for partly on this basis. Another possibility is that the sex training of females, with its emphasis on the very real danger of pregnancy, results in more anxiety about sex in general than does the sex training given to males. However, the difference in anxiety level between male and female parents might have been reduced, or even reversed, if daughters, rather than sons, had been discussed. Several mothers depicted their husbands as more anxious about sex than they in fact appeared to be from their own interviews and commented on their husbands' embarrassment when sexual matters were brought up. It is possible these mothers were projecting their own anxiety on their husbands. On the other hand, the sex training of males undoubtedly includes teaching them that there are some things which they do not talk about in front of women, the most important of these matters being sex. Thus, it is possible that some husbands were embarrassed to talk about sex in front of the woman with whom they had presumably been having intercourse for years, yet could talk relatively freely about this topic to a male whom they had never previously seen.

Correlations between measures (Table 4-3) clearly indicated that parents whose sex anxiety was low tended to be more permissive of all forms of sex behavior and also less punitive for such behavior than parents whose anxiety about sex was high. Of course, the anxiety rating was not entirely

TABLE 4-3

INTERCORRELATIONS BETWEEN PARENTS' SEX ANXIETY
AND THEIR HANDLING OF SEX BEHAVIOR

Scale	2	3	4	5
1. Parent sex anxiety	−.51 −.67	−.45 −.58	−.40 −.68	.51 .60
2. Permissiveness: early sex behavior		.74 .66	.35 .45	−.59 −.74
3. Permissiveness: masturbation			.38 .44	−.50 −.52
4. Permissiveness: heterosexual behavior				−.27 −.58
5. Punitiveness				

Coefficients for the fathers are in the upper left corner of the cell; for the mothers, in the lower right corner of the cell. Correlations equal to, or greater than .37 are significant at the .01 level. Correlations equal to, or greater than, .28 are significant at the .05 level.

independent of the other ratings of sex training; the inter-correlations nevertheless seem to reflect consistent differ-ences between high-anxious and low-anxious parents in their handling of sex behavior.

Fathers who were highly anxious about sex tended to be less acceptant of their sons ($r = -.35$; $p < .05$) and less warm towards their wives ($r = -.41$; $p < .01$) than fathers who were low in sex anxiety. The following excerpts from the interview with the father in Case 17 illustrates very clearly how high sex anxiety, apparent from the father's avoidance of discussion of sex matters with his son, may be accompanied by an avoidance of any open demonstration of affection for the wife.

I. Suppose you found him doing this now (masturbation), how would you feel about it?

F. (Case 17) At this age, now? If I saw Ben doing a thing like that, I'd call—I'd get a hold of the oldest boy and have a talk with him and tell him to explain it to Ben, because Ben is a little bit young yet. He's not too young that I couldn't talk, you know. But I'm kind of a little bit yet on the embarrassed side, because he's so young yet. I talked to the brother and told him the facts of life and every-thing when he was about eighteen. Of course he was embarrassed, red and everything, and I told him, "Son, somebody's got to tell you so you know." So I'd get hold of Ben and I would tell Jack to talk to him. I've told him, "Whenever you get in a bind, when-ever you get in a bind about sex, you don't want to come to me. Go to your brother. Ask your brother, and he'll help you out. . . ."

I. Would you tell us also about the relationship between you and your wife? Do you express affection toward each other freely or are you somewhat reserved?

F. She's more reserved than I am. Once in a while I kiss her when I go to work and I kiss her when I come back, and that's all. In fact, I never kissed my wife until I got married (laughs). That's the old-fashioned way. I don't know, they say it's old-fashioned. We don't show any of that in front of the children. You know what I mean. We don't kiss or hug or anything like that in front of the children.

Parents' Estimate of Boys' Sex Anxiety

Very few mothers, and still fewer fathers, thought that their sons were worried about sex. While few boys, as judged by their interviews, showed excessive anxiety over sexual matters, many of them were much more confused and anxious than their parents apparently believed. The parents undoubtedly failed to perceive many of their sons' problems in this area. This is not surprising in view of the reluctance of many parents even to mention sexual matters to their sons. Boys who were worried or confused over sexual matters could have received little help from the majority of the parents, in whom consultation would have produced only evasion and other signs of uneasiness.

RESULTS FROM BOYS' INTERVIEWS

Masturbation

The two groups of boys did not differ significantly in the extent to which they engaged in masturbation (Table 4-4). Of the fifty-two boys in the total sample, only thirteen said they had never masturbated. Possibly some boys were being untruthful. However, there were several late maturing boys who might not have experienced ejaculation, and some of these may have interpreted the interviewer's question as referring only to masturbation resulting in orgasm. The

TABLE 4-4

Boys' Sex Behavior: Differences between
Aggressive and Control Boys

	Aggressive Group		Control Group			
Scales	Mean	S.D.	Mean	S.D.	t	p
Masturbation	5.52	1.84	4.71	2.66	1.47	N.S.
Heterosexual behavior	6.46	2.55	4.15	1.30	4.03	<.001
Homosexual behavior	2.31	0.87	2.17	0.54	0.66	N.S.

These scales were not used as bases for prediction.

median frequency of occurrence for those boys who admitted masturbation was between once and twice a week, as estimated from the ratings of individual boys.

Very diverse attitudes about masturbation were expressed. At one extreme were those boys who denied having practiced masturbation at all. Some of these boys expressed the belief that masturbation was a sign of mental illness or abnormality.

I. How do you feel about playing with yourself?
B. (Case 48) I don't do it myself. A person who does, I think, is sick in mind.

.   .   .

B. (Case 26) I don't. I think you'd have to have a couple of screws loose.

Other boys admitted some masturbation in the past, but denied that they practiced it currently. At least one boy seemed to have been frightened away by the thought that he might go insane.

I. How do you feel about playing with yourself?
B. (Case 22) Well, it can drive a person nuts. I found that out from a friend of my dad's. He went nuts like that. He had a wife but he'd still, he'd lock himself in the bathroom and it ain't right. I didn't do it very often because I found out what it did to this other guy. He went nuts, so I left it alone as long as I could. My dad said there was no real harm in it by itself, but in a way it can really make you go nuts.

A very different reason for not masturbating at the present time was given by a few of the aggressive boys. Since they could get all the sexual outlet they needed from intercourse, they had no longer any need to masturbate.

I. How do you feel about playing with yourself?
B. (Case 23) I don't.
I. When did you first learn about this?
B. I walked in on a friend of mine who was throwing a hank.
I. How often would you say you had done this?
B. I get interested in girls. Why have that if you can have girls?
I. How about before you had girls?
B. Oh, every week, two weeks. I wasn't very much of a kick on it.

A similar view was put forward by one of the control boys who said he had never had intercourse.

I. How about petting? How far have you gone with this?
B. (Case 36) Oh, I've made out (laughing) up to where I guess I should. I'm not going to become a father until I'm married. I have that in my mind and I'll never try to put me in that category.

I. Have you ever gone all the way with a girl?
B. No. . . .
I. How do you feel about playing with yourself?
B. No, I don't do that.
I. What are your feelings about it?
B. Well, I see no need for it. If you want to do it, you might as well take a girl out. I mean, that's ridiculous.

It seems likely that this boy satisfied his sexual urges by petting to climax or by some kind of sex play that stopped short of intercourse.

Another group of boys admitted masturbation quite readily and stated that they considered this to be a natural or normal activity for an adolescent.

I. How do you feel about playing with yourself?
B. (Case 28) Well, it's part of growing up. I can't express it in words. I think most teenagers do it. If they don't do it, I think there's something wrong with them.

•   •   •

I. How do you feel about masturbation?
B. (Case 45) You've got to do it or you're going to get wet sheets, that's all.
I. How did you first learn about this?
B. Well, when I was maybe about nine or ten, these guys started talking about it. I didn't know what they were talking about. They were my age. And they just told me to keep on rubbing. "It feels good." I don't know, so naturally I tried and nothing happened. I may have been reading comic books and doing it. And then one day, I remember the day, a summer day, hot. I was sitting up in my room sweating and just started playing around. And all of a sudden, whew (laughs)!
I. How often would you say you did this?
B. Now? Once or twice a week. When I first started I just went crazy on it. I used to do it every chance I had.
I. Does this sort of thing ever get you worried?
B. No, I'm not ashamed of it or anything. You've got that stuff in you and it's got to get out one way or another.
I. Do you talk about this to your friends?
B. It's just a natural thing. Everybody knows that everybody does it, and they just expect it.

A boy's reactions to masturbation, or any other sexual activity, are probably a complex product of numerous environmental influences and of his earlier sexual experiences.

As excerpts from the parents' interviews have illustrated, a boy may, even within his home, be subject to inconsistent training. The following excerpts from the interviews with one family indicate how parental confusion and anxiety may be communicated to a boy.

I. How do you feel about playing with yourself?

B. (Case 2) Well, I mean, everybody does it or has done it, so I feel it's natural.

I. When did you first learn about this?

B. Oh wait! I'd say three or even—I was pretty small when I did it, I can tell you that.

I. How did you find out about it?

B. I really don't know. I can't remember.

I. When did you last do this?

B. Oh, I guess—I don't know—Probably in the last two days, I guess.

I. How often would you say you did this?

B. Pretty often. Is that unusual or . . . ?

(At this point the interviewer, in order to allay anxiety, made a statement to the effect that there were considerable individual differences in the frequency of masturbation among normal people.)

B. But what does it actually mean, though? What does it actually mean? Why do you do it?

I. I guess you'd say it's natural. Now you say you do it pretty often. Do you mean several times a week?

B. Oh, yes.

I. More than once a day?

B. Well, it depends on how you feel.

I. What's the most you do it in a day?

B. Well, I don't know. Two to three, I think, sometimes.

I. Has it ever got you worried?

B. Yes.

I. Why do you worry about it?

B. Well, I didn't think much about it myself, because I didn't think it was natural and I didn't know about it. I guess everybody goes through that. I mean, they didn't do it, they don't know what they are doing. They think it's something wrong.

I. Did any adult ever speak to you about this sort of thing?

B. My parents.

I. What did they say?

B. Well, my father got me and said it's just a natural thing; and if ever anybody said they've never done it, he's a liar. If they don't

want to be frank about it when they actually have, and so I don't
feel so bad about it.

I. Do you ever talk about this to your friends?

B. Yes, but I mean—I might—but I don't usually tell them.

The father of this boy was quoted earlier as saying, "Well,
we're supposed to believe it's a normal thing, but I would
discourage him all I could." It is possible that this father
had been somewhat vacillating in his attitude, reassuring
the boy at one time yet by other expressed attitudes raising
doubts in the boy's mind. On the other hand, the boy's conflict may well have been generated by the father's permissive
verbal comments and the attitudes of a mother whose sex
anxiety was apparently somewhat high.

I. When David was a small child, how did you feel about letting him
run about indoors without clothes on?

M. (Case 2) Well, he always had clothes on. He always had a diaper
and maybe a tee shirt. He always had clothing. I never had him
running around with no clothes.

I. What did you do when you found him playing with himself?

M. Not very often, but I just put his hand aside.

I. Suppose you found him doing this now, how would you feel about
it?

M. Well, I've had my husband talk to him, but I wouldn't know what
to say, how to go round it.

Most boys stated that, even if they discussed masturbation with their friends, they did not reveal their own habits
in this matter. Only a very few of the boys said they were
quite frank with their friends on this subject. One of the
aggressive boys, however, apparently mixed with a group
who considered sexual performance, including masturbation,
to be a token of masculinity.

I. Do you ever talk about this to your friends?

B. (Case 47) We talk. We say, "Did you make it last night?" "Yeah,
yeah." You'd tell them, "Well, I made it every night you know."
They figure, "Sure, this guy is mighty."

Although the aggressive boys reported very little more
masturbation than the controls, perhaps because many of
them were having intercourse, some evidence was produced

that boys who are rejected by their parents tend to engage in frequent masturbation. For the control families, the fathers' warmth and acceptance, as measured from the parent interviews, correlated —.35 and —.37, respectively, with correlations between parental warmth and acceptance and the extent to which the boys masturbated. The corresponding correlations for maternal warmth and acceptance were —.37 and —.44. When mid-parent ratings were used, the extent of the boys' masturbation were —.49 and —.48 ($p <$ .02 in each case). Moreover, there were positive correlations for both the aggressive and the control families between the boys' masturbation and the extent to which their parents used threats of withdrawal of love as a means of disciplining them. The average correlation of .38, based on both groups, is significant at the one per cent level. As will be shown in Chapter 5, the use of this technique of discipline appears to be symptomatic of parental rejection.

Correlations within the boys' interviews also to some extent supported the view that masturbation and feelings of rejection are associated. Boys who felt rejected by their peers tended to masturbate more freely than boys who felt accepted ($r =$ .44; $p <$ .01). No significant correlations were found between the boys' expressed feelings of rejection by their parents and their masturbation, but this may have been in part due to their difficulty in expressing such feelings. On the other hand, the extent to which the boys masturbated correlated .36 ($p <$ .02) with their hostility toward their mothers and .28 ($p <$ .05) with their hostility toward their fathers. In addition, extent of masturbation correlated .34 with anxiety about dependency on the mother and .31 with anxiety about dependency on the father. Both correlations are significant beyond the .05 level. Since this kind of anxiety can be symptomatic of a fundamental disturbance in the parent-child relationship (Chapter 3), the obtained correlations are additional indirect evidence of a relationship between the extent to which a boy masturbates and his feelings of lack of parental love and support.

Heterosexual Experience

There was a clear-cut difference between the aggressive
and the control boys in the extent to which they had had sex
relations (Table 4-4). Not a single control boy claimed to
have had intercourse, though a few of them, as a prior
excerpt has illustrated, had engaged in some heavy petting,
possibly to climax. Since the boys were not asked if they had
ever reached climax during petting, there is, however, no
definite evidence that any of the control boys had actually
done so. In contrast, thirteen of the twenty-six aggressive
boys admitted intercourse, and nearly all of them had engaged in heavy petting. Two-thirds of the aggressive boys
who were sixteen or older had experienced intercourse, some
of them on numerous occasions.

Moreover, there were indications that the aggressive boys
tended to associate aggression and sex. This association was
reflected in the correlations between heterosexual behavior
and aggression toward peers, which were generally high for
the aggressive group (.53 with physical aggression, .58 with
verbal aggression, and .60 with directness of aggression) but
negligible for the control group (.09, —.09, and —.16, respectively). For the control group heterosexual behavior was
more closely associated with affiliative activities ($r = .47$
with group activity for the control boys, —.09 with group
activity for the aggressive boys). This difference between
the aggressive and the control boys reflects the heteroge-
neous character of sexual behavior in adolescence as it passes
from dating patterns to actual intercourse. The aggressive
boys tended to seek an aggressive expression of their masculinity through sexual intercourse. Their sexual acts usually
were unaccompanied by any affectional response; in fact
they sometimes expressed hostility toward, and depreciation
of, their sex partners.

I. How far have you gone with this (petting)?
B. (Case 47) Oh, I guess I've gone as far as any other guy.
I. What do you think of a fellow who goes all the way with girls?

B. Well, it depends on the girl, I think. If a guy likes a girl a lot, he won't do too much. But then, if he's just taken a girl out to see what he can get, it's her fault if anything does happen, because she should know a lot better, because it's her reputation as far as reputation among guys goes. You're king of man if you do, you know. But a girl, she's just nothing if she does. So actually it's more responsibility to them than to I.

The control boys, on the other hand, satisfied their heterosexual interests primarily through companionship and shared activities and were unlikely to engage in more direct sexual expression, such as petting, unless they were fond of the girls.

I. How about petting?
B. (Case 26) I usually don't do it on the first day. As a matter of fact, I don't do it at all unless I really like the girl.

Several of the aggressive boys were extremely frank, almost boastful, about their sexual conquests and sometimes went into considerable detail.

I. Have you ever gone all the way with a girl?
B. (Case 49) Yeah.
I. When was the last time you did this?
B. I don't know. A couple of weeks ago, and I was all crocked up.
I. How did this come about?
B. I don't know. We picked her up down at Joe's. You know where Joe's is? You've seen that big drive-in? Round here that's the teenage hangout, you know. On the weekend everybody goes down and hangs out one. We picked up a couple of girls down there. We was in a '49 Plymouth and they was in a '56 Dodge. And they asked us to go for a ride with them, and we went for a ride with them. And there was three of them and there was three of us, and they took us up. From Joe's up here they took us up in Oakland Hills up by Greenoaks. You know where that park is up there? Well anyway, they went up there and they parked up on that big flat up there where you can see out over all the Bay Area. You know, you can see the Bay Bridge, Golden Gate, and all around here, you know, and Hayward and all over. I know it was some big hill. And one of my buddies grabbed hold of some girl, started making out with her. I wasn't going to be left alone, so I did the same deal and my other buddy did the same thing.
I. How often would you say you had gone all the way?
B. Not too often. Depends on the girls we find, I mean. We go once a week, twice, three weeks or so. It all depends on the girl.

Judging from the accounts of the aggressive boys, intercourse quite frequently occurred when two or three adolescent girls went out together with two or three adolescent boys. The feeling that there is someone else involved perhaps gives the adolescent greater courage in this matter. If this is correct, some of the parents' trust in double-dating as a precautionary measure against sex relationships may have been misplaced.

The importance of sexual conquest as a proof of masculinity was often verbalized by the aggressive boys.

I. O.K. just one more question. Suppose you had three choices you could make for yourself for the future. What are the three things you'd most like to happen?
B. (Case 23) First, I'd like to move out and get a job. Second, I'd like to get another car. Third, I'd like to drop a full load in it.

. . .

I. What do you think of a fellow who goes all the way with a girl?
B. (Case 25) More power to him, I guess.
I. What do you think of girls who go all the way?
B. That's a different situation there. I'd just like to take her out.
I. Have you ever gone all the way with a girl?
B. Yeah.
I. When was the last time you did this?
B. When I was home at Christmas.
I. How did that come about?
B. She was hung up on me. She had a crush on me, so I took her out.
I. How often would you say you'd gone all the way?
B. Three or four times.
I. Suppose a friend of yours got a girl you knew into trouble, what would you think of him?
B. He ought to have used a rubber.
I. Suppose you go all the way with a girl, how do you feel afterwards?
B. You feel sharp when you do it, but after, you know, you might be wrong. You might knock her up.

Not all the aggressive boys were as ready to engage in sex relations as those quoted above. Here is an interesting example of one boy whose aggressive orientation comes through even while he is defending conventional morals.

I. How about petting? How far have you gone with this?
B. (Case 7) Well, as far as I've got is kissing.
I. What do you think of a fellow who goes all the way with a girl?

B. I wouldn't trust him.
I. What about girls who go all the way? How do you feel about them?
B. I wouldn't trust them either.
I. Suppose a friend of yours got a girl you knew into trouble, what would you think of him?
B. Well, there's three things. One, if I ever saw him again, I'd scar up his face something terrible so he'd have to go to the hospital. And if I like that girl, I'd scar up his face something terrible so he'd have to go to the hospital. Or else I wouldn't hang around with him, or else I wouldn't ever see the girl. I wouldn't even talk to her.

The most impressive difference between the aggressive and the control boys was perhaps in their attitudes toward girls who engaged in premarital intercourse. The aggressive boys typically held to a double standard: you have sex relationships if you can, but you don't marry girls who have already had sex experience.

I. How about petting? How far have you gone with this?
B. (Case 49) Some girls we go a long ways with and some, if you like them a lot and you're a real coolhead, you don't try anything. There's a difference there. A girl you've taken out for some specific reason, that's all right. If you like a girl a lot, or something like that, you won't do anything against her.
I. What do you think of a fellow who goes all the way with a girl?
B. That depends on the girl again, see. If she's a real nice kid and all that, you know, I don't particularly like it, but if she's a broken-up old character, I don't give a good goddam what anyone does to her.

Control boys, on the other hand, were much more likely to say that premarital relations were understandable and acceptable only if the boy and the girl liked one another very much.

I. Have you sometimes felt you'd like to have more sex experience than you've had so far?
B. (Case 26) Oh, a couple of times. I haven't gone on a date for a couple of months and you get so darn lonely that you wish you had a girl-friend, almost wish you had a wife and everything else. Get to feel that way sometimes. But if you go out normal dating, you don't feel that way.

This attitude contrasts very strongly with that of those aggressive boys who would not forego a chance of sex relations unless they liked the girl.

I. Have you ever had the chance of going all the way with a girl and deliberately held yourself back from doing this?
B. (Case 47) Yes.
I. How often have you done this?
B. Oh, only a few girls that I liked a lot and I didn't want to, well, spoil their reputations.

Some boys in the control group were inclined to put the blame for pregnancy partly on the girl.

I. Suppose a friend of yours got a girl you knew into trouble, what would you think of him?
B. (Case 30) I'd think he was pretty rotten, but unless she was pretty dumb, why, it's kind of her fault.

None of them, however, showed the almost complete lack of sensitivity to the social consequences of their acts that was displayed by some of the aggressive boys.

Homosexual Behavior

Since mutual masturbation is the commonest form of homosexual behavior among adolescents (Kinsey, Pomeroy, and Martin, 1948), the boys were asked if they had ever masturbated in the presence of other boys. It was hoped that this question, together with the request for information about how the boy had learned about masturbation, would be sufficient to bring out some material on homosexual behavior. Only six boys, however, admitted any sex play at all with members of their own sex, and it was evident, even in these cases, that anxiety about such behavior was very high.

It is almost certain that the estimate of homosexual behavior obtained from the ratings is by no means an accurate one. In the first place, the scale does not utilize all the information that was given in the interview. For example, a boy who had been shown how to masturbate by older boys certainly had had a homosexual contact. Yet, if he denied masturbating in the presence of other boys, he was not rated for the kind of contact involved in learning sexual acts unless his description had left no doubt concerning what precisely had occurred. Secondly, since the inquiry into sexual behavior was subordinate to the general purposes of the study, no attempt was made to get the boys to give any details of their experiences.

Moreover, although the question leading into this topic was deliberately worded in such a way as to be as little threatening as possible, in the total context of the sex questions it was probably interpreted as a direct threat to the boys' masculinity. It usually elicited a flat denial or even an expression of indignation. To be labelled as a "queer" would undoubtedly be one of the most threatening experiences these adolescent boys could have. This was very evident from the response of one boy (Case 19) who, when asked if he had ever masturbated, responded with indignation, "I'm not a queer." This response, of course, also illustrates the extreme sexual confusion that was displayed by a few of the boys.

On the other hand, the interviewer did not get the impression that the boys were being deliberately dishonest. While it is likely that many, if not the majority of, adolescents do occasionally find themselves physically aroused by members of their own sex and do engage in some mutual sexual experimentation, openly homosexual incidents leading to orgasm may be rarer than has sometimes been supposed. The taboo on such relationships, and particularly the doubts they may raise about a boy's masculinity, may be adequate to inhibit for the most part direct expressions of homosexual impulses.

Sex Anxiety

As predicted, the aggressive boys showed significantly less anxiety about sex than did the control boys (Table 4-5). The greater anxiety of the control boys perhaps reflects the greater effectiveness of their parents' training into social conformity and will be discussed in more detail in Chapter 6.

The measure of anxiety was based in part on the boys' answers to questions asking whether they had ever felt tempted to masturbate or to go beyond their customary dating patterns, and had deliberately held themselves back

TABLE 4-5

Boys' Sex Anxiety: Differences between
Aggressive and Control Boys

	Aggressive Group		Control Group			
Scale	Mean	S.D.	Mean	S.D.	t	p
Sex anxiety	5.50	2.25	6.62	1.86	2.19	<.05

from doing so. Most boys did admit temptation of some
kind, though one seventeen-year-old boy, who showed no
evident signs of being a late maturer, denied having experienced any sexual impulse whatsoever. On the other hand,
some boys who reported little sexual activity reported frequent temptation.

I. Have you ever felt like playing with yourself and deliberately held
yourself back from doing this?
B. (Case 15) I stop myself from playing with myself all the time, that's
all.
I. How often would you say this happened?
B. A lot of times, I guess. I read that it was habit-forming, so I
decided I wouldn't do it again.

This boy said that he had not masturbated during the six
months preceding the interview.

Sex Information

Boys had obtained their sex information from various
sources, but mainly from their peer group and from reading
(Table 4-6). Almost all boys in both groups felt that their
parents either had given them little, or no, sex information
or had been too late in giving it. Thus the boys' accounts
confirmed the impression left by the parent interviews that
most parents were reluctant to face the task of imparting
adequate sex information.

I. From whom have you got most of your information about sex?
B. (Case 48) Well, twelve or thirteen, my father told me the facts of
life, but I knew a lot before then. I mean in school, if you don't

TABLE 4-6

AMOUNT OF SEX INFORMATION RECEIVED FROM PARENTS: DIFFERENCE
BETWEEN AGGRESSIVE AND CONTROL BOYS

Scale	Aggressive Group		Control Group		t	p
	Mean	S.D.	Mean	S.D.		
Amount of sex information from parents	4.33	2.37	4.86	1.96	0.83	N.S.

This scale was not used as a basis for prediction.

know anything by the time you're ten, you're considered ignorant.
But before we knew all the scientific facts I usually, I read on my
own, read different books.

I. How much (information) have you gotten from your parents?
B. (Case 22) I knew everything ahead of time, but I got the same thing
over again.

Parents rarely admitted that they directly refused to answer their sons' requests for information on sex matters.
From the boys' statements, however, it was apparent that
such refusals sometimes occurred.

I. From whom have you got most of your information about sex?
B. (Case 23) My friends. You mean, have my parents ever talked to
me about it? No. They never told me much about it. They said,
"Learn it for yourself." And that's what I did.

Excerpts from this boy's interview, cited elsewhere in this
chapter (pp. 167, 174, 182), make it evident that, on this one
occasion at least, he had complied with his parents' wishes.
The boys' responses to the question about sex information
provide further evidence of the confused and misinformed
way in which many parents handle their children's sex education. It seems that, if parents are going to take the responsibility of imparting sex information to their children, they
must begin as soon as a child is capable of understanding
and must continue his education stage by stage as the child's
capacity for understanding increases.

RESULTS FROM THEMATIC TEST

Sex responses to the thematic test pictures and stories were scored under two categories, physical expressions of sexuality and psychosexual references. The categories were defined as follows:

Physical Expressions of Sexuality: Any act such as kissing, fondling, etc., that implies contact of an erotic nature. Any response that explicitly or implicitly indicates that intercourse has taken place or will take place.

> He put his arm around her and started kissing her.
>
> So they start dancing a little bit, and he starts feeling around.
>
> And they probably feel pretty hot and they go further than necking.

Psychosexual References: Any references to dating, to seeking the company of girls, or to affectionate feelings for girls.

> Well, George, he had a job and made lots of money, so he decided to take his girl out.
>
> This is at a party, and he told the girl that he liked her and everything, and the girl told him that she liked him too.

There was no difference between the aggressive and the control boys in the number of psychosexual references that they made within the stories. The aggressive boys, however, gave a significantly greater number of responses that involved references to physical expressions of sexuality (Table 4-7).

There were three test items, Pictures 6 and 10 and Story 1, that were designed to elicit sex content (Appendix E). The pictures each depicted a scene in which physical contact between a girl and a boy was taking place and therefore did not allow much variation in the form of the sex responses that could be attributed to the story characters. The incom-

TABLE 4-7

FREQUENCY OF SEX RESPONSES TO THEMATIC TEST: DIFFERENCES
BETWEEN AGGRESSIVE AND CONTROL BOYS

		Aggressive Group		Control Group			
Category	Rater Reliability	Mean	S.D.	Mean	S.D.	t	p
Physical expression of sexuality	.80	3.57	2.04	2.16	1.75	2.46	<.02
Psychosexual references	.75	2.38	2.70	2.68	2.65	0.37	N.S.

Probabilities remained the same when Mann-Whitney U-tests were employed. These categories were not used as bases for prediction.

plete story, on the other hand, merely depicted a girl, who was at home alone, inviting a boy to come into her house.

Story 1. One night about eight o'clock Jack is walking home from a friend's house. As a general rule he has to be home by nine on week nights. He sees Sally, who is sitting all alone on the front steps of her house. Sally is known as the girl in the neighborhood who looks most like Marilyn Monroe. All the boys go out with her a lot. Sally asks Jack why he doesn't come on in and talk with her for a while. She says that she's all alone because her parents have gone to Los Angeles for several days.

In this case the storyteller could either depict some sexual interaction or he could depict the boy as doing no more than talk with the girl, either inside or outside the house. When this story was scored according to these two possible outcomes, it was found that the aggressive boys were much more likely to depict the boy as entering the house and having some form of erotic contact with the girl (Table 4-8). Moreover, some of the aggressive boys who depicted the boy in the story as having to go home on time on this particular occasion, and consequently not entering the house, indicated that he would nevertheless return as soon as an opportunity offered itself.

TABLE 4-8
Boys' Responses to Sexual Temptation Theme: Incomplete Story 1

	Aggressive Boys	Control Boys
Physical contact	10	2
No physical contact	11	23

$$\chi^2 = 9.29; \, p < .01$$

B. (Case 37) He figures he better make it home, so he says, "Goodnight," and says, "Would it be all right if I come over tomorrow night instead?" So he goes home, gets in trouble with his parents, and then comes over there right after dinner the next night.

Stories with blatant sexual themes were given by some of the aggressive boys, but not by any of the control boys.

B. (Case 23) Well, if I was that stud Jack, man, I'd make it in the house and start wailing with her like mad, you understand. Nah, the hell, the hell with gettin' home. I mean, I'd phone my parents and tell them I wouldn't be home all night if her parents weren't home.

I. And how are the people in your story thinking and feeling?

B. I hope he's feeling with his hand; I don't know how she's feeling.

• • •

B. (Case 45) Well, naturally he goes in whether he's gotta be home or not, because ya just can't pass that up. And so he figures, "Well, I'll go in and just get started now and, you know, get her ready and everything and be home by nine-thirty. And I'll tell her I'll make it over on Friday night. I'll tell my parents I'm gonna sleep over at some friend's house and I'll just sleep over there. (I. And how are they thinking and feeling?) They both know what's gonna, the girl knew that she was gonna ask him that. She knows he knows she knows it, so (laughs), so ain't nothin' more to that.

In most of the stories given by the control boys, the story-character never even entered the house. If he did, he resisted any overtures that the girl might make.

B. (Case 36) Jack, who is a very, boy of very high standards who has never gone out with a girl like Sally, does not know what to do at the moment. But finally he sees no harm in just coming in and talking, because it's only eight o'clock. He enters the house and sits down. Sally comes in and she has a very tight sweater on, and Jack begins to realize, think if, if he was doing the right thing. Sally is sorta playing. She knows the type of boy Jack is, and she is sort of planning on seeing if he has his high morals because she does not care what happens to her. She sits down next to Jack and starts curling his hair, and Jack begins to feel uncomfortable. When Sally asks him if he'd like to do anything, Jack says, "Well, I'd like to talk." And so they start talking. During the conversation Sally turns down the light and Jack realizes that he is doing something wrong. He gets up and he says, "I must go now. It is getting late and I want to be home on time."

More often the control boys presented the boy as avoiding the girl or as merely conversing with her outside the house. Very frequently they described him as naive in sexual matters or as having strong moral principles.

B. (Case 48) Well, Jack, being rather shy of girls asked her why and what they can do when he goes up there—assuming he hasn't had too much experience with girls. Sally said, "Well, just come up and talk with me, look at TV together." Behind her mind she's just looking for a good time where, I would say, Jack is innocent and more or less he's just not the type for girls, and I would say that he says, "Bah!" and walks off.

· · ·

B. (Case 46) Oh, oh (sigh) he's, he was loyal to his parents' rules of not being late, because they had driven it into him all his life. So he just stood at the gate and talked to her for a while, and tried to talk her out of her talking him into coming in, see. And he finally succeeded, but not too tactfully, and so she turned around in a huff and went into the house, and he went home. She seemed to have the personality that she could turn it hot or cold as she wished and she got mad easily from his refusal. She wasn't used to being refused. And he was on the spot really; he didn't know what to do. He wanted, he was torn between a loyalty to his parents and a friendliness toward the girl, and his loyalty to his parents won out.

In the stories of some of the aggressive boys there was further evidence of their association of sex and aggression that was noted earlier in this chapter. The following story was given to Picture 10.

B. (Case 23) Well, this looks like what I was doing over the week-end. Looks like these kiddies are going up to the hills. Or they're parked, no, they're parked, they're parked. Excuse me, they're parked. And they're lushing it up like mad, got themselves some brew. Two broads and two guys, got all kinds of brew. The broads probably, the guys probably, want to get drunk and the broads probably want to get gassed too. This guy is thinking he'd like to go for a walk with this broad, and she's thinking she don't want to go for a walk with him. And these two people are thinking they want to get gassed. So these two people here get gassed. This guy slaps the hell out of her and she slaps the hell out of him and everybody is happy.

While the aggression does not here take a physical form, the excerpt below reflects the hostility that the aggressive boys sometimes displayed toward the girls with whom they had sex relations.

B. (Case 21) She acts like Marilyn Monroe in a way, coy or naive. You know what I mean. She's kind of corny, man. She sees pictures all the time, you know. So he starts kinda making a play for her. He doesn't want to pass up a nice chance. Her folks are gone and everything. He says, "Well, I gotta go. Could I come over tomorrow? Come back?" She says, "Well, if you don't want to come over, if you don't want to stay here tonight, just forget about it. I mean, I can take a hint, you know." She's like that; you know—rotten. So he stays there with her a while. It starts getting pretty close, you know, and everything, man. Finally winds off, man. . . . I think the girl, she doesn't really care. She just figures the more boys she can get hooked on her, it's more of a game with her, try to hook more than the next girl. She doesn't really care for him at all. I mean, she cares; you know, she doesn't want him to get really mad at her. But he wants, he wants, you know what I mean (laughs).

In general, then, the stories suggested that the aggressive boys were more ready to engage in heavy sex play and intercourse than the control boys and that they did so with relatively little guilt. Thus, although the test items were not specifically designed to obtain information about the boys' sexual behavior, they elicited material that seemed to confirm the findings from the boys' interviews.

DISCUSSION

There was only one clear-cut difference between the parents of the aggressive boys and the control parents in their handling of their sons' sexual behavior. The fathers of the aggressive boys were considerably more permissive of adolescent heterosexual behavior than were the fathers of the controls.

Mothers and fathers did not greatly differ in their attitudes toward early forms of sex behavior. On the other hand fathers were much more tolerant than were mothers of sex behavior during the boys' adolescent years. Mothers were typically nonpermissive of any overt expressions of sexuality. In contrast, the fathers showed much more understanding of the sexual problems of the adolescent boy. It is interesting that most fathers showed greater tolerance of heterosexual behavior than of masturbation. Possibly they regarded masturbation as something completely under the boys' control. Many, however, viewed the dating situation as one in which the boys would be faced with strong sexual temptations that would prove hard to resist. The mothers were inclined to emphasize both the dangers of pregnancy—in other words, the consequences for the girl—and the possible harmful effects on the boy's future. It was evident that most mothers felt that their sons should maintain self-control under all circumstances.

The majority of parents showed considerable confusion and lack of perspicacity in their handling of their children's sexual curiosity. Many of them failed to provide their children with adequate sex information, and those who attempted to fulfill this task usually left it so late that the boys had already gained their basic information (or misinformation) from other sources. Some parents clung to outmoded and untenable views about the possible consequences of sexual behavior. Others gave lip service to sounder views based on modern knowledge, for example, that masturbation is natural and not harmful physically or mentally, but still could not accept the implications for their own sons' behavior.

In discussions of sex education the focus is almost inevitably on the problem of imparting sex information to the child. Training in sex attitudes and behavior, however, commences even before much verbal communication is possible. Almost from the very beginning of a child's life he will manifest forms of sexuality which his parents are obliged to handle in some way. Early conditioning, for example, through the prompt removal of the child's hands from his genitals, insistence on modesty, and control of early sex curiosity, may play a large part in determining basic sexual attitudes. These attitudes may be further reinforced by the parents' avoidance of open discussion of sex topics throughout the boy's childhood. Under these circumstances it is unlikely that an attempt to impart sex information in a single session with the father or the family doctor, or by the provision of a book, will have much effect in counteracting anxieties and confusion which early training may have produced.

The aggressive boys engaged much more freely in heterosexual relations, leading to intercourse, than did the control boys. They also displayed somewhat less anxiety about sexual behavior. These differences may be in part produced by the greater permissiveness for heterosexual behavior of the fathers of the aggressive boys.

Sexual and aggressive impulses were closely associated for the aggressive boys, whereas for the control boys heterosexual impulses were more likely to be affiliative in character and to stop short of intercourse. The aggressive boys' sexual exploits in many cases seemed to represent an aggressive assertion of their masculinity. The aggressive boys were inclined to voice a double-standard philosophy, whereby one secures one's sex gratification from women one does not care for but rejects the idea of having sex relations with a woman one likes. On the other hand, the control boys were much more inclined to take the diametrically opposed view that the only valid reason for having sex relations, or even for petting, with a girl is that one is emotionally involved with her. The aggressive boys' attitudes toward heterosexual behavior may also reflect their anxiety about dependency. Certainly, they characteristically showed no integration of sex and affection. Both their casual, short-term relationships with girls, and their association of sex and aggression, may represent a form of defense against close dependency attachments.

On the whole, the adolescents seemed to show much more anxiety about masturbation than about heterosexual activities. They showed still more anxiety about homosexual behavior. This is perhaps understandable in view of the obvious concern of many of these adolescent boys to demonstrate and prove their masculinity. Very divergent views about masturbation were, in fact, expressed. Some adolescents considered masturbation dangerous to one's physical and mental health, or even more frequently as a sign of mental disturbance. Others considered it natural, and one categorically stated that a boy who did not masturbate was not normal. A few of the boys thought that masturbation was a superfluous form of behavior, since one could get greater sexual satisfaction from intercourse, or some activity which barely stopped short of intercourse, by going out with girls.

Some indication that extent of masturbation is associated with feelings of loss of love or lack of acceptance was provided by correlational findings. Very little empirical evidence, except that contained in case histories, has been previously brought forward in support of this relationship. While the evidence from the present study is not by any means conclusive, it suggests that further tests of this relationship might be fruitful. In addition, the correlational analysis suggested that parents who are anxious about sexual matters may tend to reject children of the same sex as themselves. Consequently it would be reasonable to suppose that children whose parents are highly anxious about sex might engage in more than the average amount of masturbation. Some support for this latter hypothesis was provided by a positive correlation between the fathers' sex anxiety and the extent of the boys' masturbation ($r = .29$; $p < .05$).

Chapter 5

Restrictions, Demands, and Disciplinary Techniques

During his infancy and early childhood, a child's needs are gratified and little is asked of him in return. As he acquires greater motor control and becomes better able to direct his behavior, his parents begin to limit and channel his activities. There are undoubtedly many reasons why a child cannot be permitted unlimited freedom. Some restrictions and guidance are necessary in order to protect him from danger. For instance, he cannot play ball in heavy traffic or play with sharp instruments or fire. Moreover, as his needs become more complex and he becomes more mobile, his wishes inevitably come into conflict with those of others. No longer can he express his needs when and how he pleases, but instead he must learn to adjust to the demands of those around him. Often this involves giving up the more direct and effective ways of gratifying his needs that he had utilized earlier for more complicated and indirect modes of behavior (Whiting and Mowrer, 1943). He must learn new habits of eating, he must exercise bowel and bladder control, he must give up infantile clinging dependence for more independent forms of behavior, his anger must be channeled into certain socially acceptable forms, and he must inhibit for some time almost all forms of sexual behavior.

Although the adolescent has usually been freed from many of the restrictions that were imposed on him in childhood, some of the limitations that remain may become increasingly irksome as a result of his increased maturation and development. These include restrictions relating to his heterosexual activities and to the degree of personal freedom and independence that he may enjoy.

Some parental demands and restrictions have been considered in previous chapters, notably restrictions on aggression, dependency, and sexual behavior. This chapter is concerned with restrictions and demands not related to these specific motivational systems, and also with the disciplinary methods that the parents used to enforce their demands and otherwise control their sons' behavior.

At this point, perhaps, some distinction should be made between what were regarded as restrictions and what were regarded as demands. In general, restrictions involve limitations put on a child in order to prevent him from engaging in disapproved activities. Thus a boy may *not* be allowed to remain out of doors beyond the hour of 10 P.M., he may *not* drink alcohol, he may *not* play the phonograph loudly. Of course, these restrictions could be rephrased as demands. A parent may demand that a child be in by 10 P.M., refrain from drinking alcohol, or play the phonograph softly. Even so, the essential function of the parental rule is to prevent behavior that the parent considers to be undesirable.

On the other hand, parental demands are concerned with the fostering of behavior that the parent considers to be socially desirable. Thus, the child *should* do well in school, *should* behave in a sex-appropriate manner, *should* show some degree of self-reliance. Restrictions, then, serve to curb behavior that is likely to occur if the child's impulses are allowed free expression; demands serve to elicit behavior that might not otherwise be manifested and to help develop secondary motives of a socially approved kind. This distinction is not always clear-cut; for example, the enforcement of obedience may be considered primarily as a restrictive measure. Nevertheless, since obedience to authority is generally regarded as a socially approved form of behavior, there is justification for speaking of parental demands for obedience. Of course, in a sense, every restriction implies a demand and vice versa. The distinction, however, appears to be more than a verbal one and serves to differentiate between two aspects of child-training—on the one hand the control of motivational systems, whether primary or acquired, that may result in socially disapproved behavior, and on the other hand the acquisition of other secondary motivational systems that lead to socially approved behavior.

Techniques of discipline are methods of securing compliance with demands and restrictions. Some of these are techniques of reinforcing approved behavior, while some are techniques for handling noncompliance. While parental demands and restrictions refer primarily to what a parent wishes his child to do or not to do, techniques of discipline refer primarily to the manner in which the parent insures that his wishes are respected.

HYPOTHESES

The investigation of parental restrictions was largely exploratory. It was felt that the information gained through the inclusion of scales measuring restrictions might throw additional light on some of the expected differences between the aggressive and the control boys. For example, if the parents of the aggressive boys proved to be excessively demanding or restrictive, one might expect to find strong resentment by their sons on this account. If they proved, on the other hand, to be extremely lax and undemanding, this might indicate a general laissez-faire attitude reflecting a lack of interest in their sons and a disinclination to take the trouble to control their behavior.

Three kinds of parental demands are considered in this chapter—demands that the boy should take on responsibilities in and around the home, demands for achievement, and demands for obedience. Predictions were made only about obedience demands. It was predicted that the parents of the aggressive boys would make fewer demands for obedience, and would be less consistent in following through with these demands, than would the control parents. This prediction was based in part on prior research findings. For example, the Gluecks (1950) found that more parents of delinquents, than of nondelinquents, were erratic in their handling of their sons; while Sears, Maccoby, and Levin (1957) found that mothers who were below average in warmth to their children tended both to be inconsistent in handling them and to have children who were above average in aggression.

The general hypothesis regarding disciplinary techniques was based on a theory put forward by Whiting and his collaborators (1954). This theory assumes that socialization involves the development of self-control through the internalization of parental standards, and that internalization can be thought of as a dimension with fear at one end and guilt at the other. When internalization is low, control is maintained through fear of external punishment; when internalization is high, behavior is controlled by feelings of guilt.

The various disciplinary techniques may, according to Whiting, be divided into two broad categories. On the one hand are the *love-oriented disciplinary techniques*. These are forms of discipline by which the child is rewarded with love and punished by withholding or withdrawing love. Included in this category are praise, threats of withdrawal of love, and ostracism. On the other hand are the *nonlove-oriented methods*. These involve primarily physical methods of discipline, exemplified in the use of tangible rewards, physical punishment, and deprivation of privileges through forcibly restricting a child's activities or confiscating his possessions.

According to the theory proposed by Whiting, the love-oriented disciplinary methods are more effective than the nonlove-oriented methods in developing conscience control in the child. If the parents reward the child with genuine love, the child will do what his parents wish in order to obtain this reward. At the same time, if the child should misbehave and the parents punish him by withholding love, the child will try to conform to and adopt the parents' demands and standards in order to regain their love and approval. Although love-oriented techniques temporarily frustrate and threaten the child, they nevertheless keep him in the love relationship. The control function of threats of withdrawal of love is well demonstrated by the mother in Case 39.

I. Do you sometimes ignore him or refuse to speak to him until he does as you want?

M. (Case 39) Mmm, huh. Yes, I do that sometimes if they talk rough to me; and not very long ago he answered me, and I said, "All right, if you want to do that, there's no sense in your asking me, because if I say, 'No,' you're going to do it. All right, go ahead and do it." And I just don't talk to him and I get mad at him. I say, "You kids don't care; go ahead and do it. See if I care." And he said, "You just think we don't love you. We love you, you know, and now you don't want to talk to me." But sometimes I get mad at them and I don't want to talk to them; they talk to me, they come around, and they behave more.

By contrast, the nonlove-oriented techniques of discipline, such as physical punishment and deprivation, tend to foster fear and avoidance of the parents and thus to weaken their child's dependency on them.

I. Suppose Tim has been behaving very badly and giving you or his mother a hard time, what kind of things do you say to him?

F. (Case 19) I'm afraid I used to—he's given his mother a bad time once that I can remember—I gave him, I worked him over a bit for it. I think maybe that's why he might be a bit afraid of me.

Whiting's theory has received considerable support from a series of empirical studies that have issued mainly from Harvard's Laboratory of Human Development (Allinsmith and Greening, 1955; Faigin, 1952; Hollenberg, 1954; Heinicke, 1953; Sears, Maccoby, and Levin, 1957).

 Eight main techniques of discipline were chosen for investigation. Six were methods for handling behavior of which the parents disapproved, i.e., physical punishment, deprivation of privileges, ridicule, nagging and scolding, threats of withdrawal of love, and reasoning; two were techniques for securing and reinforcing desired behavior, i.e., praise and material rewards. In addition, the use of models, i.e., holding up someone as a good or a bad example of the type of behavior the parent does or does not want the boy to learn, was included as an additional technique that could be employed in guiding the boy.

On the basis of Whiting's theory it was predicted that the parents of the aggressive boys would, in disciplining their sons, rely more on physical punishment, deprivation of privileges, and ridicule than would the control parents. It was assumed that ridicule, as a technique particularly damaging to self-esteem, would be an extremely painful experience, giving rise to resentment and fear rather than to guilt. It was predicted, on the other hand, that the control parents would tend to resort more to reasoning and threats of withdrawal of love as means of control. It was felt that reasoning —a technique involving disapproval of a child's action expressed in a constructive manner—would be extremely effective in developing and supporting conscience development. It was further predicted that in rewarding their sons the parents of the aggressive boys would utilize material rewards more than the control parents, whereas the latter, relying more on the love relationship, would tend to bestow more praise and approval.

Support for the predictions about praise, reasoning, and physical punishment was provided by Sears, Maccoby, and Levin (1957), who found that the degree of conscience development in children was positively related to their mothers' use of praise and reasoning and negatively related to their mothers' use of physical punishment. Strong support for the predictions regarding physical punishment and reasoning was also provided by the Gluecks' (1950) finding that parents of delinquents used physical punishment more often than parents of nondelinquents, whereas parents of nondelinquents relied more on reasoning as a means of controlling their sons.

No prediction was made about nagging and scolding, since their import seemed to be somewhat ambiguous, nor about the use of models as a means of training.

In addition to the scales relating to demands, restrictions, and specific forms of discipline, measures were taken of the degree of consistency and agreement between the parents in their training of their sons. Parents' efforts to socialize their children should be facilitated by a high degree of consistency between husband and wife. Learning proceeds most rapidly when behavior is followed by consistent consequences. When husband and wife handle their children in quite different ways, the inconsistency may create conflicts in the children, particularly if the same general kind of behavior is rewarded by one parent and punished by the other. Moreover, such disagreement provides children with opportunities to maneuver one parent against the other and thereby render parental discipline still more ineffective. It was consequently predicted that the parents of the aggressive boys would show a greater degree of interparental inconsistency and disagreement than would the control parents, both in regard to what they required of their sons and in the way in which they enforced their limits and demands.

Finally, it was predicted that the aggressive boys would show greater resistance both to their parents' discipline and to their parents' restrictions and demands than would the control boys. Such resistance might be symptomatic of the boys' hostility toward their parents and also of their reluctance to be placed in a dependent role.

RESTRICTIONS AND DEMANDS: RESULTS FROM PARENT INTERVIEWS

Parental Restrictions

Ratings were made of the extent of parental restrictions on the boys' behavior both outside and inside the home.

Restrictions outside the home involved limits placed on the boys concerning when they could go out and when they had to be in and restrictions on their activities and choice of associates. No differences were found between the groups of parents in respect to these outside restrictions (Table 5-1).

TABLE 5-1

PARENTAL RESTRICTIONS: DIFFERENCES BETWEEN PARENTS
OF AGGRESSIVE AND CONTROL BOYS

Scales	Aggressive Group		Control Group			
	Mean	S.D.	Mean	S.D.	t	p
Data from Father Interviews						
Restrictions outside the home	6.37	1.50	6.19	1.07	0.65	N.S.
Restrictions in the home	5.33	1.75	5.90	1.29	1.56	N.S.
Data from Mother Interviews						
Restrictions outside the home	6.31	1.29	6.48	1.39	0.65	N.S.
Restrictions in the home	5.33	1.53	6.01	1.58	2.21	<.05 (.07)[a]

[a] The probability in parentheses is based on the Wilcoxon Test.
These scales were not used as bases for prediction.

The parents' reports, however, pointed to several factors that might account for the lack of any significant difference. In the first place, many of the control parents indicated clearly that their sons were well socialized and quite capable of guiding and assuming responsibility for their own behavior. These parents had almost complete trust in their sons' judgment and felt that externally imposed limits were, therefore, largely unnecessary. Here are some typical parental replies to the inquiry concerning the restrictions they placed on their sons.

M. (Case 50) Well, he has very few restrictions because it's been unnecessary for him to have any.

• • •

M. (Case 22) I don't have to do anything like that any more. I think he's getting so mature now, he's sort of happy medium. I don't have to do much with him. He's well trained.

• • •

M. (Case 34) He's not a boy who has required any particular amount of restrictions. He's very reasonable. He's allowed to do pretty much as he pleases.

At the same time, however, some of the control parents gave the impression that definite restrictions had been imposed on their sons during childhood and that, if the boys were to fail to meet current expectations, they would be promptly reprimanded.

I. What are some of the restrictions you have for him? How about going out at night?

F. (Case 30) We trust the boy. We never question him.

I. Are there any things you forbid him from doing when he is with his friends?

F. At his age, I would hate to keep telling him that he mustn't do this or mustn't do that. I have very little trouble with him in that regard. Forbidding I don't think creeps into it because he knows, he ought to know at this age, right from wrong. It's certainly been drilled into him, I mean, through the years. I don't think there's anything in particular. Of course, I mean, if there was anything definitely wrong, I would certainly, but the little things that happen around the home and the little forbidding around the home, there's nothing that he does that is really seriously wrong.

I. Are there any friends with whom you have discouraged him from associating?

F. No, not up to now. They are very lovely boys.

I. How about smoking or drinking, how do you feel about these?

F. Drinking, he doesn't drink; and up to the moment, to my knowledge, he doesn't smoke.

I. How about using bad language?

F. Only once, only once have I. Of course, I'm a little bit hard of hearing in one ear, and sometimes he gets around the wrong side and takes advantage of that. But only once had I to reprimand him, and that was very recently when he lost his temper; and he had to apologize—very, very definitely.

A second reason for the failure to find any differences between the groups of parents in regard to outside restrictions may be simply that parental restrictions can be easily imposed on adolescents only when they are at home. They are old enough to go off on their own and their parents cannot effectively control their behavior when they are away from home.

The picture is somewhat different for the parents' restrictions within the home. The findings from the parent interviews showed that, although the groups of fathers did not differ in the amount of restrictions they placed on their sons, the control mothers were somewhat more restrictive in the home than were the mothers of the aggressive boys (Table 5-1). The control mothers tended to be less tolerant of noise, bad language, smoking, or drinking; they were more likely to insist that their sons should do their homework, and they placed more emphasis on orderliness and care of household property.

I. How about smoking and drinking, how do you feel about these?
M. (Case 34) No, definitely not for a boy his age.
I. Are there times when Peter has to do his homework?
M. Yes. It's not a question of his having to do it; he does it. Right after dinner he goes up to his room and does his work.

Many of the control mothers indicated that their sons showed a good deal of responsibility and self-control in the home, as well as outside, and therefore needed no restrictions. This factor undoubtedly made the control parents' ratings on this restriction scale lower than they would otherwise have been and has to be taken into account in the interpretation of the findings.

I. How about smoking and drinking, how do you feel about these?
M. (Case 50) He doesn't smoke or drink. He has no desire. He has a great aversion to smoking and also he doesn't like drinking.
I. How about using bad language?
M. No. He's very mild in his language.
I. Are there times when Keith has to do his homework?
M. Well, he takes that responsibility on himself. I give him a bonus of $2.00 when he brings his report card home, and he's on the honor roll and he's been on the honor roll all along, and so I give him a free hand on his studies. He knows what he has to have in on time, and he does.
I. Are there times when he has to refrain from being noisy about the house?
M. No. Well, he has times when he's been in high spirits. He's a great one, a good sense of humor and lot of fooling around, but as a general rule he's quiet.

On the other hand, it was clear that in a few of the control families the boys were subject to a pattern of strict control. The parents prescribed extensive and precise limits and exercised strict supervision over the boys' activities. Not only were such parents very explicit in what they expected of their sons, but they also clearly exemplified in their own conduct the pattern of behavior they wished their sons to follow.

I. What are some of the restrictions you have for him?

M. (Case 16) Well, he can go out at night providing we know where he's going, with whom he's going, what time he will be home, and whether or not there is supervision. But he's very definitely not permitted any floating. We know where he is all the time.

I. Is Eric allowed free use of the family car?

M. He's just learning to drive, so we haven't met that problem yet. But no, he certainly won't have free use; I mean there will be restrictions on it, of course. It'll be a long time before he'll be able to take it at night because a child has to be taught the responsibility, and we feel that's when children get into trouble when they are not properly supervised and they don't have proper restraints at home.

I. How about smoking and drinking, how do you feel about these?

M. We've never had to meet that problem. It's never been a problem in our family. He's not interested in the sort of people who do that in the first place, and that might be the reason. Or it might be the high moral standards in our own family, I don't know. Hardly anyone—his father smokes a pipe—but other than that no one else in the family smokes; none of the women smoke at all, and no one with whom he associates smokes to my knowledge.

I. How about using bad language?

M. Well, that's not a problem.

I. Can he use the radio and TV as freely as he likes?

M. We don't prevent the radio. We don't have a TV, which will be amazing, I suppose, to many people. He can play his radio whenever he wishes unless he's studying, but I don't permit him to study with his radio on.

In general, the mothers of the aggressive boys were inclined not only to put few limits on their sons' behavior but also to assume an attitude of resignation and passive tolerance about habits of which they expressed some disapproval.

I. How about smoking and drinking, how do you feel about these?

M. (Case 33) Well, when he decided to smoke, we naturally tried to discourage it. You know, for about a week we talked with him about it. Of course, he had been trying cigarettes off and on since he was seven years old at different times and then, when he decided, when he started smoking regularly, he was out at Juvenile Hall. He asked if he could go ahead and smoke; and we knew he had been behind our backs, but we didn't say anything. We just ignored it and thought, "Well, if he's going to smoke, he's going to smoke." My husband smokes; there isn't much you can say or do if you do the things yourself (laughs). And we've always told him if he wanted to take a drink it was perfectly all right for him at home, than to be going out and maybe getting in a wrong place and get in trouble.

I. How about using bad language?

M. Well, the only thing we tried to instill in him was that there were just certain times that it might be all right to use bad language but there were other times when he shouldn't.

The intercorrelations of the parent measures threw some light on the personality correlates of restrictiveness. In general, mothers who placed high restrictions on their sons' behavior within the home tended to be intolerant of aggression toward themselves ($r = -.46$; $p < .001$) and nonpermissive of heterosexual behavior ($r = -.33$; $p < .05$). They tended also to be demanding in the standards they set for obedience ($r = .45$; $p < .001$) and for being responsible for household tasks ($r = .55$; $p < .001$). At the same time they were inclined to encourage their sons to spend time in their company ($r = .33$; $p < .05$). This cluster of relationships suggests the picture of a mother who is generally strict yet who fosters a close relationship with her son.

Fathers who were restrictive in the home were also inclined to suppress most forms of aggression and sexual behavior. For instance, they were punitive of aggression toward adults ($r = .34$; $p < .05$) and toward peers ($r = .27$; $p < .06$), and were relatively nonpermissive of masturbation ($r = -.32$; $p < .05$) and heterosexual behavior ($r = -.36$; $p < .02$). Restrictive fathers also tended to show a high degree of sex anxiety ($r = .39$; $p < .01$). It is possible that some fathers had experienced considerable anxiety about sex during their own adolescence, and that their anxiety had been reactivated by their sons' sexual maturation and by the

increased possibility of the boys' engaging in sexual behavior. These fathers may thus have attempted to allay their
own sex anxieties by maintaining strict control over their
sons' behavior.

Resistance to Restrictions

In training a child, the parents often require him to modify
his behavior. He has to refrain from doing some things that
he likes to do and must do other things that he finds distaste-
ful. He has to delay gratification of his needs or fit them into
elaborate schedules and routines. Socialization is inevitably
frustrating and naturally elicits some resistance from the
child.

The prediction that the aggressive boys would prove more
resistant to the socialization demands made on them by their
parents was confirmed (Table 5-2). The aggressive boys

TABLE 5-2

PARENTS' ACCOUNT OF BOYS' RESISTANCE TO RESTRICTIONS
AND DEMANDS: DIFFERENCES BETWEEN PARENTS
OF AGGRESSIVE AND CONTROL BOYS

Scales	Aggressive Group		Control Group		t	p
	Mean	S.D.	Mean	S.D.		
Data from Father Interviews						
Boy's resistance to father's restrictions	6.17	2.06	4.15	1.65	5.09	<.001
Boy's resistance to respon- sibilities	4.83	2.20	4.04	0.68	1.62	<.10
Data from Mother Interviews						
Boy's resistance to mother's restrictions	6.60	1.66	4.23	1.87	5.24	<.001
Boy's resistance to respon- sibilities	5.38	1.98	4.17	1.26	2.42	<.02

generally responded with resentment to their parents' restrictions and demands. More often than not, they would simply

ignore or refuse outright to follow the parents' requests. Occasionally they would do the very opposite of what was expected of them. Here is a description given by a mother of her son's defiance of her restrictions.

I. Does George seem to accept the restrictions you place on him or does he resent them?

M. (Case 9) If you hold him too tight, yes, he does get resentful. He does; he does get resentful.

I. Does he ever ignore them?

M. He'll just go out the front door. If I told him he couldn't go, he'll just go out and slam the door.

I. How often?

M. Sometimes he'd be awfully good, and then again I did notice it. If he did get into any trouble or had done anything, it would sort of build up. You know, he would get a bad temper, shouting, hollering and shouting all the time, and then he'd get more defiant if he'd done something wrong. Whenever he got real defiant and downright nasty, he just wouldn't. Whenever he'd get real defiant and stubborn, he had done something, and then he'd get worse if he'd done something maybe a week before. Two or three days he'd get unbearable. We could always tell.

The parents of some of the aggressive boys had little knowledge of their sons' activities outside the home. The boys would leave home without the permission of their parents who knew little of where they were going, what they would be doing, or with whom they would be associating.

A few of the most blatantly rebellious boys seemed to come from homes of considerable interparental inconsistency. The parents would present conflicting standards of behavior and make conflicting demands. In such homes the fathers were usually highly restrictive, severe, and critical. The mothers, on the other hand, tended to be lenient and protective. The boys strongly resented their fathers' severity and harshness, and the mothers often supported the boys' resistance to their fathers. The net result was that the boys developed defiant, oppositional patterns of behavior which they carried over into their relationships with people outside the home.

I. In general, do you and your husband agree about the restrictions you place on Donald?

M. (Case 33) We did fine until 4 or 5 years ago. And I don't know, never could understand. My husband said he couldn't do this, he couldn't do that. But other boys could do this. The other boys were nice friendly boys and well, you know what I mean, they would just like being mischievous, but they would never have thought of stepping over the bounds and really doing bad things. We had an awful time with his clothes and his hair; and the other boys were beginning to wear peggers, and my husband just, Donald just was not going to wear it and that was all there was to it; and he was very sensitive about it, his clothes and hair. I kept still to a certain point. I don't like to see anyone disagree over a youngster, and they eventually feel it. And finally, when Donald asked me why his father didn't agree with what he did, I told him we had talked about it and I just couldn't make him understand and for it not to let it bother him. But it made him awfully nervous. Really, many times I felt that Donald could have ignored it a little bit (laughs). It seemed like it was a constant pull one way or the other. He was determined Donald was going to do what he said; and Donald was determined he was going to do like the rest of the crowd did; and I was trying to keep a balance between the two of them and between my husband and myself at the same time.

I. Does Donald seem to accept the restrictions you place on him or does he resent them?

M. Well, that's another thing I don't understand about Donald now. He argues with his father and he really, everything that his father told him he couldn't do, Donald was just that much determined that he was going to do. And out here (Juvenile Hall) he made a remark one day that, "Nobody can fight with my father but me" (laughs). Looks like he kind of enjoyed it or something (laughs).

I. Does he try to get around the restrictions in any way?

M. Yes, he tries to get around them. He'll really go and finally get around something that he knows someone doesn't want him to do. Even school teachers said that. If he would put as much effort in learning as he did to get around all of these things, he would be an A student (laughs).

I. How much do you keep after him to see that these things (responsibilities) are done?

M. Well, we got so that we'd give him a couple of days. We'd tell him a few days ahead of time so that he knew that it was up to him to do that; and finally, after the time was set, we'd say that that has to be done by such and such a time, and 2 or 3 days to give him time to work it in with any plans that he might have made. And invariably he would make other plans; and we'd have to, we'd give him a little more time, and he'd make some more plans; and he'd just keep that up until eventually one of us would have to do it ourselves because we couldn't wait any longer (laughs).

I. Does he ever seem to resent having to do them?

M. Well, he got so he resented doing anything, period.

The control boys, according to their parents' accounts, were considerably more willing to accept the restrictions and demands that were imposed on them. For the most part, they complied with their parents' requests without question and spontaneously informed their parents about the activities in which they engaged. Most of the control parents nevertheless indicated that at times their sons were not happy about restrictions. However, in contrast to the resentful, defiant reactions of the aggressive boys, the control boys' resistance was usually expressed in much milder forms. For example, they might at times attempt to evade their parents' restrictions or try to talk their parents out of enforcing them.

I. Does Vincent seem to accept the restrictions you place on him or does he resent them?

F. (Case 48) I've never seen resentment. We've shown him, if he feels that his rights have been infringed upon, he has a right to talk it over with us. We've never raised the children with the idea of fear. They have no fear of us, certain of that.

I. Does he try to get around them in any way?

F. I would say at times he tries to outwit us, yes. He doesn't believe in everything we say. He tries to outwit us. But normally he accepts our opinion.

I. Do you feel in general that Vincent is frank and open with you about where he has been and the sort of things he does outside the home?

F. Very definitely feel that way.

I. Does he ever seem to resent your asking him about these things?

F. No, he never has. He usually broaches the subject himself. He tells us where he's going, how long he'll be gone, who he'll be with.

In general, then, the control parents' accounts indicated that the majority of the control boys had, by the time they had reached adolescence, more or less adopted their parents' standards and expectations as their own and were therefore in very little serious conflict with their parents.

I. Does Bruce seem to accept the restrictions you place on him or does he resent them?

M. (Case 22) We've had no indication of resentment as far as that goes because, whenever we say anything, I think it's usually for his good, and he has agreed all the time. We never have any arguments.

Parental Demands

OBEDIENCE DEMANDS

Both groups of fathers were inclined to demand obedience and were quite firm in following through with this demand. Indeed, the two groups of fathers did not differ in this respect. The control mothers, however, were more demanding of obedience and were more consistent in enforcing their demands than were the mothers of the aggressive boys (Table 5-3).

TABLE 5-3

OBEDIENCE DEMANDS: DIFFERENCES BETWEEN PARENTS OF
AGGRESSIVE AND CONTROL BOYS

Scales	Aggressive Group		Control Group			
	Mean	S.D.	Mean	S.D.	t	p
Data from Father Interviews						
Obedience demands	7.17	1.52	7.46	1.50	0.67	N.S.
Consistency of obedience demands	8.75	1.86	8.79	1.22	0.01	N.S.
Data from Mother Interviews						
Obedience demands	6.25	1.78	7.56	1.05	3.00	<.01
Consistency of obedience demands	6.81	2.57	8.85	0.93	3.67	<.001

The control mothers, like their husbands, expected their sons to do what they were asked to do and were quite firm in seeing that their requests were heeded. Though many of the control mothers indicated that they might be somewhat more lax when they were busy or if they felt that the matter was not of immediate importance, some of them expected almost instant obedience regardless of circumstances.

These mothers who viewed obedience as an end in itself were in effect establishing a secondary motivational system.

I. Some mothers expect their children to obey immediately when they tell them to do something; others don't think it is terribly important for a child to obey right away. What is your feeling about this?

M. (Case 16) Well, I feel it's important to do it fairly soon. I certainly wouldn't be happy about anybody putting it off for half an hour if I asked him to do something. When I usually ask him to do something, it's important.

I. If he doesn't do what you ask, do you ever drop the subject or do you always see to it that he does it?

M. If I tell him to do something, he does it. I see to it that he does it because I think it's part of his training.

The mothers of the aggressive boys made fewer demands for obedience and were more inclined to overlook noncompliance. Consequently, their sons had become inclined to ignore their mothers and to obey only at times when extra pressure had been brought to bear. The mothers' mounting anger usually served as the cue that they expected compliance and that they would brook no further delay.

M. (Case 11) Well, I'm not strict. I'm more or less lenient. I expect them to mind, but I don't expect them to mind like little robots, you know. I mean there's a give and take. They're doing something of their own interest, I don't expect them to drop it and come to my beck and call. I give them a reasonable time to do it, then I start getting mad.

A few of the mothers of the aggressive boys felt, in retrospect, that their laxness had only made the task of handling their sons more difficult. Each time they requested something the boys would test the limits set by their mothers to see whether or not they might be able to get away without complying.

M. (Case 9) Well, I think sometimes I've been too easy. You know, sometimes I think, if you make them do everything you say and never renege on anything, you're better off.

I. If he doesn't do what you ask, do you ever drop the subject or do you always see to it that he does it?

M. Oh, half the time I drop it.

Although the picture most frequently presented by the mothers of the aggressive boys was that they had been fairly lax with their sons throughout the boys' childhood, in a few cases it seemed that the mothers' laxness represented capitulation to boys who had defeated all earlier attempts at control. These mothers' attempts to get their sons to obey them had become a power struggle in which they had inevitably lost. The more pressure they had applied, the harder the boys had resisted, until eventually the mothers had to give in. They consequently tried to keep the rules and orders to a minimum. They had learned to be very careful in timing their requests so they would not interrupt or interfere with anything their sons might be doing. They were now afraid of their sons, who had apparently gained control of the relationship. Consequently, they had lost hope of, and interest in, guiding and controlling their sons; instead, they would struggle to prevent any conflicts from arising.

I. Are there times when Philip has to do his homework?
M. (Case 37) No. Not for the past years. I'm not having the house stirred up every, every night with that arguing. I'd rather have a peaceful home than every, every night. I've just given it up and won't argue about it. It makes it much more pleasant.
I. Some mothers expect their children to obey immediately when they tell them to do something; others don't think it is terribly important for a child to obey right away. What is your feeling about this?
M. It isn't important to me.
I. If he doesn't do what you ask, do you ever drop the subject or do you always see to it that he does it?
M. Well, now, I think I've mostly—now that he's older I'm very careful what I ask him to do. I try not to ask him to do anything that will get him off the phone or away from his records or program, because he might resent it and it'll just go on and on, and then I would have to take a definite stand if I really mean it. I find it easier, well, he doesn't have to do anything for me.

How much Philip's resistant pattern of behavior was reinforced originally by his mother's laxity is of course a matter for speculation. There were certainly definite indications in other interviews that the mothers' laxness fostered a pattern of disobedience which later made it even more difficult for them to get their sons to obey. The mother in Case 23 is such an example.

M. (Case 23) Well, I don't want him to do it right away because, if you try to make Earl do it, he won't do it. If you ask him, he'll do it, but not just right away. But you don't boss him—he won't do it.

I. If he doesn't do what you ask, do you ever drop the subject or do you always see to it that he does it?

M. Yes, I don't bother; I don't bother. I just forget it; just forget it. . . . Sometimes my husband wants Earl to do this, do that, and I feel—well, he's only a boy, can't expect as much from a boy as you would from a grown man, you know. But it's nothing serious, you know. . . . I don't know—sometimes I get a little bit hurt; my husband is too strict, you know. He's just a young boy. I'd be more lenient, you know, to let him a little more freely than his dad is, and then we have a misunderstanding about that. Dad is a little more stricter with Earl than I would be. Naturally, the mothers, always, sometimes, instead of keeping him in I'd say, "Let him go," or something like that. He's more strict than I am. He's not mean or anything, but he wants Earl to obey and do what he's told, that's all.

The son, in his interview, indicated that he had found non-compliance a successful way of defeating his mother's attempts to control him.

B. (Case 23) I don't do what she says. I can talk her out of anything in three minutes.

RESPONSIBILITY DEMANDS

One might expect that as the boys grew older they would be assigned increasing responsibilities by their parents. In a great majority of the families, however, the boys had very few regular duties that they were expected to perform. For the most part they were assigned some minor household chores and a limited amount of yard work. Although many of the parents felt that responsibilities would be desirable in preparing their sons for adulthood, they were nevertheless reluctant to give the boys too much to do for fear that this might interfere with the boys' schoolwork. In the hierarchy of activities, "studies come first." Moreover, some of the boys came from quite well-to-do homes where the presence of modern conveniences and, in some instances, the part-time employment of a gardener and maid service left little in the way of responsibilities that might be assigned to them. Thus, for a variety of reasons no differences were found between the two groups of parents in the extent to which they placed responsibilities on their sons (Table 5-4).

TABLE 5-4

ACHIEVEMENT AND RESPONSIBILITY DEMANDS: DIFFERENCE BETWEEN
PARENTS OF AGGRESSIVE AND CONTROL BOYS

Scales	Aggressive Group		Control Group		t	p
	Mean	S.D.	Mean	S.D.		
Data from Father Interviews						
Responsibility demands	5.12	2.11	5.67	1.29	1.01	N.S.
Achievement demands	4.92	1.07	6.71	1.72	7.10	<.001
Data from Mother Interviews						
Responsibility demands	5.42	1.31	5.37	0.98	0.14	N.S.
Achievement demands	5.21	1.27	7.19	1.62	5.32	<.001

These scales were not used as bases for prediction.

ACHIEVEMENT DEMANDS

In the area of achievement demands, one marked difference was found between the two groups of families; the control parents, both the mothers and the fathers, had higher expectations for their sons in the way of school achievement (Table 5-4). The difference probably reflects, for the most part, realistic appraisals of the boys' current motivation for academic success. In view of the very similar intelligence level of the two adolescent groups, it is nevertheless somewhat surprising to find that, in spite of the generally poor academic performance of most of the aggressive boys, their parents did not exert any more pressure on them for school success than did the parents of the control boys. Of course, if a child has accepted his parents' values, parental expectations can themselves constitute pressures. For the most part the control boys were doing adequately in school, allowing for limitations in intelligence in some cases; a few may in fact have been overachieving. Consequently, the moderate amount of pressure exerted, on the average, by the control parents requires a different interpretation than the similarly moderate amount of pressure exerted by the parents of the aggressive boys. One might say that, in spite of relatively good school progress, the control boys were subject to continued pressure; whereas the aggressive boys, in spite of generally poor progress, were being urged on no more than their much more successful controls. In other words, the motivational levels of the parents, as well as of the boys, seemed to be quite disparate.

DEMANDS AND RESTRICTIONS: RESULTS FROM BOYS' INTERVIEWS

The picture became more interesting when the boys' reports of parental restrictions and demands were taken into account (Table 5-5). While the findings from the interviews

TABLE 5-5

Boys' Accounts of Their Parents' Restrictions and Demands: Differences between Aggressive and Control Boys

Scales	Aggressive Group		Control Group			
	Mean	S.D.	Mean	S.D.	t	p
Father's responsibility demands	5.37	1.10	6.29	1.35	3.04	<.01
Mother's responsibility demands	5.46	1.07	6.58	1.34	4.09	<.001
Father's restrictions: in home	5.50	1.41	5.65	1.53	0.37	N.S.
Mother's restrictions: in home	5.31	1.56	5.88	1.47	1.26	N.S.
Father's restrictions: outside home	6.17	1.53	6.27	1.60	0.44	N.S.
Mother's restrictions: outside home	6.15	1.30	6.35	1.43	0.51	N.S.

These scales were not used as bases for prediction.

with the parents did not agree in detail with those from the interviews with the boys, the two sets of results, taken together, suggested that the control parents were, in general, more restrictive and demanding than the parents of the aggressive boys. Moreover, the adolescent interviews provided no evidence that the aggressive boys perceived their parents as excessively demanding or restrictive.

Most of the boys, like their parents, reported relatively few regular responsibilities. A few of the control boys, however, described somewhat more extensive duties that they were expected to perform.

I. What kind of jobs does your mother make you responsible for around the house?

B. (Case 18) Oh, breakfast dishes, sweeping the kitchen, mopping the kitchen, bathroom. Taking care of that. I got to take care of my own bed. Every other week I clean the bedroom up. My brother and I switch off on that and on dinner time; every other day my brother and I switch off on dishes and things like that. Taking care of the box, emptying it, cleaning up, cleaning the incinerator.

I. How about the garden?

B. Well, the garden, I got a job to take care of the lawn. During the summer we have a lousy lawn. It usually dries deader than a door nail. Next spring it turns up beautiful. I don't figure it.

I. What about your father?

B. Yes, he expects me to get it done in reasonable time. He wants me to do the same things. They both kind of go together on these things.

In spite of the fact that the control boys reported significantly more responsibilities than did the aggressive boys, they rarely protested or complained (Table 5-6). Some quite clearly felt that they should accept such responsibilities as one way of contributing to the family welfare. "Oh, I feel it's necessary. . . . I think I should do something around the house." Most of them felt resistant only when their duties conflicted with some other more attractive activity, and it was at times like these that they might attempt to evade their assignments.

I. How do you feel about having to do them?

B. (Case 42) Oh, well, regular routine jobs I'm used to it now. I just get them done as soon as I can, all the better.

TABLE 5-6

Boys' Resistance to Restrictions and Demands: Differences
between Aggressive and Control Boys

Scales	Aggressive Group		Control Group		t	p
	Mean	S.D.	Mean	S.D.		
Resistance to father's restrictions	4.73	2.00	3.15	1.37	2.93	<.01
Resistance to mother's restrictions	4.67	2.19	3.44	1.79	2.15	<.05
Resistance to father's responsibility demands	5.54	2.22	5.48	2.21	0.11	N.S
Resistance to mother's responsibility demands	6.00	1.90	5.48	2.04	1.20	N.S

I. Do you ever try to get out of doing them?
B. Once in a great while, if I have something else planned to do and I have to do the dishes, I don't like it. I try to get out of it. Ask my mother if she'll do it. My dad usually ends up saying he'll do it.

In contrast, the aggressive boys tended to resist and resent any demand that they should accept responsibilities, no matter how minor these might be.

I. What kind of jobs does your mother make you responsible for around the house?
B. (Case 21) I really don't have any responsibilities around the house. I just come home and play the piano and that's all; practice the piano.
I. Does she expect you to look after your room?
B. Yes. I don't. I'm expected to. I usually don't. I usually throw things in there.
I. How about the garden or car?
B. No. Never.
I. What about your father?
B. No. He never—he expects me to, but he really never asks me about it. If I don't do it, I don't do it.

The boys' accounts provided no evidence of differences between either the groups of mothers or the groups of fathers in the amount of restrictions they placed on their sons, at home or outside. Such small, nonsignificant differences as there were, however, all suggested that the control parents were slightly more restrictive. On the other hand, the aggressive boys were much more resentful of restrictions than were the controls; the boys' reports thus confirmed those given by the parents.

I. Do you ever feel like doing something your mother forbids just in order to assert yourself?

B. (Case 25) Yeah. Especially on Saturdays. She'll tell me, "I got a lot of work planned for you." "No, you don't. Uh, uh, I'm going out."

I. What about your father? How often do you feel this way about him?

B. When I do something, he stands right over me and watches me do it.

I. Do you feel like not doing it sometimes?

B. I feel like not doing it all the time.

I. How do you feel about your mother's attitude about the things you should do and the things you shouldn't do?

B. She's a pretty fair woman.

I. Do you think she gives you as much freedom as other fellows get?

B. More.

I. And your father?

B. Him, too.

.   .   .

I. Do you ever feel like doing something that your father forbids just in order to assert yourself?

B. (Case 49) I do that quite a bit. I mean he'll tell me to stay home or something like that. I'll leave anyway. He'll say, "Be in by a certain time." Just out of plain meanness sometimes I stay as late as I want.

I. How about your mother? Do you ever feel this way with her.

B. No. I don't feel like that. I mean, if I'm going to be out late, I tell her I'll be in kind of late. She'll expect it.

I. How do you feel about your mother's attitude about the things you should do and the things you shouldn't do?

B. She's pretty reasonable with me. She's not strict or anything like that.

I. How about your father?

B. Oh, he's a strict old miser.

I. You feel he's stricter than your mother?

B. Oh, he tries. That's about all he does.

The control boys tended to perceive their parents' regulations less as a burden imposed on them than as evidence of their parents' positive interest in their welfare.

I. How do you feel about your mother's attitude about the things you should do and things you shouldn't?

B. (Case 48) I'd say both of them have a healthy attitude. They take interest in me and they want to know what I'm doing or what I'm going to do. They usually try to tell me if I'm going to do something; and if it's wrong, they usually try and tell me why.

I. How honest do you feel you can be to them about where you have been and what things you have done?

B. I'm completely honest with them. I mean, they trust me fully, I know, so there's never any problem.

While they generally accepted and complied with the limits that their parents set for them, most of the control boys felt free to express their own opinions and to assert themselves when they felt that they were in the right.

I. How do you feel about your mother's attitude about the things you should do and things you shouldn't do?

B. (Case 26) Well, lots of things my mother tells me I should do and lots of things my dad tells me I should do, and I kind of make my own conclusions, too. I take their wise advice. I know they're older and they've gone through a lot. Yet I still have some ideas myself, and there's only a couple of things that I do wouldn't agree with them.

I. Do you think they're pretty reasonable or do you think they give you less freedom than other fellows get?

B. They're pretty reasonable. They are, both of them.

I. How honest do you feel you can be to your mother about where you have been and what things you have done?

B. Completely. I can be completely honest with them.

The greater resistance of the aggressive boys seemed to arise neither from the onerous nature of their parents' restrictions and demands nor from a mistaken belief that they were unusually extensive. Since the aggressive boys had experienced no more, and in all probability fewer, restrictions than had the control boys, their resistance and resentment must have been due to other factors.

On the assumption that secondary rewards in the form of parental nurturance and approval are important, if not indispensable, for the effective social training of a child, one would expect that a child's resistance to socialization demands might be a function both of the strength of his dependency on his parents and of his anxiety about being placed in a dependent role. If his parents' love and approval are more important to him than the sacrifices he has to make in accepting their limits and demands, he probably will not resent the control over his behavior that his parents exercise. The anticipation of dependency and affectional gratifications may motivate him to conform to his parents' wishes. On the other hand, if a boy's affectional dependent tie to his parents is weak—as it was found to be in the families of the aggressive boys (Chapter 2)—he has less reason to accept restrictions on his freedom. Where there is relatively little affectional compensation for compliance and where noncompliance does not threaten the boy's dependent security (since there is little dependency present), the parents are forced to rely to a much greater extent on coercion. Under these circumstances the boy experiences no compensatory reward for compliance, and he is therefore likely to resent and resist the parents' interference.

The expectation of an inverse relationship between the boys' dependency and their resistance to prohibitions was partially confirmed. The correlations, for both the mother and the father data, were all negative in direction, and several of them were significant beyond the .10 level (Table 5-7). There was thus some direct evidence that dependency on the parents is an important factor in the socialization of the child. Although these correlations are not for the most part large, one must remember that the boys in this study were already adolescent and that they were probably less dependent on their parents for emotional gratifications than they had been at an earlier age.

Although coercive methods might have had some influence on the behavior of the aggressive boys during their childhood, it was clear that their parents found the problem of controlling their sons increasingly more difficult. Some of the older boys had reached the stage where they were almost completely independent and quite capable of caring for themselves. Meanwhile, they had developed physically to

TABLE 5-7

CORRELATIONS BETWEEN MEASURES OF THE BOYS' DEPENDENCY
ON THEIR PARENTS AND THEIR RESISTANCE TO THE
PARENTS' SOCIALIZATION PRESSURES

Scales	Resistance to Responsibilities	Resistance to Restrictions	Resistance to Discipline
Data from Father Interviews			
Extent seeks father's help	—.02	—.19	—.24
Extent seeks father's company	—.07	—.18	—.30
Extent seeks father's praise	—.21	—.18	—.18
Data from Mother Interviews			
Extent seeks mother's help	—.23	—.04	—.17
Extent seeks mother's company	—.27	—.17	—.29
Extent seeks mother's praise	—.16	—.12	—.19

Correlations equal to, or greater than, .37 are significant at the .01 level.
Correlations equal to, or greater than, .28 are significant at the .05 level.

the point where their parents could no longer force them to comply. Consequently, a number of the boys showed a blatant indifference to their parents' wishes about which the parents could now do little or nothing.

I. What sort of things does your mother object to your doing when you are out with your friends?
B. (Case 23) She don't know what I do.
I. What about staying out late at night?
B. She says, "Be home at 11 o'clock." I'll come home at one, 'cause my father's always the person who says what goes. I mean she always wants me in early. My father says, "12:30, son. Try to make it home on time." He always gives a reasonable time to stay out to.
I. How about using the family car?
B. No. I wrecked mine, and my father wrecked his a month before I wrecked mine, and I can't even get near his. And I got a license and everything. I'm going to hot wire it some night and cut out.
I. How honest do you feel you can be to your mother about where you've been and what things you have done?

B. I tell her where I've been, period.
I. How about what you've done?
B. No. I won't tell her what I've done. If we're going out in the hills for a beer bust, I'm not going to tell her. I'll tell her I've been to a show or something.
I. How about your father?
B. I'll tell him where I've been, period.

Since to submit to, and comply with, their parents' demands would involve acknowledging their dependent status, it is reasonable to suppose that the resistance of the aggressive boys in part reflected their anxiety about dependency. The intercorrelations of the boys' measures supported this interpretation (Table 5-8). In general, boys who showed most anxiety about dependency on their parents also showed the greatest resistance to parental demands and restrictions.

TABLE 5-8

CORRELATIONS BETWEEN MEASURES OF THE BOYS' ANXIETY ABOUT
DEPENDENCY ON THEIR PARENTS AND THEIR RESISTANCE
TO THE PARENTS' SOCIALIZATION PRESSURES

Scales	Resistance to Responsibilities	Resistance to Restrictions	Resistance to Discipline
Data from Father Interviews			
Resistance to father's suggestions	.36	.61	.40
Resistance to father's company	.18	.28	.35
Resistance to confiding in father	.38	.42	.26
Data from Mother Interviews			
Resistance to mother's suggestions	.48	.48	.33
Resistance to mother's company	.29	.48	.53
Resistance to confiding in mother	.37	.42	.17

Correlations equal to, or greater than, .37 are significant at the .01 level. Correlations equal to, or greater than, .28 are significant at the .05 level.

TECHNIQUES OF DISCIPLINE: RESULTS FROM
PARENT INTERVIEWS

Methods of Reward

The prediction that the parents of the aggressive boys would make relatively more use of material rewards, whereas the control parents would make relatively more use of praise, was not confirmed (Table 5-9).

TABLE 5-9

USE OF REWARDS: DIFFERENCES BETWEEN PARENTS OF
AGGRESSIVE AND CONTROL BOYS

Scales	Aggressive Group		Control Group			
	Mean	S.D.	Mean	S.D.	t	p
Data from Father Interviews						
Material rewards	4.54	2.13	4.27	1.20	0.48	N.S.
Praise	7.04	1.87	7.63	2.66	0.83	N.S.
Data from Mother Interviews						
Material rewards	5.38	2.07	4.42	1.90	1.60	<.10
Praise	7.48	1.76	7.17	2.17	0.56	N.S.

Both groups of parents made relatively little use of *material rewards* as a method of training. Indeed, the majority of parents felt that the use of rewards was not a good practice. Some were of the opinion that good behavior should be taken for granted and they feared that, if it were rewarded, the boys would not behave as the parents desired unless they were continuously paid to do so. As one mother expressed it, "No, I would be paying all my life." Another common attitude was that rewarding a child with material things represented a form of bribery.

I. Do you have any system of rewarding him for good behavior?
M. (Case 21) Oh, we've tried to bribe him, which I guess is not the right thing to do, to make good grades; that he would get so much if he would get A's and B's. But that doesn't work at all.

By far the most common form of reward was money and this was usually given for scholastic achievement, the rate of exchange varying considerably from 10¢ to $2.00 per A. In fact, school achievement seemed to be of such great importance to some of the parents that they would offer their sons anything that might increase their motivation to do well in school. One father, for instance, offered to make a down payment on a car if his son would obtain a B average, even though the boy had just wrecked a car which he had had for only two weeks.

Praise was employed much more frequently than material rewards as a way of rewarding behavior of which the parents approved. A good deal of variation was found among the parents in the extent to which they praised their sons. Some parents felt that praise would only make the boys complacent or egocentric. Others felt that it was an essential and effective means of guidance. These latter parents often commented on the effectiveness of praise for increasing their sons' motivation to conform to their demands and for bolstering the boys' self-esteem.

In attempting to influence and modify the behavior of children, parents may rely primarily on methods of punishment or primarily on methods of reward. If parents punish disapproved behavior, but do not reward the behavior they desire, they provide little positive guidance for their children. In other words, the children may learn perfectly well what they should not do, but will remain uncertain of what it is they should do. Consequently, it is rather surprising that so many parents viewed the use of rewards unfavorably.

There was a good deal of variability among both groups of parents in the readiness with which they used rewards. Intercorrelations among the parent measures suggested that the use of rewards was associated with the affectionate, nurturant qualities of the parents. Mothers who praised their sons tended to display a high degree of warmth for their husbands ($r = .42$; $p < .01$); they tended also, though within the control families only, to show a good deal of warmth for their sons ($r = .45$; $p < .05$) and to have spent considerable time in affectionate interaction with them during the boys' childhood ($r = .39$; $p < .05$). The relationship between praise and affectionate demonstrativeness was even more apparent for the fathers. Fathers who made frequent use of praise tended to be acceptant of ($r = .28$; $p < .05$), and warm towards ($r = .49$; $p < .001$), their sons and to show little hostility toward them ($r = -.37$; $p < .01$). In addition, these fathers displayed a good deal of warmth for ($r = .45$; $p < .001$), and little hostility to ($r = .31$; $p < .05$), their wives. Moreover, mothers who provided their sons with material rewards tended to show warmth for them ($r = .33$; $p < .05$) and to be permissive of their sons' requests for help ($r = .30$; $p < .05$). Among the mothers of the aggressive boys, those who made use of material rewards were also permissive of the boys' spending time in their company ($r = .45$; $p < .05$). Similarly, fathers who rewarded their sons were permissive of the boys' seeking their company ($r = .32$; $p < .05$). For the fathers of the aggressive boys, the use of tangible rewards was also positively associated with the amount of affectionate interaction with their sons in early childhood ($r = .40$; $p < .05$); on the other hand, these measures were found to be negatively related for the control fathers ($r = -.42$; $p < .05$).

The negative, rejecting attitude of some parents who used little praise was sometimes apparent in their comments on this technique of training. It is interesting to note that the mothers in the cases quoted below had experienced the same cold treatment themselves during their own childhood.

M. (Case 9) I don't think you ought to have a halo on your head just 'cause you're good. That's the way you are supposed to be. That's the way I was raised.

· · ·

M. (Case 13) No. I don't get down on my knees and praise my children. I've always tried to teach them right from the beginning, the way to behave and how to act, but I've never praised them for doing it. I guess I was raised more or less to do what you're supposed to do.

The prediction concerning the use of material rewards

was based on the assumption that this practice is less closely related to the parents' affectionate qualities than is the use of praise. The intercorrelations given above suggest that this assumption was false, and in retrospect it is easy to see why this may be so. When one adult bestows a gift on another it is often a very special token of affection and respect. In the same way, a parent's use of material rewards may be a sign of his regard and affection for his children. Thus, when an adolescent receives money or other tangible rewards from his parents, these may be important to him primarily as tokens of his parents' affection and only secondarily for their material value.

Methods of Punishment

Physical Punishment

Although the parents were asked to give an account of the extent to which they used physical punishment during the boys' earlier years as well as currently, the ratings largely reflected the parents' earlier practices. Both mothers and fathers reported little current use of physical punishment. In the first place, the boys were getting too big physically to be handled in this manner. Then, too, some of the parents of the aggressive boys feared that their sons might counter-attack if they were to punish them physically. In the boys' earlier years, however, physical punishment had been used to some extent by both groups of parents; indeed, from the apologetic way in which many parents admitted its use, it seemed possible that it had been used more frequently than the parents actually reported.

The hypothesis concerning physical punishment was in part confirmed. The fathers of the aggressive boys were more prone to resort to physical punishment to discipline their sons than were the control fathers (Table 5-10). The mothers, however, did not differ much in this respect. It is possible that the greater use of physical punishment by the fathers of the aggressive boys may have been to some extent forced on them by the nature of their sons' behavior. On the other

TABLE 5-10

USE OF METHODS OF PUNISHMENT: DIFFERENCES BETWEEN PARENTS
OF AGGRESSIVE AND CONTROL BOYS

Scales	Aggressive Group		Control Group		t	p
	Mean	S.D.	Mean	S.D.		
Data from Father Interviews						
Physical punishment	5.62	1.91	4.19	1.64	2.38	<.02
Deprivation of privileges	7.10	1.76	5.40	1.82	4.42	<.001
Withdrawal of love	3.92	2.23	3.27	1.67	1.03	N.S.
Ridicule	2.94	1.25	2.62	1.15	0.93	N.S.
Nagging and Scolding[a]	5.65	2.12	4.50	1.45	2.55	<.01
Data from Mother Interviews						
Physical punishment	5.19	1.69	4.67	1.32	1.32	<.10
Deprivation of privileges	6.35	0.94	5.40	1.27	3.75	<.001
Withdrawal of love	5.81	1.90	5.13	1.90	1.37	N.S.
Ridicule	3.50	1.02	3.10	1.45	1.22	N.S.
Nagging and Scolding[a]	5.52	1.78	5.17	1.83	0.70	N.S.

[a] This scale was not used as a basis for prediction.

hand, there was evidence that some of the most punitive fathers had themselves experienced corporal punishment during their own upbringing and were repeating their parents' practice. In these cases, physical punishment was clearly a method of preference rather than a method of last resort.

I. How often have you found it necessary to slap him or give him a licking?

F. (Case 39) Well, in recent years it's getting further apart all the time. But it used to be where—we were brought up in a German family and the yardstick was the first thing we used, which wasn't too often, but we tried to use it as authority and not to harm the child. I don't think that any of them ever did suffer anything in the sense that there were marks. Several times they have had examinations, and there's been nothing said about it or remarked about it. I feel in my own mind, my own heart, we did spank him too hard. At the same time they have no marks from it, so I don't think we've been wrong there.

I. What do you find most effective?

F. Well, I think in later years his privileges has had the most effect. The lickings, so to speak, are getting further and further apart all the time because he's starting to be a man, and when you go into that, why, they feel that they are beatings rather than spankings. I know that Philip has told me himself several times that he considered it as a beating because he was getting too big for that, and I tried to impress on his mind that he was a man before he would not get any more beatings, because in my mind I thought that was the way to punish him. But as I say, we felt that it wasn't doing any good, so we went to restrictions more than punishments.

The general impression given by a number of the control parents was that they had used physical punishment for the most part only when their sons were too young for verbal controls to be effectively employed. At this time, physical punishment was used largely in conjunction with verbal commands for the definite purpose of training the child to respond to verbal cues. Gradually these verbal cues, through their association with punishment, came to elicit anxiety which served to inhibit the disapproved actions as effectively as the physical punishment itself. Later, the verbal commands themselves were sufficient to control the child. The mother in Case 34 gave a good example of such a conditioning process.

I. How often have you found it necessary to slap him or give him a licking?

M. (Case 34) No. Well—when he was a baby, when he'd go to touch things that aren't to be touched. I'm not too much of a believer in putting things away. I think if something is there and they're not to touch it, then they shouldn't touch it. But when you have a baby before it's of a reasoning age, I don't think that there is anything more than just a quick pat on the hand, nothing that hurts or injurious, just—that's it—"Don't touch." Same thing when they're doing something and you have said, "No," two or three times, to which there has been no attention paid. You say, "No," and you give them a whack and the next time "No" means something. Of course, this is with babies. Once they get to the point where you can talk with them, unless they get beyond the reasoning point, then they should go off by themselves.

Whether or not the parents of the aggressive boys employed physical punishment in a different manner from the control parents cannot, of course, be determined from the ratings alone. However, the intercorrelations of the parent measures suggested that physical punishment might have been sometimes employed, not so much as a specific tech‑. nique of training (as it seemed to have been used by the control mother quoted above), but rather as an expression of a generalized rejecting attitude. Mothers who had frequently spanked their sons tended to reject them ($r = .45$; $p < .001$), to be hostile toward them ($r = .46$; $p < .001$), and to ridicule them ($r = .39$; $p < .01$). In addition, they were inclined to show little warmth for ($r = -.34$; $p < .05$), and more hostility to ($r = .38$; $p < .01$), their husbands.

A somewhat similar picture emerged from the father data. Fathers who frequently punished their sons physically tended to lack warmth for them ($r = -.39$; $p < .01$) and also to discourage close emotional relationships between their sons and themselves through a lack of permissiveness toward the boys' bids for their company ($r = -.31$; $p < .05$).

Correlations between the ratings of the parents' use of physical punishment, made from the parent interviews, and ratings of the boys behavior, made from the adolescent interviews, suggested that boys who had experienced a good deal of physical punishment tended to be hostile and aggressive outside the home. Boys whose mothers had frequently used physical punishment tended to be hostile toward teachers ($r = .38$; $p < .01$). In addition, though for the control boys only, the boys' total aggression toward teachers correlated $.42$ ($p < .05$) with their mothers' use of physical punishment, and their hostility toward teachers correlated $.49$ ($p < .02$) with their fathers' use of physical punishment. Moreover, control boys whose mothers used physical punishment showed relatively little guilt about aggression toward their mothers ($r = -.48$; $p < .02$) and were more resistant to accepting the suggestions of their parents ($r = .43$; $p < .05$; mid-parent ratings).

It has been suggested that the parents' use of physical punishment may have hindered some boys from forming dependency relationships. The correlational findings, however, do not consistently support this suggestion. Indeed, aggressive boys who received a good deal of physical punishment from their fathers tended to show relatively high dependency on them ($r = .46$; $p < .05$). While this relationship received no support from other data, it could perhaps indicate that some of the aggressive boys had formed relatively close relationships with hostile, punitive parent models. In contrast, control boys whose parents made relatively frequent use of physical punishment showed less dependency on their teachers ($r = -.49$; $p < .02$), and more anxiety about being dependent both on their teachers ($r = .38$; $p < .06$) and on their peers ($r = .27$; $p < .16$), than control boys whose parents did not favor the use of this method of discipline.

DEPRIVATION OF PRIVILEGES

Depriving a boy of certain possessions and privileges was a very common mode of punishment among both groups of parents. Both the mothers and the fathers of the aggressive boys used this form of discipline to a significantly greater extent than did the control parents (Table 5-10). Depriving the boys of the use of the family car and restricting them from going out were favored disciplinary measures.

I. Which of these things are you most likely to do?

M. (Case 23) We take the TV away, take the shows away. He can't go out, and that hurts him more than anything. That's worse than —I think he'd sooner take a spanking than punishing.

It was interesting to find that deprivation of privileges was often combined with isolation. The following excerpt, taken from an interview with the father of one of the aggressive boys, illustrates a rather extreme use of both methods.

I. What do you find most effective?

F. (Case 17) When he doesn't want to do something we don't want— don't want—don't like—the best punishment that I've found, and the best punishment I think, is to deprive him of everything that he really likes. Just put him in his room and he can't use nothing. He can't even read—he can't do nothing, just stay there. I think that's the best. Probably different parents don't like it, because it's rude or something like that; that's their opinion. My opinion—that's about the best way because it deprives him of the phonograph, of the radio. They can't use it because they've done something.

Unfortunately no rating was secured of the extent to which the parents were inclined to send the boys to their rooms or otherwise isolate them, since it was thought that such a method of discipline would be used very infrequently by the time the boys had reached adolescence. The parent interviews, however, seemed to indicate that isolation was still commonly used, particularly by the parents of the aggressive boys. It may be that, by removing the boys from their presence, the parents did not have to deal with the resentment that punishment might elicit.

It was noted in a previous section that material rewards may be primarily important as tokens of parental affection and approval. In a similar manner, deprivation of privileges may sometimes be primarily important as a sign of the parents' disapproval and withholding of love. This is perhaps especially true when a young child is deprived of a toy or a pastime as an indication of his parents' displeasure. However, for the parents of the adolescent boys in this study, the use of deprivation as a method of discipline appeared to be primarily associated with a rejecting, punitive attitude toward their sons.

Fathers who frequently deprived their sons of privileges tended to lack warmth for them ($r = -.37$; $p < .01$), to be rejecting ($r = .35$; $p < .02$), and to be hostile toward them ($r = .36$; $p < .02$). They also tended to make frequent use of physical punishment ($r = .28$; $p < .05$). There was also some evidence that fathers who used deprivation tended to discourage dependency. For the fathers of the aggressive boys the use of deprivation of privileges correlated $-.41$ ($p < .05$) with the encouragement of help-seeking, while for the control fathers its use correlated $-.42$ ($p < .05$) with the amount of time the fathers had spent with their sons during the boys' early childhood. For the mothers also, the use of deprivation of privileges was associated with rejection of their sons ($r = .32$; $p < .05$) and with hostility toward them ($r = .29$; $p < .05$). Moreover, the extent to which the control boys sought help from their mothers, as estimated from the boys' interviews, showed a high negative correlation with the mothers' use of deprivation of privileges ($r = -.53$; $p < .01$), as measured from the parents' interviews. This latter correlation constitutes further evidence that the use of deprivation may serve to weaken a boy's dependency on his parents.

WITHDRAWAL OF LOVE

The hypothesis that the parents of the control boys would make more use of withdrawal of love as a disciplinary technique than would the parents of the aggressive boys was not confirmed (Table 5-10). This failure to find any difference between the two groups of parents may, however, be partly due to shortcomings in the method of inquiry. The more subtle withdrawal-of-love techniques were not explicitly investigated, but only the more openly rejecting forms, involving the parents' refusing to speak to their sons or telling them that they wanted to have no more to do with them or that they were ashamed of them. Consequently, the questions usually elicited strong denial and even expressions of disapproval of the use of such techniques. Indeed, those parents who reported withholding love as a way of punishing their sons usually did so apologetically and sometimes expressed guilt and self-criticism.

I. Do you sometimes ignore him or refuse to speak to him until he does as you want?

M. (Case 9) Sometimes I swear at him. I know you shouldn't be—gee, you get so mad at them. Sometimes I tell him I'm sorry I ever had him; "You brought me nothing but grief." I know you shouldn't, but you do—sometimes you get so mad.

I. Do you ever tell him you don't want any more to do with him until he changes?

M. Yeah, I've told him. I've said some terrible things to him sometimes.

I. How often?

M. When he's hurt me so and I'd tell him, 'cause he's often told me that, "You don't love me. You told me you wish you never had me."

The correlational data suggested that the use of withdrawal of love was associated with the fostering of dependency relationships in the boys' early years, but with rejection during the boys' later years. Mothers of aggressive boys and fathers of control boys who had spent much time in affectionate interaction with their sons during the boys' early years tended to make relatively frequent use of threats of withdrawal of love ($r = .46$; $p < .05$, and $r = .53$; $p < .01$, respectively). On the other hand, mothers in both groups who used threats of withdrawal of love tended also to be rejecting ($r = .26$; $p < .06$). Moreover, when used by the fathers of the aggressive boys, such threats seemed likely to arouse feelings of rejection. Ratings of withdrawal of love made from these fathers' interviews correlated .47 ($p < .02$) with the boys' expressed feelings of rejection by their fathers.

It is, of course, possible that only if a child has a close dependent relationship with his parents will threats of loss of love increase guilt feelings. Sears, Maccoby, and Levin (1957) found that children whose mothers were relatively affectionate and used withdrawal of love methods fairly often presented a high degree of conscience development; whereas, if mothers were lacking in warmth, their use of withdrawal of love had little effect on their children's conscience development. Unless a child has a secure feeling of being loved and accepted, he is apt to regard his parents' threats of withdrawal of love as hollow or to interpret them as evidence of his parents' rejection. Under these circumstances, the use of threats of withdrawal of love by the parents, rather than fostering conscience control, may actually reduce the probability of the child's identifying with his parents and thereby accepting their values and standards.

The use of threats of withdrawal of love in a punitive and manipulative way is illustrated in the following excerpt from an interview with a father of an aggressive boy.

I. Do you sometimes try to make him feel ashamed of himself by pointing out that he is ungrateful and doesn't appreciate what you've done for him?

F. (Case 13) Absolutely, that's what we've based it on, right there. That's when I say he breaks down and feels awfully bad. We used to use a little strategy, using his mother. He loves his mother very dearly, and if he thinks my wife is kind of—she carries her feelings on her shoulders, especially toward the children. They do something wrong, it just breaks her heart. She's crying and they go to crying with her. So I kind of use that as a weapon and sometimes it works. I think it works terrifically. Then, "Oh," I think, "I hit the nail right on the head." I think, "Well, buddy, I did it." But I guess, a week later . . . it takes them about a week to get over it.

If threats of withdrawal of love were perceived by the boys as evidence of rejection, one would expect them to respond with hostility and aggression. As a matter of fact, parents who used such threats tended to have sons who were relatively hostile toward them ($r = .31$; $p < .05$) and who tended to be aggressive toward their peers ($r = .27$; $p < .06$). Moreover, in the control families, boys whose parents used threats of withdrawal of love tended to be aggressive toward their teachers ($r = .44$; $p < .05$). In addition, the boys' resistance to their mothers' suggestions was greater if their mothers disciplined them by using threats of withdrawal of love ($r = .41$; $p < .05$).

RIDICULE

The two groups of parents did not differ in the extent to which they employed ridicule as a method of discipline. Most parents, especially fathers, were as quick to deny the use of any form of ridicule as they were to deny the use of threats of withdrawal of love. Nevertheless, some interesting correlations were obtained between the use of ridicule and other qualities of the parents which further confirmed the finding, previously reported, that parents who used punitive methods of discipline were lacking in warmth and affection. For example, mothers who were inclined to ridicule their sons were more rejecting of them ($r = .35$; $p < .05$), had low esteem for them ($r = .41$; $p < .05$), and were punitive of their help-seeking ($r = .31$; $p < .05$). They had little warmth for their husbands ($r = -.45$; $p < .001$), felt hostile toward them ($r = .49$; $p < .001$), and tended to disagree with them regarding disciplinary practices ($r = .33$; $p < .05$). In addition, fathers who ridiculed their sons tended to have a low evaluation of their wives ($r = -.29$; $p < .05$).

Both mothers and fathers who used ridicule tended also to use deprivation of privileges ($r = .43$; $p < .01$, and $r = .41$; $p < .01$, respectively). Moreover, the fathers' use of ridicule correlated very highly with their use of withdrawal of love ($r = .63$; $p < .001$). This latter correlation provided further evidence that some fathers tended to use withdrawal of love in a punitive, rejecting manner.

NAGGING AND SCOLDING

There was no difference of note between the groups of mothers in their use of nagging and scolding. On the other hand, the fathers of the aggressive boys nagged and scolded their sons considerably more often than did the control fathers (Table 5-10). Nagging and scolding are frequently thought to be predominantly maternal prerogatives. However, to judge from their ratings, the aggressive boys' fathers nagged and scolded as much as, if not somewhat more than, either of the groups of mothers.

It was found that mothers who made considerable use of nagging and scolding tended to feel little warmth for their sons ($r = .37$; $p < .01$), to reject them ($r = .52$; $p < .001$), to be hostile toward them ($r = .49$; $p < .001$), and to have spent little time in affectionate interaction with them during the boys' childhood ($r = -.32$; $p < .05$). They also tended to be lacking in warmth ($r = -.30$; $p < .05$) for their husbands and to be more at odds with them concerning disciplinary policies ($r = -.36$; $p < .02$). Moreover, these mothers made frequent use of other disciplinary techniques that were found to be associated with punitiveness and rejection. They tended to deprive their sons of privileges ($r = .29$; $p < .05$), to ridicule them ($r = .30$; $p < .05$), and to threaten them with withdrawal of love ($r = .33$; $p < .05$).

A similar cluster of correlations was obtained for the fathers. Fathers who nagged and scolded tended to reject ($r = .57$; $p < .001$), and to be hostile toward ($r = .57$; $p < .001$), their sons. They also tended to deprive them of privileges ($r = .41$; $p < .01$) and to threaten them with withdrawal of love ($r = .29$; $p < .05$). In addition, fathers of aggressive boys who nagged and scolded had little warmth for their sons ($r = -.56$; $p < .01$) and were unlikely to encourage their sons to come to them for help and advice ($r = -.40$; $p < .05$).

Reasoning

The control parents employed reasoning as a method of training and control to a much greater extent than did the parents of the aggressive boys (Table 5-11). In fact, most of

TABLE 5-11

Use of Reasoning: Differences between Parents of Aggressive and Control Boys

Scales	Aggressive Group		Control Group		t	p
	Mean	S.D.	Mean	S.D.		
Fathers' use of reasoning	7.33	1.72	8.25	1.01	2.41	<.02
Mothers' use of reasoning	7.33	1.04	8.35	0.92	4.06	<.001

the control parents indicated that in more recent years they had relied almost entirely upon reasoning in the handling of any problems of misconduct that arose. In answer to questions concerning the frequency with which they resorted to other forms of discipline, they were inclined to point out that explaining to their sons why they did not want them to act in certain ways usually sufficed to modify their behavior.

I. What do you find most effective?

M. (Case 40) Well, I would say talking to him, reasoning things out with him at different times.

I. What other ways have you used to discipline Samuel since he has been in high school?

M. I couldn't say that I have had much problem with him. He's always, as far as I'm concerned, very good to listen to reason.

I. How often have you found it necessary to slap him or give him a licking?

M. No. I don't think—I try never to hit my children. I try to, you know, reason with them. If they are naughty, I try to take them to one side and talk to them. Perhaps I'd take them into their room and explain to them that they aren't doing right and they all have to cooperate to get along in this world together. If they can't get along in their homes, how are they ever going to get along outside? I use that approach with them. I always, you know, try to reason to them and to tell him that he wasn't right and change his attitudes toward things.

・　　・　　・

I. Suppose Alec has been behaving very badly and giving you or his mother a hard time, what kind of things do you say to him?

F. (Case 32) Well, I'd try to point out to him why we want it done. There is a reason, and I'll explain to him that probably he doesn't understand now, but as he gets a little older we'll tell him why he would possibly tell his youngster the same thing.

I. How often have you found it necessary to slap him or give him a licking?

F. Right now, I'd say I haven't. I never have with him, because I found that even when he was very, very small I could take him into the bedroom and talk to him and try to explain to him. I've never had to lick him.

Not only did the two groups of families differ in the extent to which they reasoned with their sons, but there seemed also to be some interesting qualitative differences between them in the ways in which they employed reasoning. The parents of the aggressive boys appeared more likely to point out the external punishments that the boys might bring upon themselves through their behavior, in the hope that this would deter them from acting out their impulses. In contrast, a number of the control parents made a direct appeal to the boys' guilt feelings. They portrayed the consequences of the boys' behavior, not so much in terms of external punishment, but rather in terms of the injury or suffering that such behavior might bring to the parents.

I. Suppose Tony has been behaving very badly and giving you or his mother a hard time, what kind of things do you say to him?

F. (Case 30) Well, I sit down and talk to him man to man. Explain to him that he's being very, very unfair and, "It could be serious if you carry this on and keep doing it. It won't affect me, my boy; it will affect your mother's health because, you know, your mother is a nervous type of person." And I think I said, "Cut it out," and since this day forward he's been very nice about it. He's seen the serious point. I said—one of the things I told him one day made him think. "If anything would happen to your mother you would hate to go through life thinking that you're partly the cause of what happened, and it could happen if you go too far." That's the way we try to bring it home to him seriously.

Another qualitative difference in the use of reasoning was apparent. Control parents quite frequently utilized reasoning, not so much for the direct control of their sons' behavior, but as a method of helping them to label, and so modify, their feelings.

I. Suppose Dan has been behaving very badly and giving you or his mother a hard time, what kind of things do you say to him?
F. (Case 26) First of all we mention that we don't think he's normal under the circumstances and must be feeling kind of low about something or another and try to draw it out of him—want to know why he's acting that way. Sometimes he'll—there will be a reason for it, such as not feeling well or things going bad on certain activities. There's usually a basis for it, if you draw it out of him.

In any disciplinary problem, handling a child's *actions* is one aspect of management, handling the *feelings* that instigate his actions is another. Discipline is often ineffective because it is directed solely toward the control of undesirable behavior and ignores the underlying motivation. In the long run, the most effective way of controlling such behavior may be to label the feelings that instigate it and then to attempt to alleviate, or otherwise modify, these feelings or the conditions that produce them. One would expect that this therapeutic use of reasoning, an example of which is provided in the excerpt quoted above, would be highly effective in preventing and handling disciplinary problems. In contrast, the use of physical punishment and other punitive techniques may serve only to intensify hostile feelings and thus may further instigate the child to display the very behavior that his parents are attempting to bring under control.

While all other techniques of control—physical punishment, deprivation of privileges, ridicule, withdrawal of love, and nagging and scolding—were associated with rejecting and punitive qualities of the parents, the use of reasoning was alone associated with parental warmth, nurturance, acceptance, and nonpunitiveness.

Mothers who emphasized the use of reasoning were highly accepting of their sons ($r = .46$; $p < .001$), felt little hostility toward them ($r = -.41$; $p < .01$), and were unlikely to punish them for seeking their help ($r = -.31$; $p < .05$). In addition, control mothers who used reasoning not only were unlikely to punish their sons' attempts to secure their help but actively encouraged them to seek it ($r = .42$; $p < .05$). In both groups, mothers who used reasoning tended to handle aggression toward themselves in a nonpunitive way ($r = -.32$; $p < .05$). They tended also to avoid the use of physical punishment ($r = -.43$; $p < .01$), deprivation of privileges ($r = -.47$; $p < .001$), nagging and scolding ($-.34$; $p < .05$), and threats of withdrawal of love ($r = -.37$; $p < .01$).

The picture was essentially the same for the fathers. Fathers who emphasized the use of reasoning were accepting of their sons ($r = .44$; $p < .01$); they showed a good deal of warmth for ($r = .49$; $p < .001$), and little hostility toward, them ($r = -.35$; $p < .02$). They tended also to foster dependency. For example, they had spent a good deal of time in affectionate interaction with their sons during the boys' early years ($r = .30$; $p < .05$) and currently encouraged the boys to spend time in their company ($r = .28$; $p < .05$). Moreover, they tended to avoid the use of physical punishment ($r = -.32$; $p < .05$), deprivation of privileges ($r = -.38$; $p < .01$), and nagging and scolding ($r = -.38$; $p < .01$) in disciplining their sons. There were indications that the use of reasoning was more closely associated with nonpunitiveness for the control fathers than it was for the fathers of the aggressive boys. Control fathers who used reasoning were nonpunitive in their handling of aggression toward themselves ($r = -.48$; $p < .02$), toward other adults ($r = -.53$; $p < .01$), and toward peers ($r = -.71$; $p < .001$). They were also unlikely to threaten their sons with withdrawal of love ($r = -.41$;

p < .05). The fact that reasoning was not associated with nonpunitiveness and avoidance of the use of withdrawal of love for the fathers of the aggressive boys supported the impression that there were qualitative differences between fathers of aggressive boys and control fathers in the way in which they employed reasoning.

Of all the techniques of control that have been considered in this chapter, reasoning alone appeared to be associated with the development of guilt. Boys whose parents used reasoning (as assessed from the parent interviews) tended to show high guilt about aggression toward their parents ($r = .30$; $p<$ .05), about aggression toward teachers ($r = .27$; $p<$ .06), and about aggression toward peers ($r = .25$; $p<$ .10). Although these correlations are not high, their consistency gives them increased weight in supporting the hypothesis that parental reasoning is an important antecedent of guilt control.

Use of Models

No significant differences were found between the two groups of parents in their use of positive or of negative models (Table 5-12). As a matter of fact, the parents made very little use of positive examples of behavior, either as exemplified in themselves or in others. They were, however, inclined to make relatively frequent references to examples of how not to behave.

I. In training Harry have you ever said, "Your father does it this way"?

F. (Case 5) I try not to. I may have on occasions, but I don't try to hold myself as an example. In fact, I try to do just the opposite. I'd like him to get a little further than I am.

I. Is there anybody else whom you might hold up as an example?

F. Yes, on occasion I have. I mainly try to introduce him and let him figure it out for himself; this guy got somewhere because of what he did. Usually do it through hints, rather than yakking at him. Sometimes it gets out of hand, and you start yakking about it before you realize it.

TABLE 5-12

USE OF MODELS: DIFFERENCES BETWEEN PARENTS OF
AGGRESSIVE AND CONTROL BOYS

Scales	Aggressive Group		Control Group		t	p
	Mean	S.D.	Mean	S.D.		
Data from Father Interviews						
Positive models	3.90	2.31	3.83	2.35	0.10	N.S.
Negative models	6.94	1.85	6.00	2.12	1.81	<.10
Data from Mother Interviews						
Positive models	4.25	2.05	3.88	2.78	0.49	N.S.
Negative models	6.38	2.39	6.38	1.83	0.00	N.S.

These scales were not used as bases for prediction.

I. Is there anyone you mention as an example of what not to do?
F. Yes, definitely. Usually it's a—well, I try to show him some of the
seamier side of some of the fellows that have fallen apart, some
bums. Take him to skid row and let him make sure he sees what
goes on down there. At the same time I show him what happens to
kids that fall apart. He's very susceptible to being tempted by
other kids. But that's got to go, too. He's got to more or less make
his own way and not be tempted too much. Temptation is going
to come in from every angle more and more.

As the excerpt above illustrates, the negative models were
usually extreme examples such as notorious criminals, delinquents, and alcoholic or psychopathic relatives.

Some reasons for the parents' reluctance to use positive
examples of behavior were provided by the parents themselves. Many of them regarded the use of such examples not
as a form of guidance but rather as a form of punishment or
rejection.

I. In training Arnold have you ever said, "Your father does it this
way"?
M. (Case 21) That's something that I never believed in, because as a
youngster my mother always held up some of her good girls to me,
which made me absolutely dislike them. "Somebody did this and
somebody did that, why don't you do that?" I know how it hurt

me and I've never used that on Arnold because I don't think it's fair.

Some of the parents, too, seemed to be somewhat self-deprecating and consequently felt that they were not good enough models for imitation. They hoped to see their sons become more adequate persons than they felt themselves to be.

I. In training Vincent have you ever said, "Your father does it this way"?

F. (Case 48) No. I try to stay away from that. I recognize my own blunders and weaknesses too much, so I wouldn't do that.

Moreover, a few of the parents felt that with the rapidly changing patterns of life, their attitudes and ways of doing things could no longer suffice as examples for their sons to follow.

I. In training Peter have you ever said, "Your father does it this way"?

F. (Case 34) No. I don't think I've ever tried to say—to do that, because I know things have changed so fast nowadays. The old-fashioned ways are on the way out, and there's not much point trying to uphold something that's gone.

Parental Agreement about Child-Training Practices

The prediction that the parents of the aggressive boys would show greater interparental disagreement about aspects of the child-training process than would the control parents was only in part confirmed (Table 5-13). The fathers of the control group reported significantly more agreement with their wives about the enforcement of restrictions than did the fathers of the aggressive boys, but other differences, though generally in the predicted direction, failed to reach significance.

Parents who are essentially in agreement about their child-training practices are more likely to share the responsibility of making and enforcing decisions about the ways in which their children should be handled. Moreover, such sharing of responsibilities should provide a greater degree of consistency between the parents in their handling of their

TABLE 5-13

PARENTAL AGREEMENT: DIFFERENCES BETWEEN PARENTS
OF AGGRESSIVE AND CONTROL BOYS

Scales	Aggressive Group		Control Group		t	p
	Mean	S.D.	Mean	S.D.		
Data from Father Interviews						
Agreement: responsibilities	9.06	1.45	8.83	1.43	0.58	N.S.
Agreement: enforcement of restrictions	7.60	1.85	8.56	1.58	1.81	<.05
Agreement: discipline	7.10	2.09	7.62	1.85	0.91	N.S.
Degree of joint participation in training policies	7.67	1.74	8.71	1.54	2.12	<.05 (.02)[a]
Data from Mother Interviews						
Agreement: responsibilities	8.75	1.40	8.79	1.34	0.10	N.S.
Agreement: enforcement of restrictions	7.81	1.87	8.29	1.53	0.80	N.S.
Agreement: discipline	6.38	2.20	7.31	1.96	1.53	<.10
Degree of joint participation in training policies	6.44	2.40	6.52	1.53	0.19	N.S.

[a] The probability in parentheses is based on the Wilcoxon Test.

children. It is consequently of considerable interest to find that the fathers of the control boys reported more joint participation by themselves and their wives in setting policies and making and enforcing decisions about their children than did the fathers of the aggressive boys (Table 5-13).

More marked differences between the groups of parents might have been expected. Ratings on the agreement scales were, however, primarily based on very specific questions that were probably far too direct and tended to elicit rather stereotyped accounts of high agreement from most of the parents. Indeed, the interviews with some of the parents of the aggressive boys provided quite obvious indications of interparental disagreement, which these parents were nevertheless inclined to deny when they were directly questioned on this topic.

In order to study the correlates of parental agreement, ratings on the three agreement scales were combined for each parent. Mothers who showed high agreement with their husbands tended also to show a good deal of warmth for ($r = .38$; $p < .01$), and little hostility toward ($r = -.69$; $p < .001$), them. Not only did these mothers express positive attitudes toward their husbands, but they were also less rejecting of ($r = -.41$; $p < .01$), and less hostile toward ($r = -.49$; $p < .001$), their sons. Moreover, they tended to foster their sons' dependency by spending a good deal of time with them during the boys' early years ($r = .26$; $p < .06$), by encouraging them to spend time in their company ($r = .30$; $p < .05$) and to seek their help ($r = .44$; $p < .02$), and by avoiding punishing their sons for wanting to spend time with them ($r = -.26$; $p < .06$). They tended to rely on reasoning as a means of control ($r = .38$; $p < .01$), and to avoid the more punitive disciplinary techniques such as withdrawal of love ($r = -.36$; $p < .02$), ridicule ($r = -.33$; $p < .05$), physical punishment ($r = -.22$; $p < .15$), and deprivation of privileges ($r = -.33$; $p < .05$). They were also inclined to set firm and consistent limits on their sons' behavior by demands for obedience ($r = .32$; $p < .05$) and by consistently following through with these demands ($r = .36$; $p < .02$).

There was no evidence that fathers who showed high agreement with their wives had attitudes toward their sons that differed from those of fathers who showed low agreement. On the other hand, they tended to show a good deal of warmth and affection for their wives ($r = .41$; $p < .01$) and to display little hostility toward them ($r = -.65$; $p < .001$).

Boys' Resistance to Discipline

The mothers of the aggressive boys reported much more resistance to their discipline than did the mothers of the control boys. From the fathers' reports it appeared that the aggressive boys might be also somewhat more resistant to their fathers' discipline than were the control boys (Table 5-14).

TABLE 5-14

PARENTS' ACCOUNT OF BOYS' RESISTANCE TO DISCIPLINE:
DIFFERENCES BETWEEN PARENTS OF
AGGRESSIVE AND CONTROL BOYS

Scales	Aggressive Group		Control Group			
	Mean	S.D.	Mean	S.D.	t	p
Resistance to father's discipline	6.38	2.01	5.60	1.92	1.67	<.10
Resistance to mother's discipline	7.33	1.05	5.90	1.83	3.40	<.01

The majority of the control boys would feel some resentment when they were disciplined but this resentment was fairly mild and short-lived.

I. When you punish or tell him off, how does he react?

M. (Case 4) Sometimes he just listens, and then sometimes he gets a little annoyed with me if I scold. He'll give his opinion on it if he thinks I'm not being fair, or he'll ask why—except with his dad. He'll never question him at all. He'll just stand there and listen. If I scold him, he'll say, "Well, Mother, that isn't fair. I think such and such," and gives his viewpoint on it.

I. Do you think he resents being punished?

M. Well, I think sometimes he sort of resents it, but he knows it should be and he accepts it. He knows he has it coming. If he resents it, he'll go up to his room and work it out of his system there in some manner. And then he'll come down, and everything is as friendly as if it had never occurred.

Some of the control parents reported that their sons would feel guilty about their resentment and would apologize or otherwise attempt to make amends.

I. When you punish or tell him off, how does he react?

F. (Case 30) He doesn't like it at first but he finally—lots of times he's been reprimanded and he comes up and says, "Well, Daddy, I'm sorry. I was wrong," and he apologizes. I made him apologize to his mother sometimes, and he's seen the light. He knows he's been wrong.

I. Do you think he resents being punished?

F. Yes, he doesn't like it, but he doesn't mind it if he's wrong. He's a man about it.

On the other hand, many parents of aggressive boys, particularly mothers, reported that their sons strongly resented any punishment they received. Moreover, they sometimes described their sons as harboring a grudge and seeking ways in which they might retaliate.

I. When you punish or tell him off, how does he react?

M. (Case 33) Sometimes he'll pout for a little while, go to his room. He would pout and carry that grudge, that feeling, until he felt he got back at you some way.

•   •   •

I. When you punish or tell him off, how does he react?

M. (Case 15) He doesn't react very gracefully to a bawling-out. He reacts more favorably to being deprived of money or not being allowed out. But bawling-out doesn't do Duncan any good. Makes him very resentful. Then he, in turn, turns around and does something else to show his resentment.

METHODS OF DISCIPLINE: RESULTS FROM BOYS' INTERVIEWS

Estimates of the frequency with which the parents used certain disciplinary techniques were made from the interviews with the boys. The data secured from these interviews were, however, far less adequate than the parent data. In the interviews with the boys less time was spent on the subject of the parents' disciplinary practices, and cues from other sections of the interviews were not plentiful. Moreover, the boys tended merely to contrast their two parents rather than to give a detailed description of each parent's disciplinary practices. Conclusions about the influence of parental discipline were therefore drawn primarily from the parent data. Nevertheless, the boys' interviews provided some valuable supplementary information.

The differences reported in Table 5-15 indicated that the aggressive boys tended to give a more unfavorable picture of their fathers than they did of their mothers. The two groups of boys did not differ significantly in their accounts

TABLE 5-15

BOYS' ACCOUNTS OF THEIR PARENTS' DISCIPLINARY PRACTICES:
DIFFERENCES BETWEEN AGGRESSIVE AND CONTROL BOYS

Scales	Aggressive Group		Control Group			
	Mean	S.D.	Mean	S.D.	t	p
Father's use of:						
Material rewards	4.88	2.07	5.10	2.19	0.35	N.S.
Praise	4.79	2.07	5.27	1.81	0.84	N.S.
Physical punishment	6.15	1.59	5.31	1.88	2.06	<.05
Deprivation of privileges	6.00	1.90	5.48	2.04	1.20	N.S.
Ridicule	3.41	1.71	2.89	1.44	1.79	<.05
Nagging and scolding[a]	4.96	2.42	4.15	1.26	1.38	N.S.
Withdrawal of love	3.56	2.28	4.06	1.82	0.89	N.S.
Reasoning	2.67	1.31	4.15	2.78	2.50	<.01
Mother's use of:						
Material rewards	4.42	1.96	5.15	2.09	1.23	N.S.
Praise	5.92	1.72	5.81	1.91	0.20	N.S.
Physical punishment	5.67	2.55	5.42	1.95	0.36	N.S.
Deprivation of privileges	5.54	2.22	5.48	2.21	0.11	N.S.
Ridicule	3.19	2.07	2.65	1.09	1.21	N.S.
Nagging and scolding[a]	5.31	2.43	5.94	1.53	1.13	N.S.
Withdrawal of love	4.06	2.60	4.52	2.34	0.68	N.S.
Reasoning	2.94	1.68	3.23	2.20	0.54	N.S.

[a] This scale was not used as a basis for prediction.

of the frequency or nature of the disciplinary practices of
their mothers. On the other hand, the fathers of the aggressive boys were reported to use more physical punishment
and less reasoning than the control fathers. These findings
are confirmatory of the differences that emerged from the
ratings of the father interviews. The fathers of the aggressive boys were, in addition, depicted by their sons as using
a significantly greater amount of ridicule, a difference that
was not evident from the ratings of the father interviews.

The boy in Case 9 provided a description of a father who
was inclined both to ridicule his son and to punish him
physically.

I. If you do something your father doesn't like, something he thinks
is wrong, what sort of things does he do?

B. (Case 9) He usually won't let me go to the show and, if it's bad enough, he'll give me a whipping.
I. What if you don't obey him?
B. He'll give me a slap in the face and tell me get out there and do what he wants me to do.
I. How often does he slap you?
B. Not too often any more.
I. How about when you were younger?
B. Well, that's when I was more bad. I used to get into all kinds of trouble and then I used to get whippings all the time. . . .
I. Has he ever made you look silly in front of other people?
B. Well, yeah, sometimes he does.
I. What does he say?
B. Well, see, I got these ears, and they call me "Ears." And then, when me and he get mad at each other, I go outside. And he says, "Come on 'Ears,' come on 'Dumbo.' " Tells me something like that, gets me all mad. He don't like that name, calls me "Ears," "Dumbo," something like that. My ears stick out, so they call me "Ears."

It is interesting to note the boys did not, according to their accounts, differ in the extent to which they expressed resistance to their mothers' discipline, but differed significantly in their resistance to their fathers' discipline (Table 5-16).

TABLE 5-16

RESISTANCE TO PARENTS' DISCIPLINE: DIFFERENCES BETWEEN
AGGRESSIVE AND CONTROL BOYS

Scales	Aggressive Group		Control Group		t	p
	Mean	S.D.	Mean	S.D.		
Resistance to father's discipline	4.27	2.04	2.90	1.62	2.61	<.01
Resistance to mother's discipline	3.73	2.37	3.00	1.74	1.24	N.S.

The boys' reports concerning parental discipline provided further evidence that in the families of the aggressive boys there had been a greater disruption of the boys' relationships to their fathers than of their relationships to the mothers. These reports were probably of greater importance from this point of view than for the information that they provided about the parents' disciplinary techniques.

DISCUSSION

The findings reported in this chapter suggest that the aggressive boys had been subjected to fewer socialization pressures than had the control boys. Their parents expected less of them in the way of school achievement and, according to the boys, were also less likely to place responsibilities on them. More important, perhaps, was the ineffectiveness of the aggressive boys' mothers as socializing influences. These mothers placed fewer limits on their sons' behavior in the home than did the control mothers. They were also less demanding of obedience and less consistent in enforcing this demand.

The effectiveness of any demands or limits that parents may impose is probably in part determined by the quality of the affectional relationships between the parents and their children. In Chapter 2 it was shown that the aggressive boys had stronger affectional ties to their mothers than they had to their fathers. Thus, although the fathers of the aggressive boys were more demanding of obedience, and more consistent in enforcing this demand, than were their wives, these demands had probably less effect on the boys than if they had been exerted by their mothers. Indeed, their mothers' failure to exert strong and consistent socialization pressures may have been an important factor contributing to the lack of self-control that characterized the aggressive boys.

Although the restrictions and demands imposed on the aggressive boys were, both according to themselves and according to their parents, somewhat less extensive than those placed on the control boys, they were much more inclined to resist and resent them. Their resistance seemed partly to reflect their hostility toward their parents and partly to be a manifestation of their anxiety about being placed in a dependent role. Indeed, by the time their sons had reached adolescence, the parents of the aggressive boys were faced with a dilemma. On the one hand, the boys required close surveillance and control to keep them out of further trouble;

on the other hand, they tended to develop further resentment and hostility when any attempt was made to control them. Moreover, because of their increasing physical maturity and independence, they could, as the years went by, increasingly ignore and even control their parents, who were rapidly losing their potential effectiveness as the primary socializing agents.

It is possible that there is a certain critical period during which socialization pressures will be most effective and beyond which they will be of little avail. During the early years of his life, a child is almost entirely dependent on his parents for food, shelter, protection, entertainment, love, and acceptance. Since the parents are at this time the main sources of the child's primary and secondary rewards, they are in a position to exercise a great deal of control over him. If socialization demands are applied during this period when the parents' nurturance and approval are very important to the child, he should be strongly motivated to do what his parents expect of him in order to maintain his dependent security. By the time of adolescence, however, the child is relatively self-sufficient. He can gain employment and provide for his physical needs. Even in the satisfaction of his emotional needs his parents occupy a less important position than they did earlier, since he is likely to rely more and more on his peers for affection and acceptance. If socialization pressures are strongly applied only at this stage in the child's development, he is unlikely to accept parental demands that conflict with his desires, since the parents' withdrawal of physical or emotional support for noncompliance is no longer as threatening as it would have been during his childhood. Some evidence for a critical period in the development of self-control is provided by Whiting and Child (1953), who found a negative relationship between age at onset of socialization pressures and strength of guilt feelings. In other words, the earlier the pressures were applied, the stronger was the conscience development as measured by their cultural index of guilt.

In their disciplinary practices, the parents of the control boys were more likely to employ methods that seemed to foster the development of internal controls, while the parents of the aggressive boys were more prone to rely on coercive methods. It is evident that the frequency of occurrence of parental disciplinary activities depends not only on the readiness with which the parents respond in a disciplinary manner but also on the frequency of behavioral episodes that require disciplining. A greater frequency of disciplinary activities by the parents of the aggressive boys could therefore be, in part, a response to the aggression and recalcitrance of their sons. Since, however, differences were found between the groups of parents in respect to some forms of discipline and not in respect to others, it seems reasonable to conclude that the differences that were found between the parent groups reflect a different relative preference for certain techniques. Moreover, some evidence was obtained that the degree of parental warmth and affection may play an important part in determining the type of disciplinary methods a parent is likely to favor. For example, parents who were lacking in affectional nurturance were prone to favor methods of punishment rather than methods of reward.

Of all the methods of correction that were investigated, only reasoning was associated with parental warmth and nurturance, and reasoning alone was associated with measures of the boys' guilt. In contrast, all other disciplinary measures—physical punishment, deprivation of privileges, ridicule, nagging and scolding, and withdrawal of love— were associated with parental rejection and punitiveness. It was, therefore, of considerable interest to find that while the parents of the control boys made greater use of reasoning as a method of control, the parents of the aggressive boys (either the mothers or the fathers or both) made more frequent use of all other disciplinary methods with the exception of withdrawal of love. The relationship of these latter methods with other aspects of the parents' behavior, and also with measures of the boys' behavior, suggested that they were associated with the development of hostility and aggression.

While it was assumed at the outset of this study that the use of threats of withdrawal of love would foster the development of control by guilt, it now seems likely that such threats, at least when used in disciplining an adolescent, are not only indicative of parental rejection but may actually foster aggression.

Of considerable interest from the general standpoint of the study was the fact that the groups of boys did not greatly differ in the picture they gave of their mothers as disciplinary agents, while they differed considerably in the picture they presented of their fathers, with the control fathers being placed in a much more favorable light. Indeed, the total evidence from all three sets of interviews suggested that the aggressive boys had experienced fathers who were harsh and punitive in their handling of their sons and mothers who placed fewer limits on their behavior and were somewhat inconsistent and vacillating. While the fathers' behavior provided the boys with predominantly aggressive and punitive models for imitation, their mothers' tendency to make relatively few demands and to overlook noncompliance may have fostered the development of aggressive, defiant patterns of behavior.

Chapter 6

Identification and the Internalization of Controls

It is now apparent that parental demands and discipline greatly influence the socialization of the child. The parents, however, cannot be continuously present to guide and direct the child's behavior. Successful socialization therefore requires the gradual substitution of internal controls and direction for external sanctions and demands. Once such self-direction is achieved, laws and outer authority are for the most part no longer required to deter the individual from antisocial behavior. His own self-demands and self-respect serve as his main guides and deterrents. In the absence of such internalized values and controls, the individual behaves much like a weathervane, continuously changing with the varied environmental pressures that impinge upon him and, whenever his desires conflict with the demands of society, external restraints in the form of laws, penalties, and enforcing agents are necessary to insure that he does not completely disregard the rights and wishes of others.

It has been suggested in Chapter 3 that the aggressive boys were restrained from aggression in the home primarily through fear of retaliation by their parents, whereas the control boys were restrained primarily through anticipation of the guilt that they would feel if they aggressed. In

Chapter 4 evidence was provided that the aggressive boys were more likely to deviate sexually when there was little danger of being caught; this, too, suggested that they had weaker internal controls than had the control boys. In this chapter, data both from the boys' interviews and from the thematic deviation test will be examined for evidence that the aggressive boys had failed to internalize parental standards and values. In addition, some of the child-training factors that appear to be conducive to the internalization of parental standards will be discussed.

A Theory of the Acquisition of Internal Controls

All children are subject to the process of socialization involving the subjugation of impulses to the demands of society. At first, control is necessarily external; the infant or very young child is restrained only through the direct intervention of his parents. It is not long, however, before the child learns to discriminate between actions that are approved and actions that are disapproved and to anticipate rewarding or punishing consequences of his behavior. Although the child may now try to conform to his parents' demands and prohibitions, the control they exercise is still largely external. The child is, at this stage of his development, primarily *fear-controlled*. Since the child's self-control is dependent upon anticipation of external punishment, the continual presence of a controlling adult is still essential to insure that he does not transgress. The fear of punishment alone is therefore not a very effective deterrent to antisocial behavior. In situations in which there is little risk of getting caught or the punishment that the child anticipates is mild, he may not hesitate to transgress.

It is only when his parents' standards of behavior have been accepted as his own that the child will observe their prohibitions at times when it is likely that a transgression will be undiscovered. The achievement of such internalized prohibitions is a gradual process and is probably never, for most individuals, completely achieved. Even the normal adult may at times be restrained from transgressing only by fear of external consequences. Nevertheless, over a gradually widening range of behavior and with more and more consistency, the actions of the developing individual become subject to a new kind of restraint, that of *conscience* or *control by guilt*. The anticipation of guilt feelings, involving remorse, self-criticism, and loss of self-esteem, now deter him from acting in socially disapproved ways.

The operation of conscience-control is manifested in two principal ways. In the first place, the individual will *resist performing acts* that run counter to his standards of behavior even when the deviation is unlikely to be detected. Secondly, if he does temporarily yield to impulse, he will *feel guilty* and attempt restitution even when his transgression remains undiscovered.

Inhibition of antisocial tendencies can be most clearly illustrated by means of the boys' stories to the deviation test that will be described in some detail shortly. The story quoted below was elicited to an item describing a boy who went out to buy a baseball mitt; upon discovering that he had lost his money, he is tempted to steal the mitt instead.

B. (Case 46) Well, he was just about to, to tuck it under his jacket and walk out, when he changed his mind. He decided to be honest with himself and so he kept on looking at the mitt; and when the clerk came up, he explained the situation to the clerk. The clerk lets him get it on the—with written I.O.U. that he would pay him in, within a certain time. He was torn between a, uh, desire to be on the team and, uh, have the catcher's mitt and his moral outlook on life. And his moral outlook on life won.

By contrast, in the story quoted below the boy deviates quite readily. This story was given to a picture depicting a boy about to steal some auto parts.

B. (Case 23) Looks like me (laughs). Well, this here looks like it's in an auto shop in school or an auto shop in the Grand Auto Store, man. This looks, looks like he's in there and looking around, trying to boost something, you know. He looks like he's getting it, too. He probably thinks he needs it for his car. And nobody's going to see him and, what, it only costs two dollars or something. If he gets caught with the stuff, he's going up for six months. But it looks like he's playing it pretty cool now. He's gonna walk out of the store with what he's got. But he's feeling, he's feeling pretty good. He's thinking nobody saw him or anything, which most probably they didn't, 'cause there's only about four people working in the Grand Auto Store and it's a big store.

In both of the preceding examples the boys apparently experience relatively little conflict; in the first case the anticipation of guilt is so strong that the boy is not too readily tempted to deviate, while in the second case there is little or no guilt to conflict with, and thereby inhibit, the tendency to transgress. The next example is one in which the competing tendencies are equally strong. The boy is caught between his strong desire for the baseball glove and his equally strong guilt over stealing. As he starts to steal the glove, guilt feelings are aroused that motivate him to return it. Thus he vacillates in a conflict which he finally resolves by removing himself from the temptation altogether.

B. (Case 17) So Dave picks up the glove, looks around, sees the guy is still downstairs. He puts—grabs the glove and puts it under his jacket and starts, starts to walk out. He thinks, "Well, I'm not gonna get nowheres this way because it's, this isn't the right way to do it." So he goes back, and the clerk sees him. So he stays back to see if he will take the glove. So he goes, Dave walks back to the counter and puts the glove down. He looks around and doesn't see anybody; and he picks it back up and starts to walk out. And he gets as far as the door and he thinks, "Aw, I better not take it. It's not right." So he walks back and puts the glove down. He looks around. The clerk's still down in the—"Gee, I had a lot, a lot of chances to take this glove. The clerk would never miss it and he's got a lot of gloves here." So he picks it up and starts to walk out again. Thinks, "Well, probably if I took this glove, I wouldn't, I wouldn't feel right. My parents wouldn't feel, feel too good about it if they ever found out." So he walks back and he puts the glove down and he starts to walk out. . . .

The second way in which the operation of conscience is manifested is well illustrated by a story given by a control boy to Card Number 2. This card depicts a boy about to pick up a purse that is lying on a sidewalk.

B. (Case 12) This boy, Tom, he was walkin' down the street. He started to think how he could get some money to take his girl out and he's coming down the street and looks down and found a purse. He looked in the purse and got to thinking about he could use the money. But he looked at the person's name. It was, he started to think it over; and the more he thought, the more he could use the money. So he put the money in his pocket and kept the purse, though. He got home and he was getting ready and he looks at the purse again. He sort of, conscience bothers him about taking the money, so he phoned up his girl and told her he couldn't come and get her tonight. He went and took the purse back to the lady. When he tried to find the place, it was pretty down in the Styx. The more he looked at where the address was, the more he knew he should take the money back. So when he got down to the pretty, pretty beat, run down—so he took the money up, and this little old lady came out and thanked him very much. After he gave her back the money, he knew he did the right thing.

In the above story the boy yields to temptation, but then *feels guilty* and attempts to repair the situation even though his transgression has not been noticed. The following story, told by an aggressive boy, stands in marked contrast to the one just quoted. In this story the deviator intellectually recognizes that the act of stealing is wrong, but is not motivated by feelings of guilt to attempt restitution.

B. (Case 23) This kid looks like he's coming along the street, and he sees this purse down there and he don't know what to do. I think he's going to bend down and pick up the purse, and he smiles and looks in to see who it belongs to and take it back again. But he probably boosts the purse and makes out with the money, you know. But he ain't even got the purse, he just thought of it. Probably looks for identification. He'll take the money and leave the purse. That's what I would do. He probably thinks it's going to be easy money, makes himself some easy money. Why work if you can steal it? That ain't the right attitude, but it's one way of getting it.

The operation of conscience, then, involves both *inhibition of impulse,* and *feelings of guilt* when restraints have temporarily broken down. Indeed, when conscience has adequately developed, the mere thought of a transgression is sufficient to arouse feelings of guilt. Internalized controls have by this time to a large extent replaced the purely external controls of an earlier period of life.

Identification

The development of internal controls is accomplished largely through the process of identification. As defined by Sears (1951*b*), identification is an acquired drive for which the satisfying goal response is *acting like another person.* This process appears to be a result not so much of direct training by the parents, but rather of active learning by the child of attitudes and values which his parents need not have attempted to teach directly. The child, in other words, imitates his parents' behavior. For example, his expressions of approval and disapproval of other children and the admonishments that he hands out to them often clearly reflect the attitudes and demands of his own parents. In early childhood, too, when he plays with dolls or joins in games with other children, he frequently adopts the adult role and evaluates himself and others in accordance with the standards he has acquired from his parents.

Identification greatly hastens the socialization process. Through imitation the child learns from his parents a good deal of his behavioral repertoire without having to go through an extensive trial and error procedure to determine which patterns of behavior are rewarded in the particular society in which he lives (Miller and Dollard, 1941).

According to psychoanalytic theory as elaborated by Sears (1957) and Whiting (1954), the process of identification originates in the dependency relationship. Since the mother is repeatedly associated with the satisfaction of the young child's physical needs, many of the mother's qualities and actions take on secondary reward value; in other words, the child grows to need and value the presence and qualities of the mother for their own sake. The mother's attention, however, cannot remain completely centered on the child; there is inevitably some gradual withdrawal of support and attention. Moreover, training in independence, though a long process, begins early in life. The child, however, wants to retain his mother's affection and attention and will do whatever he can to maintain them.

One means of obtaining attention and approval is to imitate the behavior of the parents. Since the parents are likely to be pleased, and even flattered, whenever the child expresses their attitudes or emulates their behavior, such imitation is likely to bring the rewards that the child is seeking. Moreover, expressions of self-disapproval or self-criticism following misbehavior will often serve to reinstate the parents' love and approval and thereby reinforce the imitation of their negative evaluations.

Imitation is rewarding to the child in still another way. The child learns early to reproduce the parents' affectionate behavior and thus to reward himself by expressions of self-approval and self-love. Whiting and Child (1953) present an excellent description of this process.

> We suggest that the basic process responsible for socialization through identification is one of the child's learning to substitute self-love for love from others when and if the latter is withheld at a time when the child strongly needs to be loved. The reward of self-love is obtained by imitating the evaluative behavior of the parents, and is provided by the child to itself in situations similar to those in which the parents have provided special indications of love. Under these conditions self-love is thus tied to conformity with cultural rules, for it is conformity rather than non-conformity which has previously led to parental love. Self-blame thus serves an instrumental role in inhibiting the child's transgressions of cultural rules and facilitating the conformity which will provide the cue for his self-love.
>
> At the same time self-blame can serve the same instrumental role in relation to the child's striving still in actuality for the love of the parents. Like the striving for self-love, this striving too would be expected to be more intense when parental love is withheld at a time when the child strongly needs to be loved. Reinforcement of self-blame through renewed parental love may be a powerful influence on the initial development of feelings of guilt, though we would suspect that their continued maintenance throughout life is dependent upon the taking over of the parent's role by the person's own imitation of their evaluative responses (Whiting and Child, 1953, pp. 260-261).

Through the repeated association of imitative behavior with reward, the child becomes motivated to behave like the parent. In other words, imitative behavior has become rewarding in itself.

HYPOTHESES

Clinical case studies of aggressive antisocial boys have seemed to indicate that an outstanding characteristic of these children is an absence of, or defective, conscience development (Aichhorn, 1935; Bender, 1947; Friedlander, 1947; Goldfarb, 1955; Greenacre, 1943; Jenkins and Hewitt, 1944; Johnson, 1949). These clinical observations have received some support in such systematic studies as, for example, that of the McCords (1956), who used an incomplete story method to assess guilt. Each of the McCords' stories described a situation in which the central character violated some standard of behavior. This fantasy measure of guilt successfully differentiated groups manifesting differing degrees of self-control. Nondelinquent school children gave, on the average, 82 per cent guilt responses; neurotic and psychotic children gave 67 per cent; children diagnosed as behavior disorders gave 54 per cent; finally, psychopaths, who presumably are characterized by a very weak conscience development, gave only 46 per cent guilt responses.

On the basis of such considerations, the hypothesis was put forward that the group of aggressive boys would present weak internal controls stemming from a lack of internalization of parental standards. This hypothesis implied that the control boys would be deterred from socially disapproved acts mainly by feelings of guilt, whereas the aggressive boys would be deterred primarily by fear of punishment by others. It also implied that the aggressive boys would show less identification with their parents, both mother and father, than would their controls.

In addition to the more general hypotheses concerning the deficient conscience development of the aggressive boys, other more specific hypotheses were advanced. These related to child-training factors believed by Sears and Whiting to be determinants of identification.

Sears and Whiting consider that the degree of *affectional nurturance* that a child receives plays an important role in the identification process. If the parents are continuously present and always gratify the child's needs, he will have little incentive to perform the parent behavior himself or to comply with the parents' demands. The parents in this case exact no price for their approval. Some of the findings of Levy's (1943) study of maternal overprotection are relevant in this connection. Levy found two patterns of maternal overprotection, an indulgent and a domineering pattern. The overprotected children who later developed aggressive, acting-out behavior were found exclusively in the group that had received a good deal of indulgent nurturance coupled with few socialization pressures. In contrast, the behavior of children who had experienced the domineering form of overprotection was largely characterized by anxious submissiveness.

If, at the other extreme, the parents are cold and rejecting, the child will experience little or no reward for adopting the parents' behavior and attitudes. One might expect, therefore, as Sears (1951*b*) has pointed out, a curvilinear relationship between parental warmth and the child's identification, with strong identification being associated with moderate warmth and weak identification with very low or very high parental warmth. Such a relationship has, in fact, been reported by Shaplin (1954) in a study of pre-adolescent boys. Children of cold and of extremely warm mothers showed less self-control, estimated from a composite score of guilt on a sentence-completion deviation test and a measure of the degree to which the child had adopted the parents' demands and characteristics, than did children whose mothers were moderately warm. No significant relationship, however, was found between the fathers' warmth and the boys' self-control.

Several additional studies have yielded results suggesting that there is some relationship between identification and parental warmth. Sears, Maccoby, and Levin (1957), for example, found that a high degree of conscience development was less often encountered among children who were rejected than among children who were accepted. Similarly, Heinicke (1953) found that children who showed high guilt in a doll-play deviation test and an interview dealing with reactions to transgressions had mothers who were significantly warmer than the mothers of children who responded with little guilt. P.S. Sears (1953), in another doll-play study, found that boys of warm, affectionate fathers tended to play the father-role in doll-play activities more frequently than boys whose fathers were relatively cold.

In a study of father-identification among adolescent boys, Payne and Mussen (1956) obtained analogous results. Boys who showed high or low identification with their fathers, as measured by father-son similarity in response to items on a personality questionnaire, were administered an incomplete stories test designed to assess the boys' perception of the parent-child relationship. Analysis of the data revealed that high father-identification was associated with the perception of the father as a highly rewarding and affectionate person.

The hypothesis that there is a curvilinear relationship between parental warmth and degree of identification, and Levy's finding that indulgent overprotective mothers tend to produce aggressive sons, could lead to the prediction that parents of aggressive boys might be either very warm and accepting or very cold and rejecting. However, the majority of investigations cited above, as well as the results of studies of delinquency to which reference has been made in previous chapters, suggest that parents of antisocial aggressive children are likely to be lacking in warmth and affection. For this and other reasons given in Chapter 2, it was predicted that the parents of the aggressive boys would show less warmth for their sons than would the parents of the control boys.

The *methods of discipline* that parents employ in handling their children may also influence the development of identification. It was predicted in Chapter 5 that love-oriented disciplinary methods should be more effective in the development of guilt-control than the physical forms of discipline. The withholding of love and approval until the child performs the behavior that his parents desire is likely to lead him to adopt his parents' demands and standards of behavior as a way of reinstating and maintaining their love.

Since a child's basic attitudes and patterns of behavior are acquired through imitation of what he sees in others, his socialization should be facilitated if his parents themselves exemplify the behavior they wish him to exhibit. Merely providing a model for imitation is not, however, sufficient. Whether or not the model of behavior that the parents provide will be imitated will in part depend upon the *affectional relationships* within the family and the *prestige of the parent models*. Consequently, the parents' affection for each other and the boys' affection for his parents should be important factors in promoting identification.

One would expect a child to learn more rapidly to copy a model with high prestige than a model with low prestige, since the imitation of a highly regarded person is likely to be more rewarding (Miller and Dollard, 1941). If the mother and father have a good deal of affection for each other, imitation of parental models should be facilitated. The mother's attitude and feelings toward the father may be particularly influential in the development of the masculine-role identification of a male child. If the mother loves and admires her husband, she is likely to welcome the boy's imitation of the father's behavior and attitudes. The boy's father-identification will therefore be rewarded not only by his father but by his mother as well. On the other hand, if the parents have little affection for each other, the boy will be less motivated to identify with the father. Moreover, such a situation places the boy in a dilemma. If he tries to emulate his father, he is apt to lose his mother's approval and acceptance. That parental antagonism may influence the boy's identification even during his early years is suggested by the finding of P. S. Sears

(1953) that five-year-old boys who adopted the mother's role most strongly in doll-play activities had mothers who were warm and affectionate, but who also were critical in their evaluation of their husbands. It was predicted, therefore, that the parents of the aggressive boys would have less warmth for each other than would the parents of the control boys.

In order to motivate a child to imitate his parents, not only must the parents love and admire each other but the child must also love and admire them. Even if the parents exhibit the kinds of behavior that they want their child to learn, this is likely to have little influence on him if he rejects them as models. This reasoning is supported by the Gluecks' study of delinquency (1950), in which it was found that delinquent boys did not identify themselves with, or strive to emulate, their fathers as much as did nondelinquent boys. In fact, many delinquent boys felt that their fathers were entirely unacceptable as models on which to pattern their own behavior. Such considerations led to the prediction that the aggressive boys would show less warmth toward their parents than would the control boys.

Every culture includes, to some extent, a differentiation of sex roles. Consequently, if a male child is to make an adequate sociosexual adjustment, he must eventually model his behavior on that of adult males. Of the factors that have been discussed in the paragraphs above, the most important may be the mother's warmth for her husband and the husband's warmth for the boy, since these factors should promote identification with the male parent. Such an identification may, in addition, be facilitated in families that strongly emphasize the learning of sex-appropriate behavior by the male child. This emphasis should appear most readily in families in which there is a close affectional tie between husband and wife and in which both parents encourage the boy to model himself after the father. Thus, a greater *encouragement of male-appropriate behavior* was expected from the parents of the control boys than from the parents of the aggressive boys.

MEASURES

A number of the parent measures that are relevant to the discussion of identification have already been presented. The *warmth* scales, one of which has already been described in Chapter 2, were measures of the extent to which affection was demonstrated by the parent to the boy, by the boy to the parent, or by one parent to the other.

The *hostility* scales were based upon the relative number of favorable and unfavorable statements which the interviewee made about the parent's or boy's behavior, as the case might be. In other words, these scales reflected the degree to which the parent (or boy) perceived the other members of the family as having predominantly praiseworthy or predominantly reprehensible characteristics. Thus, they provided indirect estimates of the prestige of the parent models.

A negative, though by no means perfect, relationship between the warmth and the hostility measures was to be expected. The intercorrelations obtained from the adolescent data showed that warmth for the mother correlated —.72 with hostility to the mother; the corresponding figure for the boy's warmth and hostility to the father was —.64. In the case of the fathers, hostility to, and warmth for, the boy correlated —.54; hostility to, and warmth for, the wife correlated —.67. The corresponding correlations for the mother's warmth and hostility were —.47 and —.73.

The scale measuring *parental demands for masculinity* was based on the extent to which parents emphasized differential social training for boys and girls in such matters as dress, household responsibilities, leisure-time activities, and general deportment.

A measure of *identification* is somewhat difficult to obtain from a single interview. It is possible, however, to secure a good deal of indirect information suggesting that much or little identification has taken place. For example, it might be reasonable to infer identification with a parent from the occurrence of guilt when aggression toward that parent has been shown. In order, however, not to confound the measure

of identification with other measures with which it might
have proved to be related, ratings of identification were
based solely on the boy's expressed statements that he felt,
acted, and thought to a greater or lesser extent like one or
the other of his parents. There was thus a danger that the
essential aspect of identification, i.e., the unconscious internalization of the value-system of the parents, might be
missed. Fortunately, within a somewhat lengthy interview,
much of which was taken up by a discussion of family relationships, a boy would often by incidental remarks reveal,
at a time when he was not being directly questioned on the
subject, that he did or did not think and act like his mother
or his father. This supplementary material proved very helpful for securing a rating. A much more adequate measure
would, however, be one which assessed the extent to which
there was congruence between the boy's and the parents'
attitudes and opinions, as expressed in the separate interviews. Unfortunately, the questions were not framed in such
a way as to make a measure of this kind feasible.

A scale was introduced to measure the *boy's relative
preference for living with his mother or his father,* if they
were to separate. Such a preference may well indicate, better than direct questioning on the subject, with which parent
a boy has primarily identified.

Feelings of guilt were assessed in two ways. One set of
estimates was made from the boys' interview data. Separate
ratings were made concerning the amount of guilt that the
boy experienced concerning aggressive and sexual behavior;
in the case of aggression, specific ratings were made for
guilt about aggression toward mother, father, teacher, and
peers. In addition, ratings were made of guilt feelings about
general antisocial behavior.

The other measure of guilt was obtained by means of a
projective test. Each test item depicted a boy either in a
temptation situation or actually violating some commonly
held moral standard (Appendix E). The deviation items depicted hostile-aggressive and sexual behavior; antisocial acts

such as cheating, stealing, and property destruction; and violations of general rules and restrictions.

For each of these situations the boys described the feelings and reactions of the deviating character. Their responses were categorized in two general classes. On the one hand were the reactions that were considered indicative of *guilt feelings*. In general, these were responses in which the deviating character felt remorseful, was punished by himself or by some unspecified agent, or attempted to make restitution in some way. On the other hand were *fear responses* in which the deviator tried to avoid detection or punishment for his behavior.

Guilt Reactions

The following specific categories of response were interpreted as signs of guilt.

Restitution: The deviator spontaneously attempts to make reparation or restitution, i.e., attempts to fix, replace, or "undo" the deviation. The story quoted below is an example of a boy's attempting to make restitution after having expressed death wishes toward his coach.

> Well, Dave would probably try to pitch a real good game. Then, if he did pitch a good game, he'd be feeling awful bad because he did get to pitch, and then the coach did get into an accident when he was hoping it. So he'd probably go out and buy the coach a gift or something. Go to the hospital and see the coach, and come visit him all the time and cheer him up and try to make up to him for wishing that he would, would drop dead when the coach did get hurt bad.

Reformation: The deviator attempts to make up for the damage or injury involved by changing his attitudes, conduct, or pattern of life. Here is an example from a story given to the first picture.

> This guy, he's got himself a new convertible and he's cattin' around on the thing, you know. And he was driving pretty

fast in it and keeps it up for about two weeks. And this picture shows about, uh, goin' a little too fast on a side street. He's coming across and hit this little kid on a bike. . . . The guy doesn't feel like driving again. After the accident he swears he will never drive recklessly again in his whole life.

Apology: The deviator spontaneously apologizes for the deviant act.

Well, he feels pretty bad about what happened to his friend Johnny, so he goes over and tells her (Johnny's mother) he's sorry about what happened. He says, he says, "Well, I'm sorry about what happened."

Injured Feelings: The deviator feels distressed, unhappy, guilty, and remorseful over what he has done.

He probably feels terrible about it all his life. . . . Maybe the psychological effect would be, uh, so profound maybe that, uh, he'd never live it down or, uh, his conscience would hurt him for the rest of his life and his—I think it would change his whole life in that whenever he saw a wrestling match or something he, it would bring back to memory when he saw maybe a couple of kids fighting or wrestling.

Self-Punishment: The deviator criticizes, belittles himself, holds himself in low esteem, or punishes himself in material ways such as imposing penalties on himself.

Well, he's probably very ashamed of himself and, uh, not too surprised because I think he knew. I mean, of course, if the coach told him before, and he was probably more ashamed of himself than surprised. I think he would, he knows the coach didn't forget him and he was just terribly, terribly silly. Maybe a little ashamed to face the coach and ashamed to get—go out and pitch because he, he did, uh, really do an injustice to the coach and probably to himself.

·   ·   ·

After finding out that his friend had drowned because he knocked him overboard, he just hit himself again and again.

Impersonal Punishment: Some general misfortune befalls the deviating character; the agents of the punishment remain unspecified.

> So he took the mitt and went to the game and he started playing the game. He was catching with the glove. And after the game was over, team lost and he couldn't figure out how come they'd lost because they figured they had a pretty good chance of winning, more than the other team, but still they lost. And so he went home and he went to his room and took his glove into his room with him. And he was thinking about how come they lost the game. He couldn't figure it out. And then he happened to think of stealin' that glove. He kept thinking about it and finally figured the reason they had lost the game was probably 'cause he stole the glove instead of paying for it.

Spontaneous Confession: The deviator confesses, without being questioned, that he is responsible for the deviant act.

> Well, Bill put it (mitt) under his jacket and walks out of the store and goes home and tells his father he bought it. He's got it for three, about three weeks, then it starts to get on his conscience and he, he goes in the store and tells the clerk about it.

Critical Evaluation of the Deviating Character: The boy, in telling the story, criticizes, depreciates, or otherwise indicates disapproval of the deviating character.

> This guy and his friend on Friday in school planned to get together that night and have a "drink-up." So, uh, these were unsavory characters here. There weren't many like them, but they were the *bad* of the school.

Moralizing: The boy focuses on the issue of right and wrong, states moral codes, or abstracts the moral of the story.

> Bill puts the mitt under his jacket and he walks out of the store with it. As Bill walks outa the store, he realizes that, if the clerk finds out that he was in the store or somebody sees him, that he's going to get himself in a lot of

trouble, and his parents. Now he isn't gone more than ten feet outa the store and he realizes that he better not take the glove and he comes back and puts it down. By that time the clerk is outa the cellar. Bill tells the clerk what glove he wants. The clerk wraps it up for him, and Bill pays for it. And Bill sees that honesty is the best policy.

In four of the test items, Picture 3 and Stories 1, 3, and 4, the story-character is presented in a situation in which he is strongly tempted to deviate although he has not as yet transgressed. The boys' accounts of the outcome of these situations—whether or not the story character deviates—provided still another estimate of the degree of conscience-control. Furthermore, it was assumed that in these situations reward for not deviating, particularly if given by the boy himself, also reflected the operation of conscience-control. Excerpts to illustrate these two response categories are given below.

Does Not Deviate: The story-character views the situation as a deviation situation, but does not deviate.

> Oh, oh, he was loyal to his parents' rules of not being up late because they had driven it into him all his life. So he just stood at the gate and talked to her for a while and tried to talk her out of her talking him into coming in, see. And he finally succeeded, but not too tactfully; and so she got, she turned around in a huff and went into the house, and he went home. He was on the spot, really. He didn't, he didn't know what to do. He wanted, he was torn between a loyalty to his parents and a friendliness toward the girl, and his loyalty to his parents won out.

Rewarded for Not Deviating: The story-character is rewarded by others for not deviating, e.g., he obtains approval or material rewards; or the rewards are self-administered, e.g., he feels proud of himself, holds himself in high regard.

> He thinks about taking it, but then he decides not to because there's always a chance for him getting caught. And he leaves the store and goes back to look for his money. And he feels pretty good because he avoided the chance of stealing something, and he feels like he has some will-

power. And he goes looking for his money and he finally
finds it. He comes back and buys the mitt. And he thinks
about the way he fought off the temptation for days, and
it gives him a good feeling.

Fear Reactions

The following response categories were interpreted as
signs of fear.

Denial of Deviation: The deviator denies any responsibility for the deviant act when questioned about it.

The auto-dealer finally takes his inventory and he finds that
an auto part is missing. And he has seen the boy in the store
the day that he thought it was taken. So he tells the police
about it. The police come out to the boy's house. The boy
says, "No, I didn't take a thing." He says, "Search my
house. I don't have it." So maybe they take his and his
parents' word for it. So the boy gets away with it.

Flight: The deviator tries to make a quick getaway in
order to avoid detection or punishment.

Well, he starts walking out of the store, sees no one's
around, so he keeps going. He gets around the corner and
starts runnin'. And he, then he went down to the next street
and he waits for the bus, and the bus comes and he gets
on the bus. And all the time he keeps wondering if anybody
ever seen him, but he don't think so and he finally gets
home. So he waits a coupla days and nothing happens.
So he knows they ain't seen him.

Hiding or Concealing: The deviator conceals the evidence
of the deviant act in order to avoid detection or punishment.

Since he's already gotten the mitt, I might as well continue.
He takes it home and hides it in his garage where his
father wouldn't see it, because his father would know it
cost more than ten dollars that he had.

Fear: The deviator is described as feeling apprehensive
or fearful during, or following, the transgression.

He feels nervous and he walks outa the store and then starts
running, still feeling nervous. He loses his glove on the way

when he's running, but he is too scared to go back and look for it.

Additional Categories

Some responses could not be clearly interpreted either as signs of fear or as signs of guilt but seemed nevertheless relevant for a study of conscience control. For example, it was considered a sign of weak conscience development if the story character transgressed and then rewarded himself for deviating successfully.

Rewarded for Deviating Successfully: The story character expresses self-approval, self-praise, and/or other positive feelings for deviating successfully.

> Well, he walks out of the store and he plays in the game with the mitt; and everybody's complimenting it because it's good lookin'. He probably feels proud that he was able to walk out of there (store) and conceal it so well.

Punishment by a specified external agent was a frequent outcome of the stories and was scored under two subcategories.

Physical or Verbal Punishment: Physical or verbal punishment is inflicted upon the deviating character.

> There is this boy, he has exams today, but the night before he went with his girl to a dance. He didn't have a chance to study for the test. When it came time for the test, he didn't know what it was about. So he opened the book; and while he was cheating, the teacher came by and caught him and made him look pretty funny before the rest of the kids and called him a cheater and all that.

Other Punishment: The deviator is ostracized, isolated, or deprived of privileges, e.g., rejected by peers, imprisoned.

> He took the mitt and shows all the fellows, and they ask him where he got it and he says, "Well, I made some money and I bought it." They started to wonder, "Did he really buy the mitt or did he steal it?" So the rest of the boys have a meeting that night and they won't, they decide that Bill couldn't play because they thought that the mitt was taken.

Since the aggressive boys were thought of as being deterred from antisocial acts mainly by fear of consequences, it seemed possible that their stories would contain frequent references to external punishment. Such references may, however, be indicative of high conscience development if the punishment is presented as an appropriate outcome of a deviant act or as a means of reforming the story character, and especially if it takes the form of loss of reputation or social acceptance.

Since the content of the test items dealt with anxiety- and guilt-provoking situations, it was likely that some boys might attempt to alter or distort the stimulus in one way or another. Two forms of distortion were scored.

Redefinition Minus: The boy alters the presented deviation situation in such a way as to make the deviant act *less* serious by changing the responsibility or the seriousness of the act, or by inventing extenuating circumstances. For example, here is a story told to Picture 4 which shows a boy sneaking into his father's liquor cabinet.

> This boy is in the kitchen. And his mother tells him to get the catsup because she's too short to get it. So he reaches up and gets the catsup. So, uh, the mother is very happy that the boy is tall so he can do it for her. And they sit down and eat.

Redefinition Plus: The boy alters the presented deviation situation in such a way as to make the deviant act *more* serious. In the story given below, for example, the boy magnifies the seriousness of the depicted transgression (a driver looking back at a crumpled bicycle) by developing it into a hit-and-run theme in which a child is killed.

> Well, uh, a lady's going down the street speeding; and this boy on a bike comes darting out of a driveway, and she hits him, consequently. And she jams on her brakes; but it's too late—she's already hit him. Before this time, she had been in traffic and she'd just gotten outa the traffic and she was in a hurry to get home to her children, which had a baby-sitter and were costing her money all the time. And she is coming out of the driveway; he came, and she hit

him. He was taken to the hospital and died five days later. She went to court and she was, uh, sentenced to life imprisonment for hit-and-run.

There is no a priori basis for regarding such redefinition, either plus or minus, as a guilt sign. It may be supposed that a guilt-oriented person is inclined to perceive any transgression, even a minor one, as more serious than it actually is. On the other hand, if the test content evokes anxiety and guilt, the subject may attempt to reduce the threat by minimizing or denying the obvious guilt-provoking cues. However, it is equally reasonable to suppose that a person who experiences *few* guilt feelings will also tend to minimize the seriousness of a given transgression. Consequently, no predictions about differences between the two groups of boys were made for these two response categories.

RESULTS FROM PARENT INTERVIEWS

Affectional Relationships between Parents

It has already been shown in Chapter 2 that in the families of the aggressive boys there was a disruption of parent-child affectional relationships, and that there was a more marked break in the father-son relationship than in the boys'

TABLE 6-1

PARENTS' AFFECTIONAL RELATIONSHIPS: DIFFERENCES BETWEEN
PARENTS OF AGGRESSIVE AND CONTROL BOYS

	Aggressive Group		Control Group			
Scales	Mean	S.D.	Mean	S.D.	t	p
Wife's warmth for husband	7.23	1.78	8.50	1.18	3.10	<.01
Husband's warmth for wife	7.90	1.32	8.77	0.81	2.66	<.01
Wife's hostility toward husband	4.04	1.52	3.19	1.19	2.15	<.05
Husband's hostility toward wife	3.87	1.42	3.08	0.90	2.28	<.02 (.05)[a]

[a] The probability in parentheses is based on the Wilcoxon Test.

relationship to their mothers. From the data presented in Table 6-1 it is evident that in these families not only was the affectional relationship between the parent and the boy less positive than in the control families, but the affectional bond between husband and wife was, in addition, relatively weak. As predicted, the parents of the aggressive boys felt significantly less warmth for each other than did the parents of the control boys. It is probable that this difference would have been even larger were it not for the fact that a good number of the parents, particularly those of the aggressive boys, seemed quite defensive and guarded in responding to the questions concerning the quality of their marital relationships. Nevertheless, it was clear that the parents of the aggressive boys, more often than not, enjoyed the company of their marital partners only under limited circumstances and mutually rejected each other's values and interest patterns.

I. Do you enjoy each other's company?

M. (Case 15) I enjoy his up to a point but, after that, if I had to spend all my time around my husband, I think he'd get on my nerves.

I. How well would you say you and your husband get along together?

M. I'd say as well as average. We're different temperaments. We don't have a lot in common. He likes to go out fishing and be in the outdoors all the time; and I like movies, the theatre, and things like that which he doesn't particularly enjoy.

I. In what ways do you get on one another's nerves?

M. Well, I guess from differences of opinion on different things.

I. Would you wish your husband to change in any way?

M. Yes, I would. I'd like for him to take more of an interest—well, he has changed in that he's taking more of an interest in our little girl at school and different things than he did with Neal. I'd like to be able to go more places and have more of a fifty-fifty basis for the things we like to, for the things I like to do, rather than doing everything he likes to do.

In some cases, the parents' marital relationship was characterized by marked estrangement and antagonism. The case cited below is one such example. In this particular case the burden of eight children undoubtedly aggravated the problems, though there were signs that there had been some discord even during the early phases of the marital relationship.

I. Would you tell me also about the relationship between you and your wife. Do you express affection toward each other freely or are you somewhat reserved?

F. (Case 11) Well, that's a hit-and-go proposition. It's a moody proposition. She's a very moody person. I'm not saying that to say it's all bad, you know what I mean. But she's very moody. She's either up in the clouds or she's down. When she's up in the clouds, she's a very lovely person and very loving. But when she's not, she's just the other way. So we have a hit-and-go proposition that way. Sometimes we don't get along at all for days. Other weeks we get along like a couple of first-year-marriage-life, even at our age.

I. Do you spend much time together?

F. Not as much as we would like, no. I fall down on that. I am home. I don't take her out like I should. I don't have the money with which to go. I don't hang around bars. I have. I don't any more. I don't hang around bars. There's not much place for us to go anymore except to a show or something like that or stay home and watch TV. Or she goes to her girl friend's house two or three nights a week, and I hit the ceiling about that. We've had lots of arguments and fights about it and I've finally given up lately. Now, I don't care. It's gotten to the point where I don't care. If she wants to go and stay with her, if she enjoys that much better than being home with me, that's where she should go. I think that's caused a lot of our arguments in the past. Time means nothing to her. If she wants to go to her friend's house and stay over there until three o'clock in the morning, that's perfectly all right. Well, I don't see it that way.

I. In general, do you and your wife enjoy one another's company?

F. Not as much as we should lately.

I. How well would you say you and your wife get along together?

F. That's broad. Well, I've said, as good as can be expected under the circumstances, I guess. Not as good as it should be, no. We don't get along as good as we should. Things are pretty, pretty rough at times. Although, we haven't hauled off and knocked one another down or anything like that. It isn't that rough by any means. Not saying she wouldn't like to once in a while. You know what I mean. We do respect one another to the point where we're not going to really come out and make fools of ourselves. There's something, after you have eight children, there's something there you can't go too far. I don't know whether you can grasp that idea or whether anyone can grasp that idea unless they've gone through it. It's like that fellow who said, "I just got through; I wrote a book

all about love," and the fellow never had a girl in his life. Well,
it's that kind of problem here. It's hard to explain until you have
eight children on one hand, and you don't have the time to give
to your husband 'cause you're trying to wash the faces of eight
children. That's her side of the story. And I don't have time to give
you 'cause I'm trying to bring home the bacon, you might say. It's
a tough life to live. It's a hit-and-go proposition. Half the time it
doesn't go over as well as we would like it. The conditions, circumstances do a lot of things to us that we don't want done to us,
but we can't help it.

I. In what ways do you get on each other's nerves?
F. Just like I say, she runs off to the neighbors to play canasta or something with the girl friend and stays to three o'clock in the morning.
I don't approve of that. I don't know of any husband that would.
But maybe I'm wrong. Then, on the other hand, she's so worn out
with the children all day long that she wants to get away from the
house about nine o'clock and getting to relax. Maybe she doesn't
relax until midnight and doesn't have any fun until two in the
morning. I don't know, but I still don't approve of it, and we get
into an argument. It's led to a lot of arguments. I don't like it. I
still don't like it, but I don't fight about it anymore. I've come to
the point, well, there are other things in life that are worthwhile.
Forget about it. The children are growing up. Now maybe I can
give them a little more of my thoughts.

In contrast, the control parents for the most part expressed
a close attachment and fondness for each other. The modal
quality of warmth, however, was more that of a close companionship than spontaneous affectional demonstrativeness.
Many parents seemed to feel very strongly that open demonstrations of affection, such as kissing and embracing,
should be avoided when the children were present.

I. Would you tell me also about the relationship between you and
your wife? Do you express affection towards each other freely or
are you somewhat reserved?
F. (Case 30) Well, we, we're somewhat reserved. We don't, uh, if
I may say, misbehave ourselves in front of our children. Far be it,
I think that's the general rule in our family. We, the wife assists
the girls, and of course it's got the time when I don't have to help
the boy. We behave ourselves. In other words, we don't run around
naked in front of our children or do things like that. I think there's
a place for everything and everything in its place.
I. Do you spend much time together?

F. Well, we're, you mean the wife and I? Near every night I come home from work and I'm there 'til I go to work in the morning. In fact, I have in my twenty-two years of married life, I don't think I have slept (pause), three weeks out of my—wherever I've been, I've been with my wife.

I. What sort of things do you do together?

F. Well, at the moment there's not much that we can do except we stay home, we work together, we do things around the house, we assist one another as much as we can, and I assist her all I can with the heavy work; and, at the same time, anything that she thinks would be an asset to the house that we can't afford to have done. why, I go ahead and do it myself. And that's how we've got along for years.

I. Do you enjoy one another's company?

F. You bet your life we do.

I. How well would you say you and your wife get along together?

F. Well, I would say 98½ per cent. There's very, very little in it (laughs).

I. In what ways do you get on one another's nerves?

F. Well, there's quite a lot of things that I do. I bite my fingernails quite a bit, and that gets on my wife's nerves. My wife smokes too much, and that gets on my nerves. There's no serious things but there's very, very little that we do, we don't, uh, we do make it, get going a wee trifle forward.

There were several control families in which the parents were very demonstrative in their affection for each other; such demonstrativeness was not encountered in any of the families of the aggressive boys.

I. Would you tell me also about the relationship between you and your husband? Do you express affection toward each other freely or are you somewhat reserved?

M. (Case 22) Well, when we're together, which is only on weekends right now, it's a perfect, we're on a continuous honeymoon, I'm afraid.

I. What sort of things do you do together?

M. We're always busy. He and I like to do a lot of work. We're fixing up, as I say, the downstairs. And we like to paint or to do yard-work and so forth. Or if not, we like to drive, drive to movies. We both like to go to shows.

I. Do you enjoy each other's company?

M. Certainly.

I. How well would you say you and your husband get along together?

M. I think we get along wonderfully.

I. In what ways do you get on each other's nerves?

M. I don't know. Actually, that's the truth. I don't know. We never argue. We don't have much time to argue. It's the only thing, if there were any arguments about bringing up the children, we'd discuss that and get a happy medium there. There's no argument. My mother says we're honeymooners and she says it makes her feel bad because of being with us, and on the other hand it makes her feel good because she likes to be where there's a lot of accord.

The control parents showed considerably less hostility toward one another than did the parents of the aggressive boys (Table 6-1). Although the cues of the whole interview were utilized in making the ratings, the parents' evaluations of each other were often reflected in their answers to the question asking in what ways they would like their spouse to change. Although the control parents sometimes mentioned minor irritations or sources of friction, they more often responded with very favorable evaluations of their marital partners.

I. Would you wish your wife to change in any way?

F. (Case 46) Wish her to change? Oh, no. She's just as sweet as any female you ever saw. Very nice disposition, pleasing voice, good housekeeper, and a very good mother. Couldn't ask anything more.

. . .

I. Would you wish your husband to change in any way?

M. (Case 22) No. I'd like him to stay just the way he is. . . .

I. If your fondest dreams could come true, what things would you wish for Ralph when he grows up?

M. I hope that whenever he gets married, some day when he grows up, that his wife will feel the same way that I do about my husband.

I. Does Ralph know you feel this way?

M. I think so. He knows that there's quite a bit of love between the two of us.

The parents of the aggressive boys, on the other hand, were often critical of, and dissatisfied with, their marital partners. Although, in most cases they described specific areas of irritation and dissatisfaction, for some the problems seemed so generalized that they did not wish to document them.

I. Would you wish your wife to change in any way?

F. (Case 23) Oh, that's too big an issue to go into.

                              •   •   •

F. (Case 11) Oh yes, I wouldn't care to describe that too much. But
    naturally there's a lot of little things after twenty years of married
    life that you would like changed that you can't. You come to the
    point where you either take them or you walk away from them.
    You can't change people unless they want to be changed.

The mothers' dissatisfaction with their husbands was
sometimes elicited by questions referring to the use of
models.

I. Is there anyone you mention as an example of what not to do?

M. (Case 49) Well, there's, yeah (laughs). There's things about his
    father I don't want him to be like, like this overbearing quality.
    I don't want him to be like that, which he's getting to be more and
    more. Then I don't want him to do any drinking. We've seen
    enough of that.

Open criticisms of this kind are unlikely to promote identification with the father.

The correlational data suggested that the boys who came
from families in which relationships between the parents
were strained were likely to experience rejection. Mothers
who lacked warmth for, and felt hostile toward, their husbands tended to reject their sons ($r = .32$ and $.30$, respectively; $p < .05$ in each case); in addition, a tendency to reject
their sons was shown by fathers who were hostile toward
their wives ($r = .27$; $p < .06$).

Demands for Masculinity

There was no difference between the mothers of the aggressive boys and the control mothers in their emphasis on
training in sex-appropriate behavior. The control fathers,
however, made significantly greater demands for masculinity from their sons than did the fathers of the aggressive
boys (Table 6-2).

For the large majority of the adolescents sex differentiation in respect to such obvious factors as dress, recreational
activities, mannerisms, and general deportment had already

TABLE 6-2

MASCULINITY DEMANDS: DIFFERENCES BETWEEN PARENTS OF
AGGRESSIVE AND CONTROL BOYS

Scales	Aggressive Group		Control Group		t	p
	Mean	S.D.	Mean	S.D.		
Mother's masculinity demands	5.50	1.65	5.77	1.64	0.73	N.S.
Father's masculinity demands	4.85	1.88	6.02	1.69	1.94	<.05

been well established. Ratings of the parents' demands for masculinity consequently depended, for the most part, on the extent to which they emphasized the need for different responsibilities for boys and girls or encouraged specifically masculine vocational and leisure-time activities. Most mothers put only a moderate amount of stress on the need for sex-role differentiation; the more extreme attitudes can therefore be best illustrated by contrasting excerpts from the father interviews.

At one extreme were those fathers who thought that their sons should be quite versatile in taking on responsibilities and should be able to carry out even traditionally feminine activities.

I. Are there things you would expect of him that you might not expect of a daughter?
F. (Case 7) No. I'd expect the same things of a daughter.
I. Do you think boys should have different responsibilities in the home from girls?
F. Yes and no. I can answer two ways. My boys can cook. They can bake and they do dishes just as well as the girls. So I think all in all it doesn't hurt them to have the same responsibilities. As far as sewing is concerned, I wouldn't say anything about that. But being able to cook and bake and other responsibilities, I think they should.

In contrast, there were some fathers who made strong demands for masculinity and who actively fostered their sons' masculine identification by drawing them into the circle of their own adult male friends.

I. Most fathers want their sons to grow up into very manly persons. What do you expect of your boy in this way?

F. (Case 6) Yes, I want him to be manly and, I think, when he had the long hair, I told him he looked a lot better with the butch. We didn't insist that he go get a butch haircut, but we told him how much better he looked and we kept at him on how much better he'd look with one. Of course his height, he's tall; we brag about his height to other people, other adults. We tell them how big he is for a fifteen-year-old boy. He seems to like that. On his own now he goes out and gets a butch haircut. He tries to appear manly. He's meeting a lot of adults running around with me and, of course, the policemen that come over to see me and visit with me. He's their friend too. He's not left out. . . .

I. Are there things you would expect of him that you might not expect of a daughter?

F. Well, girls are entirely different. You have to be a little bit more careful when you raise them.

I. Do you think boys should have different responsibilities in the home from girls?

F. Yes, I think the boys' responsibilities should be of the outside nature. Girls' responsibilities should be to help the mother.

The significance of a high emphasis on training in sex-appropriate behavior may be more complex than was assumed in the section on hypotheses (p. 258). In the aggressive boys' families, mothers who placed emphasis on training for the male role tended to show little warmth for, and considerable hostility to, their husbands ($r = -.43$ and $.45$, respectively; $p < .05$ in each case). In this group, therefore, a high demand for masculinity from the son accompanied dissatisfaction with the husband. From these correlations it appeared that some mothers emphasized sex-typing, not so much because they wished their sons to be like their husbands, but because they looked upon them as partial substitutes for husbands whom they could not fully accept.

Under these circumstances, however, the mother's pressures are likely to endanger her own relationship with the boy. If a boy feels that his mother is cold and rejecting toward his father, he is also likely to feel that she responds similarly to all males, including himself. It is interesting, therefore, to find that aggressive boys whose mothers lacked warmth for, and were hostile to, their husbands themselves felt rejected by their mothers. The correlation between the boys' feelings of rejection, as measured from the adolescent interviews, and the mothers' warmth toward their husbands was $-.61$, which is significant well beyond the .01 level. In addition, the boys' feelings of rejection by their mothers, and their anxiety about being dependent upon them, were both stronger if their mothers showed hostility toward their husbands ($r = .43$ and .40, respectively; $p < .05$ in each case).

Relatively high correlations were found also, but again only for the families of the aggressive boys, between the fathers' demands for masculinity and their warmth for, and hostility to, their wives ($r = -.38$; $p < .06$, and .41; $p < .05$, respectively). In addition, a very high negative correlation was found between the fathers' demands for masculinity and the extent to which they agreed with their wives ($r = -.67$; $p < .001$). Obviously, these correlations cannot be explained in the same way as the correlations that were found for the mothers. It may be that husbands whose respect for their wives is relatively low feel hostile toward feminine traits, and consequently encourage a masculine identification in their sons even when the father-son relationships are themselves quite markedly impaired.

Within the control group no consistent relationships were found between the parents' demands for masculinity and the other variables discussed in the above paragraphs. In part, this may be due to the absence of any marked discord within the control families. High positive correlations were, however, found between the control fathers' warmth and acceptance of their sons and their demands for masculinity ($r = .48$; $p < .02$, and $r = .52$; $p < .01$, respectively). In addition, these fathers tended to make fewer masculinity demands if they expressed hostility toward their sons ($r = -.50$; $p < .01$). The corresponding correlations for the aggressive boys' fathers, although in the same direction, were considerably smaller and failed by themselves to reach significance.

RESULTS FROM BOYS' INTERVIEWS

Affection for Parents

The data from the aggressive boys' interviews (Table 6-3) provided further evidence that in the majority of cases a

TABLE 6-3

Boys' Affection for Their Parents: Differences between
Aggressive and Control Boys

	Aggressive Group		Control Group			
Scales	*Mean*	*S.D.*	*Mean*	*S.D.*	t	p
Warmth to mother	5.62	1.96	6.33	1.51	1.48	<.10
Warmth to father	4.98	2.05	6.79	1.24	3.72	<.001

severe break had occurred in the father-son relationship. There appeared, in fact, in most families to be a consistent and pervasive disruption of the emotional ties between father and son which was more clearly perceived as such, and presumably more keenly felt, by the boy than was the disruption of the relationship with the mother. While the two groups of boys differed little in the amount of warmth they showed for their mothers, the aggressive boys showed very much less warmth for their fathers than did their controls. Evidence has already been provided (Chapters 2 and 3) that the aggressive boys were also more hostile to their fathers than to their mothers, and less ready to relate to them in a dependent manner.

In general, the control boys expressed a fairly high evaluation of, and a good deal of fondness for, both parents.

I. Are there times when you really enjoy your mother?
B. (Case 28) Yeah, yeah. She's funny and she has a good personality. She, lots of times someone's dancing on television or something funny, and she gets up and starts doing the show. You know, really funny.
I. Do you have any way of showing her how you feel?
B. Oh, yeah. Try to do, you know, what she tells me, not talking back, try not to get into any arguments. . . .

I. Are there things you really enjoy about your father?
B. He doesn't get angry at me. I mean, he's easy going. He does things
    with me, jokes around, never gets angry with me if I make a
    mistake.
I. How do you go about showing him how you feel?
B. Yeah, same way as my mother.

Almost without exception, the aggressive boys expressed
strong dissatisfaction with one or both parents. Typically,
the boys had something positive to say about their mothers
but were indifferent, critical, or hostile toward their fathers.

I. Are there times when you really enjoy your mother?
B. (Case 15) Yeah.
I. What sort of things do you especially like about her?
B. Well, she's got a good sense of humor, and I find that she and I
    think alike.
I. How much do you feel she understands you?
B. Like I say, we think alike, and she's able to put herself in my place.
I. Does she enjoy having you around?
B. Yes, when I'm behaving myself (laughs).
I. How much interest do you think she takes in you?
B. She takes quite a bit of interest.
I. Are there things you really enjoy about your father?
B. No. Not actually, I don't think.
I. How much do you feel he understands you?
B. I don't think he understands me at all. We think exactly opposite.
I. Does he enjoy having you around?
B. I don't know. He might. He keeps me in enough (laughs).
I. How much does he try to help you?
B. I don't know. I don't understand him and he don't understand me.
I. In general, would you say you and your mother get along well
    together?
B. Yes.
I. And how well would you say you and your father get along to-
    gether?
B. Well, I think we're just two different people. We don't match.
I. Of all the people you know, whom do you most want to be like
    when you get older?
B. I don't know.
I. How about your father?
B. No. I don't think so.
I. How about your mother?
B. Yes. She's able to do things. She can build things, figure out all dif-
    ferent things. Like we've done most of the work on our house.

When the relationship between the father and boy is as distant and strained as that depicted above, identification with the father is virtually impossible.

Identification

The control boys were more inclined to identify with their fathers than were the aggressive boys. They tended also to identify more with their mothers, but the difference between the groups in this case failed to reach significance.

TABLE 6-4

Boys' Identification with Their Parents: Differences between Aggressive and Control Boys

Scales	Aggressive Group		Control Group		t	p
	Mean	S.D.	Mean	S.D.		
Identification with mother	4.37	1.83	5.08	1.17	1.60	<.10
Identification with father	5.02	1.60	5.79	1.34	1.71	<.05 (.06)[b]
Preference for father[a]	3.62	1.21	4.62	1.24	2.58	<.02 (.02)[c]

[a] This scale was not used as a basis for prediction.

[b] The probability in parentheses is based on the Wilcoxon Test.

[c] The probability in parentheses is based on a chi-square test using only those cases in which a definite preference for one or the other parent was expressed (N = 26).

Although at this stage in their development both groups of boys were inclined to single out some star in sports as their idol, many of the control boys also strived to model themselves after their fathers. From their accounts it was evident that they felt they possessed some of the values and behavior patterns that they admired in their fathers. An example of a strong father-identification is provided by the boy in Case 48. In this particular excerpt it is interesting to note that conditions that would foster strong identification, for example, a good deal of mutual affection and esteem in the parent-child relationships, were clearly present.

I. Are there times when you really enjoy your mother?

B. (Case 48) Yes. She's really a good mother. She sacrifices, and I like to do things for her. She's a good person.

I. How do you go about showing her you feel this way?

B. I show affection when I'm around her, show her that I love her and I'm glad to be around her.

I. How about your dad, what sort of things do you enjoy about him?

B. Well, more or less, he's the way a father should be. Good head, takes an interest in me, does things with me occasionally like fighting, fooling around. Wonderful sense of humor. He's very well educated, high I.Q. You can talk to him about anything. He understands.

I. How do you go about showing him how you feel?

B. Occasionally I do something for him. I just talk to him and that's the way I show affection; wrestling and something. . . .

I. Of all the people you know, whom do you most want to be like when you get older?

B. Of all the people I know? I don't know; I'd like to be a few traits out of everybody.

I. How about your father? In what ways would you like to be like him?

B. Well, I'd like to be about like my dad. Have his sense of humor, wisdom, his judgment, work with his hands like he does, like to have speaking ability.

I. How much do you think you are like him already?

B. Well, I've picked up his trait of thinking things out for myself and acting; I get a kick out of being or doing dry humor, crack jokes without smiling, fooling around, enjoying good books. He enjoys doing that, too.

I. In what ways would you like to be like your mother?

B. Her personality, always has a smile, cheerful person. Person you like to be around.

I. How much do you think you are already like her?

B. In some mannerisms, but not too many.

I. Whom do you think you are more like in your ways, your mother or your father?

B. I'd say my father.

Here is another example of a boy who looked upon his father as a prototype of what he himself wanted to be. From his report it appeared that he already resembled his father in his attitudes and specific skills.

I. Of all the people you know, whom do you most want to be like when you get older?

B. (Case 26) Like my dad, I think.

I. In what ways would you like to be like him?

B. Oh, my dad could do most anything. He does his own repairing. He can paint, repair. He can do anything as far as that goes. He can do any kind of odd jobs.

I. How much do you think you are like him already?

B. Well, I'm learning how to paint like he does. I'm learning a little in carpentry and doing odd jobs and how to save money by certain types of paints.

I. Do you think you are alike in your ways at all?

B. In ways, yes, I am.

In contrast, a number of the aggressive boys were quite critical of their fathers' attributes and had, for the most part, rejected their fathers as suitable identification figures. Instead, they took an older brother or some other male adult as their model.

I. Of all the people you know, whom do you most want to be like when you get older?

B. (Case 27) My uncle.

I. Why do you choose your uncle?

B. I like him best.

I. How about your father? In what ways would you like to be like him?

B. I can't think of any.

I. Are there any things about him you admire and would like to be the same way?

B. No. Not at all.

Since dependency ties to adults outside the immediate family are likely to be less intense than those that ordinarily develop between parent and child, one would expect that such substitute figures would usually be less influential in fostering the development of internal controls.

Additional supporting evidence for the stronger father-identification of the control boys was provided by the scale that measured the boys' preference for living with one parent rather than with the other (Table 6-4). The aggressive boys were apparently much less likely than the control boys to have chosen their fathers to live with, had they been forced to make a choice between their parents. Here are the contrasting replies of a control boy and an aggressive boy.

I. Let's turn to your family now. Let's suppose your mother was living in one place and your father in another, which would you choose to live with?

B. (Case 22) It would be hard to say. I mean, I guess I'd probably end up choosing my dad.

I. What makes you prefer to live with your dad?

B. Oh, I don't know. I guess most boys would probably choose their dad because they're real close, you know.

· · ·

B. (Case 47) I don't know. That's a hard thing to say, to answer, because, well, I never was too intimate with my father. I mean, I never did go out with him too much or anything like that. Well, I never did with my mother, either. I don't know what I'd do if they separated.

The difference obtained by this measure might have been even larger, were it not for the fact that a good number of the boys in both groups refused to register a preference. Interestingly enough, the reasons given for the difficulty in making such a choice differed for the two groups of boys. Usually the control boys could not choose because of their close attachment to both parents.

I. Let's turn to your family now. Let's suppose your mother was living in one place and your father in another, which would you choose to live with?

B. (Case 40) Gee. I've never been confronted with that. I'd never know. Both have been nice.

The aggressive boys' difficulty in making a choice seemed to be more a problem of double avoidance.

I. Let's turn to your family now. Let's suppose your mother was living in one place and your father in another, which would you choose to live with?

B. (Case 19) If I had to live with one or the other, I wouldn't live with any of them.

As can be seen from Table 6-5, fairly consistent positive relationships occurred between the identification and dependency measures; most of the correlations were significant beyond the .01 level. The identification and dependency measures were in turn related, also in a highly consistent manner, to the boys' feelings of rejection, and to their

TABLE 6-5

INTERRELATIONSHIPS BETWEEN DEGREE OF THE BOYS' IDENTIFICATION
WITH PARENTS AND OTHER THEORETICALLY RELATED
VARIABLES: DATA FROM BOYS' INTERVIEWS

Scale	2	3	4	5	6	7
1. Identification with parent	.64 .54	-.35 -.36	-.52 -.49	.44 .57	.43 .33	.38 .33
2. Warmth toward parent		-.44 -.69	-.58 -.72	.38 .62	.42 .63	.43 .50
3. Feelings of rejection by parent			.47 .73	-.17 -.67	-.30 -.56	-.18 -.30
4. Hostility to parent				-.38 -.61	-.44 -.60	-.33 -.43
5. Help-seeking from parent					.45 .59	.16 .31
6. Seeking parent's company						.41 .56
7. Praise-seeking from parent						

Coefficients for the fathers are in the upper left corner of the cell; for the mothers, in the lower right corner of the cell. Correlations equal to, or greater than, .37 are significant at the .01 level. Correlations equal to, or greater than, .28 are significant at the .05 level.

warmth for, and hostility to, their parents. Assuming that a boy's feelings toward his parents are to a large extent determined by their feelings toward him, and in view of the evidence previously set forth that parental warmth arouses and maintains dependency behavior in a child, the intercorrelations given in this table may be interpreted both as supportive evidence for the hypotheses considered in this chapter, and as further justifying the focus that has been placed on the dependency relationship in this study of the aggressive boy.

Some further supportive evidence was obtained by correlating the identification measures with relevant parent variables. Small, but nevertheless significant, relationships were found between the mothers' warmth and encouragement of dependency and the boys' identification with their mothers ($r = .30$ and $.28$, respectively; $p < .05$ in each case). In addition, a significant correlation ($r = .29$; $p < .05$) was obtained between the fathers' encouragement of help-seeking behavior and the boys' identification with their fathers.

Quality of Parent Model

So far, in the treatment of identification, the quality of the parent model has been disregarded. It is, of course, important to consider the adequacy of the pattern of behavior provided for the boy to copy, since a child's delinquency may stem, not so much from a failure to internalize parental standards, but rather from the internalization of essentially dissocial values. In fact, a number of authors have described cases of antisocial behavior in which a boy had developed a close identification with a parent, the major problem being that the parent with whom the decisive identification had been made was himself antisocial (Aichhorn, 1935; Fenichel, 1945; Johnson and Szurek, 1952).

Although a direct attempt was not made to assess the adequacy of the parents' values and behavior patterns, a good deal of relevant information was elicited both from the parents' own interviews and from the interviews with the boys. No blatant antisocial incidents were reported, but there were indications that some of the parents of the aggressive boys themselves displayed an antisocial orientation. A few spontaneously described minor delinquencies in their own histories.

F. (Case 13) See, for the last eleven years, up to a year ago, I was a railroad man. . . . I tore up a little equipment down there at the railroad company and I'm being punished now. I'm being punished now. They pull you out of service, six months, seven months. I've been out about six months now. I'll probably be back in a couple of weeks.

Occasionally, in the course of an interview with one or other of the family members, there was a reference to the father's heavy drinking.

I. How about your father, do you ever deliberately avoid going out with him?
B. (Case 49) Well, when he goes out, a lot of times I won't go with him because when he goes out he winds up with one of his buddies, this guy that usually stays with us. He winds up with him down in the bar. I wind up driving home with him crapped out in the back seat.

Even more frequent were expressions of antisocial attitudes, some of which have already been illustrated by quotations in the sex and aggression chapters. A further example is provided by the father in Case 11 who expressed a very permissive and condoning attitude toward his son's defiance of school authorities and at the same time revealed that he, too, had played truant in his childhood.

I. Some youngsters play hookey from school; what about Edward?
F. (Case 11) I don't think he does. He might cut class once in a while. I guess he has. He said he had to stay an hour after school and make up some time, but I've never paid a great deal of attention to that. Lots of worse things than cutting class once in a while. Unless it's reported by the teachers, I wouldn't pay much attention to it. You have to give children a little devilment once in a while. I mean, that's one of the little things that they might get away with once in a great while. I wouldn't care too much about it unless the teachers reported that he was cutting class a great deal and something had to be done about it. Then I would do something. I cut class when I went to school, several times, and I got a kick out of it. You got to have a kick at something. They gotta have a little cut class once in a while. Take the teacher an apple with a worm in it or something else. That's part of life.

In Chapter 5 it was suggested that the fathers of the aggressive boys, with their relatively frequent use of physical punishment, provided more physically aggressive models for the boys than did the control fathers. Moreover, it was shown in Chapter 3 that both the mothers and the fathers of the aggressive boys tended to display an aggressive orientation in their encouragement of their sons' aggressive behavior. Thus, identification with their parents could, in itself, have made these boys somewhat aggressive. There was, in fact, evidence in some of the interviews with the aggressive boys that a partial identification with the father may have taken place and that this identification was almost exclusively with the aggressive, dissocial aspects of his personality.

I. How well would you say you and your father got along together?
B. (Case 49) I don't know, he's kinda got a temper, you know. He's always bubbling about something. . . .
I. How much do you think you are like him?
B. I got a hot temper (laughs).
I. Any other ways.
B. No, I don't think so.
I. Who do you think you are more like in your ways, your mother or your father?
B. Probably more like my father because he's hot tempered, you know. I don't lose my temper; but when I do, it slides all the way out.

Guilt

The strongest evidence of the aggressive boys' defective conscience development was their lack of guilt feelings when they transgressed. Although the measures of guilt based on the interview data showed that the aggressive boys were not completely guilt-free, their guilt feelings were considerably weaker than those of the control boys (Table 6-6).

TABLE 6-6

FEELINGS OF GUILT: DIFFERENCES BETWEEN
AGGRESSIVE AND CONTROL BOYS

Scales	Aggressive Group		Control Group			
	Mean	S.D.	Mean	S.D.	t	p
Guilt over aggression toward:						
Mother	4.69	1.88	6.10	1.85	2.92	<.01
Father	4.27	1.71	6.21	1.82	4.02	<.001
Teachers	3.46	1.18	5.38	1.38	5.89	<.001
Peers	3.71	1.28	5.27	1.23	4.74	<.001
Guilt over antisocial behavior	3.48	1.45	5.42	1.64	3.48	<.001
Anxiety over sex behavior	5.50	2.25	6.62	1.86	2.19	<.05

GUILT OVER ANTISOCIAL BEHAVIOR

Approximately half the control group reported no antisocial behavior of an illegal or semi-illegal kind, thus reducing considerably the number of cases on which a comparison could be made for the amount of guilt felt about such behavior. Nevertheless, the boys in the control group who had so transgressed showed significantly more guilt than did the aggressive boys. Even though the acting-out incidents described by the control boys were typically minor in nature, these boys customarily responded with self-disapproval.

I. Have there ever been times when you've felt you've got to do something foolish just for the hell of it, for example, driving a car at 90 m.p.h. or starting a brawl, or smashing up?

B. (Case 52) Yeah. I can't remember; oh, one time I dropped a match out the window and to my horror it caught fire. Dry grass started. I ran into the kitchen and got a pan full of water and dumped it out, and every time I go by that burnt place I sort of wince. And I'm tempted to, uh, run across the street. Traffic is coming; and when I'm half way across, maybe I can beat it. I run a little faster. I think that's kind of foolish. Nothing much. Except sometimes I get the urge to take my dad's car. Otherwise, that's about it.

I. How do you feel afterwards?

B. I think, ashamed and a little bit worried about the consequences. Sometimes, gee, I broke records once and, gee, I didn't know whether to tell my mother or just leave them there or put the blame on somebody else. And so I finally put them in a wastebasket. She came in and said, "O.K., who did this?" I kept my mouth shut for a little while. Then my sister, she kind of talked my mom out of her guilt, see. I knew she didn't do it. She knew. I guess my mom knew. So I just told her. She said, "Well, don't do that." I was surprised. She didn't get really mad at me because I was so young at that time.

By contrast, the aggressive boys would in most cases show little or no guilt about their antisocial behavior, even when it involved rather serious destructive activities. Perhaps the most extreme example was the boy in Case 23 who carried out unprovoked vindictive assaults on strangers with little apparent guilt.

I. Have there ever been times when you've felt you've got to do something just for the hell of it?

B. (Case 23) Yeah.

I. What kind of things?

B. Well, I feel like going out and getting drunk, and going and beating the shit out of some guy.

I. How often have you done this?

B. About five or six times.

I. How do you feel about it afterwards?

B. I feel good. I always pick on a person bigger than me, so I can't think I was picking up some guy smaller. I don't care if he's that much bigger. He's always bigger than me.

Stealing a car for a joy ride and "rolling" it seemed to be one of the most frequent antisocial activities engaged in by the aggressive boys.

I. Have there ever been times when you've felt you've got to do something foolish just for the hell of it?

B. (Case 31) Yes. I know sometimes I feel like doing something wrong, doing something to keep from getting bored. Wrecked a car one day like that.

I. How do you feel afterwards?

B. After it's all over I feel better. I mean, I feel better. The car, I forgot about it, but I feel better inside. I don't feel bored anymore.

I. How often does that happen?

B. By myself, a couple of times—not many: with my friends, we did it a lot.

From the boys' accounts it seemed as though such activities represented a cathartic relief from frustration, the source of which they found hard to specify.

I. Have there ever been times when you've felt you've got to do something foolish just for the hell of it? For example, driving a car at 90 m.p.h. or starting a brawl, or smashing up?

B. (Case 21) Car? Yes, yes, lots of times.

I. What have you done?

B. Things I felt like doing, like tearing a car up in the hills or something. I did that. I rolled a car. Oh, lots of things. I feel like leaving home. Go away. I did that once. Once I went to Fresno.

I. What makes you feel this way? What happens before you feel this way?

B. Nothing especially happens. The day, I don't know, seemed to be a boring day. Nothing to do, just sitting around. So let's do something different. No really big thing behind it.

I. How do you feel afterwards?

B. I don't know. I don't feel bad about it.

Temporary boredom is a frequent phenomenon of adolescence. This is, perhaps, in part due to the fact that the adolescent can no longer engage, without losing face, in many of the pastimes which were available to him in child-hood. On the other hand, many adult leisure-time activities are not yet permitted him. Nor has the average adolescent yet developed stable and absorbing activity and interest patterns in the service of long-term goals. Moreover, as was shown in Chapter 4, there are at this stage of development many unresolved sex tensions which adolescents are not trained to identify and which they have no socially approved means of reducing. Feelings of this kind may be experienced as generalized frustration and may prompt activities which are unplanned and which bring no apparent gain.

The behavior that such frustration and boredom elicits will vary according to environmental influences and to the adolescent's past experiences and internal resources. If, in the past, aggressive behavior has brought rewards—in other words, if a good deal of antisocial learning has occurred; if the adolescent's interests have not been directed to con-structive activities inside and outside the home; if he has little motivation for formal education or organized social activities; if, above all, there is little or no anticipation of guilt for antisocial behavior—under these circumstances, his response is especially likely to take the form of an aggressive-destructive reaction.

For the aggressive boys, guilt about antisocial behavior correlated .39 ($p < .05$) with dependency on the mother. The correlation between this guilt measure and identification with the parents, though positive ($r = .31$), failed to reach significance.

GUILT OVER AGGRESSION TOWARD PARENTS

It was reported in Chapter 3 that the two groups of boys did not differ appreciably in the amount of overt aggression that they showed toward their parents. They differed con-siderably, however, in the amount of guilt that such aggres-sion evoked (Table 6-6).

For most of the control boys any show of aggression, no matter how attenuated, was accompanied by feelings of remorse and attempts to make restitution. Restitution typically took the form of a conscious effort to behave in a way they knew their parents would approve.

I. What if you fail to do something you were supposed to do, how does this make you feel?

B. (Case 12) Not too good.

I. What do you do?

B. I try to make it up some way.

I. I guess everybody gets angry with their parents sometimes. What sort of things make you angry with your father, for example?

B. If I keep harping on the same subject, he'll get mad at me. Sometimes I won't be able to go someplace and I get mad.

I. What do you usually do when you get mad at him?

B. Go outside. Go to my friend's house or something.

I. Have you ever struck your father?

B. No.

I. Thrown things around the house?

B. Yes. Not too often. Sometimes I slam the door.

I. Stomped out of the house?

B. Yes. Most of the time I stomp out of the house.

I. Shouted at him?

B. If I get angry or something.

I. Talked back?

B. No, I haven't talked back.

I. What sort of things make you angry with your mother?

B. Sometimes I want to do something, and she doesn't want me to do it or something like that. I tell her I want to go, and she says, "Better stay home," or I want to buy something and she don't let me get it. Stuff like that.

I. What do you usually do when you get angry at her?

B. Go outside and don't do the dishes if she asks me to.

I. Have you ever struck your mother?

B. No.

I. Thrown things around the house?

B. Yes. Probably more than with my dad.

I. Slammed doors and things like that?

B. Yes.

I. Sworn or shouted at her?

B. Yes, sometimes if I get mad.

I. Talked back?

B. Maybe, once in a while.

I. After this happens, do you sometimes feel very sorry and try to make it up or do you usually let things go?

B. I usually try to make it up.

I. How do you do this?

B. Do something—go out of the way to do something for them, and they'll sort of forgive me then. Do something that I don't ordinarily do around the house or something.

From the interviews with the aggressive boys it was apparent that their strongest motive for restraint was fear of their fathers' counteraggression. Even when they felt strong hostility and gave little indication of any internalized controls, they had evidently learned that it would be unwise to express their aggressive impulses in a direct fashion.

I. After you've done something that your mother disapproves of without her knowing about it, do you ever feel sorry and go and tell her afterwards?

B. (Case 45) No.

I. What if you fail to do something you were supposed to do, how does that make you feel?

B. I don't care about it.

I. Is it the same way with your father?

B. Yeah.

I. I guess everybody gets angry with their parents sometimes. What sort of things make you angry with your father, for example?

B. Sometimes he'll be listening to me and my mother argue. He'll come in and tell me to keep quiet or something.

I. What do you usually do when you get mad at him?

B. I just look at him. I feel like I'd like to go over and hit him in the mouth, but I know if I did, I'd go through the wall. No, I've never hit him. No. No. I might get mad, but I've got enough sense.

I. Have you ever thrown things around the house?

B. No.

I. Sworn at him?

B. I've got enough sense not to do that, too.

I. Shouted at him?

B. Well, I sort of raise my voice.

I. Talked back?

B. Yes, if I feel I've been wronged, I do.

I. How often have you raised your voice or talked back?

B. Couple of times a week.

I. Have you ever slammed doors?

B. No. I usually just walk into another room, sit down.

I. What sort of things make you angry with your mother?

B. Oh, her asking stupid questions. Boy, that depresses me. She asks me the same things a hundred times. I say, "You've asked me that already and I've told you."

I. What do you usually do when you get angry with her?

B. Talk to her. Tell her, tell her how I feel.
I. Have you ever thrown things around the house?
B. No.
I. Sworn at her?
B. No.
I. Shouted or talked back?
B. Yeah.
I. How often?
B. Couple of times a week.
I. After this happens, do you sometimes feel very sorry and try to make it up or do you usually let things go?
B. No. I don't care about it.
I. Same with your father?
B. Yeah.

Significant negative correlations were found for the control families between the extent of the boys' guilt about aggression toward their parents and the parents' rejection of, and hostility to, the boys. The boys' guilt about aggression toward their fathers correlated $-.42$ ($p < .05$) both with their fathers' rejection and with their fathers' hostility. Their guilt about aggression toward their mothers correlated $-.45$ ($p < .05$) with their mothers' rejection and $-.50$ ($p < .01$) with their mothers' hostility. When correlations were based on mid-parent ratings and an over-all estimate of the boys' guilt for aggression in the home, the correlations between the boys' guilt and the parents' rejection and hostility were $-.59$ and $-.55$, respectively. Both these correlations are significant well beyond the .01 level. In addition, a significant correlation was found between the boys' guilt and a mid-parent measure of warmth ($r = .47$; $p < .05$). No such correlations were found for the aggressive boys' families. However, for the aggressive boys, guilt about aggression toward their mothers correlated .60 ($p < .01$) with their identification with their mothers and guilt about aggression toward their fathers correlated .36 ($p < .07$) with identification with their fathers.

GUILT OVER AGGRESSION TOWARD TEACHERS

In comparison to their controls, the aggressive boys showed considerable direct aggression toward their teachers.

In the school situation there is considerably less threat of severe punishment for aggression than there is in the home. Teachers are prohibited from counteraggressing with the more drastic measures to which parents can turn, if need be, for controlling their sons. In fact, the most severe punishment that can be administered by school authorities is suspension from school, a punishment that was not entirely unwelcome to some of the aggressive boys. With the fear of external punishment largely removed and in the absence of adequate guilt control, some aggressive boys felt little need for self-restraint.

I. If you dislike a teacher, do you ever try to get back at him?

B. (Case 49) If I dislike them, I don't do anything against them, I just give them a bad time. I just mess around and do things that she can't mark me off for, but she don't like. When we go to the library or something, I'll just talk loud enough where she could hear me and say something about her, and she can't say nothing about it.

I. When did you last get mad at a teacher?

B. One teacher last year I got mad at. He threw an eraser at me. I was talking in the back of the room with some guys I know. I picked up an old rubber eraser and cut loose with it and let him have it.

I. Have you ever struck or thrown something at a teacher?

B. In grade school I threw a ruler at a teacher. One of those wooden rulers with a metal edge. I was talking, and she came along and stopped me. I picked up an eighteen-inch ruler, a big heavy one; I just cut loose with it and hit her across the forehead with it. I cut her forehead. . . .

I. When you've done something to annoy a teacher, how do you feel about it afterwards?

B. It don't bother me one little bit. I don't have that much, that kind of conscience.

* * *

I. When you've done something to annoy a teacher, how do you feel about it afterwards?

B. (Case 23) I don't feel any different than when I started to annoy her. I mean, I don't feel silly for it.

I. How many suspensions have you had?

B. Westview, I got suspended four times; Oakdale, I got suspended about six or seven; Mayfair, I got suspended three; and here I got suspended twice.

I. What were you suspended for?
B. Swearing at teachers, mostly cutting up in class. Once for hitting a teacher. Once for swearing at teachers and smoking on school grounds and stuff like that.
I. How about the police?
B. Petty theft, attempted burglary, shooting B.B. guns. Picked up plenty of times on curfew, attempted car theft.
I. How do you feel about this?
B. I don't feel no different.

Even though the control boys' aggressive reactions were relatively mild, they nevertheless tended to feel guilty about them and to atone in some way. It was quite clear that the absence of many of the external threats that exist in the home made little difference to their conduct.

I. How often have you gotten angry at a teacher in high school?
B. (Case 52) Never. Well, I groan about it if the lesson is too hard. I groan about it. I make comments outside class. Say he's an old slave driver and all that, but it's never anything serious because I find the teachers are pretty nice people.
I. Have you ever struck or thrown something at a teacher?
B. No.
I. Slammed doors or desks or things like that?
B. No. I might have when I was pretty young. I can't remember that.
I. Sworn at them?
B. No.
I. Talk back?
B. Well, you mean talk back or serious?
I. Serious.
B. Very little.
I. What have you found the best way of dealing with a teacher you don't like?
B. So far I haven't, because I get along pretty well with teachers. I find that in things like that, if I don't bother them, they don't bother me. But I ran across a few that really take it that way . . . they seemed like they were out to get me or something like that. Maybe they start on the wrong side of the bed or the taxes were too high that year and they got to get back at somebody (laughs).
I. When you've done something to annoy a teacher, how do you feel about it afterwards?
B. Well, gee, I suppose I'd have a twinge of conscience.
I. Do you just forget about it or do you sometimes try to make up for it in some way?

B. Well, I certainly recall one time where the teacher was explaining something and I whispered out loud or commented on his English or something like that. I think I apologized. Yeah, the teacher wasn't too riled about it, but I still, I didn't feel too good about it.

Many control boys displayed considerable empathy for their teachers; some even remarked that a teacher might be hurt by aggressive acts on the part of his pupils. Such sensitivity to the social and interpersonal implications of aggressive and other socially disapproved acts should facilitate the control function of guilt.

I. When you've done something to annoy a teacher, how do you feel about it afterwards?

B. (Case 42) Well, if it's a teacher that I usually get along with and I do something to irritate her, I feel bad about it later on, because they have just as much feeling as we do.

I. What do you do about it?

B. I think I try to make up.

Boys who felt guilty about aggression in their homes tended also to feel guilty about aggressing toward teachers; the correlation between the boys' guilt about aggression toward their mothers and their guilt about aggression toward their teachers was .29 ($p < .05$), while that between their guilt about aggression toward their fathers and their guilt about aggression toward their teachers was .45 ($p < .001$).

Once more there was evidence of a relationship between dependency and guilt; boys who were dependent on their teachers tended to feel more guilty when they aggressed against them ($r = .37$, $p < .01$). In addition, the boys' guilt about aggression toward their teachers correlated .36 ($p < .02$) with their dependency on their mothers. No relationship was found between the boys' guilt about aggression toward their teachers and their dependency on their fathers, but there was some indication that their identification with their fathers might be related to their guilt about aggression to school authorities ($r = .25$; $p < .08$). In addition, though for the aggressive boys only, their guilt about aggression toward their teachers was related to their identification with their mothers ($r = .44$; $p < .05$).

As might be expected, boys whose parents were permissive for aggression toward adults tended to show little guilt about aggression toward teachers ($r = -.32$; $p < .05$).

GUILT OVER AGGRESSION TOWARD PEERS

When they aggressed against one of their peers, most of the aggressive boys were likely to experience relief rather than guilt. Others appeared to be little moved one way or another by their hostile feelings or acts.

I. How about blowing your top at a guy?

B. (Case 39) Well, it all depends on what kind of mood I'm in. If I'm in a bad mood, I'll just haul off and pop him. But if I'm in a good mood, I'm likely to brush it off.

I. When did you last hit a guy?

B. I think it was when they walked out of the wood shop during the class. You see, I had a big argument with the teacher and the teacher said, "If you don't like me, just get going," so I walked out. And after school a kid was smarting up to me about it. And I asked him if he didn't like it; and he said, "No." So I hit him.

I. What was the last time before that?

B. There weren't many times except the time when a kid jumped on me. All I had to do was slip him on his back because I know a little bit of ju-jitsu.

I. How often have you gotten into a fight?

B. Well, like little scraps, you know, there isn't too much bloodshed. When I really get wound up, that's when I'm really mad. That doesn't happen very often. Usually when I get wound up, I get mad at a teacher or mad at what some kid done or something.

I. Have you gotten into any real fights since you've been in high school?

B. Oh, there was this one little guy. He was always messing off. He comes up and starts to shove me around; and he was a little bit smaller than me, and I just wasn't going to take it. So we batted around. Finally I got, put a cut down his nose and the coach stopped it.

I. Do you ever feel like doing something mean to another fellow?

B. If he's a boy and always picking on somebody else, well, I usually find some way of sticking my big mitts into it.

I. When you've got mad at a guy and hit him, how do you feel afterwards?

B. Well, after the fight's over I'm usually still a little bit mad and I don't think of it, and by the time I cooled off I forgot all about it.

In Chapter 3 it was shown that the control boys typically manifested aggression in more indirect, and consequently less guilt-provoking, forms. If, however, hostile feelings toward a peer precipitated more direct aggression, feelings of remorse or an attempt to make reparation almost inevitably followed.

I. When did you last hit a guy?
B. (Case 26) Oh, ages ago. Ages ago. Since grammar school, when I didn't know any better.
I. How often did you do it in grammar school?
B. At Emerson I got into lots of fights because there were a lot of kids ready to jump other kids and I got into fights pretty regularly, about once a week or two a week, average.
I. How about blowing your top at a guy? When was the last time you did that?
B. Oh, I don't know. I don't blow my top easily. I mean, not at my friends at least. I don't remember blowing my top.
I. Do you ever feel like doing something mean to another fellow?
B. Oh, when you get—occasionally everyone feels like doing something, but not really mean. I don't think I ever do anything really mean. I wouldn't want anyone doing anything mean to me.
I. When you've gotten mad at a guy and hit him, how do you feel afterwards?
B. I guess I feel pretty bad about it. I mean, I know I lost my head and I apologize. I guess, tell them I'm sorry in some way. I tell them, "Forget it, it won't happen again. I just didn't know what I was doing."

This boy's statements indicate that he had, over the years, developed internal controls. As he looks back, his earlier aggressive behavior appears quite incompatible with his present value system. If his controls still occasionally break down, he feels his aggressive acts to be somewhat alien to himself.

The boys' guilt about aggression toward their peers did not directly relate to any parent variables. However, boys who felt guilty about aggressing toward their parents also tended to feel guilty about aggressing toward their peers ($r = .33$; $p < .05$). There was also a relationship between the boys' guilt about aggression toward peers and their guilt about aggression toward teachers ($r = .37$; $p < .01$).

GUILT OVER SEXUAL BEHAVIOR

The aggressive boys' lack of guilt about sex behavior was most apparent in their statements about premarital sex relations. Judging from their accounts, whether or not they would go all the way with a girl depended primarily on opportunity and self-interest; they were rarely deterred by anticipation of guilt.

I. How about petting. How far have you gone?
B. (Case 23) How far have I gone? All the way.
I. In what kind of situation was this?
B. In the back of a car, back seat.
I. How often have you gone all the way with a girl?
B. Every other week.
I. What do you think of girls who go all the way?
B. Eh, they'll do.
I. When you've gone all the way with a girl, how do you feel afterwards?
B. Oh, I don't feel no different. It don't hurt me a bit. . . .
I. Have you sometimes felt you'd like to have more sex experience than you've had so far?
B. I think I've had about as much as anybody my age.
I. Have you ever had the chance of going all the way with a girl and deliberately held yourself back from doing so?
B. No, never.

While many of the aggressive boys regarded most females as "fair game," they would on some occasions refrain from sex relations on account of fear of consequences.

I. Have you ever had the chance to go all the way with a girl and deliberately held yourself back from doing so?
B. (Case 13) Yeah.
I. What sort of things make you hold yourself back?
B. Well, lots of times you know, if too many guys get to screwing her, you know, you can get syphilis or some kind of disease like that. All these guys, you see, I had nothing to worry about because I was the first one that had intercourse with her. That was it. The other guys got her after I did, so all these guys had the intercourse, three or four of them after I did.

In contrast to this, the control boys set clearly defined limits to their heterosexual activities. The presence of self-imposed restraints was most clearly evident in situations in which the boys had opportunities for sex relations. That such restraints were primarily guilt-motivated is suggested not only by the boys' anticipation that any disregard of these restraints would give rise to guilt feelings, but also by their spontaneous introduction of moral judgments and by their deliberate avoidance of situations in which control might be threatened.

I. How about necking, how far have you gone with this?
B. (Case 22) Well, I go as far as I think I ought to, and that's it.
I. . How far is that?
B. Well, as far as kissing a girl, that's all right. That's as far as I think you ought to go.
I. Have you ever gone all the way with a girl?
B. No.
I. What do you think of a fellow who goes all the way with girls?
B. I don't go for it.
I. Well, what about girls who go all the way? How do you feel about them?
B. Well, I feel this shouldn't be, you know, hanging around with a bunch of guys. Couple of them up there, couple of chippies up at Bayfield, all the time they're with boys. I try to shake them off. It don't work out. They keep following. Like a fungus on your finger or something. Just keep growing.

Most control boys made it quite clear that they were unlikely to deviate under any circumstances; at the same time they indicated that they would lose respect for, and be critical of, those who might transgress in this way. Reactions of this kind are a further indication of an internalized value system.

I. Have you ever gone all the way with a girl?
B. (Case 48) No, I haven't. I don't think a person should do that. I feel more or less that's for married life. Why fool around beforehand?
I. What about girls who go all the way? How do you feel about them?
B. Well, I try to keep away from them, because I know that also they can communicate diseases that way, so that I keep away.
I. Suppose a friend of yours got a girl you knew into trouble, what would you think of him?
B. I think it would lower my opinion of him.

Fear of consequences undoubtedly serves to reinforce internal controls, as can be seen from the above quotation. However, if fear is alone present, deviations will occur when dangers can be circumvented or forestalled. The inadequacy of controls that are entirely external was illustrated by the boy in Case 13 who gained a false sense of security from preceding his companions when they all had sex relations with the same girl.

The correlational data suggested that there was some relationship between parental handling of sex behavior and the amount of anxiety and guilt about sex shown by the boys. The boys' sex anxiety tended to be high if their mothers were non-permissive for sexual behavior ($r = -.32$; $p <.05$) and if their fathers were punitive for sexual behavior ($r = .29$; $p <.05$).

While boys in both groups who were anxious and guilty about sex tended also to be guilty about showing aggression toward their parents ($r = .33$; $p <.05$), the correlations between sex anxiety and the aggression measures again suggested that sex and overt aggression were associated for the aggressive boys, but not for the control boys. For the aggressive boys the correlation between their sex anxiety and the directness of their aggression toward their parents was $-.54$ ($p <.01$), and that between their sex anxiety and their total overt aggression toward their fathers was $-.52$ ($p <.01$); for the control boys the corresponding correlations were $-.07$ and zero.

While no direct relationship was found between the boys' identification with their fathers and their anxiety about sex, boys who were warm and affectionate toward their fathers tended to experience more anxiety and guilt about sex than boys who showed little warmth and affection for their fathers ($r = .37$; $p <.01$). In contrast, mothers who were rejecting and lacking in warmth for their sons tended to have sons who were anxious about sex ($r = .34$; $p <.05$, and $r = -.26$; $p <.07$, respectively). Although, in general, maternal rejection is likely to interfere with the process of identification with the mother and to prevent acceptance of her values and standards, it may at the same time serve to make a boy anxious about relating to members of the opposite sex.

RESULTS FROM THE THEMATIC TEST

The analysis of the thematic test data in part corroborated the results obtained from the interviews. On the over-all measure of guilt the control boys scored significantly higher than the aggressive boys (Table 6-7). It is very likely that this difference would have been even more marked had not several factors, themselves probably indicative of guilt, operated in such a way as to reduce the total guilt scores of the control boys.

In the first place, the control boys often depicted the deviating character as an unscrupulous delinquent with whom they had little sympathy. While this way of structuring the situation elicited a good deal of moralizing and criticism of the deviator, it precluded the use of many of the other guilt categories. Most of the guilt signs were based on the assumption that the storyteller would identify with the deviator. As the story below illustrates, many of the control boys did not identify.

B. (Case 42) This boy's been studying for a test. And he hasn't gotten much out of it, what he's studied. And so he, instead he decided that he'd cheat on the test. And here he's holding a book and he's taking answers out of the book. I don't think he's too smart. He'd know that it isn't any good to cheat, because he's not gonna get anywhere anyway. Beside that, there's a girl sitting behind him watching. And I don't think this girl's very smart, because she's not saying a word about it. And I can't see why the teacher can't see this, so obvious. . . . If someone doesn't speak up the boy might do it again. I imagine he will. He'll get into the habit, taking these tests and not studying for them, just cheating. After the test they're probably gonna think about it more. And, uh, they'll, the boy that's cheating now, if he realizes it, if I did it, I'd certainly, uh, have my conscience bother me. I think, this girl sitting behind him is probably thinking about it, and she'll think, "Why didn't I say anything? I got a lower grade than he did. I was quite stupid not to say anything."

TABLE 6-7

FREQUENCY OF GUILT RESPONSES TO THEMATIC TEST: DIFFERENCES
BETWEEN AGGRESSIVE AND CONTROL BOYS

Response Category	Rater Reli-ability	Aggressive Group		Control Group		t	p
		Mean	S.D.	Mean	S.D.		
Redefinition[a]		3.71	2.39	6.36	3.86	2.76	<.01 (.02)[b]
Plus[a]	.79	1.95	1.37	3.28	2.85	1.88	N.S.
Minus[a]	.61	1.76	1.87	3.08	2.77	1.81	N.S.
Total Guilt Responses		42.86	17.38	54.20	19.56	2.02	<.05
Restitution	.89	6.24	3.42	5.72	3.50	0.49	N.S.
Apology	.95	2.38	2.94	2.24	1.33	0.21	N.S.
Reformation	.93	4.19	3.38	4.40	4.30	0.21	N.S.
Injured feelings	.89	11.24	5.70	13.20	5.96	1.07	N.S.
Self-punishment	.93	2.25	2.65	5.32	4.66	2.61	<.01
Impersonal punish-ment	.67	1.00	1.45	1.68	2.01	1.26	N.S.
Spontaneous con-fession	.91	3.05	3.03	2.68	2.62	0.44	N.S.
Criticism of de-viator	.73	1.67	1.89	3.16	2.77	2.05	<.05
Moralizing	.83	4.43	3.08	8.32	6.73	2.39	<.02 (.03)
Doesn't deviate	.90	3.24	2.37	3.92	2.41	0.93	N.S.
Rewarded for non-deviation	.86	3.29	2.99	2.40	2.61	0.81	N.S.
Total Fear Responses		8.71	5.86	9.44	5.73	0.41	N.S.
Denial	.80	1.24	1.51	2.40	2.15	2.02	<.05 (.06)
Flight	.77	1.14	2.05	1.16	1.80	0.04	N.S.
Hiding	.89	2.43	2.44	2.84	2.44	0.55	N.S.
Fear	.92	3.04	3.78	3.90	3.53	0.78	N.S.
External Punishment[a]		9.10	7.42	8.84	4.41	0.14	N.S.
Physical and verbal[a]	.85	3.05	4.26	1.72	1.61	1.41	N.S.
Other punish-ment[a]	.91	6.05	5.11	7.12	4.20	0.78	N.S.
Rewarded for Deviation	.86	3.29	4.33	2.40	2.89	0.81	N.S.

[a] These categories were not used as bases for prediction.
[b] Probabilities in parentheses are based on the Mann-Whitney U-test.

As depicted, the deviator is completely guilt-free, and consequently the only guilt category in which this story was
scored was the storyteller's criticism of the deviator. However, it is quite clear from his comments that, if this boy

had identified with the deviator, the story would have contained many more indices of guilt.

Another factor that may have affected results was the much greater frequency with which the control boys restructured the picture or story. In some cases the control boys changed a deviation situation to such an extent that it no longer presented a deviation; when this occurred, the test item could no longer serve as a stimulus for eliciting guilt feelings. The following story to Picture 7, usually perceived as a boy in the act of shaking his fist at his father, is a good example of this kind of distortion. In fact, the storyteller in this case appears to be consciously avoiding the usual type of interpretation.

B. (Case 10) Well, he was going out for the boxing team and he wasn't doing so good in it. And he, uh, so he came home and asked his father to show him some pointers, because his father was a boxer once. And so he showed him how to hold his hands and that. So that's what he's doing here, practicin'. And, uh, he turned out that he's one of the best, and he was glad that he asked his father for help (laughs). I changed that one all the way around.

A redefinition that altered the deviation situation in such a way as to make the deviant act *more* serious might have been expected to result in increased guilt responses for a guilt-controlled boy. However, such a redefinition at the same time made identification with the deviator less likely, thus tending to limit the boy's guilt responses to moralizing and criticism of the deviator. Moreover, rather than eliciting guilt, redefinition in this direction sometimes elicited an almost frantic fear reaction.

B. (Case 4) Well, Bill takes down the boxes and takes 'em down, and she has things that she's been cherishing for a long time that—she didn't want nobody in because they are very valuable and easy to break, like china and that. And he grabbed one of the boxes and he starts to bring it down and he drops the box and it breaks all the china. And he don't know what to do; he's frantic. He cleans it all up and he's hoping that she won't notice it. So he throws it all away, what he broke, and he arranges it all nice and neat. And he's all scared. He feels that, oh boy, if he gets caught, he's killed (laughs).

Occasionally, a control boy would depict a moral conflict which was acted out in two different characters, one a delinquent character and one a moralizing commentator. Although a greater degree of identification took place than when a guilt-free delinquent was alone depicted, this way of structuring the situation tended also to confine guilt responses to the moralizing and criticizing categories. It could, however, elicit a relatively large number of fear responses, for example, denial and hiding.

B. (Case 50) "Better hi-tail it down the street here. Well, nobody around. What'll I do with this big catcher's glove? I've gotten away with things before; this isn't the first time. Nope, he doesn't see me. That's great, boy. Get in the car and just cut outa here. I got the glove here, Jim. Don't show it, don't show it to them. Put it under there. Yeah, I bought it. You don't have to worry. Just do as I say. It's my glove. Now you can look at it. The ten dollars, you've got it? Well, O.K., I'll go back. For cryin' out loud, you're always the most honest man in the world. I'll take the glove back. Here, *you* take the glove back, all right? Give it to them. I'm not going to go back there. I don't care what you say, I'm not gonna take this glove back." "All right, you can get out of the car then; you can walk home." "Okay, I don't care. You're too righteous anyway, for cryin' out loud." "You can walk home. Here's twenty cents. Take the bus home." "Well, I lost a friend but I still got this mitt —free. I got ten dollars, I got my mitt." Couple of days later. "Hey, I got the glove, guys; let's get goin'. Whaddaya mean I'm not on the team anymore? He told the coach? Wait 'til I get my hands on that guy! There goes my baseball career. I don't think any team will sign me now. I can't play for anybody. Doggone that guy, I'll get him."

Moralizing also occurred in stories in which the control boys fully identified with the deviator. In this case, however, the moralizing became, in effect, self-criticism. In the following story, the self-reactions attributed to the story character are reminiscent of a parent's admonishments to a child.

B. (Case 26) Oh, Bill takes no more than a couple steps and he decides right there, "Bill, what's gotten into you? You can't change that much. Just because your father doesn't give the money to buy a glove, that's not the end of the world. You don't have to go out and get the mitt." He says, "Just think what that clerk has to go through. He has to go through bills and checks and whatnot and all kinds of accounts just to find where that little mitt went to, all because of me. And what am I gonna get out of it? Everytime I see that mitt, I'm gonna think about the time I stole it." So Bill walks right back in that store and lays it down. The clerk is still downstairs. He says, "I'm gonna feel a heck of a lot better after doing this." Says, "I guess I can wait until I get my catcher's mitt."

In view of the above considerations it is not surprising that two of the three guilt categories that individually differentiated the two groups of boys were *Moralizing* and *Criticism of the Deviator*. The third of these categories, *Self-Punishment*, perhaps most clearly reflected the operation of a well-internalized set of sanctions. In the stories, self-punishment frequently took the form of self-devaluation and a loss of self-esteem resulting from a failure to live up to the standards that the storyteller attributed to the main character.

B. (Case 52) He takes it (mitt) home and, uh, he's not proud of himself. If he really was honest, I don't think he woulda taken it. But then, if he did, I think his friends would sorta mistrust him, and he would probably not respect himself for doing that.

The close relationship between feelings of guilt and self-punishment was well illustrated by the following excerpt, in which the storyteller emphasized that, although the boy in the story had done no deliberate wrong, he nevertheless could not avoid the reprimands of his own conscience.

B. (Case 24) Well, anyway, he has the feeling any time when he goes down the street that he has a guilty conscience. You know what I mean. He feels that everybody is sorta looking down at him as to what has actually happened. And he's actually punishing himself. You know what I mean. And well, I mean, the people around him aren't actually punishing him. He just punishes himself, thinking that they think that he's done wrong. But they actually say he's okay, he didn't do it on purpose. And he's always going around punishing himself, but actually he hasn't done anything.

While, in some categories, the aggressive boys' guilt responses were as frequent as those of the control boys, in most instances their guilt seemed far less pervasive and intense. The guilt scores of some of the aggressive boys, in fact, derived largely from conventional gestures of repentance which they attributed to the story characters. In such cases, one or two stories in which the customary reactions to deviations were completely absent rather dramatically revealed their antisocial orientation.

B. (Case 45) This guy got a car. He wants to lower it but he doesn't have enough brass, enough money to do it. So he just goes around to an auto parts place and buys some little things, maybe four bits worth of stuff, just so he can hang around there long enough time so he can get a part that would cost a few dollars. He sticks it in his jacket and goes out and puts it in his car. The auto parts guy, he just turns it in to his insurance. I guess they got insurance like that. So if their insurance pays it, they don't care. So they're happy. The boy's happy 'cause he's got a faster car.

The difference between the aggressive and control boys on the over-all measure of fear was small and not statistically significant. Only one of the fear categories individually differentiated the groups; in this category, *Denial*, the control boys produced significantly more responses. Thus, the thematic material suggested that the aggressive boys might be somewhat less fearful of consequences than their controls. Although no measure of fear, as opposed to guilt, was secured from the interview data, the interviews, too, left the impression that the aggressive boys might be relatively less concerned about the possible consequences to themselves of their antisocial acts.

The aggressive and control boys did not differ significantly in the extent to which they represented the deviator as being punished by some external agent. It is interesting, however, that the aggressive boys made more reference to physical and verbal punishment, while the control boys more frequently referred to forms of punishment involving deprivation, isolation, social ostracism, or loss of the respect of others. The latter kinds of punishment include those that are predominantly psychological and thus, according to the hypothesis advanced in Chapter 5, are more closely associated with the development of conscience than are physical punishment or certain forms of verbal punishment, such as ridicule or nagging.

While differences for the remaining three categories, *Doesn't Deviate, Rewarded for Nondeviation,* and *Rewarded for Deviation,* were all in the expected direction, not one of them was statistically significant. Thus, the only individual categories for which predictions were confirmed were the three guilt categories, *Moralizing, Criticism of Deviator,* and *Self-Punishment.* It is probable that discomfort about antisocial acts, perhaps reflecting a high degree of conscience development, was also indicated by the control boys' more frequent redefinition of the situations depicted in the test items.

DISCUSSION

It was found that the two groups of boys did not differ in the extent to which they identified with their mothers. The aggressive boys, however, showed significantly less identification with their fathers than did the control boys. This weaker identification was evident not only from the direct measure of identification but also from consistently supportive findings arising from comparisons on other measures.

The defective conscience development of the aggressive boys was shown in their lack of guilt feelings when they deviated. To be sure, the aggressive boys were not completely guilt-free; however, as both interviews and thematic data showed, their guilt feelings were considerably weaker than those shown by the control boys. For the control boys guilt-avoidance was a strong motivating force to keep their behavior in line with social sanctions, whereas for the aggressive boys control had still to be largely maintained by fear of external punishment.

The development of conscience has been presented as the gradual replacement of controls based entirely on fear of consequences by an internalized system of values that prevents social deviation even when a deviant act is unlikely to be discovered. This does not, however, imply that the predominantly guilt-controlled person has little fear of consequences. Ordinarily such fear remains, and serves to fortify the effects of conscience when temptation is particularly strong.

On the other hand, most fear-controlled persons are not entirely guilt-free; during the long socialization period of childhood some internalization of values almost inevitably takes place. The aggressive boys, almost without exception, indicated both by their interview responses and by their thematic productions that they were at times motivated by anticipation of guilt and afflicted by feelings of remorse. This sporadic functioning of conscience is characteristic of the aggressive boy and makes him unpredictable and consequently difficult to handle (Redl and Wineman, 1952). Occasional spells of contrition or remorse often lead well-disposed adults to place more faith in such a boy than his history would warrant. Under these circumstances, the boy is likely to be accused of deception or bad faith if he commits further antisocial acts. Such an accusation, however, may be quite unfair; the boy may have temporarily experienced guilt as genuine as that which is more habitually felt by the well-socialized adolescent.

From the material presented in this chapter, as well as from that presented earlier, it is evident that the aggressive boys experienced many conditions that were particularly unfavorable for identification with their parents and for conscience development. It was shown in Chapter 2 that they lacked security in their emotional relationships with their parents; consequently, they had become fearful of, and resistant to, relating to others in a dependent role. The correlations reported in this chapter support the view that dependency and identification are closely related and that a disruption of the dependency relationship will make less probable the internalization of parental standards and values. It seems, therefore, that in the families of the aggressive boys one of the conditions for producing identification, a close dependent interaction between the parents and the child, was lacking.

In addition, the parents of the aggressive boys showed less

warmth for, and more hostility toward, their marital partners than did the parents of the control boys. The aggressive boys showed as much warmth for, and as little hostility toward, their mothers as did the control boys; they showed, however, considerably less warmth for, and a good deal more hostility toward, their fathers than did their controls. Since both the mothers and the boys showed relatively little warmth for the fathers and were also hostile toward them, the fathers were unlikely to serve as important models for imitation.

It was shown in Chapter 5 that the parents of the control boys made more use of psychological disciplinary methods. In contrast, the parents of the aggressive boys resorted more freely to such methods as ridicule, physical punishment, and deprivation of privileges. The use of these latter methods may have further weakened dependency relationships and thus have impeded the development of internalized controls.

A child's first identification is presumably with his mother or mother-substitute. The male child, however, must eventually identify with a male adult in order to fulfill the masculine role that is demanded of him very early in life. In fact, continued parental approval will ordinarily be dependent upon a successful transfer of identification.

Nothing has been said so far of the boy's competition with the father for the mother's love, or of the resolution of the Oedipus complex through identification. This is not because such a process is thought to be unimportant or never to occur, but because there are always cultural pressures for a child to behave in a sex-appropriate way, and these pressures would appear to be adequate to force a shift in identification, whether or not the psychoanalytic theory of identification through the resolution of the Oedipal complex holds true in every case. Psychoanalytic theory regards identification as a child-initiated defensive maneuver (Freud, 1936); however, from the point of view presented in this book, this process is initiated primarily by the parents. In this study, in fact, greater father-identification was found in the group of boys whose fathers made relatively high demands for male-appropriate behavior. Parental pressures for a male-identification are, of course, reinforced by the expectations of other adults who are significant figures in the boy's early childhood, as well as by the peer group.

A shift in identification should be facilitated if the father accepts the boy, rewards him with affection and approval, and spends sufficient time with him for imitative behavior patterns to be established. It was found that the fathers of the aggressive boys had spent relatively little time in affectionate interaction with their sons in early childhood, were lacking in warmth for them, and were more hostile, rejecting, and punitive than were the control fathers. In turn, the aggressive boys were critical and disparaging of their fathers. This disruption of the father-son relationship undoubtedly made identification with the father difficult, and consequently internalization of parental values was not completely achieved.

Chapter 7

Antisocial Aggression: An Overview

The findings of this study afford new insights into the underlying dynamics of antisocial aggression. Not only were the majority of hypotheses that were most strongly supported by theory and prior research adequately confirmed, but, in addition, new understandings emerged from the focal interest in the dependency conflict, which no previous study of antisocial behavior has thus emphasized. For the most part, however, it has been necessary to present the findings in a somewhat fragmentary fashion; an attempt is now made to integrate the findings previously reported and to discuss some of their more general implications.

An over-all view of the typical characteristics of the aggressive boys shows how they emerged from comparison with their more adequately socialized counterparts. In the first place, they expressed their aggression in a much more direct and uninhibited manner, particularly outside the home; they were more openly antagonistic to authority and less positive in their feelings toward their peers. They felt somewhat rejected by both parents, but retained a good deal of affection and respect for their mothers. In contrast, they were critical and resentful of their fathers, with whom they showed only limited identification. They were markedly distrustful; they feared and avoided situations in which they might have become emotionally dependent on others. Their sexual behavior was likely to be less inhibited than that of the average adolescent, and they tended to confound sex and aggression. Aggressive and sexual behavior aroused in them fewer guilt feelings than they did in the control boys and, in general, their impulses were more likely to be controlled by fear than by guilt. They were, in many respects, like small children whose impulses are held in check by external, rather than by internal, restraints. Their behavior, moreover, was apparently self-defeating, because it alienated them from the affection of which they already felt deprived and brought them under the more direct control of the authority figures whom they distrusted and resented.

Several aspects of the child-training process were separately considered, and an attempt was made to identify some factors that might be conducive to specific socialization defects. The conjoint operation of some or all of these factors is probably necessary in order to produce a boy of the kind described in the previous paragraph. The interplay of factors can be best illustrated by presenting, together and in detail, all the material obtained from a single family. A detailed presentation of the material from two families, one in which the boy had a record of antisocial aggressive behavior, the other a control family, has consequently been undertaken. The boys in these families were both approaching their seventeenth birthdays, and both were only children; they lived in the same middle-class neighborhood, and had attended the same schools. Both families were apparently in comfortable economic circumstances.

CASE 33: DONALD

Court and school records indicated that Donald had shown an antisocial aggressive pattern of behavior throughout adolescence. It was evident, however, from the interviews with his parents that his difficulties did not emerge in adolescence, but were present even in very early childhood.

M. Well, when he was about three years old, it seemed like we had to be constantly doing something. We just tried everything in the book to keep from having to spank him so much. It didn't do any good.

About this time Donald displayed both distance and hyper-aggressiveness.

M. He was awfully shy and backward and he'd stand off to one side and watch the activities and play, but he, after he got out of kindergarten and started in school, he began to, at times, would join in and do things; but a lot of times he did stand back and he could never get up in school and talk before a class. He said, "Mother, I just go blank. I can't think of a thing to say."

.   .   .

M. I always felt that he always was just a bit too handy with his fists (laughs), because even when he first started to school he didn't want anyone to touch him, anyone to bump into him. He was just that quick. Fly up and maybe hit him or do something to them before they could bat an eyelid (laughs heartily).

It would seem that Donald, by the age of three or four, was already anxious about, and avoidant of, any close interaction with others. His mistrust was manifested in his aggressive responses; he seemed to anticipate aggression from others and to retaliate in advance. By the time of adolescence this pattern was firmly entrenched.

I. What kind of things make you like a fellow?
B. I kind of hate them when I first meet them.

Yet in the first year or two of his life Donald had at times made very strong overtures for dependency gratification. His mother's early nurturance had sufficed to develop a dependency motive which was manifested when she attempted to leave him to himself.

M. Well, before he walked, I usually, when he was up and playing, we'd go out. When it was nice weather, we'd go for a walk and go to the store. I would play with him and talk with him, and I tried to have him entertain himself a certain amount, but he would never at any time stay by himself in his room. He had to see someone (laughs).

There were already signs, as the above quotation illustrates, that the mother was, to some extent, inclined to discourage Donald's dependency behavior.

M. I always rocked him to sleep until he was a little past a year old.
. . . I just, when I noticed that he'd go to sleep quicker by just
putting him to bed, I just quit rocking him.

It is clear from the accounts of both parents that by the time
Donald was seven or eight years, at the most, he was actively
inhibiting the affectionate, dependent behavior that he had
displayed during an earlier period.

M. Well, he was never (affectionate); he was up until he was eight
years old. He didn't want you to kiss, to hug him or anything like
that, so I just would gradually, I would talk instead of hugging
him or kissing him like we used to. Like he'd come and crawl on
my lap, put his arms around me and kiss me on the cheek. He'd
want to be loved a little bit, you know, and then he'd go to play.
After he got to where he didn't want you to make over him, why,
I tried to more or less, when I felt it was right to show him my
affection in other ways.

While Donald had early in life made attempts to obtain
dependency gratification from his mother, he manifested,
even at that early age, an active avoidance of close contact
with his father.

F. You see a lot of boys, they'll squeeze their mothers or come up and
bite them on the neck. You know, hug them, love them a little bit.
You never see Donald do it. He never has. Even when he was a
little kid he never wanted to be held. He never did that. He didn't
like my lap. All you needed to do was to squeeze that boy and he'd
wiggle right out and he wouldn't come back.

Although the mother's subtle discouragement of Donald's
dependency behavior may have played some part in producing the change, the father's almost complete rejection was
probably a decisive factor in the development of the boy's
dependency conflict.

M. They (children) get on his nerves, it seems like. Of course his
mother was that way, and he can't seem to help it. I kind of felt
sometimes that he could be a little bit more understanding of
children and their ideas and ways of doing things.

The father's interview yielded little information about his
handling of early forms of dependency behavior; however,
he constantly stressed the desirability of the boy's being

independent in a way which suggested he wished to have little to do with him.

I. Do you ever tell him he should work things out for himself and not rely too much on his parents?

F. Yeah, make up your mind. You're the one that's got to live with it.

His rejective, punitive attitude was most clearly revealed in his comments to Donald after the boy had been in trouble with the police.

F. "Brother you're here now. When you get so you want to get home and behave yourself, you're perfectly willing, but we're all washed up with this. You're on your own now. You think you're a big shot. You go right along and peddle your own papers, just the way you want to." We left him alone for about a month, then we went out to see him and, boy, he was really a different kid altogether. He didn't have that—I don't know what you call it—a snotty attitude —the kind of word you'd use—but he had a little who-do-you-think-you-are—but he didn't have that. He looked like he was, you'd say, he looked like he was whipped.

After Donald's return home, his father found him a job at the same place of work as himself, but nevertheless took the precaution of reducing Donald's dependency on him to a minimum.

M. And my husband told them, "Now don't put him anywhere where I will have to have any jurisdiction over him. I want him in another department where someone else will be his boss and I'll have nothing to do with it and he'll be on his own. He'll have to make good on his own. He won't expect me to help him."

Although Donald was a boy of high average intelligence and a competent musician, his father constantly referred to him as being a boy of limited capabilities who deserved little of the teachers' attention. "He just didn't have it . . . he just didn't absorb anything." Even when Donald was in grade school, his father felt that the boy was incapable of progressing at the same rate as his classmates, and his vocational expectations for Donald had evidently always been low.

F. We always pumped, always tried to pump it into him that he ought to have at least a high school diploma, if he only wants to use a pick and shovel.

His disparaging attitude, as well as his aggressive, punitive orientation, was reflected over and over again in the terms which he used to describe his attempts to change his son's behavior.

F. Well, I think we did (make him feel ashamed) about three or four weeks ago. And I think it really soaked in. The first time that he realized that we had been trying to keep something knocked in his head without knocking it into him.

In answering questions about the desirability of Donald's spending time with them, both parents were inclined to focus on the advantages of his being with other persons. When they did insist that he should stay in their company, it seemed primarily for the purpose of keeping him from getting into trouble.

I. Some parents feel that boys of Donald's age should go on trips and vacations with their families; others think it is better that they should go off with their friends. How do you feel about this?
F. I think it's a good idea for Donald to go with his friends, too.

. . .

M. I think it does him good to go with other people. . . . There were times when we just couldn't let him stay at home by himself. He'd have to go with us because there was no place else for him to go. But if there were other activities that we thought were all right then, safe enough, we let him go on his own.

The interview with Donald left no doubt that he had experienced strong feelings of rejection, particularly in relation to his father.

I. How much do you feel your father understands you and tries to help you?
B. Not at all. I don't understand him.
I. Do you think he likes having you around?
B. By the way he acts, I don't think he does.
I. How much interest do you think he takes in you?
B. Not too much.

Although Donald had retained some affection and respect for his mother, he had become distant and distrustful even with her.

I. Are there things you especially like about your mother and that make you happy in her company?

B. She has a good personality . . . she's always very nice.

I. How much do you feel she understands you?

B. I don't think she understands me, period. I never rely on her. You know what I mean.

In view of the father's openly rejective attitude and the mother's more subtle discouragement of dependency behavior, it is not surprising that Donald showed an extreme reluctance to display any dependency whatsoever on his parents.

I. When Donald is in difficulties does he ever come to you to talk things over?

F. He'll talk them over with his mother first.

       •   •   •

M. No. He got so that he wouldn't. He always says afterwards that he was afraid to. And we would ask him why he was afraid to, he'd say he was just afraid to.

       •   •   •

I. Does Donald know what you expect of him (type of work)?

M. Well, we had talked some when he would talk with us. That was our main problem. He kept everything to himself as far as we were concerned in knowing his thoughts and what he wanted to do.

       •   •   •

I. How well do you think Donald and his mother understand one another?

F. I think a lot better than I do. They talk more. I think they understand one another a lot better.

       •   •   •

I. How well do you think you and Donald understand one another?

M. Well, at times I felt that I really understood him and could follow along his pattern of thinking and his ideas, and like I said, it seemed all of a sudden, as my sister made the remark, I just lost contact. That was all.

       •   •   •

I. How often would you say you went to your father to talk things over?

B. Never.

I. How about getting him to help you with your schoolwork?

B. No.

I. How about if you were worried about something or had gotten into a scrape? Do you go to him then?

B. No. I never went to my parents.

I. When your parents make a suggestion, do you usually accept it or do you prefer to work things out for yourself?
B. I'd rather work things out for myself. . . .
I. Some fellows go around with their parents quite a lot, for example, on trips or to movies. Others don't like this very much. How do you feel about this?
B. I don't go.

Donald, in fact, showed a generalized inhibition of dependency behavior. He rarely, if ever, consulted his teachers or school counselors about any kind of problem and expressed a strong uneasiness about having to do so.

I. Does it ever make you feel uncomfortable if you have to get help from a teacher or counselor?
B. Yes.
I. What makes you feel this way?
B. Well, I feel very stupid.
I. If a teacher or counselor offers you advice or makes a suggestion, do you generally follow it, or do you prefer to work things out for yourself?
B. I prefer to work things out for myself.

One way in which Donald's father expressed his negative feelings toward his son was through a constant disparagement of Donald's intellectual capacity; it is therefore possible that attempts by Donald to seek help or advice from his father in earlier years sometimes elicited a critical or disparaging response. Under these circumstances, it is not surprising that Donald felt "stupid" when he had to seek help from teachers.

Donald's uneasiness about dependency was, however, most strikingly revealed in his answers to the questions about his relationships with peers.

I. How do you feel about asking favors of friends, like lending you money or fixing you up with a date?
B. I don't go for that. I'd rather do it myself. . . .
I. When a friend suggests something to you, do you generally do what he suggests, or do you prefer to work things out for yourself?
B. I prefer to work things out for myself.
I. Does it ever make you feel uncomfortable if you have to get help from another fellow or can't make up your mind for yourself?

B. Yes it does. It makes me feel like I need somebody around me.

I. How do you prefer to spend your time, alone or in the company of friends?

B. Alone. . . .

I. When you are with a group of friends, what kind of things do you like to do?

B. If they feel like talking to me, they talk to me. And if I feel like talking, I talk to them. . . .

I. Suppose you disagree with a decision, do you usually go along with them (friends), or do you go off by yourself and do what you want to do?

B. Once in a while I go with them, but most of the time I go off by myself. . . .

I. If your friends don't like some ways you act, do you try to change, or do you think that's your business and not theirs?

B. I try to avoid them. If they don't like the way I act, then I try to avoid them.

I. Would you say you like to have friends to talk things over with and trust in, or do you think it's better to rely on nobody but yourself?

B. I want to rely on myself. I don't want to rely on others.

I. How much do you think you can trust other guys?

B. Not too far. . . .

I. Have there ever been times when you felt you weren't wanted by your friends?

B. I've never even thought about it. . . . If they want to be my friends, well, they can be my friends. If they don't, why, it's up to them.

The hesitancy about relating to peers that Donald had displayed during childhood had by adolescence developed into a calculated and hostile avoidance.

Throughout Donald's life the socialization pressures imposed upon him by his parents were weak and fluctuating. Few limits were set on his behavior; even these tended to be poorly defined and inconsistently enforced.

I. If you had your time over and had to bring up Donald again, would you do things differently from the way you have done them?

M. Well, I think in my way of handling him when he was, oh, say, around three. I didn't realize at the time that that is the stage when they begin to have ideas of their own and start asserting them, and he and I used to go round and round (laughs) until I began to think maybe I was too hard on him, and then I would let up on him and I tried to, instead of saying "No" to him so much, as much as possible let him do things. I felt that would help him out. Of course once in a while you did have to say "No" to him.

• • •

I. How strict was your wife with Donald?

F. Oh, gee. You couldn't say she was downright strict. He could always soft-soap around her a little bit (laughs). She gives in to him a little bit. But, you know, she'd stick to what she told him, but she would kind of kick over the traces by the end of the week, or something like that. In fact, we both kind of did that.

Donald's father delegated the task of positive social training almost entirely to his wife. "I figure she's the housekeeper, so she keeps the house up. Whatever she wants him to do, I figure that was all right." The mother, however, failed to force obedience and to follow through the few demands that she made.

I. Some mothers expect their children to obey immediately when they tell them to do something; others don't think it is terribly important for a child to obey right away.

M. You can't, you can't expect that (laughs). I don't, I don't. I like to, I always felt they should have a little forewarning and I always give them a little time to arrange themselves a little bit so they could do what was expected of them at times.

• • •

I. How much do you keep after him to see that these things (responsibilities) are done?

M. Well, we got so that we'd give him a couple of days. We'd tell him a few days ahead of time so that he knew that it was up to him to do that; and finally, after the time was set, we'd say that that has to be done by such and such a time, and 2 or 3 days to give him time to work it in with any plans that he might have made. And invariably he would make other plans; and we'd have to, we'd give him a little more time, and he'd make some more plans; and he'd just keep that up until eventually one of us would have to do it ourselves because we couldn't wait any longer (laughs).

I. Does he ever seem to resent having to do them?

M. Well, he got so he resented doing anything, period.

She had adopted an attitude of passive resignation to much of Donald's behavior of which she did not particularly approve.

I. How about smoking and drinking, how do you feel about these?

M. Well, when he decided to smoke, we naturally decided to discourage it. You know, for about a week we talked to him about it.

Of course, he had been trying cigarettes off and on since he was seven years old at different times and then, when he decided, when he started smoking regularly, he was out at Juvenile Hall. He asked if he could go ahead and smoke; and we knew he had been behind our backs, but we didn't say anything. We just ignored it and thought, "Well, if he's going to smoke, he's going to smoke."

Apparently if Donald asserted himself with sufficient force and regularity he eventually got his own way. Thus there was considerable reinforcement of self-assertive behavior.

While Donald's father did little in setting limits, he freely punished behavior of which he disapproved. In view of the mother's laxness and inconsistency, many of the father's punishments must have appeared unjustified and irrational to Donald and had given rise to strong feelings of resentment.

I. How do you feel about the way your father has dealt with you in regard to punishment?
B. I don't like him. I don't like the way he's handled it.

In fact, there are indications that the mother supported Donald in his feelings.

I. In general, do you and your husband agree about the restrictions you place on Donald?
M. We did fine until 4 or 5 years ago. And I don't know, I never could understand. My husband said he couldn't do this, he couldn't do that. But other boys could do this. The other boys were nice friendly boys and well, you know what I mean, they would just like being mischievous, but they would never have thought of stepping over the bounds and really doing bad things. We had an awful time with his clothes and his hair; and the other boys were beginning to wear peggers, and my husband just, Donald was just not going to wear it and that was all there was to it; and he was very sensitive about it, his clothes and hair. I kept still to a certain point. I don't like to see anyone disagree over a youngster, and they eventually feel it. And finally, when Donald asked me why his father didn't agree with what he did, I told him we had talked about it and I just couldn't make him understand and for it not to let it bother him. But it made him awfully nervous. Really, many times I felt that Donald could have ignored it a little bit (laughs). It seemed like it was a constant pull one way or the other. He was determined Donald was going to do what he said; and Donald was determined he was going to do like the rest of the crowd did;

and I was trying to keep a balance between the two of them and between my husband and myself at the same time.

During Donald's childhood both parents had tried varying forms of discipline with little apparent effect on the boy's behavior.

I. Suppose Donald has been behaving badly and giving you or his father a hard time, what kind of things do you say to him?

M. Well, when, for example, he was smaller, it didn't do any good to spank him because he would invariably go right back and do the same thing again as soon as you turned him loose. Then we would try, oh, maybe depriving him of doing some little thing; or we have even taken maybe a toy from him or something like that that he thought quite a lot of. We would never keep them too long away from him if we did anything like that. But never at any time would he ever ask for them back. Once you took something away or deprived him of doing something that he liked, he'd never mention it again.

When parents deprive a child of a toy that he prizes, they are not only taking away an object that has some intrinsic value as a plaything but, in doing so, they are also symbolizing the withdrawal of their love and approval. Usually the child will strive for the return of the toy, largely because he wishes to be reassured of his parents' continued affection, and he will ordinarily promise to conform to the parents' wishes in order to obtain this reassurance. Thus Donald's behavior suggested that he had already begun to give up attempts to win the parents' love and approval.

It is quite evident even at this stage that deprivation was an ineffective technique for changing Donald's behavior. By the time that Donald was an adolescent, his father's use of severe deprivation had little value other than to gratify the father's own punitive and retaliatory feelings.

I. What do you find most effective (in disciplining Donald)?

F. Take his privileges away from him. Take his allowance away from him. Boy, that hurts him more than anything. We've tried to talk to him, but that doesn't do any good at all. He got to the point where he got to know more than we did. Which maybe he did. "If you're to feel that way about it, we'll take your allowance away from you this week. See what you think of that."

From the parents' accounts, it was clear that they had used a good deal of physical punishment even though they had found it ineffective. They had been slow to abandon this method of discipline, for Donald reported almost daily slappings or spankings up until his twelfth or thirteenth year. With verbal reprimands, deprivation, and physical punishment all ineffective, the parents' attempts to control Donald had become a trial and error procedure.

F. We generally always thrash things out and talk about it. Shall we do this or shall we do that? Then we kind of come to some kind of conclusion. We do a little of both and see how it works. If it works out all right, we have confidence. If it doesn't work out, we're lost.

It appeared that the parents had, in fact, lost. The relationship between the father and the boy had become one of intense mutual hostility, while the mother at times expressed a feeling that control of the situation was difficult, if not impossible.

I. Does Donald seem to accept the restrictions you place on him, or does he resent them?
M. Well, that's another thing I don't understand about Donald now. He argues with his father and he really, everything that his father told him he couldn't do, Donald was just that much determined that he was going to do. And out here (Juvenile Hall) he made a remark one day that, "Nobody can fight with my father but me" (laughs). Looks like he kind of enjoyed it or something (laughs).

       •   •   •

I. Does he try to get around the restrictions in any way?
M. Yes, he tries to get around them. He'll really go and finally get around something that he knows someone doesn't want him to do. Even school teachers said that. If he would put as much effort in learning as he did to get around all of these things, he would be an A student (laughs).

Donald was now too big to be controlled physically and the threat of outside intervention seemed to be the last resort left to the parents.

F. "Well, you just have to take care of it, you'll have to do this, and if you can't keep it up, we'll have to call in the Youth Authority or somebody. We can't go along with it."

Although the picture was very similar in many of the families of the aggressive boys, usually one point of bargaining remained. The boy either had a car of his own which could be taken away, or made requests for the use of the family car which could be refused. Donald, however, had never bought a car and, according to his parents, had never asked for the use of theirs. Just as in childhood Donald never asked for the prized toy, so now he did not ask his parents for one of the main pleasures of an adolescent, the use of a car. Yet car theft was one of his offences.

Although Donald verbalized strong hostile feelings toward his father, he showed little direct aggression in the home.

I. When Donald gets angry at you, what does he do?
M. He'll usually just clam up and you can't get anything out of him.

. . .

F. He generally just pouts. He never says anything, that's the trouble. He just pouts.

The interview with Donald's parents yielded little information about how they had handled aggression toward themselves during Donald's early years. The mother was currently vacillating and inconsistent in her responses to Donald's expressions of hostility, sometimes ignoring him, sometimes scolding him; it is therefore probable that she had allowed a good deal of overt aggression to occur during Donald's childhood. On the other hand, the father's generally punitive behavior and his current nontolerance of disobedience and defiance suggest that he had been severe in his handling of Donald's aggression and had finally succeeded in channeling it into indirect and displaced forms. Donald's hostility was now expressed predominantly in resistance, sullenness, and a revengeful attitude.

M. Sometimes he'll pout for a little while, go to his room. He would pout and carry that grudge, that feeling, until he felt he'd got back at you some way.

. . .

M. When he went to work he got all of a sudden, got very careless and seemed to want to get things dirty, and he wanted to mar the furniture, anything.

Some of Donald's aggression had apparently been displaced to teachers. He reported much blatant verbal aggression toward teachers and a considerable amount of disruptive behavior in and out of the classroom.

B. I give them a hard time. . . . I sass them back. . . . I've sworn at a counselor. The teacher gave me a bad time. That was the time that I was drunk. He threw me out of the room. So I went and told the Vice-Principal. He laughed and he said, "You know you'll get into trouble for making remarks like that." So I started cutting class.

Although many of Donald's disruptive activities were markedly hostile in nature, others were primarily of an attention-getting kind and were sometimes directed toward those teachers to whom his attitude was relatively favorable.

I. Do you sometimes do things openly in school for which you know you'll get told off or punished?
B. I'd start fights in school.
I. Have you ever been told off for clowning in class?
B. Yes. Goof off, make wisecracks, crack jokes, and things like that. Quite frequently.
I. How about asking silly questions on purpose? Making funny remarks?
B. Yes. If I like the teacher I do that, but not all the time.

In view of Donald's very early hyperaggressiveness, one might expect that his parents would have done all they could to discourage him from being aggressive toward other children. Instead, his mother's attitude was one of noninterference, while his father may have actively encouraged his son by his own belligerent, combative attitude.

I. Have you ever had to encourage Donald to stand up for himself?
F. No. We've always tried to pump that into him. "You don't back down to nobody. . . ."
I. Has he ever come to you and complained that another fellow was giving him a rough time?
F. No.
I. Suppose he did, what would you say to him?
F. "You're big enough. Can't you thrash it out amongst yourselves? You don't have to fight about it. Either that, or leave him alone."

I. If Donald got into a fight with one of the neighbor's boys, how would you handle it?

F. (Laughs) Well, last time he got into a fight, I let him fight it out, and they're darned good friends now. I don't know how far that one went (laughs). They both looked like chopping blocks when they came home. They both had black eyes, cut lips, and banged-up hands.

Donald's aloofness and hostility could hardly fail to evoke hostile, rejecting reactions from his peers.

I. What sort of things make you like a guy?

B. I kind of hate them when I first meet them. They generally get under my skin when I first meet them.

. . .

I. Do you think on the whole other guys like you?

B. Not too much. The way they act when I'm around. They make wisecracks and stuff.

When other boys became angry at him, Donald did not hesitate to use physical aggression in a way that must have evoked still more hostility from his peers.

I. What about the sort of fellow who blows his top at you or says things about you you don't like?

B. I generally bust him in the nose.

Donald's initial hostility probably reflected his anticipation of rejection and hostility from others. When it evoked these reactions, his expectations were confirmed. Thus his habitual pattern of aloofness and hostility was self-perpetuating.

Donald's father was generally nonpermissive of early forms of sexual behavior but indicated that he had left the handling of such behavior entirely to his wife, who, in contrast, was unusually tolerant.

I. Would you have allowed this (sex play with other children) or do you think you would have done something about it?

F. I'd nip it in the bud.

. . .

M. Well, when they're small, I look at it this way. They don't understand those things and they're more or less curious, and the less you pay attention to it, they soon go to something else. You can always, up to a certain age, distract them and get them to thinking about something else.

Both parents were remarkably permissive in their attitudes toward heterosexual behavior. The father felt that it was quite natural for the boy to engage in sexual experimentation and that the girl was responsible for maintaining control.

I. How would you feel if you found that Donald had now begun to play around with girls?

F. Well, if he didn't, I think he'd be, at his age, he'd be kinda, something wrong here (laughs). I think, a kid gets sixteen years old, why, they kind of feel out their oats.

I. How do you feel about young fellows who go all the way with girls?

F. Well, that I don't know. It's up to the girl, I guess. That's the way I look at it. If she's willing to go all the way, why, that's the way it's going to bé.

Donald's mother expressed a very similar attitude; in addition, she seemed to obtain some satisfaction from learning that Donald knew a good deal about sex and from hearing about his sexual experiences.

I. Suppose you found that Donald had now begun to play around with girls, how would you feel about it?

M. Well, in fact, I know he has been; and once or twice he hasn't come right out and said, but he did make the remark that if he was, that's one thing he wouldn't go about bragging about, and especially who the party was or anything like that. And then he said that he knows all about it.

I. How about petting, how do you feel about it?

M. Well, I think they all, all young people, especially right now, more than they used to in years back. They have more opportunity now; and I don't know, I've never thought much about it. They're all going to, more or less, some time or another.

I. How do you feel about young fellows who go all the way with girls?

M. Well, I don't think that's right, but if the two are agreeable, why, there's not much at that age that a person can say or do. . . .

I. Do you think that Donald is worried at all about matters that have to do with sex?

M. Sometimes I used to wonder a little, but my father-in-law talked with him and he seemed to feel that Donald knew more than he did (laughs heartily).

It is thus not surprising that Donald showed a matter-of-fact attitude toward sexual behavior.

I. Suppose a friend of yours got a girl you knew into trouble, what would you think of him?
B. Well, I wouldn't feel too badly about it.
I. Suppose you go farther than usual with a girl, how do you feel about this?
B. It's O.K.

According to Donald he had been initiated into intercourse at the age of eleven and at that time first learned about masturbation.

I. How did you find out about masturbation?
B. Well, I was out with a girl once.
I. Did you engage in masturbation with her?
B. No, we were in intercourse. There was something wrong with me, first half. I didn't know anything about it.

Although Donald had experienced intercourse at an earlier age than any other boy in the study, he used this form of sexual outlet only about twice a year, much less frequently than the other boys who had begun having sexual relations. He said that he masturbated about once every two weeks, and this seemed to be his main way of obtaining sexual gratification.

Donald expressed indifference toward girls and it is probable that his acts of intercourse were unaccompanied by any affectional response.

I. How do you feel about girls?
B. I don't particularly like them or dislike them.

This indifference, as well as his infrequent use of intercourse, may, in fact, reflect Donald's anxiety about dependency. In this connection, it is interesting that at the age of fourteen, long after he had first engaged in sex relations, Donald spent several nights with a girl without having intercourse with her.

B. Two years ago I ran away with a girl. That's when I was picked up for car theft.
I. Did you think you were in love with her?

B. No, she just wanted to tail along. We didn't actually go all the way. I didn't have intercourse with her.

•   •   •

F. I asked the mother to have the girl examined as soon as she came home. She had never been touched.

From the above excerpt from Donald's interview, and from his description of his first experience of intercourse, it seems likely that the heterosexual activities in which he had engaged had been largely initiated by the girls.

Donald did not display the derogatory, hostile attitude to women that was characteristic of many of the aggressive boys, nor did he give any signs of confounding sex with aggression. His aggression appeared to be focused almost entirely on males, perhaps because his attitude to his mother was generally a positive one. Moreover, Donald's parents were both so permissive of heterosexual behavior that promiscuity could hardly serve for him as a way of expressing defiance of social standards.

Many of the conditions that facilitate identification with parent models were clearly absent in Donald's home. The complete disruption of the father-son relationship and the inconsistent, punitive disciplinary techniques to which Donald had been subjected have already been illustrated in some detail. Undoubtedly other factors contributed. Neither parent made strong demands for male-appropriate behavior; in fact, both emphasized the importance of a boy's being able to carry out traditionally feminine responsibilities. The parents disagreed in what they expected of Donald and, although the relationship between them was relatively intact, there was sufficient disharmony about the handling of the boy to have undermined the boy's respect and esteem for his parents, particularly for his father. Donald's mother was highly critical of her husband's lack of patience and understanding in his handling of their son. As an earlier excerpt showed, she communicated to Donald some of her negative feelings about her husband, and thus probably fanned his hostility to his father. The parents' lack of mutual esteem seemed to be reflected in their tendency to see their admittedly difficult son as unlike themselves and as resembling the family of the other parent.

I. Whom would you say Donald is most like, personality-wise?
F. He's more her side of the family. He's a dead ringer of her brother. He's more of the wife's type.

. . .

M. Well he, I don't know. Part of the time he resembles some of my family, and then at different stages of growth he resembles his father's family. Well, I don't know; I never felt he resembled me too much.

Donald gave very few indications of having identified with his parents. At one point, however, he expressed the feeling that he had acquired some of his father's irascibility.

I. Of all the people you know, whom do you most want to be like when you grow older?
B. I wouldn't know that.
I. How about your father?
B. No.
I. Are there any ways in which you think you are like him already?
B. Well, I've been getting kind of cranky. I've been trying to break that. I mean, I talk back fast, flare up.
I. In what ways would you like to be like your mother?
B. Oh, she has a good personality. I like her. She gets along with people.
I. How much do you think you are like her now?
B. Not too much.

While it is true that Donald's father provided a hostile, aggressive model, it is unlikely that identification with the aggressive aspects of the father's personality was an important determinant of his antisocial behavior. In fact, Donald's desire not to be like his father seemed to provide some motivation for striving for self-control.

Under these circumstances one would not expect a boy to develop strong conscience-control. Neither sexual intercourse nor masturbation appeared to cause Donald any concern. Questions designed to provide material for assessing guilt about aggressive behavior merely elicited, for the most part, further descriptions of hostile acts or feelings.

I. When you get mad at a guy and hit him, how do you feel afterwards?

B. Oh, I'm just cooling off then. I generally talk to them and tell them not to do that any more. . . . If I get mad at a guy, I'm going to let him come and apologize.

. . .

I. What if you do something you know your father disapproves of, do you ever feel sorry and go and tell him afterwards?

B. I don't over-exert myself for my father.

Although Donald expressed some uneasiness about aggression toward his mother, this feeling did not lead him to lessen his defiance nor did it motivate attempts to change his behavior.

Donald grew up in a home in which he experienced rejection, punitiveness, and interparental inconsistency. As a result, he had developed into a frustrated adolescent who was seething with hostility. Not only were his affectional needs not satisfied in his relationships with his parents, but his distrust and hostility, which early deprivation had engendered, had prevented him from gaining emotional gratifications which were potentially available from other adults and from his peers. He continued to "stand off to the side," expecting and inviting the rejection and lack of security that he had always experienced, and ready to strike back at the slightest provocation. Thus, he remained unloved and unwanted. His complete alienation from his father and his distrust of his mother had prevented him from adopting social values that might have served to control and direct his behavior. While the emotional tie between Donald and his mother had never been completely severed, she was too inconsistent, and too rewarding of defiance and rebellion, to serve as an effective socializing influence.

CASE 36: RAYMOND

Raymond grew up in a child-centered home atmosphere.

F. He's always had a nice place to live and he's always had very loving parents. I think perhaps sometimes too loving. I think that basically a great deal of our push and a great deal of our living habits have been built around Ray.

In infancy Raymond received a good deal of affectionate care from both parents. In addition to carrying out the usual routines, his mother set aside some time each day exclusively for playing with the child. The father participated in care-taking when he came home from his work, among other things feeding Raymond his evening and night bottles.

M. When he'd come home, he'd get him ready for bed and he'd feed him the ten o'clock bottle. I mean that was a cut-and-dried busi-ness, but that wasn't the time that he played. But when he got older, he played with him as much as I did.

This affectionate interaction continued throughout child-hood and early adolescence.

F. When he was in scouting, I used to take all the trips with the scouts up to the snow and so forth. I participated. I was a cub-master for two years and I became active in scouting with him and we took all the scouting trips together.

While both parents were completely accepting of Ray-mond and obviously felt a great deal of affection for him, the father was the more demonstrative of the two.

I. I'm wondering if you could tell me more about the relationship be-tween you and Raymond. Do you show your affection toward each other quite a bit, or are you fairly reserved?

F. Yes, we do something that probably most fathers and sons don't do. I usually kiss him on the cheek when I leave, and a great num-ber of times when he leaves, he'll come over and kiss me on the cheek. He won't do it when there's anyone around because of the shyness of it. He'll come over and shake my hand or say, "Hello, dad." But if it's just my wife and myself and Ray in the house, he kisses us both on the cheek.

Raymond's mother was very self-demanding and was con-tinually comparing herself unfavorably with her husband. It was clear, however, both when she gave specific details about the relationship between Raymond and herself and from the accounts given by her husband and son, that she, too, was a warm and understanding parent.

M. We're not too affectionate. The fault is probably mine. I'm not affectionate. We kiss each other hello and goodbye, and we could perhaps be more affectionate if I were more affectionate.

I. Are there some things about Raymond that you really enjoy and make you like doing things with him?

M. I enjoy being with him. He's very pleasant company. He's a very nice boy. He's pleasant to have around.

I. How well do you think you and Raymond know and understand one another?

M. Very well; very, very well. I understand him, I think, perfectly because we're very much alike.

Raymond, in turn, expressed a great deal of warmth and esteem for both parents. His relationship with his father was particularly close.

I. Are there things you really like about your mother?

B. Yes. She's very intelligent. She's not bad looking. She's very friendly with my friends. They all really like her. She's real friendly. They like to talk with her.

I. How do you go about showing her you feel this way?

B. Uh, I don't know. I guess she thinks sometimes, most times, I don't love her or something like that, but I mean parents can really tell by the way their kid acts. I mean if he's good, and I'm not doing anything wrong, they can tell. Because most of the juvenile delinquency is due to the parents.

I. How much do you feel she understands you?

B. Not too much. No, I don't think—I guess she really does, but I don't feel she does.

I. Do you think she enjoys having you around?

B. Oh, we don't argue. Yeah, yeah.

I. Do you think she tries to help you?

B. Most of the time, yes. Most of the stuff she says is very good.

I. How much interest do you think she takes in you?

B. Oh, she has a very large interest.

I. Are there things you really enjoy about your father?

B. Oh, my friends really like my mother. She's the kind of person who gets along with anybody. I mean, my Dad, everybody likes him, but usually with the older people—but my friends they really like him too. I mean, he's a square guy. He's the kind of guy that understands because he was young once. He wasn't a lover or anything like that, but he was a football type and things like that.

I. How much do you feel he understands you?

B. He understands me pretty much.

I. How much interest do you feel he takes in you?

B. Oh, he takes quite a bit.

I. Do you think he tries his best to help you?

B. Oh, yes, he's always trying to help me.

I. Does he enjoy having you around?

B. He enjoys me more than I enjoy being with him. Yeah, he'd like me to be with him all the time. He likes always to do something with the family and I like to go out with my friends a lot of the time.

While the parents accepted Raymond's growing independence and his interest in peer-group activities, they nevertheless expressed some regret that they could no longer expect him to be too much in their company.

I. Do you feel that you spend as much time with Raymond as other fathers do with their sons, or more?

F. I would say about average, average being the fact that Ray and I are very close in our thoughts; but perhaps I should spend more time with him than I have, because as the years go by, I see that he's growing up into manhood and I'm losing a lot of him every year. When he was younger, I think I was with him more than I am now. . . . I think, as he gets older, he's had a tendency to get his pleasures from people his own age, and this is fine as long as he makes home his headquarters. That's all I want.

They felt that Raymond's peer-group activities were essential for his social development and encouraged them even though this meant giving up the rewards of his company.

M. Both my husband and I felt that, as much as we'd like him to be home, we don't make too much of an issue of it because we felt that by insisting on that we're being selfish . . . I do like him to be home when he's home, but if he didn't have friends, that would make me most uneasy.

Raymond was a very gregarious boy. Nevertheless, when he was not devoting time to club activities, his weekday evenings were spent at home and he still found time to participate in family activities.

F. He's home more than he is away from home. But I don't like him to be away from home too much.

Raymond's parents remarked on, and approved of, his self-reliance and independence. It seemed that they had encouraged and rewarded initiative and independent thinking, but without punishing dependency behavior. Consequently, although Raymond had become a self-reliant boy, he readily sought out the help, advice, and support of his parents when he was in difficulties of any kind.

I. When Raymond is in difficulties, does he ever come to you to talk things over?

F. Oh, yes. . . .

I. Have you ever discouraged him from coming because you felt he should stand on his own feet a little bit?

F. Well, that's a hard question to answer for the simple reason that Ray is a very independent boy, and I always told him when he was younger that, if he ever had any trouble with anything to come to me, but a majority of things he seems to work out of his own free will and seems to like to work them out himself.

Dependency is sometimes unwittingly punished when a child seeks help after doing something of which his parents disapprove. Raymond's parents seemed more concerned that he should feel free in bringing his troubles to them than to punish him for the difficulties he might have created.

I. When Raymond is in difficulties, does he ever come to you to talk things over?

M. Yes. If he gets in any kind of trouble, like once he got a ticket for not coming to a complete stop at a stop sign, and he was terribly upset because he had just got his license. He came in and wanted to know what to do. He was just beside himself. Another time I think he ripped the chrome off my car going out of a parking place, he ripped the chrome. I think, any time anything really goes wrong, he'll come and tell me about it.

I. What do you do?

M. When he does anything really wrong and he comes and tells me, I try to be as calm and sensible about it as I can. I realize that he's coming and telling me and he's asking me for advice, and I'm obligated to do the best that I can for him at the time.

Raymond's parents readily provided him with information and suggestions, but did not force their own opinions on him. In this way they both rewarded dependency and fostered the boy's self-reliance.

I. How much notice do you expect him to take of your suggestions or opinions?

M. I don't expect him to take too much notice. The only thing that would bother me would be, if he did something that was completely contrary to what I wanted of him, I'm afraid that I would tell him. But if he doesn't take advantage of what I offer, I feel that's his privilege.

I. Does he ever do the opposite of what you suggest?

M. He may not do what I suggest, but he never does the opposite.

Raymond showed a decided preference for his father and consulted him more readily than he did his mother. This preference, however, was not based on any rejection of the mother, but arose from Raymond's very high esteem for his father and his strong masculine identification which both parents had fostered.

I. How about if you are worried about something, would you go to your mother or——?

B. I'd go to my dad. I mean, it's not that I don't love her as much as my father. It's just that he, I guess, was in the same messes. He sorta understands what a boy would do.

I. How good do you think he is at helping you out?

B. Oh, whatever he tells me I think pretty much of, because he wouldn't tell me anything that wasn't well thought out. He really knew what he was saying.

I. How about your mother?

B. Like I say, she's a mom (laughs). You know, they worry a lot. I mean, she tells me a lot more specific things. Like my dad says, "Go to Tahoe, but be careful." She says, "Be careful. Don't do this, don't do this, don't do this." You know, it's just a little more, you know.

I. When your mother makes a suggestion, do you generally accept it?

B. Oh, I usually accept it. She doesn't give me foolish advice. I mean, everything she tells me is probably right. If I did it, I'd be so much better.

As a result of the parents' judicious training into independence, Raymond showed neither distance, rebelliousness, nor subservience in his relationships with other authority figures.

I. How do you feel about going to a teacher or counselor to talk over problems?

B. I think it's the only way to clear things up. I mean, I very frequently do that, especially with the teachers that I really get along with. I discuss many things outside the school even like dating, their life, why they teach and stuff like that.

I. What about asking them for help with schoolwork?

B. Whenever I don't understand, I go.
I. Do you think in general teachers can be helpful to you in these ways?
B. Oh, yeah. . . . They really can be helpful.
I. Does it ever make you feel uncomfortable if you have to get help from a teacher or counselor?
B. No.
I. If a teacher or counselor offers you advice or makes a suggestion, do you generally follow it, or do you prefer to work things out for yourself?
B. Usually, if the basic idea seems good. I like to work things out for myself a lot of times, but I will take advice. Usually it helps you work them out for yourself.
I. Do you ever feel like doing something quite different from what a teacher suggests, just because he suggested it?
B. No, I don't think so. Not that I can remember it.

Raymond enjoyed close and warm relationships with many of his peers and actively sought out a wide range of friendships.

I. Do you enjoy having very close friendships with other fellows your own age, or do you feel it's better to avoid these?
B. Oh, I have. I avoid having one or two. I don't mind having four or five close friends. I avoid having just one.
I. Why do you feel that way?
B. Oh, if you have just one friend you're always with that one friend and you sorta break away from the others. But if you have five or six you have a chance to be close to a lot more people.

Since he had no anxiety about close dependency relationships, Raymond could easily turn to his friends for advice and emotional support.

I. Does it ever make you feel uncomfortable if you have to get help from another fellow or can't make up your mind for yourself?
B. No. That's what friends are, for something. It's a good thing you have them. . . .
I. Some fellows like very much to have friends with whom they can talk things over and whom they can trust. Others think it's best to rely on no one but themselves. How do you feel about this?
B. I have a few friends I tell about everything and we discuss. It's very nice that way. They don't tell all the whole crowd. It's real nice to have someone like that, 'cause it sure helps you, 'cause

there's some things you can't discuss with your parents. They are so minute and trifling, but they're important to you now.

Raymond was very involved with a peer group that reflected the standards of his parents' social group; in fact, these adolescents' parents were themselves on friendly terms. Since Raymond was very sensitive to his friends' approval or censure, they provided an alternative source of social control at a time when he was increasingly seeking his gratifications through activities at which his parents could not be present.

I. Do you care very much what other guys think of you?

B. Oh, yes. I think it's very important. . . .

I. If your friends don't like some ways you act, do you try to change, or do you think that's your business and not theirs?

B. Well, if they don't like what you do, there's usually a few that are close enough to tell you; and if I feel it is, I feel that I'm doing something wrong, I'm acting wrong, I'll correct it.

By the time of adolescence Raymond was a well socialized boy; at this stage in his development his parents had little need to impose external restraints and controls.

I. What sort of things does your mother forbid you to do around the house?

B. Forbid me to do? Gee, I don't think there's ever anything. The house is mine as much as theirs, they tell me. . . . Oh, can't whistle, can't throw paper up in the air, and can't play the radio and phonograph too loud. Rules of the house; anybody, I mean, it's not just me. . . .

I. What about smoking and drinking?

B. I can't stand smoking, and she knows that; and if I ever drink, she'd rather I do it at home. And I do occasionally, on a real hot day I'll have a half a glass of beer with my dad or something like that. That's about all. I don't drink either. . . .

I. Are you expected to stay away from certain places or people?

B. She knows I do. I'm not expected; I mean, she figures I'm old enough to take care of myself now. They never tell me who to stay away from or where. Well, I mean, they don't expect me to sleep down on Skid Row or something like that. . . .

I. How honest do you feel you can be to your mother about where you have been and what things you have done?

B. Oh, I can be honest. . . . I'm not afraid. I mean, I can tell her because she knows nothing would happen there wrong.

Although Raymond's mother expressed some concern about what might happen to him when he was away from home, it was not primarily because she feared that he might deviate from the standards of the family.

I. What are some of the restrictions you have for him?
M. I don't worry about his morals, if that's the type of thing that you're wondering about. I mean, I feel that he's capable of making his own choices in his judgment. I restrict him more in cases where I feel he'd be doing something that is dangerous to his life and his health, because I feel that boys of that age have a tendency to stimulate each other. The ones that have good judgment lose their good judgment, and that's the only way we restrict him.

The father's confidence in the boy was even greater than the mother's, and this difference provided the only point of disagreement between the parents that came to light throughout the interviews.

I. In general do you and your wife agree about what restrictions you place on Raymond?
F. No, not all the time.
I. On what do you disagree?
F. I'd say, the amount of freedom he should have. I think a boy of his age should have a great deal of freedom in what he wishes to do, if it's within reason. My wife, I think, has a tendency to worry about him too much. In other words, I fall asleep when he's out, and she doesn't until he comes home. So she worries quite a deal about it.

It is interesting that Raymond interpreted his mother's tendency to outline precautions as an indication of her concern for his welfare.

B. I guess she loves me too much. She doesn't baby me or spoil me, but she's always watching everything I do. I mean, they're free with me. They let me do a lot, you know.

Raymond's freedom was bounded by certain definite and consistent limits about which his parents seemed very much in agreement. Both parents, however, gave the impression that these limits, for the most part, no longer needed to be enforced, and that over the years there had been a gradual freeing of the boy from restrictions as he grew more and more able to act in independent, but nevertheless socialized, ways.

I. Now we'd like to get some idea of the sort of things Raymond is allowed to do and the sort of things he isn't allowed to do. What are some of the restrictions you have for him?

F. The time that he has to be in at night. I think, too, a great deal, the persons that he chooses as friends: I'm always anxious that he has good friends, and whenever he goes with someone I don't like especially, I put my two cents in.

I. Do you expect Raymond to let you know what he has been doing?

F. He normally does. We always ask him where he's been and what he's done.

I. Are there any things that you don't let him do?

F. Yes, there are some things like taking long trips with boys. He thinks at the age of sixteen he's a grown man, you know. And, like he was all set to go to Yosemite with some boys, and I put my foot down and said, "No, you can't go." I don't think he should have that much freedom, because to me he's still a little boy.

I. Is Ray allowed free use of the family car?

F. Yes.

I. How about smoking and drinking?

F. Oh, it's entirely up to him. He frowns on smoking, frowns on drinking. In fact, he doesn't like me to smoke.

I. How about using bad language?

F. I don't go for it. . . .

I. Are there times when he has to do his homework?

F. Oh, yes.

I. Are there regular times?

F. No, not regular times. He seems to do it, and there's no questions asked, because we visit the school and his teachers are all very happy with him.

• • •

I. Does he have to check out or be in at a certain time?

M. Yes, he has a deadline. Of course, he sometimes has reasons for missing that deadline. He cannot come in later than two o'clock on a weekend, on a Friday or Saturday night, and if he's going to be home later than two o'clock, he must let us know. He must call us earlier in the evening and let us know he's going to be home later than two o'clock. And on week nights he must be home at a fairly reasonable hour, at eleven or so.

I. Is Raymond allowed free use of the family car?

M. He uses the car whenever he wants it. . . .

I. How about using bad language?

M. He doesn't. He's quite proper, because he will call me on something if I say something that he feels is not right. . . .

I. Are there times when he has to refrain from being noisy about the house?

M. He's not inclined to be a noisy child.

Neither of Raymond's parents tolerated disobedience. On matters about which they expressed concern, they were quite firm in following through with their demands.

I. Some mothers (fathers) expect their children to obey immediately when they tell them to do something; others don't think it is terribly important for a child to obey right away. What is your feeling about this?

M. Well, I guess I'm more inclined to be of the mothers who'd like to have it done soon. . . . I'm impatient. I don't like to wait. . . .

.   .   .

F. The things that I think are important, I expect immediate obedience. If it's important enough to make a stand, I think that he should follow. I really do.

Yet, in many matters that are apt to become points of conflict between adolescents and their parents, Raymond's parents gave their son complete freedom, partly because they felt them to be unimportant, partly because they trusted his judgment.

I. Do you let him wear what he likes or are there some things that you object to his wearing?

F. The majority of the time I let him wear what he likes. He has a very good taste. I don't think that he doesn't have a great deal to say. I think that basically it's his choice. It should be, because he knows what boys of his age are wearing, what's stylish, and what's acceptable. I don't want to make him unhappy about something as small as that.

Raymond's parents made only moderate demands on him for taking on responsibilities around the home. Training in keeping his room tidy and clean had, however, begun early, and the parents' current demands evoked no resentment.

I. How long have you been expected to do these jobs?

B. Oh, I've kept my room clean for about six years, I guess. They taught me how to make my bed as soon as I was tall enough to reach it.

I. How much does your mother keep after you to see that you do these things?

B. Oh, she doesn't have to. I don't leave my room until it's clean. And my car, I mean, I want it to look nice. When I go out on dates and that, I want it to look nice.

Both parents avoided the use of physical punishment. In fact, Raymond's mother had very early in his life conditioned him to respond to verbal reprimands.

I. How often have you slapped him or given him a licking?

M. Oh, I never hit or punish him. I mean, once in a year, I might lose my temper and give him a slapping. I don't usually, because it's not satisfactory at all, I mean. More than anything else that would ruin his pride, and then I'd have to apologize to him for slapping him.

I. How about when he was younger?

M. No, we never hit him to punish him. Except when he was a very small boy and we'd say to him, "No, no, no," when he would pick something up or something, we'd slap his hand lightly.

. . .

I. Has your father ever slapped you or given you a licking?

B. No. I don't think either one of them ever hit me.

During Raymond's adolescence, and probably for a long time previously, his parents had been able to rely primarily on reasoning for producing conformity with their wishes.

I. Suppose Raymond has been behaving very badly and giving you or his mother a hard time, what kind of things do you say to him?

F. I usually try to reason with him. I tell him I'm quite disgusted with with the way he's acting. Silly to act the way he does. I never scream at him. I don't believe in it. I never struck him. I never received a hitting or spanking from my dad. He was one of the most terrific guys in the world, and I think with a good heart-to-heart you can accomplish a great deal more than the losing of your temper and beating the holy daylights out of your kid. I really do.

. . .

I. If you do something your father doesn't like, something he thinks wrong, what sort of things does he do?

B. You mean punishment? Well, we don't have that much usually, though. Usually when my father scolds me—I guess that's the word you use—usually he isn't punishing me, because he doesn't do it that way.

. . .

I. Suppose Raymond has been behaving very badly and giving you or his father a hard time, what kind of things do you say to him?

M. Actually, more than anything else, I imagine, his father would tell him in one sentence, "Raymond, I am not pleased with your behavior. You haven't been acting in a manner in which I am proud of." That would be Father's story, and that would be the end of it. I would probably go on for two days . . . but I would tell him in no uncertain terms how displeased I was with the way he'd been acting.

I. What do you find most effective?

M. I think, just tell him.

. . .

I. When your mother's displeased with you, what is she most likely to do?

B. Just tell me.

Often, however, the reasoning was combined with expressions of disapproval involving covert threats of loss of love, which sometimes were calculated to raise the boy's esteem of the other parent.

I. Has your father ever told you that you don't appreciate things enough or anything like that?

B. Oh, yeah, he's told me sometimes that I don't realize how lucky I am to have such a wonderful mother. Something like that, you know, when my mom and I are arguing. Well, sometimes when I argue with my father, she'll tell me I don't realize how lucky I am to have such a wonderful father. It's the same deal. That's usually all they say.

The most severe punishment that Raymond received consisted in being deprived of going out on a Friday or Saturday. All three members of the family agreed that this happened only once or twice a year when Raymond had been unusually thoughtless. Raymond, in fact, had no complaint at all about his parents' manner of disciplining him.

B. Usually they don't punish me that much. There's not much need, though I say so myself, to punish me that much.

Parental disapproval was most frequently shown for lack of sensitivity to the feelings of others; in addition, praise was deliberately given for any thoughtful behavior.

I. Some mothers praise their children quite a bit when they are good; others think that you ought to take good behavior for granted and that there is no point in praising a child for it. How do you feel about that?

M. I don't praise him for good behavior. I praise him for thoughtfulness. . . . When he does something that is thoughtful or kind, we make an issue of praising him for it.

In fact, Raymond's parents themselves showed a great deal of sensitivity to their son's feelings and thus, in their interactions with him, provided many examples of the kind of behavior and attitudes that they wished him to adopt. This was particularly evident in their handling of aggression which was both nonpermissive and nonpunitive.

I. When Raymond gets angry at you, what does he do?
F. He usually clams up and walks out.
I. Does he ever shout or swear at you?
F. No.
I. Answer back?
F. Oh, he has answered back, which is normal.
I. How often?
F. Very seldom.
I. Has he ever struck you?
F. No.
I. Thrown things around the house?
F. No.
I. Stomped out of the house?
F. He's done that (laughs).
I. How often?
F. Very seldom.
I. How much of this sort of thing have you allowed?
F. There's a certain amount that a person has to expect. I think in my own self, when I was younger, I did a certain amount of it, and as I've grown older I've learned to accept a great number of things that I found necessary to make the happiness of the whole family. I don't say that everything makes me very happy, but you have to give and take.
I. What do you do?
F. I usually get very stern. I don't blow up at him. I don't believe in it. I get very stern, explain, try to explain to him that he has to do

it and he better do it. The quicker he does it, the easier it will be
for him.

.   .   .

M. The only time he gets violently angry is when it's something terribly, terribly, terribly important to him. But then, in twenty
minutes or half an hour, he comes out of his room as if the incident
had never taken place.

Since his parents had neither rewarded aggression nor
administered punishment that might have given rise to resentment and further aggression, Raymond now displayed
little anger or hostility. Moreover, their nonpunitive and
emphatic handling of aggression made it easy for the boy
to accept, in a good humored way, his parents' nontolerant
attitude.

I. When you are angry, have you thrown things around the house?
B. Oh, yes, slam doors and stuff like that. They always laugh, make
a joke out of it, and I usually end up laughing along with
them. . . .
I. How often do you get angry with your mother?
B. Oh, sometimes we can go over a month without arguing. I mean,
we argue over minor things. Anything serious is not an argument
in our house. We usually discuss it. It's just the minor things we
argue about.
I. How often do you get angry at your father?
B. I'd say about a half as much as my mother, because half of the
things they are mutual on, and I get mad at both of them. It's more
funny, because they make a joke of it and think it's funny, and
then it is.

While Raymond's parents wanted him to assert himself in
socially acceptable ways, they strongly disapproved of belligerence. Settling differences with teachers was presented
as a problem-solving task.

I. Has Raymond ever complained that a teacher or another adult was
being unfair to him?
F. Yes.
I. What did you do?
F. I definitely took the teacher's part, because knowing how a group
of young kids can get on your nerves sometimes, having worked
with young kids, I took it that it was mainly Ray's fault rather
than the teacher's fault. I try to explain that to him. I don't know

how successful I was (laughs). He probably didn't believe me, because they have their own thoughts, too.

I. Have you ever encouraged Raymond to stand up for himself against an adult?

F. To the extent when he complained of a teacher not being fair, I told him that the only way to attack the problem was to go to the teacher before school, or between periods, and ask what the trouble was and how could he remedy it.

• • •

I. Have you ever encouraged Raymond to stand up for himself against an adult?

M. Yes. If anybody were to ridicule him or belittle him and we were there, we would certainly tell him privately that, if anybody did that to him, he should speak back in a polite way and not be made the butt of the children necessarily, if it weren't right.

I. What would you do if you discovered Raymond was giving a teacher a hard time?

M. I'd be ashamed of him.

Raymond had transferred to his teachers many of the positive feelings and attitudes that he had developed toward his parents. When he was frustrated in school situations, he kept his anger under control; if he took action, rather than attacking the teacher, he directed his efforts toward attacking the problem that had arisen.

I. Suppose a teacher punishes you unjustly, what do you do about it?

B. Most of them are pretty just. I mean, now they're getting some really nice teachers. I'm really very happy with the teachers. I feel, if I have a teacher I can get along with, I can talk personally; also, I get more out of their courses.

I. What do you do if you feel that a teacher has given you an unfair grade?

B. Discuss it with the teacher. He usually explains why they gave it to me. I mean, I don't hold a grudge. I go and find out why I got it. . . .

I. When did you last get mad at a teacher?

B. Well, when the report card came out, one of my best friends among the teachers, really a great guy that I really get along with, he gave me a B when I thought I should get an A; and I got sort of mad but, I mean, the madness on the grades didn't have any effect on our personal friendship. . . .

I. Have you ever slammed doors or desks and things like that?

B. No, no. My anger usually stays inside until I get over it.

I. Have you ever sworn at them?
B. No.
I. Answered them back?
B. Oh, I don't think I really answer them back. I mean, I talk to them later. I go over and discuss with them or discuss with somebody else who might be able to help me; but, I mean, I don't think I could stand up in a class and say something.

The attitude of Raymond's parents about aggression within his peer group was very similar to their attitude about aggression toward adults. They wanted Raymond to express his own opinions and attitudes freely, but discouraged any disruptive hostile behavior.

I. Some people think it is very important for a boy to be able to stand up for himself, others think boys are only too ready to do this. How do you feel about this?
F. I think a boy is an individual just as much as a parent. He has his own ways of expressing, living, and thinking. He should have a part in saying what he should do. I really think he should. . . .
I. If he got in a fight with one of the neighbor's boys, how would you handle it?
F. I would stop it immediately, because it's very silly to use your fists to settle any argument.
I. What would you do if you found Raymond teasing another fellow or calling him bad names?
F. I would call him away from it and explain to him it was a very silly thing. I don't believe in that.

                    •   •   •

I. What would you do if you found Raymond teasing another fellow or calling him bad names?
M. He wouldn't be likely to; he's not that type of child. But if he did, certainly I would mention to him I thought he was not doing the right thing. He's not a bully at all.

Raymond's initial approach to his peers was a very positive one.

B. I'm real friendly when I first meet them.

This approach undoubtedly evoked positive counter-responses; consequently Raymond rarely became a target for hostility. If another boy attempted to provoke him he tried, if he could, to make light of it. Indeed, Raymond's description suggests that, like his parents, he sometimes made a joke of aggression and thus turned an originally hostile response into a positive one.

I. How do you deal with the kind of guy who likes pushing his weight around?

B. I try to just, well, I've never fought against anybody in comment, because our ideas disagree or anything. I just fight when I mess around. But when I meet a person like that and how I feel about them, I just try to say, "Hello," to them and tell them to stop messing around. I mean, I don't take any drastic steps. I try to be friendly to everybody.

I. What do you do if he starts on you?

B. Well, I've never had that happen. I don't think I'm the kind of person they are looking for particularly. I don't think I'd let it bother me. I think I'd just let him have his fun. I don't think I'd strike back. Well, I'd defend myself if worse came to worse, but, I mean, I'd just let him have his fun and go along.

I. What about the sort of fellow who blows his top at you or says things about you you don't like?

B. Well, it's just as easy to be friends with everybody as to be enemies with everybody. In fact, it's much easier for me to be friends, and so I just try and play along, let them live it up.

In their handling of sexual behavior, Raymond's parents, in their usual manner, set definite limits within which they were relatively permissive and completely nonpunitive. Early expressions of sexuality had been treated as natural occurrences to be gently discouraged, while heterosexual behavior in adolescence was expected and tolerated as long as it stopped short of intercourse.

I. What did you do when you noticed him playing with himself?

M. Nothing. Nothing.

I. Suppose you found him doing this now, how would you feel about it?

M. Oh, I'd do nothing about it. I'd feel it was perfectly normal.

I. What about sex play with children, did they ever come up?

M. Not that I ever noticed or saw.

I. Would you have allowed this or do you think you would have done something about it?

M. I think it would depend a tremendous amount on who the children were and what they were doing. I mean, if they were playing house or doctor or something like that, I don't think I'd have done anything about it because I'd have thought it was perfectly normal. If they were doing something I felt was unnatural, I'm afraid that I would have consulted a pediatrician and asked him what to do. It would depend on what they were doing.

I. Suppose you found that Raymond had now begun to play around with girls, how would you feel about it?

M. Well, I don't really know. More than anything else I would feel that, if a girl got pregnant, it would be horrible if he had to get married at this time, and that would be the thing that would upset me terribly. I understand that it's perfectly normal for a boy of his age to have sexual relationships. I guess I wouldn't be pleased, because I feel he's a little too young to know exactly what to do and how to do it. I think he's a little young. I guess I'm wrong, but that's how I feel.

I. Does Raymond know how you feel?

M. In a way, yes, I think so, because we discussed somebody at his school that had to get married, and I said to him, "Heavenly Day, I hope you don't go and have to get married, and I become a grandmother with you at sixteen" (laughs). . . .

I. What is the best way, do you think, for a young fellow to learn about sex?

M. Be told when they ask questions.

· · ·

I. What did you do when you noticed him playing with himself?

F. I just ignored it or took his hand away.

I. Suppose you found him doing this now, how would you feel about it?

F. I really don't know. I mean, it's never occurred and I'd probably say something to the effect and explain to him I didn't think it was very good for him. In a way, just try to reason with him.

I. What about sex play with children, did this ever come up?

F. No. It never has. I think I would have done something about it. I think, at a very early age we bought two books. They were in young boy's language. I explained everything to him, because I think a boy should know about these things at a very early age.

I. Suppose you found that Raymond had now begun to play around with girls, how would you feel about it?

F. It would worry me to a great extent because, I guess, it might be a normal thing for a boy his age to think of doing it, but I would worry very much about the consequences both to himself and to the girl. Consequences, not only in the fact that she might become pregnant, but also in the fact that he might go to extremes. I really mean it. It bothers me constantly.

I. How about petting, how do you feel about that?
F. That's part of the enjoyment of being a youth.

Raymond said that he had never masturbated. On the other hand, he had developed a strong interest in girls and had undoubtedly gained some sexual satisfactions from petting, though without engaging in intercourse. In fact, his views about heterosexual behavior almost exactly paralleled those of his parents.

I. How about petting? How far have you gone with this?
B. Oh, I've made out (laughs) up to where I guess I should. I'm not going to become a father until I'm married. I have that in my mind and I'll never try to put me in that category. . . .
I. How do you feel about playing with yourself?
B. I see no need for it. If you want to do it, you might as well take a girl out. I mean, that's ridiculous.

Both the parents and the boy looked forward to Raymond's getting married and raising a family, and it is probable that all three regarded his adolescent sexual experimentation as a preparation for adult life.

I. If your fondest dreams could come true, what things would you wish for Raymond when he grows up?
M. Oh, I'd like him to find a girl that would be really right for him and to be in the type of work that he would really and truly enjoy . . . and I'd like him to have a very happy married life and to have more than one child.

． ． ．

I. Suppose you had three choices you could make for yourself for the future. What are the three things you'd most like to happen?
B. Nice home and family, a good job, and to be well liked and be a leader in the community.

Much evidence has already been given of Raymond's identification with his parents' system of values. In addition, both parents expressed the opinion that Raymond possessed the praiseworthy characteristics of each of them and responded to his environment in the same way as they did.

I. Whom would you say Raymond is most like, personality-wise?
F. I think there are definite traits of both of us. In his friendliness,

great friendliness toward people, his desire to be among people at
all times, I think comes from the fact that I was an only child. He
just wants people around him at all times. I want people around
me at all times. With my wife, she is a great deal more intelligent
than I. I think he has a great deal of intelligence from my wife.
He seems to grasp things very easily, and she has a tendency to do
that. He has a very good memory; my wife has an excellent memory. I'd say he resembles both of us.

· · ·

M. Both of us. He's very observant and he's very sensitive to the environment that he's in, which is like I am. And he's pleasant,
amiable, like his father. Everybody likes him, everybody likes his
father. I think he's like both of us.

Raymond agreed with his parents in saying that he resembled each of them in some ways and, in doing so, gave
further evidence of his close identification with them.

I. In what ways would you like to be like your father?
B. I'd like to be liked by everybody, and I'd like to be a hard-working
person.
I. How much do you think you are like him already?
B. I can get along with people. When I work, I work hard. . . . I'd
like to raise a family by the same way he's brought me up.
I. In what ways would you like to be like your mother?
B. I'd like to be smart. I'd like to be very intelligent. Both of my
parents are intelligent. She knows a lot, has a lot of friends.
I. How much do you think you are like her already?
B. I guess we're both (laughs) very headstrong.

Evidence from all three interviews suggested that Raymond had very early in life transferred much of his dependency to his father and had identified with him more strongly
than he had with his mother. This process was probably
facilitated by his parents' very strong demands for masculinity, which were summarized in a single statement made
by his father: "I think, if I had a daughter, my whole
philosophy of being a father would probably be different."

As might be expected, Raymond showed considerable
guilt on the rare occasions on which he deviated from the
standards that he had so well internalized. If he aggressed,
he felt uncomfortable and usually made some effort to repair the situation.

I. After this happens (aggression against parents), do you sometimes feel very sorry and try to make it up, or do you usually just let things go?
B. I usually do something awfully nice. You know, I start talking, you know, "Can I take this down to the store for you."

• • •

I. When you have done something to annoy a teacher, how do you feel about it afterwards?
B. Gee, I feel sorry, because I try not to do anything to annoy a teacher.
I. Suppose you do?
B. I feel the only way you give a fair chance to both the teacher and yourself is if you do not do anything like that; I mean, if you do, apologize and discuss with him why you did it, and you'll never do it again.

• • •

I. When you've got mad at a guy and hit him, how do you feel afterwards?
B. I think I'd feel pretty bad. I mean, I'm the kind of person that doesn't like to do that sort of thing. I see no need to.

Although Raymond seemed never to deviate in his sexual behavior, his expressed attitudes and his avoidance of strong temptations suggested that he would have felt considerable guilt if such deviations had occurred.

I. What do you think of girls who go all the way?
B. I don't take those kind out.
I. How do you feel about them?
B. I may talk to them but I don't hold their hands, they're too dangerous.

• • •

I. Have you sometimes felt you'd like to have had more sex experience than you've had so far?
B. Oh, once in a while you get that craving. But I usually go and do something else and forget about it.
I. Have you ever had the chance of going all the way with a girl and deliberately held yourself back from doing so?
B. Yes, once.

Raymond presented a picture of a boy who had learned to maintain a great deal of self-direction and self-control through the internalization of the standards and values of his parents. He had become a self-confident boy who looked upon his parents and teachers as friends rather than as disciplinarians. Because he shared their system of values, he was not in conflict with them; because he trusted them, he could seek the benefit of their experience and greater knowledge without feeling threatened or inadequate; because his need for affection had not been frustrated, he was free from irrational and deep-seated hostility and could approach others in a friendly, trustful way. In spite of his having become highly self-reliant and capable of finding many of his gratifications outside the home, he had maintained strong emotional ties with his parents. His parents' warmth and esteem for him and for one another had provided a secure home atmosphere in which he could find emotional support in a crisis; their careful training into adult independence had made him capable of organizing his life around goals of which they and society would approve.

SOME THEORETICAL CONSIDERATIONS

The Failure of the Socialization Process

The findings reported in the previous chapters suggest that the child-training factors outlined in Chapter 1 are of considerable importance in the development of antisocial aggressive patterns of behavior. As Donald's case illustrates, the fathers of the aggressive boys were typically hostile to, and rejecting of, their sons, expressed little warmth for them, and had spent little time in affectionate interaction with them during the boys' childhood. Although the mothers' greater warmth had apparently sufficed to establish dependency needs during the boys' infancy, their tendency to punish and discourage dependency behavior reduced the boys' striving for secondary rewards in the form of dependency gratification, thus reducing the effectiveness of important sources of social control. Because of the fathers' rejection and the mothers' inconsistent handling of dependent behavior, the boys had become anxious and conflicted in dependency situations. This dependency conflict generalized to other authority figures and even to peers, so reducing their effectiveness as possible socializing agents. The parents' use of punitive methods of discipline not only further alienated their sons but also fostered the hostility and aggression with which the boys had responded to emotional deprivations. The absence of consistent socialization demands, and the failure of the parents to follow through on the demands that they made, provided some reinforcement of defiance and resistance and left the boys without any clear guides for controlling and directing their behavior.

Although there was no evidence that any of the parents in this study had displayed consistently blatant antisocial behavior, many of the fathers of the aggressive boys undoubtedly provided hostile and aggressive models for imitation. There was also evidence that many of the parents had subtly, if not openly, instigated and encouraged their sons' aggressive behavior outside the home and in some cases even toward the other parent.

In the interpretation of the findings of this study much emphasis has been placed on the disruption of the father-son relationship. Most studies of aggressive behavior, especially psychoanalytic ones, have emphasized the importance of the relationship to the mother. A typical view is that of Friedlander (1947), who considers a disturbance of the first object relationship to be crucial and who regards the antisocial character as being fixated at the anal stage of development. Clinical workers who are not essentially psychoanalytic in their orientation have also emphasized the mother-child relationship. For example, Jackson (1954), who studied the family backgrounds of aggressive children, strongly emphasizes the primary importance of the relationship with the mother. Although her experimental data would lead one to assume that the father-child relationship was at least equally important, these are largely ignored in her theoretical discussion of aggression. Whereas the psychoanalysts have tended to regard the relationship to the father as important only in terms of the Oedipal situation, child psychologists have tended until recently to pay relatively little attention to it. The former appear to be bound by their theory, even

when their case material points to the importance of non-
sexual father-son relationships; the latter have perhaps overlooked the importance of this relationship because they have
dealt in the clinical-social situation mainly, or solely, with
the mother who is the more accessible parent.

The view that one of the major sources of aggressiveness,
possibly leading to criminality, is a faulty handling by the
parents of the dependency relationship has been put forward
by Saul (1956), apparently with the additional implication
that the disturbance may be either in the mother relationship or in the relationship with the father. This view is probably correct. The pattern of family relationships and child-
training procedures varied to some extent among the families
of the aggressive boys in the present study. Greater variation
would undoubtedly have been found if the criteria for the
selection of the aggressive boys had been less stringent.
However, the inability to relate positively to the father may
be especially crucial for the formation of aggressive antisocial tendencies in male children.

The majority of boys who display repetitive antisocial
behavior come from broken homes, or live in high delinquency or deteriorated areas. Such boys were excluded from
the present study. Nevertheless, in these cases also, one
would expect such child-training factors as disrupted parent-
child relationships, inconsistent or weak socialization pressures, punitive discipline, and parental disharmony to facilitate the development of an antisocial orientation. In fact, far
from their being absent, these factors seem to occur in more
extreme forms under conditions of severe family and social
disorganization. Zucker (1943) gives the following account
of the home conditions of a group of antisocial boys from
families of rather low socioeconomic status.

> Out of the twenty-five boys in Group A (delinquent
> group) twenty-three came from families in which it would
> have been practically impossible for desirable relationships
> to predominate. These were some of the family situations:
> the father had deserted and the mother was hysterical; the
> mother was placid and unable to give affection, the father

was weak and vacillating—the handling of their boy was
on the severe, punitive side; the father and mother were
separated; favoritism was shown by the parents to another
child; the boy was unmercifully beaten by the mother;
violent and abusive father, and the boy did not live with
mother; parents inadequate; home was completely disor-
ganized as father had deserted and mother burdened children with her worries and fears; father alcoholic, no supervision and a great deal of friction in the home; father
deserts periodically and mother neurotic; illegitimate boy
viewed by mother as inferior; constant dissension in home
accompanied by open rejection; boy sent from one home to
another; mother openly maintained promiscuous relations
with other men; boy felt rejected and was badly neglected
(p. 47).

Under these circumstances, it is not surprising that Zucker
found that the boys' relationships with both parents were
considerably impaired and that the boys had failed to internalize social values. Indeed, his conclusions are essentially
similar to those reached in the present study.

Theories of Delinquency Causation

While the focus of this study has been on the development
of aggression, the findings clearly have implications for
theories of delinquency causation. Since several different
kinds of factors appear to contribute to the development of
antisocial behavior, it is not surprising that a variety of
diverse classifications of delinquency have been proposed
by various authorities. Terminologies may vary, and there
may be a particular emphasis on one or another causative
factor; nevertheless, the classifications overlap considerably
and may be reduced to four or five categories.

SUBCULTURAL DELINQUENT

A child patterns his behavior primarily on that of adults
in his immediate social environment. In a subgroup whose
behavior and values run contrary to those of the larger
community, the imitation of aggressive antisocial patterns

may be encouraged and rewarded, particularly if the home itself provides dissocial models. Antisocial personalities who have identified with subgroup standards are typically portrayed as being well adjusted within their own group (Alexander and Staub, 1931; Jenkins and Hewitt, 1944). While the crucial psychological process in most cases may be identification with a delinquent prototype rather than a hostile reaction to emotional deprivation, the extent to which subcultural delinquents manifest intrapsychic conflicts and disturbed interpersonal relationships nevertheless varies considerably according to the quality and stability of their emotional ties throughout childhood. Moreover, as the present study suggests, identification with dissocial aspects of a parent's personality may occur in children who do not reside in high delinquency areas. The social environment provides the content of the value system of the subcultural delinquent; however, the conditions necessary for internalization of values (Chapter 6) are to be found in the psychological development of the child.

NEUROTIC DELINQUENT

Some antisocial acts have been regarded as neurotic solutions of unconscious intrapsychic conflicts (Alexander and Staub, 1931; Bromberg, 1949; Friedlander, 1947; Freud, 1925). The major motivating factor is said to be a powerful and unconscious sense of guilt, which is displaced from forbidden Oedipal wishes onto acts that violate the law.

> Unable to seek punishment for the primary crime, since the nature is unknown to him, he commits an actual misdeed in order to be punished. He often unconsciously reveals the function his delinquency serves. In committing the delinquent act, be it stealing or any other type of asocial behavior, he does it in a manner that makes detection inevitable. His clumsiness belies his assumed misdemeanor or crime. He is caught and punished. If institutionalized, he is often the ideal inmate conforming because he is actually grateful to the administration for the relief from guilt which

the punishing situation offers him. Released from the institution he reverts to his former behavior pattern (Josselyn, 1948, pp. 78-79).

While it is possible that repeated antisocial behavior is sometimes motivated by severe guilt, it does not follow, as some psychoanalysts appear to say, that all behavior that carries the risk of being punished is thus motivated (pp. 363-368). Indeed, the overt pattern of delinquency associated with a strong conscience development is not obviously different from that attributed to guilt-free psychopaths.

The concept of the neurotic delinquent has, however, had a therapeutic effect on social attitudes. It has drawn attention both to the importance of motivational components in antisocial behavior and to the futility of punishment as a means of correcting many antisocial patterns.

PSYCHOPATHIC DELINQUENT

Psychopathy is frequently said to originate in severe affectional deprivation in infancy and early childhood, resulting in a complete failure of the socialization process. The psychopath is described as asocial, highly impulsive, guilt-free, and incapable of establishing and maintaining close affectional ties (Cleckley, 1941; McCord and McCord, 1956). The "unsocialized delinquent" described by Jenkins (1954) would seem to fit well into this category.

The presence of psychopathy is usually inferred from the repetitive nature of the antisocial behavior and from the inability of the offender to respond either to punishment or to treatment.

. . . These boys fit very well into the routine of the training school, are always friendly and obliging, behave irreproachably while under supervision and go out into life entirely unchanged, committing once more the same offenses for which they were sent to be reformed. . . . They continue, however, with their petty antisocial behavior regardless of how often it may land them in prison (Friedlander, 1947, p. 139).

The difficulty of distinguishing reliably the psychopath from the neurotic delinquent should be evident from the two descriptions quoted above. In the case of the neurotic delinquent, repetitive antisocial behavior which almost inevitably results in apprehension is considered indicative of severe guilt; in the case of the psychopath, it is taken as evidence of an undeveloped conscience. Moreover, the neurotic's good adjustment to the prison situation is interpreted as gratitude for relief from guilt; the psychopath's good behavior is customarily interpreted as an attempt to "con" his way out of prison or to make conditions in prison as pleasant for himself as possible.

Organic Delinquent

Gross organic pathology is found only in a small minority of delinquents. Many brain-damaged children are hyperactive, distractible, and impulsive and are undoubtedly difficult to socialize, especially when considerable intellectual retardation occurs (Strauss and Lehtinen, 1947). These children need a comprehensive therapeutic approach and there is thus justification for considering the brain-damaged delinquent as a special problem. Whether or not a brain-damaged or defective child will display a consistent antisocial orientation may, however, depend on the extent to which his shortcomings elicit rejection or hostility from his parents and other persons in his immediate environment.

> Let it be repeated: if a child of average or better intellectual endowment were subjected to similar influences, he would be in danger of quickly developing serious problem reactions (Pearson, 1949, pp. 196-197).

Neurological dysfunction has sometimes been considered the primary cause of purposeless and repetitive antisocial patterns such as have been ascribed to the neurotic delinquent and the psychopath (Thompson, 1953). Much stress has been laid on the high incidence of abnormal electroencephalograms (EEG's) found among antisocial personalities. The reported findings are, however, far from being consistent, and abnormal EEG's seem to occur no more frequently among aggressive delinquents than among social deviants who do not display aggressive patterns of behavior (Ostrow and Ostrow, 1946). It is conceivable that abnormal EEG patterns may, in many cases, be merely an accompaniment of emotional disturbance and not a direct cause of antisocial aggression. Moreover, case histories of aggressive delinquents show that the majority become involved in repeated fights, in automobile accidents, and forcible arrests that might easily result in head injuries. Indeed, many of the aggressive boys described in this book had already "rolled" cars or been involved in fights that could have resulted in serious physical injury.

I. How do you deal with the kind of guy who likes pushing his weight around?

B. (Case 23) I kick his face in. Last Friday night a guy threw a cherry bomb on the back of my friend's car. He cut down the street and I cut after him. I caught him, hit him and threw a stomp on his head. . . .

I. How about blowing your top at a guy?

B. Once in a while.

I. Do you remember the last time you blew your top?

B. Yeah, very distinctly. It was at Bayfield. This guy told on somebody and I blew my top at him. I went down to Fairview Park and I got the hell beat out of me by five guys.

Thus some cerebral dysfunction would not be a surprising product of a life of aggression.

Psychotic Delinquent

Psychotic children may commit illegal acts on account of their distorted perception of their environment and the consequent inappropriateness of their responses. Those who are apprehended by the police have often shown a markedly withdrawn and seclusive pattern of behavior that has culminated, after prolonged frustration, in an explosive outburst of aggression. The psychotic's illegal behavior is usually an incidental by-product of a pervasive personality disturbance; it rarely reflects a consistent antisocial aggressive orientation.

Dimensional Versus Type Approach

While the classification of delinquents into types has facilitated the identification of certain psychological factors that contribute to antisocial behavior, it has fostered a good deal of semantic confusion. For example, Friedlander (1947) distinguishes antisocial character formation, involving weak conscience development, from delinquency that is a manifestation of neurotic conflicts. She states, however, that neurotic conflicts may occur together with a greater or lesser degree of antisocial character formation. This statement implies that one and the same individual has a neurotic conflict involving strong conscience development and also antisocial character formation involving too weak a conscience, and is consequently hardly meaningful. It would be more meaningful to say that antisocial behavior may occur in individuals with varying degrees of conscience development.

Similarly, it is confusing to say that some delinquents are normal or adjusted to their environments if their parents are described as punitive, rejecting, or as providing inadequate models for identification, and if such parent characteristics are concomitantly said to produce a failure of socialization for other delinquent children. It would be more profitable to regard the pseudosocial delinquent described by Jenkins and his collaborators (Jenkins and Hewitt, 1944; Jenkins and Glickman, 1947; Lorr and Jenkins, 1953) as similar to the unsocialized aggressive boy in having a defective conscience development, but as different from him in his greater capacity for forming dependency relationships.

A more productive and less confusing approach to the understanding of behavior disorders is to examine carefully the process by which socialization of behavior is achieved and to select dimensions or variables of child behavior that appear to be of importance for the socialization process. Such an approach was, in fact, taken in the study of aggression that has been reported in this book. Relevant variables, for example, seemed to be the readiness with which a child forms dependency relationships, the extent of his conscience development, and the strength of his motivation to aggress. Any individual child who displays a hostile, aggressive orientation—whether "subcultural," "neurotic," "psychopathic," or "organic"—will differ from other aggressive children on one or more of these dimensions. Similarly, the parents of aggressive children will differ among themselves on variables or dimensions of behavior that, on the basis of current theory and research, seem important for the socialization of the child. The findings reported in previous chapters suggest that among the more important variables are the severity of the parents' punitiveness and rejection, the degree to which they instigate and reward aggression, and the consistency with which they enforce socialization demands.

It is possible that when certain constellations of parent variables occur, certain constellations of child variables will be found also, thus leading to conclusions somewhat similar to those reached by a classification into types. The dimensional approach, however, has certain distinct advantages. In the first place, it facilitates discrimination between children who fall, according to the typological approach, in a single category. It also avoids the contradictions into which a typology will lead when cases do not fall into clearly defined categories. Above all, it focuses on relationships between parent and child variables that are relevant to the study of the normal development of the child and its findings can thus be more readily fitted into the context of general psychological theory.

Persistence of Antisocial Behavior

The fact that antisocial behavior persists in spite of repeated and severe punishment has led a large number of workers in the field of delinquency to conclude that the persistent offender lacks the capacity to learn from experience. Another explanation that has been offered is that he is so guilty about some repressed impulse that he perpetually seeks punishment; since conscience largely operates in an anticipatory fashion to control and inhibit behavior, this explanation can be retained only on the assumption that the guilt itself has been repressed.

The statement that the repeated offender does not learn from experience lends itself to more than one interpretation. One possible interpretation is that punishment does not alter his behavior. It is necessary, however, to examine the patterns of behavior that are characteristic of habitual offenders in order to assess in what ways they are not altered. It is true that punishment does not seem to alter the offender's goals; on the other hand there is considerable evidence that it does alter the methods by which these goals are obtained. An excellent example is provided in the autobiography of Billy Hill, an habitual offender who received considerable punishment at the hands of the law yet who in no way changed the goals that he had adopted. He, nevertheless, systematically changed the forms of his crimes and the techniques that he employed in order to avoid detection.

> My prison surroundings have been completely a life apart, something so far away that at times it was my real circumstances that seemed so fantastic. In between I went over jobs which I had pulled off and mentally surveyed them to see how they could be improved upon. Then I went over my mistakes again, and learned how they had occurred and let me down. So you see there was always plenty for me to do when I lay on that board with no occupation but thinking. And plan future jobs. Oh yes, if a survey can be taken it would be proved that most of the big criminal jobs, and thousands of small ones, are planned in jail. Planned to the last detail because there is not sufficient alternative interest to occupy prisoners' minds (Hill, 1955, p. 39).

If Hill had as ingeniously directed his learning toward the more efficient attainment of socially acceptable goals, he could undoubtedly have been admired and respected for his brilliance and flexibility.

If antisocial personalities were to receive consistent and immediate punishment each time they performed an antisocial act, it is probable that they would quickly give up, or at least modify, their antisocial goals. It is evident that in many cases persistent offenders amass considerable rewards between each punishment that they incur. No adequate study is at present available concerning the relative frequency of reward and punishment in the histories of these individuals who are presumed to have no capacity to learn.

The learning of antisocial behavior is facilitated if the offender identifies with a delinquent group. In this case he not only learns new and more efficient techniques through direct instruction and imitation but he learns also from the errors of his associates. Moreover, he receives material rewards for the successful execution of antisocial acts and at the same time gains the approval and admiration of his peers. In view of the usual home background of repeated offenders, it would not be surprising if these rewards outweigh the hardships that punishment may bring.

Finally, there is some evidence to suggest that intermittent punishment may actually perpetuate the antisocial aggression that its use is designed to discourage. The punishments and deprivations inflicted by society for antisocial behavior are unlikely to differ in their effects from the penalties that are imposed by parents. As in Donald's case, they may result in further hostility and retaliation.

Probably the second most frequent explanation of the persistence of antisocial behavior is that the offender is motivated by an unconscious sense of guilt. Since the guilt is deeply repressed, the evidence on which this explanation is based is usually that some antisocial acts are performed so inefficiently that apprehension is inevitable. While it is true that some offenders appear to invite detection, it does not necessarily follow that they or other repeated offenders are motivated by a sense of guilt; other explanations are possible.

One such explanation is suggested by the findings of the present study. The guilt ratings of the aggressive boys, as assessed both from the interviews and from the projective material, showed that they were relatively guilt-free. On the other hand, there is evidence that they sometimes attempted to gratify dependency needs through disruptive, aggressive behavior. Consequently, it seems more reasonable to explain their self-defeating, repetitive antisocial behavior in terms of dependency conflict, rather than in terms of expiation of guilt.

The antisocial boy whose parents are rejecting must come to feel that attempts at gratification of his dependency needs are in themselves reprehensible, and as a defense against such needs, he aggressively asserts himself, allowing his impulses to pass into action irrespective of the needs and wishes of others. He is able to utilize such a defense only because he has been unable to internalize parental values. His self-assertive behavior represents a denial of dependency on the adult world, since he flouts its prohibitions, yet results in the gratification of dependency wishes by the punishment it brings upon him. He is forcibly made subservient to adults and is punished by an external authority just as he was in the early years when he was considered to be an irresponsible child.

Young children may frequently be observed to transgress parental prohibitions when it is quite clear that they will be seen and punished. Such behavior appears to have a twofold purpose; it both forces attention on themselves, so immediately gratifying their dependency needs, and following punishment, it frequently elicits subsequent nurturant responses from the parents, who now feel guilty for having punished. In fact, a similar process sometimes operates in the present-day treatment of the delinquent, on whom, following punishment, a great deal of attention is frequently showered. Moreover, if delinquent behavior is persistent, the boy is ordinarily incarcerated or at least made dependent on a probation officer. In such a situation dependency needs are in some respects met; if the boy is detained in custody, very adequately so. In the latter case, his day is largely planned; all major decisions are made for him; his meals are set before him at regular times; his work and recreation are provided by the authorities of the institution. Moreover, the institutionalized adolescent need not feel anv responsibility for such dependency behavior, since he presumably did not voluntarily abrogate what freedom of action he might be allowed at this stage of his development. In addition, he is dependent on the institution itself, rather than on particular individuals; the dependency relationship can be kept at an impersonal level. One may conceive of this solution of the dependency conflict as a form of response displacement in which directly dependent behavior is inhibited but dependency is manifested in a more indirect, disguised form.

Although the above interpretation of repeated antisocial behavior is based on a study of adolescent boys, it should apply all the more strongly to older offenders. Most habitual delinquents have records extending back at least to early adolescence, and by the time they have reached adulthood many of them have become almost entirely dependent on a life in a correctional institution for the gratification of their emotional needs. The institution now represents a secure haven from a society that rejects and despises them. Indeed, it is not surprising that habitual offenders often become troublesome just before the time of their release; in fact, many verbalize their anxieties about facing life on the outside. It would not, therefore, be surprising if some antisocial personalities were motivated to commit offenses in a manner that insures their return to the institution.

Another, and perhaps much less speculative, explanation of repeated antisocial behavior may be offered. There is good evidence that antisocial personalities have conscience defects and that their behavior is too little controlled by anticipation of guilt. The behavior of a person who is primarily fear-controlled will be largely governed by his estimation both of the probability of his being caught and of the severity of the punishment that may follow. There is, of course, an element of error, the magnitude of which depends to a large extent on the offender's ability to learn by experience and to assess the reality circumstances at any given moment. In fact, habitual offenders may the more readily risk punishment because they have consciously changed their techniques on the basis of prior experiences and thus have gained confidence that they will not be caught on future occasions. Moreover, detection of offenses often occurs because of some unusual event which the offender could not have predicted even after careful and prolonged study of the habits of the persons whom he wishes to thwart and deceive. It has been noted that most repeated offenders do not commit offenses that bring extremely severe penalties, nor do they ordinarily carry out their antisocial acts under circumstances in which the probability of being caught is very high, as they might be expected to do if they were motivated by a strong need for punishment.

The alternative explanations that have been offered should not be regarded either as mutually exclusive or as exhaustive. The motivating factors may, indeed, be quite complex in any particular case. In fact, when the conditions that are conducive to antisocial behavior are carefully examined, the fact that such behavior tends to persist no longer appears enigmatical. It is more surprising that a fair proportion of delinquent personalities appear to change their habitual patterns of behavior without receiving any treatment other than that dealt out to them by the police and the law.

Continuities in Learning

The process of social learning is a continuous one. A child's behavior at any stage of his development is lawfully related to the events that occurred at earlier stages, and adolescence in this respect is no exception. This picture of continuity was clearly evident among the control boys, who may be regarded as a small sample of typical adolescents. There was no less continuity in the pattern of behavior displayed by the aggressive boys; they had merely become a greater social menace as their physical size, dexterity, and self-sufficiency had increased.

There is a widely held view that adolescence is in many ways a unique period of development that is quite distinct from childhood and adulthood.

> Starting at about high school age young Americans, espe-
> cially in the urban and middle class, embark on patterns of
> behavior and attitudes which do not constitute a stage in
> continuous transition from childhood to adulthood but
> deviate from such a line of continuity (Parsons, 1950,
> p. 378).

There are several correlates of this belief in discontinuity.
The adolescent years are characterized as a period of "storm
and stress," of tension and rebellion, that emerge suddenly
with adolescence and as suddenly disappear as adulthood
is achieved.

> The radicalism of rebellious youth is a common phenom-
> enon in Western cultures, where the need for emancipation
> from parental restriction is emphasized and acted out in
> rebellion against all authority (Mohr and Despres, 1958,
> p. 107).

At adolescence the parents supposedly become more restrictive and prohibitive.

> As children grow older, there is a relative decrease in
> warmth and intellectual stimulation from their parents and
> an increase in parental restrictions (Hurlock, 1955, p. 422).
>
> . . .
>
> On the other hand, parents and teachers, frightened by
> the apparent instability of the adolescent, tend to inhibit
> where freedom formerly was implied (Josselyn, 1948, p. 94).

The adolescent resents this enforced dependency and rebels
against the controls that are imposed upon him by his parents. He emancipates himself from his parents by transfer-
ring his dependency to the peer group. He thus becomes
part of an adolescent subculture (Williams, 1952), whose
values are in conflict with those of his parents.

> Thus the compulsive independence of the youth culture
> may, according to well-established psychological principles,
> be interpreted as involving a reaction-formation against
> dependency needs, which is for understandable reasons par-
> ticularly prominent among boys. The compulsive conform-
> ity (within the peer group of age mates), in turn, would

seem to serve as an outlet for these dependency needs, but displaced from parental figures onto the peer group so that it does not interfere with the independence (Parsons, 1950, p. 381).

In spite of this compulsive conformity to the peer group, the adolescent at times shows excessive dependency on his parents. Thus he still remains under their influence and, because of the conflicting values to which he is exposed, he is confused, frightened, unpredictable, and irresponsible.

The adolescent struggles for independence, verbalizing vehemently his protest against the protective ruling of the adult group. On the other hand, he is unable to handle his independent activities as adequately as he did in the immediate past. He is impulsive in his behavior and confused about his goals. . . .

The adolescent's own group dominate his thinking and his behavior, a group composed of individuals of approximately the same emotional level of development. . . .

In spite of the iron control of the group, membership is not lifetime. . . . During periods of marked fluctuation in the individual's degree of maturation, he may have loyalty for more than one group. He will then use the standards of the particular group that is at the moment the most compatible with his emotional state, swinging with little hesitation to another group as the rise or fall of his maturity level influences his needs and capacities. . . .

At one time he rigidly adopts a code of conduct which, if really followed, would deny him all human gratification. As if by a sudden metamorphosis he then violates, or more often talks of violating, every acceptable code of behavior. . . .

In no area is the dichotomy more evident than in his relationship to his parents. At times he rejects them as if they were lepers in a community of healthy people. . . . In almost the next breath he reveals his idealization of them, picturing them as more holy than the saints, more omnipotent than God. . . .

The adolescent is characteristically secretive about himself and his feelings. Most of the time it is extremely difficult for him to express how he does feel. Furthermore, even if he can put his feelings into words, he is reluctant to expose himself to others (Josselyn, 1955, pp. 124-127).

This picture of adolescents receives little support from the detailed information that was supplied by the families who participated in the present study. It is true that in the families of the control boys dependency had been fostered a d encouraged during their childhood; on the other hand, independence training had begun early, and restrictions and prohibitions had been gradually lightened as the boys became increasingly able to control and direct their own activities. The boys, nevertheless, retained close affectional ties to their parents whose basic values they had, by adolescence, fully internalized. Since they chose their friends on the basis of these values, membership in the peer group did not bring them into conflict with their parents; rather, the peer group served to reinforce and uphold adult values and standards. Consequently, these boys did not regard their parents and other authority figures as adversaries, but rather as supporting and guiding influences to whom they could turn in times of need. To the extent that they had accepted well-defined internalized standards of conduct, situational influences had become relatively less important in determining their behavior. Consequently, they were far from being unpredictable.

An essentially similar picture of adolescents, based on a study of middle-class families, has been presented by Elkin and Westley.

Family ties are close and the degree of basic family consensus is high. The parents are interested in all the activities of their children, and the adolescents, except for the area of sex, frankly discuss their own behavior and problems with them. In many areas of life, there is joint participation between parents and children. . . . In independent discussions by parents and adolescents of the latter's marriage and occupational goals, there was a remarkable level of agreement. The adolescents also acknowledged the right of the parents to guide them, for example, accepting, at least manifesting, the prerogative of the parents to set rules for the number of dates, hours of return from dates, and types of parties. The parents express relatively little concern about the socialization problems or peer group activities of their children (1955, p. 682).

In the families of the aggressive boys there was a great deal of "storm and stress" for many years. Donald, for example, had been resistant and defiant from the age of three. As the years passed by, his behavior and attitudes had merely become more firmly entrenched. His belligerence and rebellion, at the age of sixteen, were not phenomena that had emerged with adolescence. Far from being engaged in a battle to win independence from their parents, the aggressive boys had for a long time been too independent of their parents and consequently had been little influenced by parental standards. While it is true that the aggressive boys fitted the stereotyped picture of the adolescent more closely than did the controls, in their case, too, the continuities in development were much more striking than were the discontinuities.

Workers in the field of mental health are apt to have most contact with acting-out adolescents and are thus prone to base their accounts of adolescent behavior on observation of atypical samples. It is remarkable how little reference to actual research is made by many "experts" in the field and to how large an extent they rely on unsystematic observational material. The view that adolescence is a period of rebellion is often supported by references to superficial and external signs of nonconformity such as the adolescents' fondness for unorthodox clothing, mannerisms, and language. Too often his fundamental and deep-seated acceptance of parental values is thus overlooked.

The myths that surround adolescence will probably continue to exist. The atypical adolescent excites far more interest than the average high-school student, and thus the cultural myth of adolescent rebellion is supported and maintained by literature, television, and movies, as well as by writers of textbooks.

Chapter 8

Treatment Implications

Most psychotherapeutic procedures have been developed primarily through work with oversocialized, inhibited patients. Since such patients typically suffer a good deal of discomfort and anxiety, they are motivated to seek help. In addition, their symptoms usually suggest, both to themselves and to others, that they are in need of medical care. Consequently, when their anxiety mounts or their symptoms become severe, they are likely to appear at therapeutically oriented institutions such as hospitals or clinics. As a result, theories and techniques of treatment for overinhibited patients have been relatively well worked out.

In contrast, a coherent treatment approach for the undersocialized aggressive patient has been slow in developing. A number of factors may account for this delay. In the first place, society's attitude toward aggressive adolescents is quite anti-therapeutic; their aggressiveness tends to evoke counteraggression and rejection even from the best-intentioned adults. Moreover, they act out impulses which are present, but inhibited, in other persons. Thus, while their acts provide some vicarious gratification for the conforming majority—manifested in the interest value of themes of violence and crime in newspapers, movies, and television— they at the same time evoke anxiety and guilt which are reflected in the public's demand for repression and punishment. Consequently, aggressive offenders are more likely to end up "serving time" in a reformatory than undergoing therapy in a hospital or clinic.

In the second place, although the symptoms of aggressive disorders are usually much more visible during childhood and adolescence than are early signs of a developing neurosis, they are often excused on the grounds that they represent a temporary phase of development. In some cases, no action may be taken because a child's aggression is largely displaced to situations outside the home, or because the parents gain some vicarious gratification from the child's aggressive behavior (Chapter 3). In other cases, the parents may be disinterested, neglectful, or absent from the picture. In fact, the child-training conditions that are conducive to the development of aggressive disorders tend also to prevent early treatment. Consequently, by the time that any constructive intervention is attempted, the pattern of aggression is thoroughly learned and the conditions that make possible the socialization of aggression are difficult to reproduce.

Thirdly, psychotherapists who work with undersocialized aggressive individuals tend to adopt theories and techniques that have been developed for the treatment of oversocialized neurotics. When antisocial patients prove unresponsive to the traditional methods, many therapists become pessimistic about the value of any psychotherapy for the treatment of aggressive disorders. Those therapists who have modified their techniques, apparently with some success, rarely make concomitant modifications in their theory; they are more inclined to excuse or minimize their departures from tradition.

Finally, there has been a marked absence of facilities for the treatment of aggressive disorders. The public appears more ready to support custodial institutions than treatment centers, in spite of the obvious facts that institutionalization does not change the goal-responses of antisocial personalities and that prisons are highly successful trade schools for training in antisocial activities.

Specificity of Treatment Conditions

While it is true that some of the necessary conditions for therapy, e.g., warmth, interest, acceptance, and understanding, are nonspecific and would apply equally in the treatment of all types of disorders, there are other conditions that are unnecessary, and would be inappropriate, for the treatment of neurotics but that are indispensable for the successful treatment of antisocial patients.

Since oversocialized inhibited patients suffer mainly from severe internal conflicts, the goal of therapy is to reduce the severity of the internal inhibitory controls, thus allowing the patients' impulses to find overt expression in socially approved directions. In contrast, the goal of therapy for antisocial patients must be the development of internal restraints. From the theory of antisocial aggression and the findings presented in this book, it would follow that the establishment of a close dependency relationship of the patient to the therapist, similar to that of a child to his parents, is a necessary condition for the development of internalized controls. The treatment of antisocial children can be thought of as falling into two phases. The goal of the first phase is the establishment of the dependency relationship. Once this has been achieved the therapist can work toward the final goal, the internalization of controls through the child's identification with the therapist.

FIRST PHASE

Immediately Generalized Negative Responses

In the treatment of the antisocial boy the therapist starts at a serious disadvantage. Rarely, if ever, does the aggressive boy come for help voluntarily. Usually he is brought in because his parents or the school personnel can no longer manage him; or he has been apprehended following some antisocial act and is referred by the court. The boy is likely to interpret his coming to the clinic as a form of punishment and to view the therapist as a disciplinarian; consequently, he readily generalizes to the therapist the hostility, fear, and distrust which he feels toward the authoritarian figures in his life.

Dependency Anxiety and Anticipatory Provocation

Since an important antecedent of antisocial aggression is affectional deprivation, some therapists have been led to believe that giving the patient "love" will repair this deficiency and thus almost automatically bring about a cure. However, the aggressive boy's problems cannot be reduced to the fact that he lacked love in early childhood; they arise largely because, in response to early deprivation, he has learned patterns of behavior that make it difficult for him to establish close positive relationships. Even though affectional gratifications may be potentially available from adults and peers with whom he comes into contact, his dependency anxiety forces him to remain unloved and rejected (Ackerman, 1944). This dependency anxiety is an even greater obstacle to therapy than the fact that he is usually forced into treatment by authorities with whom he has come into conflict.

Because he has experienced repeated rejection and hostility from others, the aggressive child has learned to expect disappointment and hurt, and will naturally tend to respond to the therapist in terms of these negative expectations. Since the friendliness and interest which he encounters in the therapy situation do not fit in with his previous experiences, he tends to be fearful and distrustful of the therapist's warmth and interest and to resist any closeness. Initially he may be sullen and uncommunicative. If he finds that he is becoming interested in the therapist, his distrust may lead him to test out the genuineness of the therapist's interest and acceptance. This testing usually takes the form of hostile or provocative patterns of behavior. The boy may distort the therapist's motives; become antagonistic, or actively aggressive, toward the therapist; make unrealistic demands; or in other ways produce situations that force the therapist to appear unjust, rejecting, or prohibitive.

The extremes to which such provocation may go is well illustrated in Aichhorn's account of a group of highly unsocialized and extremely aggressive boys who had throughout their lives experienced harshness and rejection. Aichhorn and his staff permitted the boys to display any behavior they wished, yet treated them with a consistently friendly attitude.

> Perhaps you will think that the children must have been very happy in this paradise where it was possible to live out their impulses without restraint, and that they showed their gratitude in good behavior. This however was not the case. Their acts of aggression increased and took on greater intensity. This contradiction is understandable when we realize that before they came to us, they had suffered physical abuse and they therefore expected corporal punishment for any provocation. They could not grasp the new situation in any terms other than those of their past experience. Since they now encountered no brutal opposition, they could evaluate our attitude in only one way: 'These workers are weaker than we are: they are afraid of us; therefore we can do as we please.' These boys had never known kindness. The only situations in which force had not been used against them were those in which they themselves had the upper hand. As a direct result of our attitude, their aggressive acts became more frequent and more violent until practically all the furniture in the building was destroyed, the window panes broken, the doors nearly kicked to pieces. It happened once that a boy sprang through a double window, ignoring his injuries from the broken glass. The dinner table was finally deserted because each one sought a corner in the playroom where he crouched to devour his food. Screams and howls could be heard from afar. The building looked as if it harboured a crowd of madmen. In spite of this, I continued to insist that the boys be allowed to work out their aggression, that there should be no intervention except when necessary to prevent physical injury. The workers were required to be absolutely impartial; they were to be equally pleasant to all and to maintain their composure. In short, they were to be a haven of peace in the midst of this chaos. The

solution of the problem of this group was due to the patient endurance of these workers (Aichhorn, 1935, pp. 173-174).

Following this period of violent aggression, the boys developed strong dependent attachments to the workers. They left the demolished quarters and moved into a newly furnished building. Because of their attachment to, and affection for, the workers, the boys were now willing to accept limits on their behavior and to take on responsibilities which could be made progressively more difficult. The process of socialization had begun.

In most situations the aggressive boy's provocative behavior evokes the hostility and rejection that he fears, and thus his anxieties are reinforced and perpetuated. Through his own behavior he elicits hostility and rejection; and he interprets this outcome as proving that he was rejected in the first place. In thus distorting the situation, he sees much of his own aggression as a form of self-defense.

At times it is difficult to maintain a warm and friendly attitude in the face of strong and persistent hostile provocations. Yet, if the therapist were to react to these provocations with hostility or rejection, as others have done in the past, he would lose the patient before he even began. The therapist's handling of the patient's initial resistance and provocative behavior should be aimed at creating a new type of social situation which will reduce the anxieties that have, in part, instigated the provocative behavior.

If the therapist adopts a consistently friendly and nonpunitive attitude, the patient's hostile provocative responses should eventually extinguish. As the patient's anxiety is reduced, he may make tentative and increasingly direct bids for dependency gratifications. This process, however, will probably take a long time. The patient may test the therapist again and again before he is fully convinced that the therapist is trustworthy.

More active measures on the part of the therapist may be employed as an aid in evoking dependent responses. It is at this stage in the treatment process that the greatest departures from traditional methods may be needed.

Rather than simply remain a friendly but somewhat ambiguous figure, the therapist may actively attempt to set up a sharp discrimination between his own attitudes and those of the punitive authority figures whom the boy has known in the past. In this way, the therapist can reduce the boy's tendency to generalize to the therapy situation the anxieties and hostilities that he has learned in his relationships with other adults.

My attitude from the very beginning lets the boy feel that I have a power over him. He is justified when he senses this as a danger. He does not feel this as an entirely new situation; he has experienced it often before. I am thus no different from his mother, father, or teacher. . . . I remain in the position of the parents but, as our association progresses, I act somewhat different. If the child is in open conflict and expecting an attack, he is disappointed. I do not ask him what he has done, I do not press him to tell me what has happened, and, in contrast to the police or Juvenile Court, I do not try to pry out of him information which he is unwilling to give. In many cases where I feel the child wants to be questioned so that he can come into opposition to me, I say that he may hold back whatever information he wishes, that I understand that one does not want to tell everything to a person he has met for the first time. When I add that I would do likewise, he is usually willing to fall into conversation with me about something remote from his difficulties but in line with his interest. To describe my attitude from the moment when I let the boy feel some activity in me, I would say that I become progressively passive the more he expects attack from me. This astonishes him, he feels uncertain, he does not know where he stands. He feels, rather than understands, that I am not an authority with whom he must fight, but an understanding ally. I avoid the word "friend" intentionally since he has no friends; he allies himself with others only because he needs them to achieve some end (Aichhorn, 1935, pp. 128-129).

Verbal expressions of friendship and interest are, by themselves, unlikely to prove convincing. Consequently, actions that provide concrete evidence of the therapist's positive attitudes, and at the same time foster dependency, are probably of considerable importance. An hour spent in playing pool with the patient may, at this stage of treatment, be more effective in developing a close attachment than many hours spent in talking about the patient's past. The therapist must adopt a nurturant attitude in order to establish the dependency relationship. For example, he can show an active interest, or even participate, in the patient's legitimate activities; he can attend to the patient's reasonable requests and do him legitimate favors (Eissler, 1950; Topping, 1943). Most of the examples of this kind of nurturant activity have been provided by therapists who have worked in institutional settings (Aichhorn, 1935; Bettelheim, 1950; Redl and Wineman, 1952). Such gratifications would seem, however, to be equally important when the patient is seen on an outpatient basis. Eissler suggests that the therapist may make unconditional gifts of money to delinquents as a tangible proof of his affection and regard. At this stage, there should be no conditions attached to any favors that the therapist may bestow; if the favors are accompanied by conditions or bargaining, the patient will interpret them, not as reflecting a genuine interest in himself, but merely as bribes to make him conform. On the other hand, if the therapist gives only when the patient demands, there is little reason for the patient to feel that the therapist's favors reflect a genuine interest; in this case, the patient may perceive the therapist only as a weak and compliant figure whom he can exploit.

Although a positive and nurturant approach generally suffices to elicit dependency, with extremely distant and non-responsive boys it may be necessary to create deliberately situations in which the therapist can clearly demonstrate that he can be a source of help and support. Aichhorn at times resorted to this device. On one occasion he subtly encouraged a seventeen-year-old boy, with whom it was extremely difficult to establish an emotional relationship, to run away in the expectation that he would return. Ten days later the boy returned—hungry, exhausted, and upset. He evidently expected to be reproached; instead, Aichhorn provided him with food and shelter and expressed sympathetic and fatherly concern. A strong, positive response, which could form the basis for further treatment, was almost immediately elicited from the boy. On another occasion Aichhorn placed an eighteen-year-old boy with a history of stealing in charge of a tobacco shop from which he might be tempted to take money. Before very long the boy had committed the theft. Aichhorn sent for the boy and steered the conversation around the topic of the tobacco shop without directly accusing the boy of the theft. The boy's anxiety kept mounting until he could no longer conceal his transgression. At this point Aichhorn merely supplied him with the missing amount and dismissed him with a friendly gesture. The boy returned almost immediately, crying and repentant. Aichhorn listened sympathetically and reassured him of his genuine interest and confidence in him. Aichhorn's nurturant behavior had become associated with the reduction of the boy's anxieties.

When the patient first becomes convinced that the therapist is a friendly and rewarding figure, his dependency feelings, which until this time have been largely inhibited, may be expressed in full force (Aichhorn, 1935; Bloch, 1952; Thorpe and Smith, 1952). The younger adolescent may now seek dependency gratifications through physical contact much like a young child. The older boy may demand the constant presence and attention of the therapist and show strong rivalry toward other patients. Nevertheless, because of residual anxieties, there may be periodic reversions to the distrustful, provocative patterns of behavior even during this period of strong dependency.

Residential Treatment

The treatment of older unsocialized delinquents is a difficult task, since they are relatively self-sufficient and do not easily become attached to a therapist. In many cases,

particularly when a boy displays extremely aggressive antisocial behavior, socialization can be accomplished only
through residential care and treatment. In an institutional
environment one can more easily reproduce, to some degree,
the psychological conditions that permit the socialization of
the young child.

In a treatment home the residential staff live in close
contact with the boys and play an important role in their
daily activities. They are thus in a position to serve almost
continuously as therapeutic influences during the boys' stay
in the treatment center. They can personally administer
many of the primary rewards and mediate between the boys'
needs and gratifications. They necessarily become important
figures in the boys' lives. Under these conditions the boys are
more ready to welcome their therapists' interest and attention. Outside such a controlled environment the boys are
quite capable of satisfying many of their needs unaided
and are consequently freer to reject a therapist's help. Moreover, the institution provides a setting in which gratifications
may be provided for aggressive boys without precipitously
forcing them into close emotional relationships with adults.
Indeed, if the boys have continuous contact with several
adults, they need not be forced to relate to one particular
person; instead, they may be allowed to develop a relationship with whatever staff member appears most effectively to
satisfy their emotional needs. In addition, if the institution
fosters positive relationships between the staff and the boys,
a newcomer's anxiety about emotional involvements may be
reduced by the readiness of other boys to trust and confide
in the staff.

If residential treatment is to be effective in socializing
aggressive boys, the staff must function primarily in the role
of substitute parents with whom these boys may in time
establish close relationships. It is unlikely that mere custodial
care or brief interview contacts with the therapist will have
much effect in changing the boys' patterns of behavior. The
type of residential program that seems most favorable for
socializing a child has been described in considerable detail

by Aichhorn (1935), Bettelheim (1950), and Redl and Wineman (1951, 1952).

It is usually assumed, perhaps because most existing institutions are not treatment oriented, that a boy should not be placed in a residential treatment program except as a last resort. This view, however, may be questioned (Lippman, 1949). The younger chronic delinquent would probably be most benefited by early residential treatment, since in childhood he is likely to be less resistant to adult influences than he will be in adolescence.

Limits and Demands

When an aggressive boy enters therapy, one should not expect him to comply with extensive limits and demands. To expect him to do so presupposes that he has already internalized an effective system of controls, when, in fact, the development of internal controls is the eventual goal of treatment. He can, of course, be forced to comply with certain restrictions; indeed, he may even obligingly do whatever he is told to do in order to avoid immediate difficulties. This does not mean, however, that he has internalized a set of sanctions and demands that will be of service to him once he is outside the treatment situation.

In the initial phase of treatment, a therapist should therefore be less interested in eliciting conformity, or in prohibiting the boy's antisocial behavior, than in creating conditions that may lead the boy to develop lasting self-control. If the boy enters treatment with a hostile, negative attitude, he will tend to interpret most limits and restrictions on his behavior as rejection or punishment. Thus, if a therapist insists on extensive conformity during the early phase of treatment, he may actually impede the development of a positive dependent attachment which might render the boy more willing to accept limitations.

Most limits and demands that are customarily imposed in institutions in no way facilitate the progress of treatment. Usually, institutions are severely overcrowded and understaffed. Consequently, they can be run efficiently only if the boys are required to observe extensive rules and regulations. Under these circumstances, the main task of the staff is to ensure conformity by constant supervision and the imposition of penalties for any breach of the rules. Rather than leading to the development of internal controls, such a system is likely only to increase the boys' reliance on external restraints. Moreover, under these conditions, the majority of the boys will develop the attitude that they will do only what they are told to do—and then often only in a half-hearted way—and that they will evade any responsibilities that they can. In fact, they are usually rewarded for successful evasion by the approval of their peers.

Certain minimal limits may be necessary to prevent unlimited destruction of property and injury to the staff or to the boys themselves. Aggressive boys are particularly prone to test out limits, in part, as the present study suggests, because they have been exposed to inconsistent demands and discipline by their parents and have learned that defiance sometimes enables them to get their own way. Moreover, they are likely to perceive adults who are inconsistent as unjust and arbitrary. Consequently, whatever limits are imposed should be firmly and consistently enforced.

SECOND PHASE

Identification with the Therapist and
the Acquisition of Internal Controls

At first an aggressive boy's dependency on a therapist is apt to be primarily of an instrumental nature. The boy may value the therapist less as a person whom he esteems and admires than as someone who will provide him with material rewards. However, through his repeated association with rewarding experiences for the boy, the therapist may become of value to the boy for his own sake. When this occurs, the boy will be motivated to seek, not merely the material rewards which the therapist is able to supply, but also the therapist's interest and approval, which now have acquired secondary reward value. The anticipation of these secondary rewards may induce the boy to conform more readily to limits and otherwise attempt to control and modify his behavior.

At this point, the boy may be expected to seek out the therapist's help, advice, and suggestions on a variety of problems, and consequently the therapist is in a position to take a more active role in guiding the boy. Moreover, if the boy strongly desires to retain the therapist's interest and approval, he will try to avoid hurting and disappointing him. In addition, if the therapist has been repeatedly associated with the boy's gratifications, many of the therapist's attitudes and actions will acquire secondary reward value, and thus the boy will be motivated to reproduce these attitudes and actions in himself. One may say that the boy has accepted the therapist's standards and values as his own. Once these values have been thus accepted, the boy's controls function relatively independently of the therapist, since to perform or not to perform certain acts may now result in self-approval or self-criticism. The boy has acquired self-control.

TREATMENT OF THE PARENTS

It is evident from material presented previously that a boy's antisocial behavior is usually associated with a general disturbance in the pattern of intrafamily relationships. Not only may the boy's relationships to his parents be disrupted but, in addition, the parents' relationships to one another may be characterized by coldness, rejection, and hostility. Moreover, the parents themselves may provide aggressive models; in this case, the boy may be faced with a conflict between his parents' standards and values and those that he may acquire through identification with the therapist. Therefore, unless the boys' parents are also included in the treatment program, therapeutic results, especially with younger boys, are apt to be limited. The parents cannot be expected suddenly to become warm and accepting toward one another and toward the boy, or to refrain from instigating and fostering the boy's aggression, unless they receive help with their own problems.

It would seem that the inclusion of the boy's father in any therapeutic program is especially important. In many cases, the disruption of the boy's relationship with his father may be the major factor in producing his aggressive orientation. Moreover, since the boy's adjustment is facilitated if he can make a masculine identification, the father is potentially a more satisfying model for him to imitate, particularly by the time the boy has reached adolescence.

Appendix A

1. What school or schools has _____ attended in recent years?
   a. How have you felt about _____'s progress in schoolwork during the past few years? (What have you said to him?)
   b. Considering _____'s ability, are you satisfied with how he is doing in his schoolwork?
   c. Have you expressed this feeling to him? (What have you said?)
   d. How far would you like _____ to go with his schooling? (Any particular college?)
   e. What kind of job would you like him to get?
   f. Does _____ know what you expect of him?
2. How well does _____ get along with people his own age?
   a. (IF NOT WELL) What have you done about this?
   b. (IF WELL) Has he ever had difficulties in mixing?
3. How about competitive sports? How important do you think it is for a boy to do well in these?
   a. If _____ does well in sports, what do you do? (Say?)
   b. What if he doesn't do too well?
   c. Has _____ come up to your expectations in these things?
   d. How much have you encouraged him to take part in sports? (How about when he was younger?)
4. Now, we'd like to get some idea of the sort of things _____ is allowed to do and the sort of things he isn't allowed to do. What are some of the restrictions you have for him?
   a. How about going out at night?
   b. Does he have to check out or be in at a certain time?
   c. Do you expect him to let you know what he has been doing?
   d. Are there any things you forbid him from doing when he is with his friends? Places you forbid him going?
   e. Are there any of his friends with whom you have discouraged him from associating?
   f. Is _____ allowed free use of the family car?

g. How about smoking and drinking, how do you feel about these?

h. How about using bad language?

i. Can _____ use the radio and TV as freely as he likes?

j. Are there times when _____ has to do his homework?

k. Are there times when he has to refrain from being noisy about the house?

5. In general, do you and your (husband, wife) agree about what restrictions you place on _____ ?

  a. (IF NOT) On what do you disagree?
    (IF YES) Are there any things of this sort about which you disagree?

  b. Do you and your (husband, wife) follow through equally in getting him to do as you wish?

  c. Does _____ seem to accept the restrictions you place on him or does he resent them? Does he try to get around them in any way? Does he ever ignore them completely? How often?

  d. Do you feel in general that _____ is frank and open with you about where he has been and the sort of things he does outside the home? Does he ever seem to resent your asking him about these things? Avoid telling you about them?

6. How does _____ get his spending money?

  a. Does he have a regular allowance? (Did he ever?)

  b. On what basis is the allowance given to him? Does he have to earn it?

  c. Does _____ earn extra money by taking on part-time jobs? Was this of his own choice or did you encourage him to earn?

  d. About how much of his total spending money does he get this way? (Very little, most, etc.)

  e. What does _____ do with the money he gets? How does he use it?

  f. To what extent do you have a say in this?

  g. Who pays for his clothes? Picks them out? Do you let him wear what he likes or are there some things you object to his wearing? What do you do about this? What does he do when you object?

  h. Does _____ ever come to you for extra money? What do you usually do about this? Does his (father, mother) usually know about this?

7. To what extent do you think a boy of _____'s age should be made responsible for taking care of his room or parts of the house and garden, or keeping things orderly and clean?

  a. What kinds of responsibilities does _____ have?

  b. How long has he been expected to do these things?

  c. How did you go about getting him to do these things?

    d. How much do you keep after him to see that these things are done?

    e. To what extent does _____ try to get out of doing these things? Does he ever seem to resent having to do them?

    f. Do you and your (husband, wife) agree about the sorts of things _____ should be responsible for?

    g. Do you and your (husband, wife) agree on the extent to which you expect _____ to carry out these responsibilities?

8. Some (mothers, fathers) expect their children to obey immediately when they tell them to do something; others don't think it is terribly important for a child to obey right away. What is your feeling about this?

9. If _____ doesn't do what you ask, do you ever drop the subject, or do you always see to it that he does it?

10. When _____ gets angry at you, what does he do?

    a. Does he ever shout or swear at you? Answer back? How often?

    b. Has he ever struck you? Thrown things around the house? How often?

    c. Stamped out of the house? Slammed doors? How often?

    d. How much of this sort of thing have you allowed? What do you do?

11. Now, I'd like you to think back to when _____ was a baby. Who took care of him for the most part?

    a. Did you have any regular help?

    b. How much did (your husband, you) do in connection with taking care of _____ when he was a baby? Did (he, you) ever change the baby's diapers? Feed him? Give him a bath? How often?

12. Did you have time to spend with _____ when he was a small child besides the time that was necessary for feeding him, changing him, and regular care?

    a. Tell me about what you did in this time? How much did you play with him and that sort of thing?

    b. Did you find some time every day for this sort of thing, or was that impossible? What about week ends?

    c. And what about your (husband, wife), how much time did (he, she) have for things like this?

13. When _____ was a small child, how did you feel about letting him run about indoors without his clothes on?

    a. What did you do when you noticed him playing with himself?

    b. Suppose you found him doing this now, how would you feel about it? What would you do?

14. How about sex play with other children, did this ever come up?

    a. (IF YES) What happened and what did you do about it?

(IF NO) Would you have allowed this or do you think you would have done something about it?

    b. Suppose you found that _____ had now begun to play around with girls, how would you feel about it?

    c. How about petting, how do you feel about that?

    d. How do you feel about young fellows who go all the way with girls?

    e. Does _____ know how you feel?

    f. How has he become aware of this?

    g. Are there any things which _____ might do in this way that would make you particularly upset?

    h. Do you think _____ is worried at all about matters that have to do with sex?

15. What is the best way, do you think, for a young fellow to learn about sex?

    a. From whom do you think it is best for a boy to get information and advice about sex matters?

    b. To what extent has _____ come of his own accord and asked you things?

    c. What sort of information have you given?

16. Some (mothers, fathers) feel that boys of _____'s age should go on trips or vacations with their families; others think it is better that they should go off with their friends. How do you feel about this?

    a. Have you expressed your feelings about this to _____? (What have you said?)

    b. What does _____ usually do?

    c. What family activities such as visiting or week-end trips do you expect _____ to take part in?

    d. Has _____ ever objected to taking part in these? What have you done about this?

    e. How much time does _____ spend at home with the family?

    f. How much have you encouraged him to do this?

    g. (IF ENCOURAGEMENT) How have you gone about doing this?

    (IF NO ENCOURAGEMENT) Would you tell me a little more about how you feel about this?

17. Do you feel that you spend as much time with _____ as other (mothers, fathers) do with their sons, or more?

    a. When you and he are alone, what sort of things do you do?

    b. Do you often take him shopping or to shows or to anything like that? (How often?)

    c. When you do this, does your (husband, wife) usually accompany you, or do you and _____ go alone?

d. What kind of hobbies does _____ have—the sort of things that can keep him interested when he's at home?

e. Do you have much time to help him in these or show him how to do things? What are you able to do in this way?

f. How about when he was in grade school, what kind of things did you do with him and how much time did you spend with him then? Was it any different?

g. In general, do you like having _____ around you, or do you think it is better for him to go off with his friends?

h. How do you suppose _____ feels about doing things with you, or being out in your company?

i. Have there been any times when you've felt that he wanted to be too much in your company? How about when he was younger? What did you do about this?

18. When _____ is in difficulties, does he ever come to you to talk things over?

a. What kind of things has he come to you about? What do you do, say?

b. Suppose he is worried about something, or has gotten into a scrape, does he come to you then? What do you do, say?

c. Are there any (other) ways in which he asks you to help him out?

d. How about asking you for help on his schoolwork? What do you say, do?

e. How much have you encouraged him to come to you for help in things like these? Have you ever discouraged him from coming because you felt he should stand on his own feet a little more?

19. When _____ has a decision to make, say about buying something or deciding what he should do for an evening, to what extent does he talk this over with you? What might he say in a case like this?

a. What (other) sorts of things might he seek your opinion on? Does he discuss his friends with you, for example? What do you say?

b. How much have you and he discussed his future? What have you said to him about this?

c. How much notice do you expect him to take of your suggestions or opinions? Do you ever tell him he should work things out for himself and not rely too much on his parents?

d. When you offer _____ advice or make a suggestion to him, what does he do? Does he usually follow it right away? Do you feel that he does the very opposite of what you suggest just because you suggested it?

20. I'm wondering if you could tell me more about the relationship between you and ———. Do you show your affection toward each other quite a bit, or are you fairly reserved?

    a. Are there some things about ——— that you really enjoy and make you like doing things with him?

    b. How well do you think you and ——— know and understand one another? Do you think you usually know how he feels, and does he seem to understand how you feel?

    c. In what way do you get on each other's nerves?

21. Can you tell me something about the relationship between ——— and his (father, mother)? How much affection would you say they show towards each other?

    a. How well do you think ——— and his (father, mother) understand each other?

    b. In what ways do they get on each other's nerves?

22. Would you tell me also about the relationship between you and your (husband, wife)? Do you express affection towards each other freely or are you somewhat reserved?

    a. Do you spend much time together? What sort of things do you do together?

    b. Do you enjoy one another's company?

    c. How well would you say you and your (husband, wife) get along together?

    d. In what ways do you get on one another's nerves?

23. Some people think it is very important for a boy to be able to stand up for himself, others think boys are only too ready to do this. How do you feel about this? (If asked what we mean by "stand up for himself," say, "assert himself when he feels he is right.")

    a. Have you ever had to encourage ——— to stand up for himself? What precisely have you done to encourage him?

    b. Have you ever encouraged ——— to use his fists to defend himself? What precisely have you done to encourage him?

    c. Has he ever come to you and complained that another fellow was giving him a rough time?

    d. (IF YES) What have you advised him to do about it?
       (IF NO) Suppose he did, what would you say to him?

    e. If ——— got into a fight with one of the neighbor's boys, how would you handle it? How far would you let it go?

    f. What would you do if you found ——— teasing another fellow or calling him bad names? How far would you let it go?

24. (IF NOT AN ONLY CHILD) How well would you say ——— gets along with his brother(s) and/or sister(s)?

    a. How do you handle things if they quarrel?

    b. Suppose ——— strikes his brother or sister, what do you do?

c. How do you deal with it if _____ is unpleasant to them in other ways? What do you say to him?
d. How do their squabbles usually start?
e. Who do you think is usually to blame?

25. Has _____ ever complained that a teacher or another adult was being unfair to him?
   a. (IF YES) What did you do? Say?
      (IF NO) Suppose this happened, what would you do? Say?
   b. Have you ever encouraged _____ to stand up for himself against an adult?
   c. What would you do if you discovered _____ was giving a teacher a hard time? What would you say?

26. Some youngsters play hooky from school; what about _____?
   a. (IF YES) How did you find out about this? What did you say?
      (IF NO) Suppose _____ wanted to stay home from school, what would you do? Say?

27. Most (mothers, fathers) want their sons to grow up into very manly persons. What do you expect of your boy in this way?
   a. Are there things you would expect of him that you might not expect of a daughter?
   b. Do you think boys should have different responsibilities in the home from girls?
   c. How have you gone about teaching _____ things that are expected of him as a boy?

28. We have been talking about how you handle _____ in many different situations. Now we'd like to know something about how you go about correcting _____ and getting him, in general, to behave the way you want him to. Do you have any system of rewarding him for good behavior?
   a. Do you ever reward him with money or special privileges?
   b. How else might you reward him?
   c. Do you always reward him when he does something good or only on certain occasions?

29. Some (mothers, fathers) praise their children quite a bit when they are good; others think that you ought to take good behavior for granted and that there is no point in praising a child for it. How do you feel about that?
   a. What if he jumps up to do something you've asked him to do, what do you say?
   b. What if _____ does something very nice, like giving you or his (father, mother) a pleasant surprise, what do you do then?

30. In training _____ have you ever said, "Your father does it this way"? Under what circumstances might you say this?
   a. Whom else have you held up as an example—older brother or sister? Grandparents? Other relatives? Friends?

    b. Is there anyone you mention as an example of what not to do? For instance, "You're acting just like so and so—you wouldn't like to be like him, would you?"

    c. Boys can pick up bad habits pretty quickly from people whom they are around a lot. Have you ever noticed _____ doing this?

    d. What have you said to him about it?

31. Suppose _____ has been behaving very badly and giving you or his (father, mother) a hard time, what kind of things do you say to him? Can you give me some examples?

    a. Are there any other things you might say?

    b. What do you find most effective in this situation?

32. What other ways have you used to discipline _____ since he has been in high school?

    a. How often have you found it necessary to slap him or give him a licking? Once a year? How about when he was younger?

    b. What about depriving him of privileges? How often would you say you have done this? Once a month? What about stopping his allowance or not letting him do things he wants to?

    c. What about making him look ridiculous in front of other people? In front of the rest of the family? Do you find it helps to be sarcastic?

    d. How often do you have to scold him or grumble at him? Do you find you have to keep on nagging at him until he does things?

    e. Do you sometimes ignore him or refuse to speak to him until he does as you want? Tell him you don't want any more to do with him until he changes? Tell him he doesn't behave like a son of yours? Try to make him feel ashamed of himself by pointing out that he is ungrateful or doesn't appreciate what you've done for him? (How often? Once a month, week, _____?)

    f. Are there any other ways in which you've gone about disciplining _____?

    g. Which of these things are you most likely to do? Which do you find most effective?

33. For what is _____ most frequently rebuked or punished? How do you handle this?

34. When you punish or tell him off, how does he react? Do you think he resents being punished?

    a. Does he get over it quickly?

    b. Some (mothers, fathers), after having to punish a boy, think it best to try to smooth things over, while others think it better to do nothing about it and let the boy get over it on his own. What do you feel about this?

35. In general, how well—would you say—do you and your (husband, wife) agree about the best way to handle _____?

    a. Can you give me an idea about the kinds of things you and your (husband, wife) might not agree about entirely?

    b. Do the children know that you and your (husband, wife) disagree? How do they know this?

36. When _____ has to be disciplined, who usually does it, you or your (husband, wife), assuming both of you are there?

    a. Do you (or does your husband, wife) punish him at all? On what occasions?

    b. How strict is your (husband, wife) with _____?

    c. Does (he, she) ever do anything in disciplining _____ that you'd rather (he, she) didn't do? Did (he, she) ever in the past?

37. We are wondering who makes the main decisions about the children? In some families it's the father, and in others the mother. How does this work out in your family?

    a. How much do you consult your (husband, wife)? OR How much does (he, she) consult you?

38. When there's a family decision to be made, like deciding where to go for a vacation, or what sort of car to buy, how is this usually reached?

    a. Suppose there's a disagreement in the family about a matter like this, how is it usually resolved?

39. Do you think _____ has been especially difficult or easy to bring up compared with other children?

    a. (IF NOT AN ONLY CHILD) How does he compare with his brother(s) and/or sister(s)?

    b. What especially makes him that way?

40. Whom would you say _____ is most like, personality-wise?

    a. What makes you say that?

    b. In what ways, if any, do you think he resembles you?

    c. What about your (husband, wife)?

41. Now, just a few more general questions about _____. Do you think _____ has had a fair chance in life?

    a. Would you tell me why you think that?

    b. What sorts of things have been hard on him?

42. If you had your time over and had to bring up _____ again, would you do things any differently from the way you have done them?

    a. What sort of things might you change?

    b. Why do you feel this way?

    c. Are there any ways in which you would especially like to see *him* change?

    d. Would you wish your (husband, wife) to change in any way?

43. If your fondest dreams could come true, what things would you wish for _____ when he grows up?

    a. Does _____ know you feel this way?

Appendix B

ADOLESCENT INTERVIEW SCHEDULE

1. Have you lived with your parents all your life?
   a. (IF NO) How did that come about?
   b. How long were you away from your home (mother, father)?
   c. Have you been separated from either of your parents at any time? (For how long? How about during the war?)
2. What grade schools have you attended?
   a. And what high schools?
3. How do you feel about your (high) school? How are things coming along there?
   a. What kind of grades do you get?
   b. Have you ever felt you'd like to move to another school?
   c. How about the teachers you've had? How do you feel about them?
   d. Do you think high school teachers are interested in helping you? (Why do you feel this way?)
   e. Are there any teachers you especially dislike, and find it difficult to get along with? (What have you disliked about them?)
   f. Have there been teachers you've really enjoyed working with? (What did you like about them?)
4. How often have you felt that a teacher has given you an unfair grade?
   a. Are there any (other) ways you've felt teachers have treated you unfairly?
   b. When this sort of thing happens, what do you do? Say?
   c. Suppose a teacher punishes you unjustly, what do you do about it? (What do you say?)
   d. What if he gives you too much homework? Tells you to do something you think is unreasonable? (Do you express your feelings about this to him? What do you say?)
5. If you dislike a teacher, do you ever try to get back at him? (What do you do? How often?)

a. When did you last get mad at a teacher? (What did you do?) When was the time before that? (What did you do then?)

b. Have you ever struck or thrown something at a teacher? (How often?)

c. Slammed doors or desks and things like that? (How often?)

d. Sworn at them? Answered them back?

e. How often would you say you got mad at a teacher?

f. What have you found the best way of dealing with a teacher you don't like?

g. Have you ever transferred out of a class because you didn't like a teacher? (Complained to the vice-principal or a counselor?)

h. When you've done something to annoy a teacher, how do you feel about it afterwards? (Do you just forget about it, or do you sometimes try to make up for it in some way?)

6. Do you sometimes do things openly in school for which you know you'll get told off or punished?

a. What sort of things? (How often?)

b. Have you ever been told off for clowning in class? (What sort of things have you done? How often?)

c. How about asking silly questions on purpose? Making funny remarks?

d. Are there any other things of this sort that you've done?

7. How do you feel about going to a teacher or counselor to talk over problems? (How often would you say you did this?)

a. What sort of things might you ask about? (What about asking them for help with schoolwork?)

b. Do you think in general teachers can be helpful to you in these ways? What about counselors? (Why do you say this?)

c. Does it ever make you feel uncomfortable if you have to get help from a teacher or counselor? (What makes you feel this way?)

d. If a teacher or counselor offers you advice, or makes a suggestion, do you generally follow it, or do you prefer to work things out for yourself?

e. Do you ever feel like doing something quite different from what a teacher suggests, just because he suggested it? (Why might you feel this way?)

8. How important would you say it was for a teacher to praise a fellow for doing something good?

a. Do you find it makes much difference to you if you get a teacher who says nothing when you've done your best?

b. Do you think a fellow should have any (other) kind of reward for good work or good behavior? (What would you suggest?)

c. How important do you think it is to get good grades in school?

d. How about getting "good" or something like that on an assignment?

e. How do you feel if you get poor grades? (What about getting
"poor" on an assignment?)

f. What kind of a fellow do you think a teacher likes best? (How
much do you try to be this way?)

9. Now, I'd like your opinion of the fellows you've met at high school.
How, in general, do you feel about them? (Do you enjoy their
company?)

a. What kind of things makes you like a fellow?

b. What kind of things makes you *dis*like a fellow? (How do you
deal with this kind of guy?)

c. How do you deal with the kind of guy who likes pushing his
weight around? What do you do if he starts on you? (Suppose
he keeps on at you?)

d. What about the sort of fellow who blows his top at you or says
things about you you don't like? (How do you deal with him?)

e. When did you last hit a guy? (How did that come about?) How
often do you find you do this?

f. How often have you gotten into a fight since you've been at
high school? (How about grade school?)

g. How about blowing your top at a guy? When was the last
time you did that? (How often does this happen?)

h. Do other fellows ever get mad at you because of things you've
said to them? (Examples?) How often?

i. Do you ever feel like doing something mean to another fellow?
(What sort of thing makes you feel this way?) What do you do
when you feel this way? (How often does this happen?)

j. When you've got mad at a guy and hit him, how do you feel
afterwards? (What if you've said something unpleasant to him?)
What do you usually do in a case like this?

10. Suppose some fellow plays a real dirty trick on you. How do you
go about getting even with him? (Can you give me some examples?)

a. What have you found the best way of dealing with a guy who
gets you into trouble? (Suppose he did this on purpose?)

11. Suppose you were in a jam and needed help. How many friends
your own age have you to whom you could go in a case like that?

a. How do you feel about asking favors of friends, like lending
you money or fixing you up with a date? (What if it were a
favor you couldn't return?)

b. What other sort of things might you ask them to do for you?
(How often?)

c. How frequently would you say you do favors for them? (What sort of things do you do?)

d. How often would you say you went to your friends for suggestions on how to do things?

e. How about getting them to help you with your schoolwork? (How often do you do this?)

f. Do you ever talk to them about what courses you should take? About what you should say to your teachers or parents?

g. When a friend suggests something to you, do you generally do what he suggests, or do you prefer to work things out for yourself? (How much notice do you take of what your friends say?)

h. Do you ever feel like doing the opposite of what a friend of yours suggests, just because he suggested it? (How often?)

i. Does it ever make you feel uncomfortable if you have to get help from another fellow or can't make up your mind for yourself? (What makes you feel this way?)

12. How do you prefer to spend your time, alone or in the company of friends?

a. What sort of things do you prefer to be alone to do?

b. Does being alone ever make you feel restless or unhappy? What do you do in a case like this? (How often do you feel this way?)

c. When you are with a group of friends, what kind of things do you like to do?

d. How do you come to decisions about how you will spend the time and so on?

e. How much do you express your opinions about what the group should do? (Do you sometimes argue the point or do you usually just go along with the others?)

f. Suppose you disagree with the decision, do you usually go along with them, or do you go off by yourself and do what *you* want to do?

13. Do you care very much what other guys think of you? (What about your really close friends?)

a. How do you go about trying to get them to like you?

b. Among the fellows you go around with, what sorts of things make a guy respected and looked up to? (How much do you try to do these things?)

c. If your friends don't like some ways you act, do you try to change, or do you think that's your business and not theirs?

d. Do you ever find that you can't be quite honest to your friends about things you've done or how you feel, because they might dislike you if you were? (About what sort of things?)

14. Some fellows like very much to have friends with whom they can talk things over and whom they can trust in. Others think it best

to rely on no one but themselves. How do you feel about this? (Are there any sorts of things you prefer to keep to yourself?)

    a. How much do you think you can trust other guys? (Confide in them?)

    b. Do you enjoy having very close friendships with other fellows your own age, or do you feel it's better to avoid these?

15. Have there ever been times when you felt you weren't wanted by your friends? (What made you feel that way?)

    a. Have you ever been thrown out of a group because the other people didn't want you? (Tell me about that.)

16. Do you find you have difficulty in keeping friends?

    a. Why do you think this is?

    b. Do you think on the whole that other guys like you?

    c. What makes you say that?

17. We haven't said much about girls yet. How do you feel about them?

    a. What about dates? How often would you say you dated a girl?

    b. How about petting? How far have you gone with this?

    c. What do you think of a fellow who goes all the way with girls?

    d. What about girls who go all the way? How do you feel about them?

    e. Have you ever gone all the way with a girl? When was the last time you did this? (How did it come about?) How often would you say you'd gone all the way?

    f. Suppose a friend of yours got a girl you knew into trouble, what would you think of him?

    g. Suppose you go farther than usual (all the way) with a girl, how do you feel about this? (How do you feel afterwards?)

    h. Do you talk with your friends much about the sort of things you've been telling me?

    i. What do you usually tell them about these matters? Do you ever tell them you've had more (or less) sex experience than you've really had?

18. How do you feel about playing with yourself?

    a. When did you first learn about this? (How did you find out?)

    b. When did you last do this? (How often would you say you did this?)

    c. Have you always done this alone, or have there sometimes been other fellows around?

    d. Has any adult spoken to you about this sort of thing? (What did they say?) Do you think this has influenced the way you feel about it? (Does this sort of thing ever get you worried?)

    e. Do you ever talk about this to your friends? (What do you tell them? The same sort of thing as you've told me or something different?)

19. Have you sometimes felt you'd like to have had more sex experience than you've had so far? (What sort of things make you say this?)
    a. Have you ever had the chance of going all the way with a girl and deliberately held yourself back from doing so? (How often?)
    b. Have you ever felt like playing with yourself and deliberately held yourself back from doing this?
20. From whom have you got most of your information about sex?
    a. How much have you got from your parents? (What have they told you?) From books? Friends? Older boys?
21. Let's talk about something else now. Do you like to take part in sports like swimming, football, and boxing and so on? (Why do you feel this way?)
    a. How do you suppose you compare physically with other guys your age?
    b. If you could change your appearance in any way, would you want to do so? (How?) Are there any other ways?
    c. Have you ever felt embarrassed because you've had to strip in front of other people? (What made you feel that way?)
22. Have there ever been times when you've felt you've got to do something foolish just for the hell of it, for example, driving a car at 90 m.p.h. or starting a brawl or smashing up? Are there any (other) things of this sort that you've done? (How often? How do you feel afterwards?)
23. Let's turn to your family now. Let's suppose your mother was living in one place and your father in another, which would you choose to live with? (Suppose all other things were equal.)
    a. What makes you prefer to live with your _____?
24. How often would you say you went to your father to talk things over? (How about getting him to help you with your schoolwork?)
    a. What (other) sort of things have you talked over with him? (How about if you are worried about something or have gotten into a scrape? Do you go to him then?)
    b. How good do you think he is at helping you out?
    c. When your father makes a suggestion, do you usually accept it, or do you prefer to work things out for yourself? (How much notice do you take of what he says?)
    d. How about your mother? How often do you go to her to talk things over? (Schoolwork?)
    e. What (other) sort of things have you talked over with her? (How about if you are worried over something or have got into a scrape?)
    f. If your mother makes a suggestion, do you generally accept it, or do you prefer to work things out for yourself?

g. If your mother suggests you do something, do you ever feel like doing something quite different, just because she suggested it?

h. What about if your father suggests something?

i. How often do you feel this way with your father? (And with your mother?)

25. To what extent do you discuss your friends with your mother? Do you like to get her opinion of your friends?

a. What about your father? Do you discuss them much with him?

b. Suppose your mother objected to your going around with someone? What would you do in this case?

c. How about if your father objected?

26. Some fellows go around with their parents quite a lot, for example, on trips or to movies. Others don't like this much. How do you feel about this?

a. How about going places with your father? (Do you go places regularly with him or only on special occasions?)

b. What sort of things do you and he do together? (How often?) What about when you and he are both at home? Are there any things you do together then? (How often?)

c. How do you feel about going places with your mother? (How often do you go places with your mother?)

d. What sort of things do you do together? (How often?) What about when you and she are both at home? Are there things you do together then? (How often?)

e. With whom do you usually go for trips or vacations? (Have you ever been away on a trip or vacation without your parents?)

f. Do you ever deliberately avoid going out with your mother, or being seen in her company? (How often do you do this?)

g. What about your father? (How often?)

27. What sort of things does your mother like seeing you do, the sort of things that make her really pleased with you? (How much do you try to do these things?)

a. Are there any things you do just in order to please your mother, things you know she'll really appreciate? (How about doing favors for her, or giving her a pleasant surprise?) How often do you do something of this sort?

b. What does she do in a case like this? (Say?)

c. When you do something that she asks right away, what does she usually do? (Say?) (What if you don't do it?)

d. On the whole, would you say your mother praised you readily when you do something good or tried to please her, or does she seem to take things like that for granted?

e. Does she have any (other) ways of showing that she's pleased with you, like giving you money or special privileges, when you do something that pleases her? (How often does she do things like this?)

f. What sorts of things does your father like seeing you do, the sorts of things that make him really pleased with you? (How much do you try to do these things?)

g. Are there any things you do just in order to please your father, things you know he'll really appreciate? (How often do you do something of this sort?)

h. What does he do in a case like this? (Say?)

i. When you do something that he asks right away, what does he usually do? (Say?)

j. Would you say your father praised you readily when you do something good or try to please him, or does he seem to take things like that for granted?

k. Does he have any (other) ways of showing you he's pleased, like giving you money or special privileges? (How often does he do things like that?)

28. How do you get your spending money? (Do you get a regular allowance from your parents?)

a. Do you earn any money by part-time jobs? (How much of your spending money do you get this way?)

b. Suppose you run short of cash, what do you do? (Suppose you need some extra money urgently?)

c. How do you feel about going to your mother for extra money? (To your father?)

d. How much freedom do you get to spend your money as you like? (Are there [any] things your parents object to your spending it on?)

e. How much do you consult your mother about how you should spend your money? (Do you usually do what she suggests?)

f. How much do you consult your father about this? (Do you usually do what he suggests?)

29. What happens when you need some new clothes? How is this handled in your home?

a. Who pays for them? (Who picks them out?) Are there any things your mother won't let you wear? (Your father?)

b. Does your mother ever criticize your taste in clothes? (What do you do in this case? Say?)

c. What if your father criticizes? (What do you do? Say?)

d. What happens if you disagree with your mother about what you should wear?

e. What if you and your father disagree?

30. What kind of jobs does your mother make you responsible for around the home? (Does she expect you to look after your own room? The garden? Clean the car?) What about your father?

    a. How long have you been expected to do these jobs?

    b. How much does your mother keep after you to see that you do them? (What if you fail to carry them out?) And your father?

    c. How do you feel about having to do them? (Do you ever try to get out of doing them? How?)

31. When you do something your parents don't like, or haven't done something you should have done, who usually handles this, your mother or your father?

    a. If you do something your father doesn't like, something he thinks wrong, what sort of things does he do? (What if you don't obey him?)

    b. Has he ever slapped you or given you a licking? (How often? How about when you were younger?)

    c. Taken something away from you or stopped you doing something you wanted to do?

    d. Made you look silly in front of other people? (Called you a baby or stupid or dumb and things like that?) (Tried to make you feel ridiculous?)

    e. Does he grumble at you very much? Keep on nagging you about things until you do as he wants? (About what things? How much?)

    f. Has he sometimes ignored you or refused to speak to you until you did as he wanted? Told you you were ungrateful or that you didn't appreciate him enough or told you all he's done for you? Told you he didn't want to have any more to do with you until you changed?

    g. When he's displeased with you which of these things is he most likely to do?

    h. If you do something your mother doesn't like, what sort of things does she do?

    i. Has she ever slapped you or given you a licking? (How often? How about when you were younger?)

    j. Taken something away from you or stopped you doing something you wanted to do?

    k. Made you look silly in front of other people? (Called you babyish or dumb or anything like that?) (Tried to make you feel ridiculous?)

    l. Does she grumble at you very much? Keep on nagging at you until you do as she wants? (About what things? How much?)

    m. Has she sometimes ignored you or refused to speak to you until you did as she wanted? Told you you were ungrateful or didn't appreciate her enough or told you all she's done for you? Told you she didn't want to have any more to do with you until you changed?

n. When she's displeased with you, which of these things is she most likely to do?

o. How do you feel about the way your mother has dealt with you in regard to punishment? (Do you think she's been pretty reasonable, or do you think she's given you a rough time?)

p. And your father? How do you feel about him?

32. What sort of things does your mother forbid you to do around the house?

a. Does she ever insist that you be quiet? Does she let you listen freely to the radio and TV?

b. Does she have any rules about when you should do your homework?

c. What about smoking or drinking? Using bad language?

d. What sort of things does your mother object to your doing when you are out with your friends or on your own? (Are there any things she prefers you not to do?)

e. How about staying out late at night? Staying overnight at the homes of your friends?

f. Does she expect you to check out or be in at a certain time? Stay away from certain places or certain people?

g. How about using the family car? How does she feel about this?

h. What sort of things does your father forbid you doing around the house?

i. How much does he insist on quiet? Limit your use of the radio or TV?

j. Does he have any rules about when you should do your homework?

k. How does he feel about smoking or drinking? Using bad language?

l. What sort of things does your father object to your doing when you are out with your friends or by yourself? (Are there things he prefers you not to do?)

m. How does he feel about your staying out late or remaining away from home for a night?

n. Does he expect you to check out or be in at a certain time? Stay away from certain places or people?

o. How does he feel about your using the car?

p. Do you ever feel like doing something your mother forbids just in order to assert yourself? (How often do you feel this way? How often do you actually do this sort of thing?)

q. What about your father? How often do you feel this way with him? (How often do you actually do this?)

r. How do you feel about your mother's attitude about the things you should do and the things you shouldn't do? (Do you think

she's pretty reasonable or do you think she gives you less freedom than other fellows get?)

s. And what about your father's attitude?

33. How honest do you feel you can be to your mother about where
you have been and what things you have done?

a. How honest do you feel you can be to your father?

b. Does it ever seem especially important not to tell your mother
where you have been and what sort of things you've been doing, even though you know she won't disapprove? (How often
do you feel this way?)

c. Do you sometimes feel this way with your father? (How often?)

d. After you've done something that your mother disapproves of
without her knowing about it, do you ever feel sorry and go
and tell her afterwards?

e. What if you fail to do something you were supposed to do, how
does this make you feel? What do you say? What do you do?

f. What if you do something you know your father disapproves
of? (Do you ever feel sorry and go and tell him afterwards?)

g. What if you fail to do something you were supposed to do?
What do you do? What do you say?

34. I guess everybody gets angry with their parents sometimes. What
sort of things make you angry with your father, for example?

a. What do you usually do when you get mad at him?

b. Have you ever struck your father? Thrown things around the
house? Sworn at him? Shouted at him? Talked back? Stomped
out of the house? Slammed doors and things like that?

c. What sort of things make you angry with your mother?

d. What do you usually do when you get angry with her?

e. What other sort of things have you done when you've been
angry with her? (Repeat probes used for father.)

f. How often would you say you get angry at your mother?

g. After this happens, do you sometimes feel very sorry and try
to make it up, or do you usually just let things go? (How do you
do this?)

h. How often do you get angry with your father?

i. Do you sometimes feel very sorry after getting angry with him
and try to make it up? (How?)

35. (IF NOT AN ONLY CHILD) How do you get along with your
brothers and sisters?

a. Do you think your mother treats you all alike?

b. And your father?

c. (IF NOT) How do you feel about this?

36. Are there times when you really enjoy your mother? Are there
things you especially like about her and that make you happy in
her company?

    a. How do you go about showing her you feel this way?

    b. How much do you feel she understands you? Does her best to help you? How much does she enjoy having you around? How much interest do you think she takes in you?

    c. Are there things you really enjoy about your father? Things that make you happy in his company?

    d. How do you go about showing him how you feel?

    e. How much do you feel he understands you and tries to help you? (Enjoys having you around? How much interest do you think he takes in you?)

    f. In general would you say you and your mother got along well together? (What makes you say this?)

    g. And how well would you say you and your father got along together?

37. Of all the people you know, whom do you most want to be like when you get older? (Why do you choose _____?)

    a. How about your father? In what ways would you like to be like him? (How much do you think you are like him already?)

    b. And in what ways would you like to be like your mother? (How much do you think you are already like her?)

    c. Whom do you think you are more like in your ways, your mother or your father?

38. Suppose you could change anything in your life, what would you first like to change? (Why do you put this first?)

    a. Are there any other things you'd very much like to change?

    b. Are there any (other) things about yourself you'd very much like to change?

    c. Are there things about yourself you're proud of, and wouldn't want to change?

    d. Are there things about yourself that make you feel angry or ashamed?

39. Most parents have some plans for their sons, about what they'd like them to do and be and so on. What, in this sort of way, have your parents expected of you? (How well do they expect you to do in schoolwork? In sports? In other school activities?)

    a. Do you feel, in general, that you've come up to their expectations?

    b. Are there *any* ways in which you feel you've let them down? (How do you think this came about?)

    c. What have you done about this? (Have you tried to make up for it in any way? Tried to be different?)

    d. How do you feel about it now?

40. O. K. Just one more question. Suppose you had three choices you could make for yourself for the future. What are the three things you'd most like to happen?

Appendix C

RATING SCALES: PARENT INTERVIEWS

Scale 1. Level of school achievement desired of boy by parent. (Q. 1)
1. Unimportant.
2. Expects boy to get high school diploma.
3. Expects boy to go to college.
4. Expects boy to go to college with selective entry requirements, or expects boy to get job involving graduate work (include school teaching here).
5. Expects boy to go to college with selective entry requirements, and to get job involving graduate work (include school teaching here, if prestige school).

$$r = .97 \text{ (M); } .89 \text{ (F)}[a]$$

Scale 2. Pressure parent has placed on boy for school achievement. (Q. 1)
1. Parent has not put any pressure on boy for school achievement and would not do so, regardless of whether or not boy's work is up to expectations.
2. Parent has not put pressure on boy because boy has been doing work up to expectations. Indication that pressure of some form would be applied if boy's work fell below expectations.
3. Mild pressure has been applied for boy to live up to expectations.
4. Moderate pressure has been applied fairly regularly for boy to live up to expectations.
5. Strong or constant pressure has been applied for boy to live up to expectations. Perhaps a demand for boy to do present work better than necessary for ultimate expectations.

$$r = .93 \text{ (M); } .73 \text{ (F)}$$

[a] Reliability of ratings for mother and father interviews, respectively.

Scale 3. Restrictions imposed on boy outside home. (Q. 4a, b, c, d, e, f)
Take into account rules about staying out at night, restrictions on
choice of friends and activities insofar as these are carried on outside the home. Also take into account restrictions placed on way boy
spends money (Q. 6f); what boy wears, if there are actual restrictions placed on this as opposed to criticisms or suggestions (Q. 6g).
1. No restrictions. Boy comes and goes as he likes, can stay out
   overnight; boy's friends and choice of activities are his own
   concern.
2. Few restrictions. Boy expected to let parents know if he is going
   to be unusually late, his approximate whereabouts, etc. Otherwise no restrictions imposed.
3. Moderate restrictions. Limits on boy's staying out late, although
   some variability. Expect to know where boy has been and with
   whom. May restrict some of his choice of friends and activities.
4. Strict. Boy expected to check out, be in at certain times, with
   very little latitude. Some limitation on boy's free choice of friends
   and activities.
5. Strict rules, rigidly enforced. Has to be in at a certain time, except on very rare occasions; has to let parents know what he is
   going to do or has done. Parents forbid a number of activities and
   pressure boy in matter of choice of friends, etc.

$$r = .87 \text{ (M)}; .66 \text{ (F)}$$

Scale 4. Restrictions placed on boy inside home. (Q. 4g, h, i, j.)
Take into account use of radio, TV; smoking or drinking in home;
noise; bad language; enforcement of homework hours, etc.
1. No restrictions. Parent would interfere only if someone else was
   being upset by boy's behavior.
2. Few restrictions. Some minor limitations set on boy's behavior.
3. Moderate. Parent sets limits to boy's activities in all or most
   areas, but some latitude allowed.
4. Strict rules in some areas. Limitations set in all or most others
   but with some latitude allowed.
5. Strict rules, strictly enforced. Boy has to be quiet around house
   (must not disturb rest of family), restrictions on use of radio and
   TV, puritanical attitude about drinking, swearing, etc.

$$r = .88 \text{ (M)}; .77 \text{ (F)}$$

Scale 5. Parent's account of boy's resistance to restrictions. (Q. 5)
1. Accepts restrictions completely. No resistance in any area.
2. On infrequent occasions tries to circumvent restrictions. Generally acceptant.
3. Tries sometimes to circumvent restrictions.

4. Often circumvents restrictions. Ignores them completely on occasion.
5. Extremely resistant. Completely unwilling to accept restrictions. Goes ahead and does what he likes.

$$r = .97 \text{ (M)}; .89 \text{ (F)}$$

Scale 6. Agreement between parents on enforcement of rules. (Q. 5)
1. Parent feels he (she) gets no support from other parent in enforcement of rules, or feels that the other is much too demanding of obedience.
2. In general, feels spouse not backing him (her) up, or is too demanding. Occasionally will get support or feel that he (she) is supported.
3. Both follow through equally well in enforcing rules, although may sometimes feel that spouse is not giving sufficient support or is going too far.
4. For the most part, enforce rules equally; on rare occasions feels that spouse is not giving sufficient support or is going too far.
5. Both enforce rules equally. Never feels that support is lacking or that spouse is going too far.

$$r = .93 \text{ (M)}; .78 \text{ (F)}$$

Scale 7. Extent to which boy earns own spending money. (Q. 6)
1. Boy earns all own spending money; for the most part pays for own clothes. Does not ask for money except in case of emergency.
2. Earns most of his spending money, but on occasion money is given or loaned by parent.
3. Regular allowance given by parents, sufficient for general expenditures. Boy earns money for extra expenditures, though additional money may be given on special occasions.
4. Regular allowance given boy. Supplemented whenever boy needs more for specific expenditures. Boy earns very little.
5. Boy gets as much money as he wants and when he wants it. Does not earn.

$$r = .93 \text{ (M)}; .88 \text{ (F)}$$

Scale 8. Pressures toward responsibility. (Q. 7)
1. Low demands, low pressure. Little or nothing expected of boy in the way of performing jobs.
2. Some demands, low pressure; or low demands, some pressure. No regular jobs, but encourages helping. One or two small jobs, not time-consuming.
3. Moderate demands, moderate pressure.
4. Moderate demands, high pressure; or high demands, moderate pressure.

5. High demands, high pressure. Many jobs, some time-consuming, expected to be performed.

$$r = .84 \text{ (M)}; .81 \text{ (F)}$$

Scale 9. Agreement on giving boy responsibilities. (Q. 7)
1. Complete disagreement as to how much responsibility should be given boy.
2. Agree that boy should have some responsibilities, but no agreement on what these should be or how responsible he should be held for these things.
3. In general, agree that boy should be given responsibilities in certain areas, but some disagreement on these areas or on degree of responsibility expected.
4. Agree on what responsibilities are to be given boy, may not show complete agreement in degree of responsibility expected.
5. In complete agreement about giving boy responsibilities, what these should be, and about degree of responsibility expected of him.

$$r = .90 \text{ (M)}; .82 \text{ (F)}$$

Scale 10. Boy's resistance to accepting responsibilities in home. (Q. 7)
1. No resistance whatsoever.
2. Boy tries to evade these on infrequent occasions, but in general accepts.
3. Tries to evade demands. On rare occasions refuses to comply.
4. Considerable resistance. Frequently evades responsibilities, sometimes refuses to accept them.
5. Extremely resistant. Evades responsibilities whenever possible. Unwilling to accept them.

$$r = .94 \text{ (M)}; .74 \text{ (F)}$$

Scale 11. Demands for obedience. (Q. 8)
1. Does not expect obedience. May say he (she) thinks one should not expect it of a boy of his age, etc.
2. Expects some obedience, but will speak several times. Parents cannot expect boy to obey immediately. Tolerant of noncompliance.
3. Will under some circumstances tolerate delay, on others not. Depends on situation. Will overlook noncompliance on occasion.
4. Generally expects obedience, but will sometimes tolerate delay. Compliance enforced for the most part.
5. Expects instant obedience, and will not tolerate noncompliance under any circumstances.

$$r = .90 \text{ (M)}; .77 \text{ (F)}$$

Scale 12. Parent's consistency of demands—Does parent ever drop subject, or does he (she) always carry through? (Q. 9)
1. Very often drops subject.
2. Sometimes follows through but more often drops it.
3. Sometimes drops subject but will follow through more often than not.
4. Usually carries through, occasionally drops subject.
5. Practically always carries through, makes strong effort.

$$r = .97 \text{ (M)}; .88 \text{ (F)}$$

Scale 13. Permissiveness for aggression against parents. (Q. 10)
Include sassing, deliberate disobedience, shouting, etc.
1. Not at all permissive. Always attempts to stop boy immediately. Never ignores it. Should not be permitted under any circumstances.
2. Generally nonpermissive. Discourages rather firmly, but would expect some aggression inevitably to occur and is not as intolerant as 1.
3. Moderately permissive. Sometimes overlooks, sometimes restrains, depending on circumstances.
4. Generally permissive. Would usually overlook this unless violent (e.g., direct verbal abuse, or displaced physical aggression likely to involve damage, or direct physical attack) or very persistent.
5. Very permissive. Would not restrain boy unless boy was likely to hurt parent.

$$r = .88 \text{ (M)}; .84 \text{ (F)}$$

Scale 14. Punitiveness for aggression against parents. (Q. 10)
1. Has never punished and would not punish even though aggression may be shown.
2. Has not punished because incidents have not occurred. Indication parent would punish if aggression were shown.
3. Mild punishment for aggression. Primarily scoldings and reprimands.
4. Moderate punishment. Perhaps deprivation of privileges, threats of more severe punishment.
5. Severe punishment, may include physical punishment. Parent may become emotional.

$$r = .84 \text{ (M)}; .82 \text{ (F)}$$

Scale 15. Parent's account of boy's physical aggression toward parent. (Q. 10)
1. No incidents reported.
2. One or two incidents of this kind.
3. A few incidents.

4. Occurs often (three or four times every year).
5. Occurs very often.
$$r = .91 \text{ (M)}; 1.00 \text{ (F)}$$

Scale 16. Parent's account of boy's verbal aggression toward parent. (Q. 10)
1. No instance.
2. Some instances, mild.
3. Occasionally objects or argues with mother (father).
4. Frequently objects, protests, argues. May express anger.
5. Frequent strong verbal protests. Loses control.
$$r = .95 \text{ (M)}; .88 \text{ (F)}$$

Scale 17. Parent's report of indirect aggression toward parent. (Q. 10)
Take account of any show of anger or resentment which does not involve direct, face-to-face, physical or verbal aggression, e.g., walking out of house, slamming doors, saying derogatory things to other parent, passive resistance.
1. No instances.
2. One or two instances.
3. Some instances, but no indication that technique is frequently used.
4. Several instances.
5. Several instances. Parent explicitly says that boy does this sort of thing often.
$$r = .93 \text{ (M)}; .84 \text{ (F)}$$

Scale 18. Amount of time father spent in care-taking during boy's childhood, as compared with mother. (Q. 11)
1. None at all.
2. Helped occasionally with feeding or changing diapers, nothing regular.
3. Helped considerably, but did not do as much as mother—perhaps some regular responsibilities such as feeding or bathing at certain times.
4. Shared equally with mother.
5. Did more than mother.
$$r = .92 \text{ (M)}; .83 \text{ (F)}$$

Scale 19. Amount of time mother spent in affectionate interaction (playing, taking out, etc.) with boy in infancy and early childhood. (Q. 12)
1. None.
2. A little, occasionally. Not much time for this.
3. Some time almost every day, although only brief periods. No time specifically set aside for this.

4. Considerable time every day, more on weekends. May or may not set specific time aside for this.
5. A great deal of time. Some time set aside for this every day. Good deal of time on weekends.

$$r = .91 \ (M); \ .87 \ (F)$$

Scale 20. Amount of time father spent in affectionate interaction with boy in infancy and early childhood. (Q. 12)
1. None.
2. A little, occasionally. Not much time for this.
3. Some time almost every day, although only brief periods. No time specifically set aside for this.
4. Considerable time every day, more on weekends. May or may not set specific time aside for this.
5. A great deal of time. Some time set aside for this every day. Good deal of time on weekends.

$$r = .94 \ (M); \ .88 \ (F)$$

Scale 21. Parent's permissiveness for sex; early years. (Q. 13, 14)
1. Nonpermissive. Stepped in and stopped any activity at once. Considered wrong, harmful.
2. Mildly permissive. May consider sex behavior wrong or harmful, but tries not to make an issue of such incidents.
3. Moderate. Would let things go, up to a point. As long as it does not become a habit, occur often. May interfere occasionally.
4. Generally permissive, but would interfere in some circumstances.
5. Entirely permissive. Natural, just curiosity, would not attempt to stop.

$$r = .94 \ (M); \ .78 \ (F)$$

Scale 22. Permissiveness for masturbation: present attitude. (Q. 13b)
1. Completely nonpermissive. Parent would tolerate no masturbation. Wrong, harmful.
2. Mildly permissive. May consider masturbation wrong or harmful, but tries not to make an issue of such incidents.
3. Moderate. Thinks some masturbation inevitable, but would discourage it.
4. Tolerant of masturbation ("part of growing up"), but would perhaps talk to the boy about this.
5. Entirely permissive. Would not talk to boy about it except perhaps to see he knows dangers and has information.

$$r = .96 \ (M); \ .93 \ (F)$$

Scale 23. Permissiveness for heterosexual activity: present attitude. (Q. 14)

1. Completely nonpermissive. Parent would tolerate no sex behavior of any kind. Wrong, harmful.
2. Mildly permissive. May consider sex behavior wrong or harmful, but tries not to make an issue of it.
3. Moderate. Might allow some necking provided this doesn't go too far.
4. Tolerant attitude. Expects some petting, but would not condone premarital sex relations.
5. Entirely permissive. Expects boy to experiment with girls. No interference, except possibly to make sure that boy knows dangers and has information.

$$r = .95 \text{ (M)}; .84 \text{ (F)}$$

Scale 24. Punitiveness for sexual behavior. (Q. 13, 14)
1. No punishment, though incidents have occurred. May distract or reason, but would not scold or make an issue of it.
2. Mild. Some scolding, not intense; some expression of disapproval. More likely to distract, etc.
3. Moderate. Some scolding, warning about consequences, but not with great intensity. No show of emotion.
4. Scolding, threats, etc., applied constantly.
5. Severe punishment. Boy beaten, threatened with extreme consequences, strong expressions of rejection. Parent becomes emotional.

$$r = .94 \text{ (M)}; .83 \text{ (F)}$$

Scale 25. Parent's sex anxiety. (Q. 13, 14, 15)
1. None evident. Matter-of-fact. Willing to answer boy's questions freely, without evasion. May find incidents mildly amusing.
2. Some anxiety shown by setting limits on boy's behavior, or admission that some things would cause worry, but generally nonemotional in handling of incidents that have occurred. Willing to give information freely.
3. Moderate anxiety. Indications of discomfort about masturbation, sex play, either through handling of situations or expression of parent's feelings about these, but parent does not become emotional or unduly disturbed. Some evasion in matter of giving information.
4. Parent emotional in handling of situations, avoids giving information.
5. As for (4) with the addition of evidence of shock or disgust or difficulty in talking about subject in interview situation.

$$r = .94 \text{ (M)}; .72 \text{ (F)}$$

Scale 26. Parent's estimate of boy's sex anxiety. (Q. 14)
1. Not at all worried.

2. A little. "I think he may be puzzled over some things."
3. Some worry. "About the same as any other boy."
4. Mother (father) feels boy is quite anxious.
5. Very worried. Mother (father) gives definite evidence to support her (his) view.

$$r = .96 \text{ (M)}; .98 \text{ (F)}$$

Scale 27. Parent's account of amount of time boy spends in his (her) company. (Q. 16, 17)

This scale assumes both boy and parent go for trips and vacations. If neither do, take account only of part of scale referring to remainder of situations.

1. Never spends time with parent other than inevitable interaction at meal times, etc. If at home, boy in own room or elsewhere in house, or following own pursuits. Boy and parent never go for trips or vacations together.
2. An occasional evening in company of parent, interacting; go places together very rarely, only on occasional visits to family or to buy something for which parent is paying, etc. Trips together very rare.
3. Some evenings at home, in interaction. Go out together sometimes, sharing activities other than those listed under (2). Some trips, vacations together.
4. Spend a good deal of time together. Regular trips in addition to activities included under (3).
5. Most of leisure time spent in parent's company. Many evenings spent in interaction; visits, trips, vacations, etc. frequent or regular.

$$r = .88 \text{ (M)}; .79 \text{ (F)}$$

Scale 28. Parent's permissiveness for boy's spending time in his (her) company. (Q. 16, 17)

1. Not at all permissive. Prefers him to go off by himself, not stay at home or be with parents.
2. Boy can please himself about this. No encouragement to spend time with parents.
3. Boy expected and encouraged to spend some time with parents, but also to go out or away with friends.
4. Boy expected and encouraged to spend time at home and with parent. Tries to make home attractive to him, etc. No active discouragement of going with friends.
5. Actively encourages boy to spend time with parent. May reward him for doing so. Discourages him from going on trips, etc., without parent.

$$r = .79 \text{ (M)}; .73 \text{ (F)}$$

5. Never interferes. Fighting natural. Lets them fight it out among themselves.

$$r = .92 \text{ (M)}; .64 \text{ (F)}$$

Scale 42. Punitiveness for aggression toward siblings. (Q. 24)
1. Has never punished and would not punish even though aggression may be shown.
2. Has not punished because incidents have not occurred. Indication parent would punish if aggression were shown.
3. Mild punishment for aggression. Primarily scoldings and reprimands.
4. Moderate punishment. Perhaps deprivation of privileges, threats of more severe punishment.
5. Severe punishment, may include physical punishment. Parent may become emotional.

$$r = .93 \text{ (M)}; .78 \text{ (F)}$$

Scale 43. Permissiveness for aggression toward adults other than parents. (Q. 25, 26)
1. Not at all permissive. Boy should respect elders, will not listen to boy's complaints about them. Tolerates no defiance of authority.
2. Generally nonpermissive. Would definitely discourage him from any direct aggression, but will let boy have say and allow possibility that he may be in the right.
3. Somewhat permissive. Would not interfere, unless boy was clearly being disruptive, insolent, flagrantly defiant. Would not let things go too far.
4. Would interfere only as last resort. Only if boy was persistent or causing serious trouble.
5. Would never interfere. Not my business.

$$r = .86 \text{ (M)}; .73 \text{ (F)}$$

Scale 44. Punitiveness for aggression toward adults other than parents. (Q. 25, 26)
1. Has never punished and would not punish even though aggression may be shown.
2. Has not punished because incidents have not occurred. Indication parent would punish if aggression were shown.
3. Mild punishment for aggression. Primarily scoldings and reprimands.
4. Moderate punishment. Perhaps deprivation of privileges, threats of more severe punishment.
5. Severe punishment, may include physical punishment. Parent may become emotional.

$$r = .94 \text{ (M)}; .86 \text{ (F)}$$

Scale 45. Demands for masculinity. (Q. 27)

1. Parent puts little value on specifically masculine activities, stresses characteristics esteemed equally in both sexes. Believes there should be little difference in household responsibilities for boys and girls.
2. In general, as for (1), except that parent spontaneously mentions some specifically masculine characteristics, or thinks there should be some differentiation in responsibilities. No specific training.
3. Parent interested in boy being masculine, but doesn't train in wide range of areas. Emphasizes characteristics esteemed in both sexes as well as purely masculine roles. Some differentiation in respect to household responsibilities.
4. Considerable demands for masculine characteristics, some specific training. Definite differentiation in respect to responsibilities, and also in some other kinds of activities.
5. Parent stresses and trains for wide differentiation in wide range of areas. Dress, activities, manners, etc., must all be appropriate to child's sex. References throughout interview to what is manly, boyish.

$$r = .93 \text{ (M)}; .84 \text{ (F)}$$

Scale 46. Use of rewards. (Q. 28)

1. None.
2. Rare, only for something exceptional.
3. Occasional rewards.
4. Frequent rewards.
5. Frequent and generous rewards. Regular for some kinds of behavior.

$$r = .92 \text{ (M)}; .85 \text{ (F)}$$

Scale 47. Use of praise. (Q. 29)

1. Practically never praises; just takes good behavior for granted.
2. Praises now and again; seldom.
3. Sometimes praises; sometimes not.
4. Usually praises, shows appreciation, admires.
5. Praises regularly, very appreciative, admiring.

$$r = .93 \text{ (M)}; .78 \text{ (F)}$$

Scale 48. Use of positive models. (Q. 30)

1. No use. May say these are undesirable. No reference to modeling in interview.
2. Does this rarely.
3. Some use, but does not do this often.
4. Uses fairly frequently.

5. Frequent use. Examples given which suggest emphasis on this technique.
$$r = .97 \text{ (M)}; .93 \text{ (F)}$$

Scale 49. Use of negative models. (Q. 30)
1. Tries to avoid this. Believes undesirable. No suggestions of use in interview.
2. Does not use, but no statement that this is specifically avoided or felt to be undesirable.
3. Uses on rare occasions.
4. Some use, not regular.
5. Uses fairly often, or regularly in some contexts.
$$r = .95 \text{ (M)}; .85 \text{ (F)}$$

Scale 50. Use of physical punishment. (Q. 32)
Take account of whole period, including earlier years. If physical punishment is still administered, rate up one point.
1. Never uses. Has never used in past.
2. Occasional cuffing in past. Nothing more.
3. Real spanking at infrequent intervals. Occasional cuffs or slaps.
4. History of frequent cuffing. Occasional real spanking.
5. History of frequent and severe physical punishment.
$$r = .88 \text{ (M)}; .84 \text{ (F)}$$

Scale 51. Use of deprivation. (Q. 32)
1. Never used.
2. Used rarely, only to control deviations connected with use of privileges.
3. Used sometimes but with moderation. Small privileges taken away, but not for long periods of time.
4. In general as for (3), but technique is used more frequently or applied in more severe manner.
5. Frequently controls defiant behavior by depriving boy of highly valued privileges for long periods of time.
$$r = .81 \text{ (M)}; .85 \text{ (F)}$$

Scale 52. Use of ridicule. (Q. 32)
1. Never uses.
2. Slight use. One or two instances given, not intense.
3. Moderate use. Several incidents reported; no indication that there is special emphasis or frequent use.
4. Much use. Several incidents reported, and evidence that the technique is emphasized, considered effective, or used quite frequently.
5. As for (4), but parent extremely derogatory.
$$r = .89 \text{ (M)}; .83 \text{ (F)}$$

Scale 53. Use of scolding, nagging, lecturing. (Q. 32)
1. Minimum use.
2. Some scolding, nagging, about one or two things.
3. Nags in limited areas, but in these areas is fairly persistent.
4. Nags about a number of things, but not as extensively as (5).
5. Constantly scolding and nagging about many things. "Have to be after him all the time."

$$r = .91 \text{ (M)}; .76 \text{ (F)}$$

Scale 54. Withdrawal of love. (Q. 32)
1. Never refuses to speak to boy, ignore him, or any other technique of this kind. No instances in interview.
2. Used rarely, or one or two instances of this kind of technique in interview.
3. Some use of the techniques, or several instances in interview.
4. Uses techniques fairly often. Include here, if parent says he makes some use, only if other examples occur in interview.
5. Frequent use of techniques. Include here some use of techniques, if these are said to be especially effective or several examples of use of these occur elsewhere in interview.

$$r = .90 \text{ (M)}; .93 \text{ (F)}$$

Scale 55. Use of reasoning as technique of discipline. (Q. 31, 32, 33)
This includes explaining why boy should not do things, listening to his arguments, and trying to give an answer on the merits of the case, describing consequences of action, etc.
1. Never uses reasoning, explicit evidence that it is not used. "It's no good to reason with him."
2. Minimal use. On rare occasions tries to explain to boy why he should do certain things or not do them.
3. While reasoning is not the regular pattern, parent will often listen to boy's reasons and explain.
4. Much use of reasoning. Used frequently, but not to the exclusion of other methods.
5. High, regular use. Parent always tries to reason before using any other technique of coercion or restraint.

$$r = .85 \text{ (M)}; .69 \text{ (F)}$$

Scale 56. Parent's account of boy's attitude to discipline. (Q. 34)
1. Acceptant. Does not complain.
2. Generally noncomplaining. Doesn't seem to resent it very much.
3. Boy resentful at times.
4. Generally resentful.
5. Very resentful. Doesn't get over it easily.

$$r = .91 \text{ (M)}; .83 \text{ (F)}$$

Scale 29. Parent's punitiveness for boy's wanting to spend time in his (her) company. (Q. 16, 17)
1. None evident.
2. Once or twice has scolded or ridiculed boy for this.
3. Evidence for some punishment of this kind of behavior in earlier or recent years.
4. Clear evidence that parent scolds, ridicules or uses sarcasm (or has done so) on occasions, e.g., "Haven't you got any friends of your own?"
5. Parent punishes or has punished on many occasions in any of the above ways. May have used more forceful methods when younger.

$$r = .84 \text{ (M)}; .00 \text{ (F)}[b]$$

[b] Due to lack of variability of the ratings of one rater.

Scale 30. Boy's resistance to spending time with parents. (Q. 16, 18, 19)
If parent says boy seems uncomfortable, even though not openly resistant, rate up one point.
1. No resistance reported.
2. Some indication of resistance; may not be directly expressed.
3. Resists sometimes.
4. Often resists.
5. Avoids going out with parent whenever possible.

$$r = .85 \text{ (M)}; .87 \text{ (F)}$$

Scale 31. Extent to which boy goes to parent for help, i.e., gets advice suggestions, reassurances. (Q. 18, 19; also note 23c, 25)
If contacts with parent are purely on matters *not* of personal significance to boy, rate down one point.
1. Never goes to parents.
2. Only on rare occasions.
3. Sometimes, not frequently.
4. Often.
5. Consults parent and seeks help or advice over wide range of topics. Goes to him (her) for help and reassurance when in difficulties.

$$r = .85 \text{ (M)}; .83 \text{ (F)}$$

Scale 32. Parent's encouragement for seeking help. (Q. 18, 19; also 6h, 23c, 25)
1. Not at all permissive. Actively discourages boy from coming for help or advice of any kind. Boy should learn to stand on own feet, must solve own problems.

2. Slightly permissive. Will be supportive or directive only in emergencies. Boy generally should stand on own feet, make own decisions.
3. Parent expects boy to work out most things for himself. Little encouragement to come for help, although may be supportive or directive when boy does come for help.
4. Generally permissive. On rare occasions encourages boy to work out things for himself. Usually encourages coming to parent.
5. Entirely permissive. Always encourages boy to come for help and advice. Always supportive or directive.

$$r = .70 \text{ (M); } .80 \text{ (F)}$$

Scale 33. Parent's punitiveness for seeking help. (Q. 18, 19, 6h, 23c, 25)
1. Not at all punitive. Parent never impatient, never scolds, ridicules, or uses sarcasm. (Encouragement of boy to be self-reliant is not punitive if done in positive manner.)
2. Some evidence of mild scolding, ridicule, or similar type of reaction on rare occasions.
3. Parents sometimes respond positively, sometimes scold, etc.
4. Evidence of frequent punitive responses.
5. Parent frequently punitive; on occasions scolds severely, is very disparaging or sarcastic.

$$r = .83 \text{ (M); } 1.00 \text{ (F)}$$

Scale 34. Boy's resistance to accepting suggestions from parent. (Q. 18, 19)
If resistance is rational rather than emotional, i.e., boy evaluates advice before acting on it, rate down one point.
1. No resistance.
2. Very little resistance.
3. Some resistance. Sometimes resists and rejects parent's suggestions; usually follows them.
4. Considerable resistance. Often resists parent's suggestions, on occasions does the opposite of what is suggested.
5. Very resistant. Takes little notice of what parent says and definitely prefers to go own way. Will do opposite of what parent suggests quite often.

$$r = .90 \text{ (M); } .74 \text{ (F)}$$

Scale 35. Warmth of mother toward boy. (Q. M20, F21. Modify rating in light of answers to previous and later questions.)
This scale is concerned with the extent to which the mother demonstrates her affection for her son. Take note particularly of the extent to which she shows pleasure in the boy's accomplishments *to the boy,* shows sympathy and understanding, is supporting and

comforting, takes pleasure in his company, and *lets him see that this is the case.*

1. Very little warmth; mother matter-of-fact, not demonstrative. Gets little pleasure or enjoyment from interaction with boy.
2. Some evidence of warmth. Not as matter-of-fact as (1), but in general is undemonstrative and enjoys interaction only under limited circumstances.
3. Moderate degree of warmth. Enjoys boy's company for the most part, but is not very demonstrative.
4. Very warm, loving. Shows similar characteristics to mother rated (5), but is more restrained in expression of her feelings.
5. Extremely warm, loving. Shows pleasure in boy's accomplishments, sympathetic when boy in difficulties. Enjoys interacting with him. Spontaneously and frequently shows affection for him.

Note: In order to be considered demonstrative a parent need not indulge in overt displays of affection which would be obvious to onlookers. It is sufficient that her response be recognizable by the boy himself.

$$r = .92 \text{ (M)}; .72 \text{ (F)}$$

Scale 36. Warmth of father toward boy. (Q. M21, F20. Modify rating in light of answers to previous questions.) (Same as for Scale 35)

$$r = .93 \text{ (M)}; .85 \text{ (F)}$$

Scale 37. Warmth toward spouse. (Q. 22. Modify rating in light of rest of interview.)

1. Very little warmth, matter-of-fact. Gets little pleasure or enjoyment from company of spouse.
2. Some evidence of warmth, seldom demonstrative. Enjoys company of spouse on limited occasions only.
3. Moderate degree of warmth. Enjoys company of spouse, although some reservations. Sometimes demonstrative, sometimes not, or only mildly demonstrative.
4. Warm and loving, although not completely free in expressing feelings. Shows pleasure in accomplishments of spouse, enjoys his (her) company.
5. Very warm, loving. Enjoys time they can spend together. Feels they communicate their feelings freely, understand each other.

$$r = .90 \text{ (M)}; .80 \text{ (F)}$$

Scale 38. Parental encouragement of aggression. (Q. 23, 24, 25)

This scale measures the extent to which the parent directly or indirectly encourages or condones combatant, defiant behavior in relation to peers or authority figures.

1. Parent never encourages or condones aggression.
2. Very little evidence of encouragement and condoning.
3. Moderate encouragement and condoning under some circumstances.
4. Considerable encouragement and condoning but with some reservations.
5. Strongly encourages and condones aggression under almost all circumstances.

$$r = .90 \text{ (M)}; .94 \text{ (F)}$$

Scale 39. Permissiveness for aggression toward peers. (Q. 23)
1. Not at all permissive. Parent always discourages boy from fighting, provoking others into arguments, etc. Would restrain him whenever possible.
2. Generally nonpermissive. Would definitely discourage him from all but the mildest forms of aggression.
3. Will not generally interfere, unless someone is getting hurt or very upset; would restrain or discourage him if this is likely to occur.
4. Would interfere only in an emergency, e.g., if neighbors complained or serious consequences are likely to result.
5. Entirely permissive. Would never interfere or discourage boy. Thinks fighting natural for boys this age.

$$r = .89 \text{ (M)}; .89 \text{ (F)}$$

Scale 40. Punitiveness for aggression toward peers. (Q. 23)
1. Has never punished and would not punish even though aggression may be shown.
2. Has not punished because incidents have not occurred. Indication parent would punish if aggression were shown.
3. Mild punishment for aggression. Primarily scoldings and reprimands.
4. Moderate punishment. Perhaps deprivations of privileges, threats of more severe punishment.
5. Severe punishment, may include physical punishment. Parent may become emotional.

$$r = .88 \text{ (M)}; .74 \text{ (F)}$$

Scale 41. Permissiveness for aggression toward siblings. (Q. 24)
1. Not at all permissive. Parent always discourages boy from fighting with siblings, provoking arguments, etc. Steps in right away.
2. Usually interferes. May ignore mild disputes, etc.
3. Interferes if someone is getting hurt or very upset.
4. Would restrain only in an emergency, i.e., if serious consequences are likely to result.

5. Never interferes. Fighting natural. Lets them fight it out among themselves.

$$r = .92 \text{ (M)}; .64 \text{ (F)}$$

Scale 42. Punitiveness for aggression toward siblings. (Q. 24)
  1. Has never punished and would not punish even though aggression may be shown.
  2. Has not punished because incidents have not occurred. Indication parent would punish if aggression were shown.
  3. Mild punishment for aggression. Primarily scoldings and reprimands.
  4. Moderate punishment. Perhaps deprivation of privileges, threats of more severe punishment.
  5. Severe punishment, may include physical punishment. Parent may become emotional.

$$r = .93 \text{ (M)}; .78 \text{ (F)}$$

Scale 43. Permissiveness for aggression toward adults other than parents. (Q. 25, 26)
  1. Not at all permissive. Boy should respect elders, will not listen to boy's complaints about them. Tolerates no defiance of authority.
  2. Generally nonpermissive. Would definitely discourage him from any direct aggression, but will let boy have say and allow possibility that he may be in the right.
  3. Somewhat permissive. Would not interfere, unless boy was clearly being disruptive, insolent, flagrantly defiant. Would not let things go too far.
  4. Would interfere only as last resort. Only if boy was persistent or causing serious trouble.
  5. Would never interfere. Not my business.

$$r = .86 \text{ (M)}; .73 \text{ (F)}$$

Scale 44. Punitiveness for aggression toward adults other than parents. (Q. 25, 26)
  1. Has never punished and would not punish even though aggression may be shown.
  2. Has not punished because incidents have not occurred. Indication parent would punish if aggression were shown.
  3. Mild punishment for aggression. Primarily scoldings and reprimands.
  4. Moderate punishment. Perhaps deprivation of privileges, threats of more severe punishment.
  5. Severe punishment, may include physical punishment. Parent may become emotional.

$$r = .94 \text{ (M)}; .86 \text{ (F)}$$

Scale 45. Demands for masculinity. (Q. 27)
1. Parent puts little value on specifically masculine activities, stresses characteristics esteemed equally in both sexes. Believes there should be little difference in household responsibilities for boys and girls.
2. In general, as for (1), except that parent spontaneously mentions some specifically masculine characteristics, or thinks there should be some differentiation in responsibilities. No specific training.
3. Parent interested in boy being masculine, but doesn't train in wide range of areas. Emphasizes characteristics esteemed in both sexes as well as purely masculine roles. Some differentiation in respect to household responsibilities.
4. Considerable demands for masculine characteristics, some specific training. Definite differentiation in respect to responsibilities, and also in some other kinds of activities.
5. Parent stresses and trains for wide differentiation in wide range of areas. Dress, activities, manners, etc., must all be appropriate to child's sex. References throughout interview to what is manly, boyish.

$$r = .93 \text{ (M)}; .84 \text{ (F)}$$

Scale 46. Use of rewards. (Q. 28)
1. None.
2. Rare, only for something exceptional.
3. Occasional rewards.
4. Frequent rewards.
5. Frequent and generous rewards. Regular for some kinds of behavior.

$$r = .92 \text{ (M)}; .85 \text{ (F)}$$

Scale 47. Use of praise. (Q. 29)
1. Practically never praises; just takes good behavior for granted.
2. Praises now and again; seldom.
3. Sometimes praises; sometimes not.
4. Usually praises, shows appreciation, admires.
5. Praises regularly, very appreciative, admiring.

$$r = .93 \text{ (M)}; .78 \text{ (F)}$$

Scale 48. Use of positive models. (Q. 30)
1. No use. May say these are undesirable. No reference to modeling in interview.
2. Does this rarely.
3. Some use, but does not do this often.
4. Uses fairly frequently.

5. Frequent use. Examples given which suggest emphasis on this technique.

$$r = .97 \text{ (M)}; .93 \text{ (F)}$$

Scale 49. Use of negative models. (Q. 30)
1. Tries to avoid this. Believes undesirable. No suggestions of use in interview.
2. Does not use, but no statement that this is specifically avoided or felt to be undesirable.
3. Uses on rare occasions.
4. Some use, not regular.
5. Uses fairly often, or regularly in some contexts.

$$r = .95 \text{ (M)}; .85 \text{ (F)}$$

Scale 50. Use of physical punishment. (Q. 32)
Take account of whole period, including earlier years. If physical punishment is still administered, rate up one point.
1. Never uses. Has never used in past.
2. Occasional cuffing in past. Nothing more.
3. Real spanking at infrequent intervals. Occasional cuffs or slaps.
4. History of frequent cuffing. Occasional real spanking.
5. History of frequent and severe physical punishment.

$$r = .88 \text{ (M)}; .84 \text{ (F)}$$

Scale 51. Use of deprivation. (Q. 32)
1. Never used.
2. Used rarely, only to control deviations connected with use of privileges.
3. Used sometimes but with moderation. Small privileges taken away, but not for long periods of time.
4. In general as for (3), but technique is used more frequently or applied in more severe manner.
5. Frequently controls defiant behavior by depriving boy of highly valued privileges for long periods of time.

$$r = .81 \text{ (M)}; .85 \text{ (F)}$$

Scale 52. Use of ridicule. (Q. 32)
1. Never uses.
2. Slight use. One or two instances given, not intense.
3. Moderate use. Several incidents reported; no indication that there is special emphasis or frequent use.
4. Much use. Several incidents reported, and evidence that the technique is emphasized, considered effective, or used quite frequently.
5. As for (4), but parent extremely derogatory.

$$r = .89 \text{ (M)}; .83 \text{ (F)}$$

Scale 53. Use of scolding, nagging, lecturing. (Q. 32)
1. Minimum use.
2. Some scolding, nagging, about one or two things.
3. Nags in limited areas, but in these areas is fairly persistent.
4. Nags about a number of things, but not as extensively as (5).
5. Constantly scolding and nagging about many things. "Have to be after him all the time."

$$r = .91 \text{ (M)}; .76 \text{ (F)}$$

Scale 54. Withdrawal of love. (Q. 32)
1. Never refuses to speak to boy, ignore him, or any other technique of this kind. No instances in interview.
2. Used rarely, or one or two instances of this kind of technique in interview.
3. Some use of the techniques, or several instances in interview.
4. Uses techniques fairly often. Include here, if parent says he makes some use, only if other examples occur in interview.
5. Frequent use of techniques. Include here some use of techniques, if these are said to be especially effective or several examples of use of these occur elsewhere in interview.

$$r = .90 \text{ (M)}; .93 \text{ (F)}$$

Scale 55. Use of reasoning as technique of discipline. (Q. 31, 32, 33)
This includes explaining why boy should not do things, listening to his arguments, and trying to give an answer on the merits of the case, describing consequences of action, etc.
1. Never uses reasoning, explicit evidence that it is not used. "It's no good to reason with him."
2. Minimal use. On rare occasions tries to explain to boy why he should do certain things or not do them.
3. While reasoning is not the regular pattern, parent will often listen to boy's reasons and explain.
4. Much use of reasoning. Used frequently, but not to the exclusion of other methods.
5. High, regular use. Parent always tries to reason before using any other technique of coercion or restraint.

$$r = .85 \text{ (M)}; .69 \text{ (F)}$$

Scale 56. Parent's account of boy's attitude to discipline. (Q. 34)
1. Acceptant. Does not complain.
2. Generally noncomplaining. Doesn't seem to resent it very much.
3. Boy resentful at times.
4. Generally resentful.
5. Very resentful. Doesn't get over it easily.

$$r = .91 \text{ (M)}; .83 \text{ (F)}$$

Scale 57. Agreement between parents on questions of discipline. (Q. 35)

Rate down one point if boy is aware of disagreement.
1. No agreement as to when and how boy should be punished.
2. Some disagreement as to techniques used, occasions when boy should be punished, and to severity of punishment boy deserves; or considerable disagreement in one or two of these areas. (If considerable in all three, rate down one.)
3. For the most part in agreement on techniques, but in specific instances feels that spouse is too lenient or severe; or punishes or omits punishment inappropriately.
4. Agree on techniques and ways of handling boy in matters of discipline. Feels that spouse may occasionally have been too strict or lenient, but not consistently so.
5. Complete agreement.

$$r = .94 \text{ (M)}; .89 \text{ (F)}$$

Scale 58. Family authority, policy setting. (Q. 37)

This scale refers to the making and enforcing of specific decisions with regard to the children.
1. One parent sets over-all policy. Other leaves all this to spouse.
2. For the most part, one parent sets policy, but other parent occasionally has some say.
3. One parent sets policy for most part, but seeks agreement from other and takes note of views.
4. In general, both parents set policy jointly, but one parent has more influence in setting policies than other.
5. Both parents set policies jointly. Have equal say in matter, work things out together.

$$r = .95 \text{ (M)}; .85 \text{ (F)}$$

Scale 59. Acceptance-rejection of boy. (Q. 39, 40, 42c, whole interview)
1. Complete rejection, expressed through excessive criticism of son's behavior and characteristics, even if these are widespread among adolescents; use of unfavorable comparisons; feeling of not wanting son, that he interferes with activities or with relationship to spouse, etc.
2. Strong rejection; in general shows similar attitude to parent rated (1), but modifies statements by mention of positive characteristics, etc.
3. Some rejection: parent ambivalent, e.g., may recognize positive characteristics in son while criticizing him in some respects.
4. Slight rejection: in general shows attitude similar to parent rated (5), but with some minor reservations.

5. No rejection; complete acceptance of boy for what he is; respects child as an individual. May be aware of boy's limitations, but is prepared to accept these.

$$r = .90 \text{ (M)}; .80 \text{ (F)}$$

Scale 60. Hostility to boy.

Measure by ratio of favorable to unfavorable comments. (Entire interview)

1. Uniformly favorable.
2. Generally favorable with a few reservations.
3. Equal number of favorable and unfavorable comments.
4. Generally unfavorable comments but some favorable ones or some comments implying some degree of regard.
5. Uniformly unfavorable comments.

$$r = .91 \text{ (M)}; .77 \text{ (F)}$$

Scale 61. Hostility to spouse. (Entire interview) (Same as for Scale 60)

$$r = .93 \text{ (M)}; .77 \text{ (F)}$$

Appendix D

RATING SCALES: ADOLESCENT INTERVIEWS

Scale 1. Boy's report of direct verbal aggression against teacher.
(Q. 4, 5)

This scale measures the extent to which boy expresses aggression directly to teacher by verbal means, e.g., swearing, arguing back, refusing directly to obey orders, protesting against treatment, etc.
1. No instances.
2. Some instances; infrequent, mild.
3. Occasionally objects or argues with teacher.
4. Frequently objects, protests, argues. May express anger.
5. Frequent strong verbal protests. Loses control.

$$r = .90^a$$

Scale 2. Boy's report of direct physical aggression toward teacher.
(Q. 4, 5)

Include only instances of boy's striking teacher, or throwing things at him, or other similar forms of physical attack.
1. No instances.
2. One or two incidents of this kind.
3. A few incidents.
4. Occurs often; three or four times every year.
5. Occurs very often.

$$r = .91$$

Scale 3. Boy's report of indirect or semidirect aggressive responses against teacher. (Q. 4, 5)

Include instances of defamation, complaining to principal or counselor, inciting of others without directly participating himself, deliberate avoidance responses, etc. Displaced aggression, e.g., slamming doors, may be considered semidirect.

ᵃ Reliability of ratings.

427

1. No instances in interview.
2. One or two instances.
3. Some instances, but no indication that this is a frequently used technique.
4. Several instances in interview.
5. Several instances. Boy explicitly says he does this sort of thing frequently.

$$r = .72$$

Scale 4. Directness-indirectness of aggressive responses to teachers. (Q. 4, 5)

Ignore absolute frequency of responses.
1. Boy expresses aggression only in a very indirect manner, e.g., by deliberately avoiding contact with teacher, by saying things about teacher (to others).
2. Boy usually expresses aggression indirectly, but sometimes aggression is semidirect, e.g., not carrying out orders properly or otherwise passively resisting.
3. Boy sometimes directly, sometimes indirectly, expresses aggression; or typically expresses aggression in a semidirect way.
4. Boy sometimes expresses aggression openly, freely, and immediately.
5. Boy typically expresses aggression openly, freely, and immediately. (Expressions need not be explosive or violent.)

$$r = .78$$

Scale 5. Indications of guilt feelings concerning aggression against teacher. (Q. 4, 5)

1. No indications.
2. Some indications, e.g., boy says he feels he acted childishly, but does not attempt to make up for this. Not defensive when reporting aggression.
3. Some indication of discomfort about aggression, defensiveness, or attempts to make up to teacher. (Rate 2 if a single indication only occurs, 4 if all three indications occur to some degree.)
4. See 3. Rate 4 also if boy indicates guilt strongly through one or other of above cues.
5. Clear indications of guilt. Boy feels uncomfortable, tries to make up to teacher. Is defensive; rationalizes when reporting aggression.

$$r = .82$$

Scale 6. Negative attention-getting behavior. (Q. 6)

1. Boy denies any behavior of this kind.
2. Boy admits to a few rare instances of this kind of behavior.

3. Some behavior of this kind admitted "now and again," but not a wide range of incidents of this kind.
4. Admits to three or four sorts of disruptive behavior "sometimes" or to fewer kinds fairly often.
5. Admits to several kinds of disruptive, attention-getting behavior, and says these occur frequently.

$$r = .91$$

Scale 7. Extent to which boy seeks advice, help from teachers. (Q. 7)
1. Never seeks advice, help.
2. Seeks advice, help rarely—only when in difficulties concerning schoolwork.
3. Sometimes goes to teacher for advice on schoolwork. One or two other things mentioned.
4. Seeks help, advice over wide range of problems, often for schoolwork, but not infrequently for other things.
5. Seeks help, advice over wide range of problems frequently, in all areas.

$$r = .77$$

Scale 8. Resistance to seeking, accepting help or advice from teacher. (Q. 7)
1. No sign of resistance, though boy may evaluate advice before accepting it.
2. Slight indication of resistance. Boy definitely prefers to work out some things for himself. May show some discomfort about having to ask for help.
3. Moderate resistance; some discomfort. On rare occasions feels like doing opposite of what teacher suggests.
4. Considerable resistance. Definitely feels uncomfortable about seeking help. Sometimes feels like doing opposite of what teacher suggests.
5. Resists strongly. Does not like asking for help; strongly resists suggestions from teachers; sometimes does opposite.

$$r = .84$$

Scale 9. Extent to which boy looks for praise, recognition from teacher. (Q. 8)
1. Praise, rewards unimportant. Grades do not matter. No indication of effort to please teacher.
2. Not very important; may help sometimes. Grades only important to get into college, etc. No special attempt to please teacher.
3. Praise, good grades, etc., helpful. No emphasis. No other tokens of recognition suggested. No special attempts to please teacher.
4. Some emphasis; suggests one or more types of reward involving recognition or explicitly says he tries to please teacher.

5. Considerable emphasis; praise, rewards definitely important. Makes effort to please teacher.

$$r = .76$$

Scale 10. Boy's attitude toward teacher. (Q. 1 through 6)

1. Boy uniformly favorable to, and accepting of, teachers. No non-constructive criticism.
2. Boy expresses mainly favorable attitudes, but makes some unfavorable remarks about teachers in general or about particular groups of teachers.
3. Approximately equal number of favorable and unfavorable statements; thinks some teachers good, some teachers bad. May avoid statements about teachers in general and stress individual differences.
4. Expresses mainly unfavorable remarks, but allows that some teachers may be enjoyable or interested in helping. "Good" teachers the exception.
5. Extremely unfavorable opinions expressed. Has never liked working with any teacher; teachers not interested in helping, etc.

$$r = .81$$

Scale 11. Boy's report of physical aggression against peers (fist-fights, hitting, pushing, etc.). (Q. 9, 10)
Take account of Q. 11 through 16, also.

1. No instances of physical aggression reported.
2. Has been in one or two fights during high school years and reports no other instances of physical aggression, or has been in no fights and reports one or two other instances of physical aggression.
3. Has been in one or two fights in high school and reports one or two other instances of physical aggression, or reports several instances of physical aggression other than fighting.
4. Several instances of physical aggression reported, including fighting. Not as favored a response as in (5).
5. Reports several instances of fighting and other kinds of physically aggressive behavior. Explicitly says he initiates attacks on other boys, or would respond with physical attack when his opponent is only verbally aggressive. "Best way of dealing with people," etc.

$$r = .90$$

Scale 12. Boy's report of verbal aggression toward peers (calling names, blowing his top, teasing, etc.). (Q. 9, 10)
Take account of Q. 11 through 16, also.

1. No instances of verbal aggression reported.

2. One or two instances, but these mild in nature. In general avoids this.
3. Admits to verbal aggression when angry.
4. Several indications of verbal aggression given. Admits to provoking others on occasions, or retorts strongly when angered.
5. Several indications of verbal aggression. Boy on occasion provokes others.

$$r = .79$$

Scale 13. Boy's report of indirect aggression toward peers. Include instances of aggression, verbal or other, which are not directly expressed, e.g., defamation, withholding favors, inciting others to aggression against a third person. *Take account of avoidance.* (Q. 9, 10)
1. No instances. All reported aggression is direct.
2. One or two instances given.
3. Some instances, but no indication that this is a frequently used technique.
4. Several instances in interview. Some emphasis.
5. Several instances. Boy explicitly says he uses such methods frequently.

$$r = .79$$

Scale 14. Directness-indirectness of aggressive responses to peers. (Q. 9, 10)
   Ignore total amount of aggression; consider only relative amount.
1. Boy expresses aggression only in very indirect ways, e.g., refuses to have anything to do with persons he dislikes, ignores them, etc.
2. Boy usually very indirect in expression of aggression, but sometimes is more direct, e.g., snubs, withholds favors, etc.
3. Boy sometimes indirect, sometimes direct, in expressing aggression.
4. Usually expresses aggression directly, but indicates that more indirect methods are sometimes preferred or that response is delayed.
5. Boy typically expresses aggression openly, freely, and immediately. (Expression need not be violent nor explosive.)

$$r = .84$$

Scale 15. Guilt feelings concerning aggression against peers. (Q. 9)
1. No indication of guilt feelings.
2. Some indication, minor in character, e.g., boy says he feels he acted childishly or stupidly. (See also 3.)
3. Some indication of discomfort about aggression; defensiveness or attempts to atone for aggressive behavior. (Rate 2 if single indication only occurs, 4 if all three indications occur)

4. (See 3) Rate 4 also if boy indicates guilt strongly through one or other of above cues.
5. Clear indications of guilt. Boy feels uncomfortable, tries to atone, is defensive when reporting aggression, rationalizes.

$$r = .64$$

Scale 16. Extent to which boy seeks help from peers. (Q. 11)
1. Never seeks advice, help, or asks favors from friends.
2. Seeks advice, help, very little. Few requests for favors.
3. Asks friends for conventional types of favors and advice, e.g., fixing dates; rides, if he has no car; on what courses are like, etc.
4. Readily goes to friends for help, advice. O.K. to accept favors if they can be returned one way or another.
5. Seeks help, advice, over a wide range of problems. Often seeks favors of friends, even if not returnable.

$$r = .96$$

Scale 17. Resistance to seeking, accepting help or advice from friends. (Q. 11)
1. No signs of resistance, though boy may evaluate advice before accepting it.
2. Slight indication of resistance. Boy definitely prefers to work out some things on his own. May show some discomfort about having to ask for help.
3. Moderate resistance. Some discomfort. On rare occasions feels like doing opposite of what friends suggest.
4. Considerable resistance. Definitely feels uncomfortable about seeking help. Sometimes feels like doing opposite of what friends suggest.
5. Resists strongly. Does not like asking for help, strongly resists suggestions from friends, sometimes does opposite.

$$r = .88$$

Scale 18. Importance of group activity to boy. (Q. 12)
1. Very independent in choice of activities. Prefers doing things alone.
2. Has number of activities he likes doing on own, but also enjoys group activities.
3. Likes to do some things on his own, but prefers being with friends.
4. Decided preference for being with friends; does little on own.
5. Finds being alone a strain. Prefers being with people. Gives way to them in order to have their company.

$$r = .88$$

Scale 19. Extent to which boy seeks approval, recognition of peers.
(Q. 13, 17j, 18d)
1. Boy does not worry what others think of him; does not try to conform to group standards.
2. Some indications of approval-seeking, but little general conformity to group standards.
3. Boy wants to be liked, makes some attempts to conform.
4. Boy generally conforms, seeks approval, but with some reservations.
5. Boy tries to win approval and recognition through conformity. Will distort to win or keep esteem of group.

$$r = .81$$

Scale 20. Resistance to confiding, trusting in peers. (Q. 14)
1. Likes to have friends' counsel. Thinks this is important, helpful. Thinks they can be trusted.
2. Similar to (1), but with some reservations, e.g., on occasions better to keep things to yourself. Most fellows trustworthy, not all.
3. Thinks there are some things that can be talked over with friends, others he would keep to himself. Wouldn't trust friends completely.
4. In general would not confide much in others. May be all right to talk over some things, not too much. Cautious about friendships.
5. Best to rely on yourself; not trust in, or get too close to, people.

$$r = .82$$

Scale 21. Boy's feelings of rejection by peers. (Q. 15, 16, but take into account responses to earlier questions.)
1. None expressed. All indications that boy feels he gets along well with other people and that they like him.
2. Slight feelings. Some doubts apparent, but boy feels he gets along well on the whole and is liked.
3. Moderate feelings. Has felt at times he hasn't been wanted or liked, but this is not his usual feeling.
4. Strong feelings. Has definitely felt not wanted on occasions and has doubted whether other people like him.
5. Extreme feelings. Boy generally feels unwanted.

$$r = .85$$

Scale 22. Boy's hostility to peers. (Q. 9 through 16)
1. Boy generally favorable to, and accepting of, peers. No unfavorable remarks.
2. Boy expresses mainly favorable attitudes, but makes some unfavorable remarks about individuals or certain groups.

3. Approximately equal number of favorable and unfavorable statements. May avoid statements about peers in general, and stress differences between individuals or groups.
4. Expresses mainly unfavorable remarks; positive attitudes also expressed toward some individuals or groups.
5. Extremely unfavorable opinions expressed. Practically no positive attitudes.

$$r = .79$$

Scale 23. Boy's warmth toward peers. (Q. 9 through 16)
Take into account spontaneous expressions of liking, enjoyment, sympathy, as well as answers to specific questions.
1. Matter-of-fact.
2. Some evidence of warmth. Not so matter-of-fact as (1), but boy expresses little positive feeling. Appears to enjoy interaction with peers to some extent.
3. Moderate degree of warmth. Enjoys others' company for the most part, but strong positive feelings absent.
4. Very warm. Enjoys companionship of peers; also expresses positive feelings about them.
5. Extremely warm. As for (4), with the addition of several spontaneous expressions of liking during the interview.

$$r = .80$$

Scale 24. Boy's report of heterosexual experience. (Q. 17)
1. None.
2. Some mild petting. Nothing more.
3. Occasional petting. No intercourse.
4. Frequent petting, intercourse on one or more occasions.
5. Considerable heterosexual experience, including intercourse.

$$r = .95$$

Scale 25. Boy's report on masturbation. (Q. 18)
1. None. Denies masturbation.
2. Admits to some masturbation, isolated incidents.
3. Admits to masturbation, regular but infrequent, e.g., once a month.
4. Admits to masturbation, once or twice a week.
5. Admits to regular and frequent masturbation, most days.

$$r = .94$$

Scale 26. Boy's report of homosexual experience. (Q. 18c)
1. None.
2. Isolated incidents, one or two only.
3. A few incidents.

4. Frequent, not regular. Several times over the past year.
5. Regular occurrences.

$$r = .91$$

Scale 27. Extent to which boy has had sex information from parents (Q. 20)
1. None from parents, all from other sources.
2. Very little from parents, mostly from other sources.
3. Some from parents, more from other sources. Parent has given some information directly, or supplied suitable source.
4. Major portion of information from parent or sources supplied by parent.
5. As for (4), except that parent has informed boy very fully, and made sure he understands.

$$r = .92$$

Scale 28. Guilt and anxiety concerning sex. (Q. 17 through 20)
1. No evidence of avoidance or worry.
2. Slight. Boy may refrain at times, but in general not disturbed.
3. Boy worries at times, occasionally refrains.
4. Clear evidence of worry, attempts to refrain.
5. As for (4). In addition, boy exhibits unrealistic fears, attempts to obtain reassurance from examiner, etc.

Note: Rate up for blocking and similar signs of embarrassment within interview situation.

$$r = .85$$

Scale 29. Guilt concerning disruptive antisocial behavior or impulse. (Q. 22)
1. No indication of anxiety or guilt.
2. Little indication.
3. Some indication that boy feels he should not do these things, some worry afterwards.
4. Clear indications of guilt, but not as strong as (5).
5. Boy feels very guilty; elaborates; self-excusatory, may try to rationalize.

Note: If no instances of disruptive behavior come to light, so that there is no occasion for guilt to be displayed, rate 0, not 1.

$$r = .80$$

Scale 30. Boy's preference for living with mother or father. (Q. 23)
1. Preference for mother.
2. No choice.
3. Preference for father.

$$r = .93$$

Scale 31. Extent to which boy talks things out with father, i.e., asks for help, information, advice, suggestions. (Q. 24, 25, 28)
Ignore boy's reactions to advice.
1. Never consults father.
2. Consults father only on rare occasions.
3. Sometimes consults father, not frequently.
4. Often consults father.
5. Consults father on wide range of topics frequently; goes to him for help and reassurance whenever he is in difficulties.

$$r = .90$$

Scale 32. Extent to which boy consults mother. (Q. 24, 25, 28) (Same as for Scale 31)

$$r = .89$$

Scale 33. Amount of time boy spends in company of father. (Q. 26)
1. Never spends time with father, other than inevitable interaction at mealtimes, etc. If at home, in own room or elsewhere in house, or following own pursuits. Never goes for trips or vacations with him.
2. Spends an occasional evening in company of father, interacting; goes with him very rarely, only on occasional visits to family or to buy something for which father is paying, etc. Trips together very rare.
3. Some evenings at home in interaction with father. Goes out in his company sometimes, sharing activities other than those listed under (2).
4. Spends a good deal of time with father. Regular trips in addition to activities included in (3).
5. Spends most of leisure time in father's company. Many evenings spent in interaction; visits, trips, vacations, etc., frequent or regular.

$$r = .87$$

Scale 34. Amount of time boy spends in company of mother. (Q. 26) (Same as for Scale 33)

$$r = .72$$

Scale 35. Resistance to going out with, being seen with, mother. (Q. 26)
If boy feels uncomfortable without actual open resistance, rate up one point.
1. Not at all resistant.
2. Some indication of resistance; may not be directly expressed to mother.
3. Resists sometimes.

4. Often resists.
5. Avoids going out with mother whenever possible.

$$r = .93$$

Scale 36. Resistance to going out with, being seen with, father. (Q. 26)
(Same as for Scale 35)

$$r = .95$$

Scale 37. Extent to which boy tries to gain praise from, approval of,
mother. (Q. 27)
Take into account extent to which boy says he tries to please her,
do favors, obey her immediately. Ignore extent to which boy receives
praise for these things.
1. Makes no, or practically no, attempt to do this.
2. Rare occasions only.
3. Sometimes does this.
4. Frequently does this.
5. Boy makes every effort to please mother.

$$r = .85$$

Scale 38. Extent to which boy tries to gain praise from, approval of,
father. (Q. 27) (Same as for Scale 37)

$$r = .84$$

Scale 39. Extent to which mother praises boy. (Q. 27)
1. Practically never praises; just takes good behavior for granted.
2. Praises now and again; seldom.
3. Sometimes praises, sometimes not.
4. Praises usually, shows appreciation, admires.
5. Praises regularly, very appreciative, admiring.

$$r = .83$$

Scale 40. Extent to which father praises boy. (Q. 27) (Same as for
Scale 39)

$$r = .90$$

Scale 41. Mother's use of rewards (e.g., money, privileges) when she is
pleased. (Q. 27)
1. None.
2. Rare, only for something exceptional.
3. Occasional rewards.
4. Frequent rewards.
5. Frequent and generous rewards.

$$r = .82$$

Scale 42. Father's use of rewards (money, privileges) when he is pleased. (Q. 27) (Same as for Scale 41)

$$r = .91$$

Scale 43. Extent to which boy earns own spending money. (Q. 28, 29h)
1. Boy earns all own spending money, pays for own clothes for most part. Does not ask for money except in emergency.
2. Earns most of his spending money, but on occasion money is given or loaned by parents.
3. Regular allowance given by parents, sufficient for general expenditure. Boy earns money for any extra expenditures, though money may be given on special occasions.
4. Regular allowance given boy. Supplemented whenever boy needs more for specific expenditures. Boy earns very little.
5. Boy gets as much money as he wants and when he wants it. Does not earn.

$$r = .88$$

Scale 44. Extent to which boy resists advice, suggestions, from mother. (Q. 24, 25, 28, 29)
1. No resistance, though boy may evaluate advice before acting on it.
2. Very little resistance. Boy definitely likes to work out some things for himself, but for the most part feels no opposition to doing what mother suggests.
3. Some resistance. Sometimes resists and rejects mother's suggestions, usually follows them.
4. Considerable resistance. Often resists mother's suggestions; on occasions does opposite of what mother suggests.
5. Very resistant. Takes little notice of what mother says, and very definitely prefers to go own way. Will do opposite of what mother suggests quite often.

$$r = .83$$

Scale 45. Extent to which boy resists advice, suggestions, from father. (Q. 24, 25, 28, 29) (Same as for Scale 44)

$$r = .85$$

Scale 46. Boy's account of responsibilities placed on him by mother. (Q. 30)
1. Low demands, low pressure. Little or nothing expected of boy in the way of performing jobs.
2. Some demands, low pressure; or low demands, some pressure. No regular jobs, but encourages helping. One or two small jobs, not time-consuming.

3. Moderate demands, moderate pressure.
4. Moderate demands, high pressure; or high demands and moderate pressure.
5. High demands, high pressure. Many jobs, some time-consuming, expected to be performed.

$$r = .64$$

Scale 47. Boy's account of responsibilities placed on him by father. (Q. 30) (Same as for Scale 46)

$$r = .83$$

Scale 48. Boy's resistance to accepting responsibilities placed on him by mother. (Q. 30)
1. No resistance whatsoever.
2. Boy tries to evade these on infrequent occasions, but is generally acceptant.
3. Tries to evade demands. On rare occasions refuses to accept.
4. Considerable resistance. Frequently evades responsibilities. Sometimes refuses to accept them.
5. Extremely resistant. Evades responsibilities whenever possible. Unwilling to accept them.

$$r = .65$$

Scale 49. Boy's resistance to accepting responsibilities placed on him by father. (Q. 30) (Same as for Scale 48)

$$r = .79$$

Scale 50. Father's use of physical punishment. (Q. 31)
Take account of whole period, including earlier years. If physical punishment is still administered, rate up one point.
1. Never used physical punishment.
2. Occasional cuffing in past. Nothing more.
3. Real spanking at infrequent intervals. Occasional cuffs or slaps.
4. History of frequent cuffing. Occasional real spanking.
5. History of frequent and severe physical punishment.

$$r = .82$$

Scale 51. Mother's use of physical punishment. (Q. 31) (Same as for Scale 50)

$$r = .88$$

Scale 52. Father's use of deprivation of privileges. (Q. 31)
1. Never.
2. Used rarely; only to control deviations connected with use of privileges.

3. Used sometimes, but with moderation. Small privileges taken away, but not for long periods of time.
4. In general, as for (3), but technique is used more frequently or applied in a more severe manner.
5. Frequently controls deviant behavior by depriving boy of highly valued privileges for long periods of time.

$$r = .82$$

Scale 53. Mother's use of deprivation of privileges. (Q. 31) (Same as for Scale 52)

$$r = .94$$

Scale 54. Father's use of ridicule. (Q. 31)
1. Never uses this.
2. Slight use. One or two instances given, not intense.
3. Moderate use. Several incidents reported; no indication that there is special emphasis or frequency.
4. Much use. Several incidents reported, and evidence that the technique is emphasized, considered effective, or used quite frequently.
5. As for (4), but father extremely derogatory.

$$r = .88$$

Scale 55. Mother's use of ridicule. (Q. 31) (Same as for Scale 54)

$$r = .89$$

Scale 56. Father's scolding, nagging. (Q. 31)
   Take note of earlier responses.
1. Minimum use.
2. Some scolding, nagging about one or two things.
3. Nags in limited areas, but in these areas is fairly persistent.
4. Nags about a number of things, but not so extensively as (5).
5. Constantly scolding and nagging about many things. "After me all the time."

$$r = .80$$

Scale 57. Mother's scolding, nagging. (Q. 31) (Same as for Scale 56)

$$r = .88$$

Scale 58. Withdrawal of love—father. (Q. 31)
1. Never uses techniques of this kind. No instances in interview.
2. Used on rare occasions. One or two instances in interview.
3. Some use of techniques.
4. Used fairly often.
5. Frequent use of techniques. Evident that this is major way of controlling boy.

$$r = .86$$

Scale 59. Withdrawal of love—mother. (Q. 31) (Same as for Scale 58)
$$r = .91$$

Scale 60. Mother's use of reasoning as a disciplinary technique. (Q. 31
and rest of interview)

This includes explaining why boy should not do things, listening
to his arguments and trying to give an answer on the merits of the
case, describing consequences of actions.

1. Mother never uses. Boy gives no answer at any time that would
suggest use of reasoning.
2. Minimal use. Very few examples given that would suggest use,
or boy says mother hardly ever does this.
3. Some reasoning evident from boy's account, but indications that
other techniques are often used immediately.
4. Parent generally reasons with boy, but not to exclusion of other
techniques.
5. Uses regularly. Boy stresses degree to which mother reasons, or
makes it clear that this is her preferred technique (at least tried
before any other method is resorted to) and that use of any other
method is relatively infrequent.

Note: If the boy gives no instances of parents' reasoning with
him, rate 1, not 0, since there is no direct question on this topic
and ratings are to be based on extent to which boy refers to reasoning in various contexts.

$$r = .83$$

Scale 61. Father's use of reasoning as a disciplinary technique. (Q. 31
and rest of interview) (Same as Scale 60)

$$r = .61$$

Scale 62. Extent to which boy resents discipline of mother. (Q. 31)

1. Acceptant. Does not complain.
2. Generally noncomplaining. Doesn't appear to resent it very much.
3. Boy resentful at times.
4. Boy generally resentful.
5. Very resentful. Doesn't get over it easily.

$$r = .94$$

Scale 63. Extent to which boy resents discipline of father. (Q. 31)
(Same as for Scale 62)

$$r = .80$$

Scale 64. Boy's account of restrictions placed on him at home by
mother. (Q. 32)

Take into account use of radio, TV, smoking and drinking inside
home, bad language, setting times for homework, etc. The boy may

say that he does not drink or smoke, etc., in such a way as to indicate that parental attitudes have been internalized. In this case, rate up accordingly.

1. No restrictions. Parent would only interfere if someone else was being upset by boy's behavior.
2. Few restrictions. Some minor limitations set on boy's behavior.
3. Moderate. Sets limits in most areas, but allows considerable latitude.
4. Strict rules in some areas. Some limitations in others.
5. Strict rules, strictly enforced. Boy must not disturb rest of family, must not drink, smoke, swear, etc.

$$r = .70$$

Scale 65. Boy's account of restrictions placed on him at home by father. (Q. 31) (Same as for Scale 64)

$$r = .78$$

Scale 66. Boy's account of restrictions placed on him outside home by mother. (Q. 32)

1. No restrictions. Boy comes and goes as he likes, can stay out at night; boy's friends and choice of activities are his own concern.
2. Few restrictions. Boy expected to let parents know if he is going to be unusually late, his approximate whereabouts, etc. Otherwise no restrictions imposed.
3. Moderate. Limits boy's staying out late, but with some latitude. A few limits on boy's choice of friends and/or activities.
4. Strict. Boy expected to check out, be in at certain time, with very little latitude. Some limitations to boy's free choice of friends and activities.
5. Strict rules, rigidly enforced. Has to be in at a certain time except on exceptional occasions, has to let parents know what he is going to do or what he has done. Parents forbid a number of activities and pressure the boy in matter of choice of friends.

$$r = .71$$

Scale 67. Boy's account of restrictions placed on him outside the home by father. (Q. 31) (Same as for Scale 66)

$$r = .78$$

Scale 68. Boy's resistance to restrictions placed on him by mother. (Q. 32)

1. Accepts completely. No resistance in any area.
2. On infrequent occasions tries to circumvent restrictions. Generally accepted.

3. Tries sometimes to circumvent restrictions.
4. Often circumvents. Ignores them completely on occasions.
5. Extremely resistant. Completely unwilling to accept restrictions. Goes ahead and does what he likes.

$$r = .83$$

Scale 69. Boy's resistance to restrictions placed on him by father. (Q. 32) (Same as for Scale 68)

$$r = .83$$

Scale 70. Boy's resistance to accounting for activities to father. (Q. 33)
1. No resistance. Boy feels he can be perfectly honest.
2. Some mild resistance. Not very important.
3. Moderate resistance. Evades telling parents now and again, but in general doesn't mind.
4. Evasive with parents. Often feels like not telling parents things.
5. Extremely resistant. Boy objects strongly to father's wanting to know, and deliberately avoids communication.

$$r = .78$$

Scale 71. Boy's resistance to accounting for activities to mother. (Q. 33) (Same as for Scale 70)

$$r = .83$$

Scale 72. Boy's report of direct verbal aggression toward mother. (Q. 34)
1. No instances.
2. Some instances, mild.
3. Occasionally objects or argues with mother.
4. Frequently objects, protests, argues. May express anger.
5. Frequent strong verbal protests. Loses control.

$$r = .86$$

Scale 73. Boy's report of direct verbal aggression toward father. (Q. 34) (Same as for Scale 72)

$$r = .90$$

Scale 74. Boy's report of direct physical aggression toward mother. (Q. 34)
1. No instances.
2. One or two incidents of this kind.
3. A few incidents.
4. Occurs often (three or four times every year).
5. Occurs very often.

$$r = .92$$

Scale 75. Boy's report of direct physical aggression toward father. (Q. 34) (Same as for Scale 74)

$$r = .84$$

Scale 76. Boy's report of indirect aggression against mother. (Q. 34)

Take account of any show of anger or resentment which does not involve direct, face-to-face, physical or verbal aggression, e.g., walking out of house, slamming doors, saying derogatory things to other parent, passive resistance.

1. No instances.
2. One or two instances.
3. Some instances, but no indication that technique is frequently · used.
4. Several instances.
5. Several instances. Boy explicitly says he does this sort of thing often.

$$r = .75$$

Scale 77. Boy's report of indirect aggression against father. (Q. 34) (Same as for Scale 76)

$$r = .78$$

Scale 78. Directness-indirectness of aggressive response toward mother. (Q. 34)

Ignore absolute frequency of response.

1. Boy expresses anger only in very indirect manner.
2. Boy usually expresses aggression indirectly, but sometimes aggression is semidirect, e.g., displaced, passively resistant.
3. Boy sometimes directly, sometimes indirectly, expresses aggression; or typically expresses aggression in semidirect way.
4. Boy sometimes expresses aggression directly, sometimes semidirectly.
5. Boy typically expresses aggression openly, freely, and immediately.

$$r = .84$$

Scale 79. Directness-indirectness of aggressive response toward father. (Q. 34) (Same as for Scale 78)

$$r = .77$$

Scale 80. Indication of guilt-feelings concerning aggression toward mother, including disobedience. (Q. 33d, 34g)

1. No indications.
2. Some indications, e.g., boy says he feels he has acted badly, but makes no attempt to make up for behavior. Not defensive when reporting aggression.

3. Some indication of discomfort about aggression, defensiveness, or attempt to make up for it to mother. (Rate 2 if a single indication only occurs, 4 if all three indications occur to some degree.)
4. See 3. Rate 4 also if boy indicates guilt strongly through one or other of the above cues.
5. Clear indications of guilt. Boy feels uncomfortable, tries to make up to mother. Is defensive, rationalizes, when reporting aggression.

$$r = .77$$

Scale 81. Indications of guilt-feelings concerning aggression toward father, including disobedience. (Q. 33e, 34i) (Same as for Scale 80)

$$r = .81$$

Scale 82. Warmth of boy toward mother. (Q. 36, but take account of all relevant answers)

This scale is concerned with the extent to which the boy demonstrates his affection toward his mother. Take note especially of the extent to which he enjoys her company and her personal characteristics, indicates sympathy and understanding.
1. Very little warmth. Matter-of-fact, not demonstrative. Shows little sympathy or understanding.
2. Some evidence of warmth. Not as matter-of-fact as 1, but in general is undemonstrative and enjoys interaction only under limited circumstances.
3. Moderate degree of warmth. Enjoys mother for most part, shows some understanding and sympathy but not demonstrative.
4. Very warm toward mother. Tries to show her he feels this way. Enjoys her as a person.
5. Extremely warm. Spontaneously expresses appreciation of her during the interview in several places, in addition to characteristics listed under 4. Sympathetic and understanding.

$$r = .82$$

Scale 83. Warmth of boy toward father. (Q. 36, and all relevant answers) (Same as for Scale 82)

$$r = .89$$

Scale 84. Boy's feelings of rejection by mother. (Q. 23 through 40, especially Q. 35, 36)
1. No feelings of rejection expressed. Feels mother wants him, enjoys him, takes interest in him.
2. In general feels accepted, but some minor qualifications.
3. Some feelings of rejection, e.g., mother does not take enough interest in him, sometimes is glad to get rid of him.

4. Strong feelings of rejection, but with some qualifications.
5. Feels completely rejected. Not wanted at home, mother doesn't like him, takes no interest in him.

$$r = .82$$

Scale 85. Boy's feelings of rejection by father. (Q. 23 through 40, especially Q. 35, 36) (Same as for Scale 84)

$$r = .86$$

Scale 86. Extent to which boy identifies with mother. (Q. 23 through 40, especially Q. 37)

Take into account the extent to which the boy says he is like his mother, the degree to which he accepts her opinions and ideas and quotes them. Spontaneous remarks, e.g., "I guess I am like my mother in that," occurring elsewhere than in Q. 23, are especially important cues.

1. Boy gives no indications of identification.
2. Some identification. May be like mother in one or two things, but not for the most part. Never spontaneously states acceptance of her ideas.
3. Moderate identification. Thinks he is like mother in some ways. Some additional evidence of identification.
4. Strong identification. Thinks he is much like her; some additional evidence in interview.
5. Thinks he is very like his mother. Clear indications of identification in various parts of interview.

$$r = .86$$

Scale 87. Extent to which boy identifies with father. (Q. 23 through 40, especially Q. 37) (Same as Scale 86)

$$r = .75$$

Scale 88. Hostility to mother. (Q. 23 through 40)
1. Boy uniformly expresses positive statements about mother. No unfavorable ones.
2. Boy expresses mainly favorable attitudes, but makes some minor criticisms.
3. Boy makes approximately equal number of favorable and unfavorable comments.
4. Boy expresses mainly unfavorable comments. A few favorable ones.
5. Boy uniformly unfavorable in comments on parent.

$$r = .82$$

Scale 89. Hostility to father. (Q. 23 through 40) (Same as for Scale 88)

$$r = .83$$

Appendix E

THEMATIC DEVIATION TEST

I. Picture-Story Test

FIGURE A–1.

FIGURE A-2.

FIGURE A–3.

FIGURE A–4.

FIGURE A–5.

FIGURE A–6.

FIGURE A-7.

FIGURE A–8.

FIGURE A-9.

Figure A–10.

II. Story Completion Test

Story 1. One night at about eight o'clock Jack is walking home from a friend's house. As a general rule he has to be home by nine on week nights. He sees Sally, who is sitting all alone on the front steps of her house. Sally is known as the girl in the neighborhood who looks most like Marilyn Monroe. All the boys go out with her a lot. Sally asks Jack why he doesn't come on in and talk with her for a while. She says that she's all alone because her parents have gone to Los Angeles for several days.

Story 2. Dave likes his baseball coach. The other day the coach promised him privately that Dave could pitch in the big game on Saturday. When the team meets for final practice, the coach doesn't say anything to Dave about pitching. Dave is afraid he has forgotten or changed his mind. He keeps thinking to himself over and over again: "The coach isn't going to keep his promise. I hope he doesn't even make the game. I wish he'd drop dead!"

When Dave arrives at the game on Saturday afternoon, he sees from the scoreboard that he is scheduled to pitch.

Story 3. Bill's friends have formed a baseball team. They promised Bill he could be their catcher if he could get a catcher's mitt. His father told him he could not buy him a catcher's mitt. Bill saved all the money he could. At last he had $10.00 saved up to get a really good glove. When he arrives at the sports store, he sees the salesclerk going down the stairs to the cellar of the store. The clerk does not see Bill. Bill decides to look at the catcher's gloves himself before calling the clerk. He finds just the one he wants. Then he reaches down for his money. It is gone. He realizes that he has lost it on the way down town. Bill feels awful. He looks around. There is nobody in the store or near it outside. The clerk is still in the cellar. It occurs to Bill that the mitt would just fit under the bulge of his jacket.

Story 4. One day Ted's mother goes visiting a friend of hers in another town. At noon just after his lunch Ted phones his mother and talks with her. She tells him to stay around the place and she will be home at supper time. Now Ted is all alone with nothing to do. He thinks of the boxes in the top of his mother's closet. She has told him *never* to take down the boxes. He knows that his mother won't be home 'til supper time.

Story 5. Dave likes his baseball coach. The other day the coach promised him privately that Dave could pitch in the big game on Saturday. When the team meets for final practice, the coach doesn't say anything to Dave about pitching. Dave is afraid he has forgotten or changed his mind. He keeps thinking to himself over and over again: "The coach isn't going to keep his promise. I hope he doesn't even make the game. I wish he'd drop dead!!"

When Dave arrives at the game on Saturday afternoon, he hears that the coach has just been in an accident and has been taken to the hospital. Every one is worried. The game is about to begin. Dave sees from the scoreboard that he is scheduled to pitch.

Story 6. Bill's friends have formed a baseball team. They promised Bill he could be their catcher if he could get a catcher's mitt. His father told him he could not buy him a catcher's mitt. Bill saved all the money he could. At last he had $10.00 saved up to get a really good glove. When he arrives at the sports store, he sees the sales-clerk going down the stairs to the cellar of the store. The clerk does not see Bill. Bill decides to look at the catcher's gloves himself before calling the clerk. He finds just the glove he wants. Then he reaches for his money. It is gone. He realizes that he has lost it on the way down town. Bill feels awful. He looks around. There is nobody in the store or near it outside. The clerk is still in the cellar. It occurs to Bill that the mitt would just fit under the bulge of his jacket. He hides the mitt under his jacket and walks out of the store. No one sees him leave.

Story 7. One day Ted's mother goes visiting a friend of hers in another town. At noon just after his lunch Ted phones his mother and talks with her. She tells him to stay around the place and says she will be home at supper time. Now Ted is all alone with nothing to do. He thinks of the boxes in the top of his mother's closet. She has told him *never* to take down the boxes. He knows his mother won't be home 'til supper time. Ted climbs up and takes down the boxes.

Story 8. Bob is practicing wrestling with his friend Johnny. They try several holds on each other. When Bob gets an arm lock on Johnny's neck, Johnny laughs and twists suddenly. Bob hears a snap. Johnny falls limp and lies still. When the doctor comes, he says that Johnny is dead. Bob tells everybody exactly how it happened, and then nobody blames him for what happened to Johnny.

Bibliography

ACKERMAN, N. W. (1944) Psychotherapy and giving love. *Psychiat.*, **7**, 129–137.

AICHHORN, A. (1935) *Wayward youth.* New York: Viking Press.

ALEXANDER, F. & HEALY, W. (1935) *Roots of crime.* New York: Knopf.

ALEXANDER, F. & STAUB, H. (1956) *The criminal, the judge, and the public.* Glencoe, Ill.: Free Press.

ALLINSMITH, W. (1954) The learning of moral standards. Unpublished Ph.D. thesis, Univer. of Michigan.

ALLINSMITH, W. & GREENING, T. C. (1955) Guilt over anger as predicted from parental discipline: a study of superego development. *Amer. Psychologist,* **10**, 320. (Abstract)

BELLER, E. K. (1955) Dependency and independence in young children, *J. genet. Psychol.,* **87**, 25–35.

BENDER, LAURETTA. (1947) Psychopathic behavior disorders in children. In R. M. Lindner and R. V. Seliger (eds.). *Handbook of correctional psychology.* New York: Philosophical Library, Inc.

BENEDICT, RUTH. (1938) Continuities and discontinuities in cultural conditioning. *Psychiat.,* **1**, 161–167.

BETTELHEIM, B. (1950) *Love is not enough.* Glencoe, Ill.: Free Press.

BLOCH, D. A. (1952) The delinquent integration. *Psychiat.,* **15**, 297–303.

BOWLBY, J. (1946) *Forty-four juvenile thieves: their characters and home backgrounds.* London: Bailliere, Tindall & Cox.

BROMBERG, W. (1948) *Crime and the mind: an outline of psychiatric criminology.* New York: Lippincott.

BROWN, J. S. & FARBER, I. E. (1951) Emotions conceptualized as intervening variables—with suggestions toward a theory of frustration. *Psychol. Bull.,* **48**, 465–495.

CLECKLEY, H. (1955) *The mask of sanity* (3d ed.). St. Louis: C. V. Mosby Co.

DOLLARD, J., DOOB, L. W., MILLER, N. E., MOWRER, O. H., & SEARS, R. R. (1939) *Frustration and aggression.* New Haven: Yale Univer. Press.

DOLLARD, J. & MILLER, N. E. (1950) *Personality and psychotherapy.* New York: McGraw-Hill.

EISSLER, K. R. (1950) Ego-psychological implications of the psychoanalytic treatment of delinquents. *Psychoanal. Study Child,* **5,** 97–121.

ELKIN, F. & WESTLEY, W. A. (1955) The myth of adolescent culture. *Amer. sociol. Rev.,* **20,** 680–684.

ESCALONA, SIBYLLE K. (1945) Feeding disturbances in very young children. *Amer. J. Orthopsychiat.,* **15,** 76–80.

ESTES, W. K. (1944) An experimental study of punishment. *Psychol. Monogr.,* **57,** No. 363.

FAIGIN, HELEN. (1952) Child-rearing in the Rimrock community with specific reference to the development of guilt. Unpublished Ph.D. thesis, Harvard Univer.

FENICHEL, O. (1945) *The psychoanalytic theory of neurosis.* New York: Norton.

FORD, C. S. & BEACH, F. A. (1951) *Patterns of sexual behavior.* New York: Harper.

FREUD, ANNA & BURLINGHAM, DOROTHY T. (1944) *Infants without families.* New York: International Universities Press.

FREUD, S. (1925) Some character types met in psychoanalytic work. In *Collected Papers, Vol. IV.* London: Hogarth Press.

FREUD, S. (1936) *Inhibitions, symptoms and anxiety.* London: Hogarth Press.

FRIEDLANDER, KATE. (1947) *The psychoanalytic approach to juvenile delinquency.* London: Routledge & Kegan Paul.

FRIEDLANDER, KATE. (1949) Neurosis and home background. *Psychoanal. Study Child,* **3–4,** 423–438.

GESELL, A. & ILG, FRANCES L. (1943) *Infant and child in the culture of today.* New York: Harper.

GEWIRTZ, J. L. (1954) Three determinants of attention-seeking in young children. *Monogr. Soc. Res. Child Develpm.,* **19,** No. 2 (Serial No. 59).

GEWIRTZ, J. L. & BAER, D. M. (1958a) The effect of brief social deprivation on behavior for a social reinforcer. *J. abnorm. soc. Psychol.,* **56,** 49–56.

GEWIRTZ, J. L. & BAER, D. M. (1958b) Deprivation and satiation of social reinforcers as drive conditions. *J. abnorm. soc. Psychol.,* **57,** 165–172.

GIFFIN, MARY E., JOHNSON, ADELAIDE M., & LITIN, E. M. (1954) Antisocial acting out: specific factors determining antisocial acting out. *Amer. J. Orthopsychiat.,* **24,** 668–684.

GLUECK, S. & GLUECK, ELEANOR (1950) *Unraveling juvenile delinquency*. Cambridge: Harvard Univer. Press.

GOLDFARB, W. (1943) Infant rearing and problem behavior. *Amer. J. Orthopsychiat.*, 13, 249–260.

GOLDFARB, W. (1945) Psychological privation in infancy and subsequent adjustment. *Amer. J. Orthopsychiat.*, 15, 247–255.

GOLDFARB, W. (1955) Emotional and educational consequences of psychologic deprivation in infancy: a revaluation. In P. H. Hoch & J. Zubin (eds.). *Psychopathology of childhood*. New York: Grune & Stratton.

GOODENOUGH, FLORENCE L. (1931) Anger in young children. *Inst. Child Welf. Monogr. Ser.*, No. 9. Minneapolis: Univer. of Minnesota Press.

GREENACRE, PHYLLIS. (1945) Conscience in the psychopath. *Amer. J. Orthopsychiat.*, 15, 495–509.

HARTUP, W. W. (1958) Nurturance and nurturance withdrawal in relation to the dependency behavior of young children. *Child Develpm.*, 29, 191–201.

HEALY, W. & BRONNER, AUGUSTA F. (1936) *New light on delinquency and its treatment*. New Haven: Yale Univer. Press.

HEATHERS, G. (1955) Emotional dependence and independence in nursery school play. *J. genet. Psychol.*, 87, 37–57.

HEINICKE, C. M. (1953) Some antecedents and correlates of guilt and fear in young boys. Unpublished Ph.D. dissertation, Harvard Univer.

HENRY, G. W. (1941) *Sex variants: a study of homosexual patterns*. New York: Hoeber.

HEWITT, L. E. & JENKINS, R. L. (1946) *Fundamental patterns of maladjustment: the dynamics of their origin*. Chicago: State of Illinois, 1946.

HILL, B. (1955) *Boss of Britain's underworld*. London: Naldreth Press.

HOLLENBERG, ELEANOR. (1952) Child training among the Ziepi with special reference to the internalization of moral values. Unpublished Ph.D. thesis, Harvard Univer.

HULL, C. L. (1943) *Principles of behavior*. New York: Appleton-Century-Crofts.

HURLOCK, ELIZABETH B. (1955) *Adolescent development*. New York: McGraw-Hill.

JACKSON, LYDIA. (1954) *Aggression and its interpretation*. London: Methuen.

JENKINS, R. L. (1954) *Breaking patterns of defeat*. Philadelphia: Lippincott.

JENKINS, R. L. & GLICKMAN, SYLVIA. (1947) Patterns of personality organization among delinquents. *Nerv. Child*, 6, 329–339.

462   ADOLESCENT AGGRESSION

JENKINS, R. L. & HEWITT, L. E. (1944) Types of personality structure encountered in child guidance clinics. *Amer. J. Orthopsychiat.*, 14, 84–95.

JOHNSON, ADELAIDE M. (1949) Sanctions for superego lacunae of adolescents. In K. R. Eissler (ed.). *Searchlights on delinquency.* New York: International Universities Press.

JOHNSON, ADELAIDE M. & SZUREK, S. A. (1952) The genesis of antisocial acting out in children and adults. *Psychoanal. Quart.*, 21, 323–343.

JOSSELYN, IRENE M. (1948) *Psychosocial development of children.* New York: Family Service Association of America.

JOSSELYN, IRENE M. (1955) *The happy child.* New York: Random House.

KINSEY, A. C., POMEROY, W. B., & MARTIN, C. E. (1948) *Sexual behavior in the human male.* Philadelphia: Saunders.

KOBRIN, S. (1951) The conflict of values in delinquency areas. *Amer. social Rev.*, 16, 653–661.

LEVY, D. (1943) *Maternal overprotection.* New York: Columbia Univer. Press.

LEWIN, K., LIPPITT, R., & WHITE, R. K. (1939) Patterns of aggressive behavior in experimentally created social climates. *J. soc. Psychol.*, 10, 271–299.

LEWIS, H. (1954) *Deprived children.* London: Oxford Univer. Press.

LINDNER, R. L. (1944) *Rebel without a cause: the hypnoanalysis of a criminal psychopath.* New York: Grune & Stratton.

LINDZEY, G. (1950) An experimental investigation of the scapegoat theory of prejudice. *J. abnorm. soc. Psychol.*, 45, 296–309.

LIPPMAN, H. S. (1949) Difficulties encountered in the psychiatric treatment of chronic juvenile delinquents. In K. R. Eissler (ed.). *Searchlights on Delinquency.* New York: International Universities Press.

LORR, M. & JENKINS, R. L. (1953) Patterns of maladjustment in children. *J. clin. Psychol.*, 9, 16–19.

LOWREY, L. G. (1940) Personality distortion and early institutional care. *Amer. J. Orthopsychiat.*, 10, 576–586.

McCORD, W. & McCORD, JOAN. (1956) *Psychopathy and delinquency.* New York: Grune & Stratton.

McNEMAR, Q. (1955) *Psychological statistics.* New York: Wiley.

MILLER, N. E. (1948) Theory and experiment relating psychoanalytic displacement to stimulus response generalization. *J. abnorm. soc. Psychol.*, 43, 155–178.

MILLER, N. E. & DOLLARD, J. (1941) *Social learning and imitation.* New Haven: Yale Univer. Press.

MOHR, G. S. & DEPRES, M. A. (1958) *The stormy decade: adolescence.* New York: Random House.

MOWRER, O. H. (1950) *Learning theory and personality dynamics.* New York: Ronald.

MOWRER, O. H. & KLUCKHOHN, C. (1944) Dynamic theory of personality. In J. McV. Hunt (ed.). *Personality and the behavior disorders.* New York: Ronald.

NOWLIS, V. (1953) The development and modification of motivational systems in personality. In *Current theory and research in motivation: a symposium.* Lincoln: Univer. of Nebraska Press.

OSTROW, M. & OSTROW, M. (1946) Bilaterally synchronous paroxysmal slow activity in the encephalograms of non-epileptics. *J. nerv. ment. Dis.,* 103, 346–358.

PARSONS, T. (1950) Psycho analysis and the social structure. *Psychoanal. Quart.,* 19, 371–384.

PAYNE, D. E. & MUSSEN, P. H. (1956) Parent-child relations and father identification among adolescent boys. *J. abnorm. soc. Psychol.,* 52, 358–362.

PEARSON, G. H. J. (1949) *Emotional disorders of children.* New York: Norton.

PHILLIPS, L. & SMITH, J. (1953) *Rorschach interpretation: advanced technique.* New York: Grune & Stratton.

REDL, F. & WINEMAN, D. (1951) *Children who hate.* Glencoe, Ill.: The Free Press.

REDL, F. & WINEMAN, D. (1952) *Controls from within.* Glencoe, Ill.: The Free Press.

SAUL, L. S. (1956) *The hostile mind.* New York: Random House.

SEARS, PAULINE S. (1953) Child-rearing factors related to playing of sex-typed roles. *Amer. Psychologist,* 8, 431. (Abstract).

SEARS, R. R. (1951a) A theoretical framework for personality and social behavior. *Amer. Psychologist,* 6, 476–483.

SEARS, R. R. (1951b) Memorandum on identification. Harvard Univer., 1951. (Mimeographed).

SEARS, R. R. (1957) Identification as a form of behavioral development. In D. B. Harris (ed.). *The concept of development: an issue in the study of human behavior.* Minneapolis: Univer. of Minnesota Press.

SEARS, R. R., HOVLAND, C. I., & MILLER, N. E. (1940) Minor studies of aggression: I. Measurement of aggressive behavior. *J. Psychol.,* 9, 275–295.

SEARS, R. R., MACCOBY, ELEANOR E., & LEVIN, H. (1957) *Patterns of child rearing.* Evanston: Row, Peterson.

SEARS, R. R., WHITING, J. W. M., NOWLIS, V., & SEARS, PAULINE S. (1953) Some child-rearing antecedents of aggression and dependency in young children. *Genet. Psychol. Monogr.,* 47, 135–234.

SHAPLIN, J. S. (1954) Child training and the identification of pre-adolescent boys with their parents. Unpublished Ph.D. thesis, Harvard Univer.

SHAW, C. R. & McKAY, H. (1942) *Juvenile delinquency and urban areas*. Chicago Univer. Press.

SIEGEL, S. (1956) *Non-parametric statistics*. New York: McGraw-Hill.

SPITZ, R. A. (1945) Hospitalism: an inquiry into the genesis of psychiatric conditions in early childhood. *Psychoanal. Study Child*, 1, 53–74.

SPOCK, B. (1946) *The pocket book of baby and child care*. New York: Pocket Books.

STRAUSS, A. A. & LEHTINEN, LAURA E., (1947) *Psychopathology and education of the brain-injured child*. New York: Grune & Stratton.

THOMPSON, G. N. (1953) *The psychopathic delinquent and criminal*. Springfield, Ill.: Thomas.

THORPE, J. J. & SMITH, B. (1952) Operational sequence in group therapy with young offenders. *Int. J. Group Psychother.*, 2, 24–33.

TOPPING, RUTH. (1943) Treatment of the pseudo-social boy. *Amer. J. Orthopsychiat.*, 13, 353–360.

WARNER, W. L., MEEKER, M., & EELLS, K. (1949) *Social class in America*. Chicago: Science Research Associates.

WHITE, R. W. (1956) *The abnormal personality* (2d ed.). New York: Ronald.

WHITING, J. W. M. (1941) *Becoming a Kwoma*. New Haven: Yale Univer. Press.

WHITING, J. W. M. (1954) The research program of the Laboratory of Human Development: the development of self-control. Harvard Univer. (Mimeographed).

WHITING, J. W. M. & CHILD, I. L. (1953) *Child training and personality*. New Haven: Yale Univer. Press.

WHITING, J. W. M. & MOWRER, O. H. (1943) Habit progression and regression: a laboratory study of some factors relevant to human socialization. *J. comp. physiol. Psychol.*, 36, 229–253.

WILLIAMS, R. (1952) *American society*. New York: Knopf.

WOLBERG, L. R. (1944) The character structure of the rejected child. *Nerv. Child*, 3, 74–78.

WRIGHT, G. O. (1954) Projection and displacement: a cross-cultural study of folktale aggression. *J. abnorm. soc. Psychol.*, 49, 523–528.

ZUCKER, H. J. (1943) Affectional identification and delinquency. *Arch. Psychol.*, 40, No. 286.

Name Index

Ackerman, N. W., 39, 459
Aichhorn, A., 254, 285, 377–78, 379, 380–81, 383, 459
Alexander, F., 141, 358, 459
Allinsmith, W., 19, 192, 459

Baer, D. M., 36, 460
Beach, F. A., 144, 460
Beller, E. K., 44, 459
Bender, Lauretta, 29, 39, 254, 459
Benedict, Ruth, 87, 459
Bettelheim, B., 380, 383, 459
Bloch, D. A., 39, 381, 459
Bowlby, J., 29, 36, 39–40, 459
Bromberg, W., 141, 358, 459
Bronner, Augusta F., 5, 39, 461
Brown, J. S., 135, 459
Burlingham, Dorothy T., 36, 460

Child, I. L., 23, 37–38, 90, 134–37, 244, 253–54, 464
Cleckley, H., 141, 359, 459

Despres, M. A., 34, 369, 462
Dollard, J., 23, 28, 88, 252, 257, 460, 462
Doob, L. W., 23, 88, 460

Eells, K., 464
Eissler, K. R., 380, 460, 462
Elkin, F., 371–72, 460
Escalona, Sibylle K., 33, 460
Estes, W. K., 26, 460

Faigin, Helen, 192, 460
Farber, I. E., 135, 459
Fenichel, O., 141, 285, 460
Ford, C. S., 144, 460
Freud, Anna, 36, 460
Freud, S., 22, 310, 358, 460
Friedlander, Kate, 29, 39–40, 141, 254, 355, 358, 359, 362

Gesell, A., 24, 460
Gewirtz, J. L., 36, 460
Giffin, Mary E., 30, 460
Glickman, Sylvia, 362, 461
Glueck, Eleanor, 3, 30, 39, 93, 191, 193, 258, 461
Glueck, S., 3, 30 39, 93, 191, 193, 258, 461
Goldfarb, W., 29, 36, 39, 40, 254, 461
Goodenough, Florence L., 91, 461
Greenacre, Phyllis, 254, 461
Greening, T. C., 192, 459

Harris, D. B., 463
Hartup, W. W., 36, 461
Healy, W., 5, 39, 141, 459, 461
Heathers, G., 34, 461
Heinicke, C. M., 192, 256, 461
Henry, G. W., 141, 461
Hewitt, L. E., 30, 41, 142, 254, 358, 362, 461
Hill, B., 364, 461
Hoch, P. H., 461

465

Subject Index